Central Asian Economies in Transition

Central Asian Economies in Transition

Edited by

E. Ayşen Hiç Gencer and Cevat Gerni

CAMBRIDGE SCHOLARS

PUBLISHING

Central Asian Economies in Transition,
Edited by E. Ayşen Hiç Gencer and Cevat Gerni

This book first published 2012

Cambridge Scholars Publishing

12 Back Chapman Street, Newcastle upon Tyne, NE6 2XX, UK

British Library Cataloguing in Publication Data
A catalogue record for this book is available from the British Library

ISBN (10): 1-4438-4035-1, ISBN (13): 978-1-4438-4035-4

For my husband, Alp: I am everything I am because you love me…
For our kids, Aylin & Alpin: We love you…
For my parents, Süreyya & Mükerrem: I know you are with me every step of the way!
—Ayşen

For my wife Mine and for Murat & Parla: They make my life complex and complete.
—Cevat

Most people acquiesce to mediocrity – not for the lack of God given potential, but primarily because they value the camaraderie of the average beyond the uniqueness of excellence.
—T.D. Jakes

CONTENTS

Part VI: Energy

PREFACE

This book is based on the series of the International Conference on Eurasian Economies (http://www.eecon.info). Organized by Beykent University's Department of Economics, the first was held on 4-5 November 2010 in Istanbul, Turkey. The second was held on 12-14 October 2011 in Bishkek, Kyrgyzstan in collaboration with Turkey-Kyrgyzstan Manas University. The third will be held on 11-13 October 2012 in Almaty, Kazakhstan in collaboration with Turan University.

We have selected papers from this conference series that specifically address the six Central Asian countries (Kazakhstan, Kyrgyzstan, Uzbekistan, Turkmenistan, Tajikistan and Azerbaijan) and their economic ties with Turkey. In addition, we feature specially invited articles by prominent academicians working on Central Asian economies. All these articles were blended together to form a complete and coherent description of Central Asian economies, their challenges, and their integration into the world economy.

The first part summarizes the current state of Central Asian economies with statistics, and details the economic and political challenges they face. The second part discusses issues related to growth and development, ranging from food security, human development, and foreign direct investments to corporate restructuring. The third part investigates international trade, as well as its relationships with economic growth, with special emphasis on their trade with Turkey. The fourth part focuses on integration of Central Asian economies with each other, whereas the fifth part discusses issues related to globalization and its effects on Central Asian economies. The sixth part details the energy sector, which is the engine of economic growth in Central Asia.

We would hereby like to convey our sincere gratitude to all contributors who have submitted their valuable work for inclusion in this book. In addition, we would like to express our genuine thanks to the co-chairs of the International Conference on Eurasian Economies, Prof. Selahattin Sarı and Prof. Jusup Pirimbaev, as well as the organizing committee members at Beykent University and Kyrgyzstan-Turkey Manas University. Specifically, we would like to deliver our appreciation to Asst. Prof. Özgür Ömer Ersin and Asst. Prof. Mustafa Ercilasun for their contribution in the paper selection process. Our special thanks go to research assistant Ainura Turdalieva for her diligent support, prompt responses, and especially for taking up the role to act as a liaison between Central Asia and Turkey. We would like to mention gratefully all the invaluable help Dominic P. Thompson provided in patiently proofreading the entire manuscript. Last but not least, we would love to gratefully mention our indebtedness to Alp H. Gencer for realizing this project on the technical sphere.

Asst. Prof. E. Ayşen HİÇ GENCER
Prof. Cevat GERNİ
Istanbul, April 2012

FOREWORD

PROF. ÖMER ÖNDER ARI[1]

The shocking news of the breakdown of the USSR in 1991 lead the way to new descriptions of political systems and to new roles of governments of the world. The radical change in the operational functions of the political system influenced the encouragement of citizens' participation and the importance of individual rights.

Researchers and theoreticians of political science and public administration pointed to various examples of this important change among the Eastern bloc of the old communist countries which were once integral parts of the USSR.

In fact, political analysts and all political scientists interested in research on Eurasian countries observed even more interesting samples of sovereign states in the Caucasus region and in Asia. Freedom of expression, respect for human rights, and individuals' rights to private ownership, free exercise of political and economic rights became normal privileges of citizens under the services of elected governments, as a result of free general elections in all of these Central Asian countries.

As widely accepted, Eurasia is described as a geographic location of countries that became independent when the hegemony of the USSR ended. This geographic area is considered as strategic because of its natural resources. Eurasia stretches from the coasts of the Black sea of Georgia and Turkey, including the area of the Caucasus that includes Azerbaijan, Armenia, and the northwest of Iran, up to the borders of China in the east. It covers the Caspian Sea basin where Russia reaches this precious oil reserve of the Caspian Sea on the north by the autonomous region of Abazia & Dagistan; and additionally Kazakhstan and Turkmenistan on the east coast of the same sea. In fact, Eurasia as a geographic term includes vast lands of Kazakhstan, stretching from the eastern coast of the Caspian Sea to the Tanrı Mountains of the Peoples' Republic of China neighbouring Siberia of Russia to the northeast, Kyrgyzstan to the southwest next to China (Urumchi and Xiang, Sincan Region) where Uygur Turks resided for ages. Common culture, the same

[1] Beykent University, Istanbul, Turkey.

etymological source of the Turkish language, and respect for similar traditions, in addition to mutually shared beliefs of Islam among the citizens of Turkish Republics, symbolize historical values dating back to the early ages of Asian tribes. They were located in and around the heart of Asia where original Turkistan covered the lands neighbouring the eastern frontier of historical Persia next to Buhara and Semerkand cities, up to Tashkent and further to Andijan province of Uzbekistan. These lands which were once the historical Turkistan include the Aral Sea to the north and the regions reaching Kyrgyzstan to the east and northeast of Uzbekistan. They also include the famous Amuderya and Sriderya rivers and their productive delta region.

In fact, Turkistan is known as the socio-cultural centre of Muslim religion among Turkish populations at large, because of the spiritual pioneer of Islam, Hodja Ahmet Yesevi, who had carried out the sacred mission of faith in the lands of Eurasia as a voluntary service to God. This new wave of religious freedom and Muslim ethics somehow must have reminded the masses of citizens of different nations about their traditional backgrounds of mutual beliefs in historical perspective. One can witness and observe these effects in their behaviour and personal gestures when passing by the graveyards and while they pray at religious shrines, covering their faces by their hands murmuring *amen* at the end of their prayer, each time they pray.

The social similarity in the behaviour of citizens in the Turkic nations seemed to bring people together among the groups within the same locations where they lived. The citizens of Eurasian countries were accustomed to identify themselves with the towns and provinces they lived in. When asked ‘Where do you consider yourself to be a citizen of?’ or ‘Which country do you belong to?’ they would answer this question by saying ‘I am a resident of Turkistan’, ‘I am a person who lives in Chimkent’, or ‘I am a Kentaurer’.

All these values and traditions shared among the citizens of Eurasian countries increased the moral strength of the leaders and the refurbishing of warm psychological feelings in their relations among the masses of people in Caucasia, as well as in Central Asian countries. These close relations of people under the initiative of leaders of Turkic states gained momentum by their cooperation in various fields of socio-political and institutional phases of development, as exercised in their contacts as new sovereign states with Turkey since 1991. The establishment of legal institutions that were adopted, similar to European models of contemporary times, such as their new national constitutions and their judiciary systems, took place during the first decade of their independence.

New national constitutions of Central Asian countries have been organized by their own decisions. Some experienced experts from different countries, such as some leading states of the European Union, the USA, England, and Turkey, helped the Central Asian countries' bureaucracies to discuss and find alternative ways to reach the most suitable methods in writing their constitutions. Although the popular Russian language has been widely used in informal transactions, the national language of each country is the fundamental (legally preferred) formal language. Russian is still valid as the second most popular language. Even so, Turkish language became the second competing popular medium of communication for the masses in these countries. Naturally, as globalisation influenced the economic relations of their contacts at international level, the English language gained momentum as preferred by their partners. In fact, English and Turkish are widely used in teaching students at lyceums as well as at universities, next to their national languages. Turkey has widely organized modern educational institutions at each level of formal education in these countries in close cooperation with their state institutions, depending upon the legal permission of each Eurasian state.

I would like to reflect my personal experience in Astana, Almaty, Chimkent, Kentau, Tashkent, Bishkek, and Baku, and an evaluation of some of the traditional Asian societies that emerged as modern nation-states gaining sovereignty after the breakdown of the USSR in 1991. Witnessing the process of establishing their democratic institutions, which started by organizing national constitutions and modern models of legislative, executive, administrative and legal organs, gave me the valuable chance of observing the community development and democratic progress in Kazakhstan, Uzbekistan, Kyrgyzstan, and Azerbaijan, between 1995-1998.

The following brief analogy is a portrait of the socio-economic structure and the interrelationship of people whose values and living standards I shared during those years as a political scientist and academician from Turkey, and whom I considered as my ancestral relatives of the bigger (family) of the Turkic population in Asia. I sincerely believe that we still share their values, use the etymological source of the Turkish language, and that the principles of the religion of Islam are accepted by the majority of citizens, documented in history. I felt the similar warm embrace of the socially humane family ties, when the following symbolic statement was repeated by the president of Azerbaijan on different occasions: 'We are citizens of one nation within two different states'.

As I observed closely during my service to their educational system at various universities, private ownership, application of the principle of equal opportunity for all citizens, equality and freedom of individuals, freedom of speech and association, private entrepreneurship, superiority of legal system and free elections, all guaranteed by a new constitution in each of these newly independent Central Asian countries, were achieved in the first era of their sovereignty, between 1991-2000, peacefully with some minor domestic conflicts of interest and few political crises.

Semerkand impressed me with its city planning and collection of historical ruins of the early Turkish culture of Uzbekistan reflecting the Islamic history. I was astonished with its modernized organization of its institutional complex for the Islamic religion, where hot water services had been in operation for male and female Muslims in 1996 at the biggest religious centre of Islam in Tashkent. All kinds of believers could freely visit Uzbekistan without a visa then by air when they travelled to Tashkent, which is the capital of this country. I felt the same degree of tolerance and warm welcome shown to me by the managers of state institutions during those years. We visited Tashkent, Semerkand, and Buhara many times, mostly during the weekends either as individuals or in groups in 1995-1996. I doubt now whether I can do so as freely as I could then, because of central control of visas now cautiously applied to newcomers, even from Turkey.

The organization of local bazaar in Tashkent was as modern as the quality of famous Boucherie de Paris when I visited this famous capital for the first time. The Turkish company Koç had opened the first shopping mall in 1995 in Tashkent, bringing all kinds of food and different Turkish products to this city. The Turkish state school of Tourism Lyceum had been opened in Tashkent to serve Uzbek students, for the modern way of learning how to attract tourists from abroad, especially from France and Germany.

The most attractive symbol of Islam shines on the tiles of the central mosque of Taskent five times a day during the *ezan* time of prayer in this land with Turkic background of Ottoman style architecture and attractive designs of state buildings in the centre of the town. Its national theatre building has a special memory in my mind, as the modern opera performance of Hodja Nasrettin had attracted my interest with its professional cast and symphonic music.

Following this phase of two years, I have to add my observations at Azerbaijan in its capital Baku, where I felt at home when serving the State

Institution of Public Management and the Faculty of Business Administration as the dean in 1997-1998. Known as the Paris of Asia, with its modern museum dedicated to the great commander Timur Han, opposite a well-designed park where there is a famous warrior's statue depicting him on a horse, which symbolizes his conquests of many lands, stretching from Tashkent to Ankara-Bursa and Moscow.

The Republic of Turkey had introduced a modern system of education both to Uzbekistan and Kazakhstan in the period of 1991-2000. The state institution TIKA is one of the best examples of Turkish projects as an important step of modern banking operations and strategic management methods, which were introduced to banks and banking personnel of Uzbekistan, Azerbaijan, Tajikistan, and Turkmenistan, reaching a total of 4500 graduates from its courses, organized and operated by the Union of Banks in Turkey. This project was managed and applied by a successful general director named Mr. Özince. In my opinion, the international prestige of this project and its functional success story should mostly be credited to this intellectual, enthusiastic general director. These courses were offered at the Turkish-Uzbek Banking Educational Centre next to Tashkent State University campus during 1995-1996. These courses achieved the most fruitful professional results in the education of many Uzbeks and other banking professionals. Professional ethics and modern banking principles were carefully taught during these courses under the leadership of the Turkish Union of Banks.

One can not hesitate to mention the mission of many schools established by different groups of individuals in all of the Central Asian countries to bring universal standards of globalization and Islam in those countries under its Turkish brand. Turkey has also introduced modern principles of private university education to these countries.

Later, European and American experts from various famous institutions followed the same influential way of multi-cultural impact in establishing a number of private universities with different quality and curricula in various fields in all Central Asian countries.

The Zaman newspaper was the first voluntary pioneering media symbol in local languages and in Turkish in tablet form of four pages, published, distributed, and sold in 14 Turkish states and autonomous provinces of the new sovereign states, as well as some regions of Russia, in 1995-1996. The first Turkish TV station broadcast in Kazakhstan, Uzbekistan and Azerbaijan via satellite was TRT, the state TV corporation of Turkey. The same Turkish model of media reached different autonomous provinces consisting of minorities with Turkic ancestry in different parts of Russia.

To conclude, I would like to offer a general summary of socio-political developments in the Central Asian countries gaining their sovereignty from the USSR:

- Legal progress of political institutions
- Social process of participation through formation of voluntary associations
- Adoption and organization of free exercise of Islamic faith at large
- Universal standards of education at every level from primary/ secondary schools to universities and university diversity
- Transfer of private sector of public enterprises at central and regional locations through local decisions, to private sector
- Harmonization of services within the new free system of political, developmental, and social change
- Freedom of expression and freedom of travel
- Freedom of private business and freedom of individual ownership
- General free elections from the members of new parliaments and presidency
- Privatization process put into use as a form of transformation to open market operations of liberal economy to encourage international capital investment flow into these countries

INTRODUCTION: MAJOR POLITICAL AND ECONOMIC PROBLEMS FACING EURASIAN COUNTRIES

PROF. MÜKERREM HIÇ[1]

I would like to begin by thanking the editors of this book not only because they have given me the opportunity to give a speech as the keynote speaker at the first International Conference on Eurasian Economies, but also because they have hit upon a wealth of political and economic problems that Eurasian countries and, in fact, the whole world is passing through today.

Let me stress at the outset that political and economic developments and problems are either directly or indirectly linked to each other. Therefore, I will be dealing here with both. But the problems are so serious, numerous, and complicated, that I can manage to present to you only a list, without deepening on any major problem.

Let me also note the obvious: that Eurasia itself, as a geographical entity, covers a very large number of countries with different historical, political and economic backgrounds. Hence, we may have to think about different regions or groups of countries. On the European side, even the EU is not homogeneous today. We have the UK, Scandinavian countries, developed continental European countries, Iberian countries, the Balkans and Eastern Europe. Even in simple developmental terms, we have at least two tiers; a first tier of democratically and economically developed countries, and a second tier with less experience in democracy and which is less economically developed. In Asia, on the other hand, we have such big countries as Russia, China, Japan, and India, as well as such regional groups as South-East Asian countries, Central Asian-origin countries, the Caucasian, Afghanistan, and Pakistan also including Bangladesh, and Middle Eastern, with Iran as a separate politico-economic entity. Similarly, Turkey, at the crossroads between Europe, Asia, and the Middle East, is yet another different, unique case.

---

[1] Emeritus Prof., Istanbul University, Istanbul, Turkey.

I should also underline here that Turkey has business relations with many of the Eurasian countries. Between the years 1991-2001, Turkey has established Business Councils with the following: Afghanistan, Azerbaijan, Belarus, Georgia, Kyrgyzstan, Kazakhstan, Mongolia, Moldova, Uzbekistan, Russia, Tajikistan, Turkmenistan, and Ukraine, plus a "Business Forum" with Pakistan. The Turkish International Economic Relations Institution (DEİK) organizes, at frequent time intervals, a General Meeting of Turkish-Eurasian Business Councils.

Major Political Problems of Eurasian Countries

Eurasian countries, and the world as a whole, recently passed through the following major political developments, changes, and upheavals:

Following Perestroika and Glasnost (1985), the demolition of the Berlin Wall (1989), reunification of Germany (1990), and the collapse of Soviet Socialist Union (1991), by which latter event member countries in Eastern Europe and the Balkans gained their independence, they have all adopted democracy and market economy.

But due to a lack of previous experience with democracy and, in some cases, due to a lack of sufficient mass education, democracy as well as economic management is far from satisfactory in many of these countries. This evaluation applies to Russia as well, particularly in terms of democracy.

On the surface, the collapse of the Soviet Union turned the bi-polar world to mono-polar. But the USA, as the remaining superpower soon learned that she is not over-powerful; there are strong limits and restraints to her use of military power and diplomatic persuasion. In fact, there is now talk of a multi-polar world in process, with the USA still the most dominant.

Another concomitant political and economic development was the enlargement and the deepening of the EU. By taking in most of the Balkan and Eastern European countries, the number of EU members now reached 27. A serious effort at economic deepening was first the "Single Market", and more recently the "Euro". The EU is, however, still far from becoming a United States of Europe, politically and militarily.

Still another Eurasian and world development is the strengthening of the religious factor in the EU and Europe. This is compounded by Islamic terror, Islamic fundamentalism, as well as difficulties of adaptation of Moslem immigrants to their host EU countries, and a confusion between real Islamic faith and "Islamism" by which I mean fanatical interpretations of Islam and its use (exploitation) for political and commercial purposes.

Communism as a political and economic regime, on the other hand, seems to be withering away, irrevocably. At present we have only 5 countries that are a "people's republic", that is, communist. Of the five, China seems to retain only the dictatorship, while it implements a mixed economic regime that is open to the world and encourages the private sector and foreign private capital flow, that is, however, with interventionism and excessive protectionism. The four remaining communist countries, of which three are in South-East Asia, are too small to flare up any major political upheaval, even the erratic North Korea. And all are set to go the way of China in the future.

The recent years also found Eurasia with persistent specific political problems pertaining directly to two countries or to a limited group of countries. These include the Israeli-Palestinian problem in the Middle East; Iraqi occupation by the USA and present withdrawal efforts; Kashmir problem between India and Pakistan; Nagorno-Karabakh issue between Armenia and Azerbaijan; the Chechen problem in Russia; and the Russian-Georgian-Abkhazian problem; not mentioning the internal problems of China.

Major Economic Problems of Eurasian Countries

In the global economic area, on the other hand, again we have very important developments and serious problems, many still in transition.

Since the '70s most of the Less Developed Countries (LDCs) had turned away from a closed economy model, import-substitution industrialization, interventionism, and protectionism, towards outward-orientation, market economy, and encouragement of private sector and foreign private capital flow. Following this change in mentality, and hence economic policies, the world entered, since the '90s, what is called a globalization process. Globalization involves vast movements of foreign private capital (that is, Direct Private Investments), short and long-term financial funds, as well as legal and illegal movement of workers, the first two not only within Developed Countries (DCs) and from DCs to LDCs, but also within LDCs and from LDCs to DCs.

It must be stressed at this point that globalization was aided by the recent technological breakthrough of the computer, the internet, and related technologies. Indeed, one may safely foresee that this technological innovation is destined to shape our future in all aspects. The magnitude of its effects will be comparable to the industrial revolution of the 18th century, the invention of the steam engine and the discovery of electricity.

As a result of globalization, growth rates of all countries rose; those of LDCs more than those of DCs. This signified that globalization is a "*win-win*" situation and not a "*zero-sum-game*".

As a result of differentiated growth, while we had only two groups of countries after World War II, the DCs and the LDCs, today we have several tiers of countries with respect to *per capita* income, as well as total income level.

Using the latter criterion we now have the BRICs (Brazil, Russia-India and China) with very high total GNP. That of China has become second only to the USA, surpassing Japan and others.

Next we have the "emerging markets" that attract large amounts of financial funds and DPIs. Turkey today is rated as an "emerging market".

But globalization also gave rise to serious, in fact, grave, economic problems. Firstly, some countries, such as Russia, Turkey, and Argentina, faced serious economic crises on a single-country basis because of wrong economic policies pursued. But then, in 1997-98, the South-East Asian countries, again because of economic mismanagement, gave rise to a global financial crisis. It was quickly prevented by IMF aid, *stand-by* agreements, and a strong US economy at the time. Following this, the globalization process started to pick up speed again.

But a much more serious global economic crisis erupted in September 2008. It emanated first in the USA in the financial sector (mortgage or financial crisis), creating a deep recession, then went on to spread to Europe and the DCs, and thence to LDCs and the entire world. The ensuing global financial crisis and global recession, which was one of the worst the world had faced, second only to the 1929 Great Depression, was alleviated by means of drastic financial aid to the financial sector, plus aid to the automotive sector, as well as macro monetary policies, tax policies, and extensive government expenditure programs. The latter-mentioned macroeconomic policies were all Keynesian in essence. The entire world and major countries acted in cooperation when taking these measures. And it is noteworthy that the medium of cooperation resorted to was not G8 but G20, that is, 20 countries with the largest GNP. Hence, the group included the BRICs, as well as Turkey.

The negative effects of drastic measures taken to prevent the global economic crisis will continue for some more time in the future. Some individual countries may falter. But a second global dip, initially feared, will likely not come to pass.

It is interesting that the 2008 global crisis will not likely cause the world to revert back away from globalization. Definitely there had been precipitous declines in the level of global flows initially, but they are picking up again. Similarly, as the base for globalization, the market economy will also remain in essence despite the contrary remarks made by the French president. The world as a whole will not move towards a French-type *dirigiste*, that is, excessively interventionist and protectionist economic model.

On the global scene again, energy supply will still continue to present problems. Petroleum and natural gas are unevenly distributed between countries, while petroleum exploration and production (extraction) is, and has been for a long time, monopolistic. Increased economic growth worldwide raises the world demand for energy, but progress in alternative energy sources is unsatisfactory. Energy-saving, on the other hand, is insufficient. Nuclear energy is one way out, but it is rightly considered prohibitive because it can easily be turned into a powerful military weapon.

PART I:

CENTRAL ASIAN ECONOMIES: FACTS AND CHALLENGES

PROBLEMS OF POST-SOVIET CENTRAL ASIAN COUNTRIES

PROF. TURAR KOICHUEV[1]

Post-Soviet Central Asia is 1.1% of the whole territory of planet Earth. The Central Asian population is 1% of the total world population. The gross domestic product of Central Asian countries is 189 billion USD, or (according to the World Bank, 2008) 0.3% of the world GDP.

As a single geo-economic space, by geographical scope (the territory is 4 million square kilometres), economic production (189 billion USD), and population (68 million people), Central Asia takes a modest place in the world. But in the modern world, regions, modest by scale and potential, take their place in politics and economics of the world community, and they have their voice in the world development process. It is true that this place should be decent, the place which is not on the sidelines of the world development, the place which actively and dynamically goes up the most upper stairs.

The collapse of the Soviet Union and acquisition of independence gave Kazakhstan, Kyrgyzstan, Turkmenistan, and Uzbekistan a historic chance for political, economic, and social climbing. Having overcome the difficult years of the economic crisis in 1992-1995 and the transit of the Soviet authoritarian economy to a social market economy, the Central Asian countries gradually acquire new features. Although not yet stable and steady, still the socio-economic development is preferred, dynamic, and is positively recognized by the society.

The Central Asian countries differ in size of territory, population, and scale of economy: Kazakhstan has a territory of 2.7 million square kilometres, its population is 16 million people, the GDP in 2008 was 132 billion USD; Kyrgyzstan respectively 199.9 thousand square kilometres, 5.4 million people, 4.4 billion USD; Tajikistan 143.1 thousand square kilometres, 7.2 million people, 5.1 billion USD; Turkmenistan 491.5 thousand square kilometres, 5.4 million people, 18.3 billion USD; Uzbekistan 448.9 thousand square kilometres, 20.6 million people, 27.9 billion USD.

[1] National Academy of Sciences, Bishkek, Kyrgyzstan.

In terms of GDP per capita, Kazakhstan (8,264 USD), Turkmenistan (3,654 USD), and Uzbekistan (1,034 USD), are middle-income countries, but Kazakhstan is on the top step of the middle level, Turkmenistan and Uzbekistan are on the bottom step, while Kyrgyzstan (880 USD) and Tajikistan (729 USD) are in the group of low-income countries. As can be seen, the Central Asian countries differ from each other in potential scale, level, structure, and dynamics of the economy. Each country makes efforts to ensure sustainability, stability, and efficiency of its own economy.

However, since the Central Asian countries represent a single geo-economic space, there are economic, social, and ecological problems, which can be solved fully and in a high-quality manner only on the basis of joint decisions.

Food security and water supply

The countries of post-Soviet Central Asia face extremely vital common problems, which concern all of them and are successfully solved only through their joint efforts. The ensuring of food self-sufficiency and security is the most important common problem. The region has a relatively high birth rate and a low mortality rate of the population. Although there is an outflow of the population from the region, its number increases. In the first half of the sovereign years (after 1991) there occurred a mass exodus of the population at the expense of non-indigenous ethnic groups, which resulted in a sharp increase in ethnic homogeneity with indigenous immigrants. Later, the outflow, to a relatively greater degree, was at the expense of indigenous residents, but not on a massive scale. Moreover, the outflow was not forever, and took the shape of temporary labour migration.

Temporarily residing in other countries, the labour migrants do not just earn and help the families, who stayed at home, but they actively participate in the expanded reproduction of the population, that is in childbirth and population growth in the republic. The increasing population should be provided with food.

Land resources of the agricultural use are limited; the same is true for the possibility of their extension. The countries do not expand geographically. There have been cases observed of removing land resources from agricultural use and construction of industrial and civil objects. Changes in agricultural specialization in favour of increased food orientation are not always possible due to climatic conditions, and they do not seem to be always economically justified. Crop yields and reproducibility, as well as productivity in cattle-breeding, are relatively low, and they have their own natural growth limits. The population is growing and it should be ensured with food stuffs.

The supply of water is essential for a solution to the food objective. The agriculture in the countries of post-Soviet Central Asia is, to a great degree, irrigated. If we exclude the North-West, North and North-East of Kazakhstan, the agricultural production of all five countries, Kazakhstan, Kyrgyzstan, Tajikistan, Turkmenistan and Uzbekistan, depends on the river basin of the Syr-Darya River (originating in the mountains of Kyrgyzstan) and the Amu-Darya River (originating in the mountains of Tajikistan). All crops need water. But the priority is given to the cultures from which food can be produced. Food security is in the hands of the rivers of Kyrgyzstan and Tajikistan. Due to the warming of the climate on the planet and speeded melting of the snow and glaciers, in future there will be a process of noticeable decrease in the mass of water. This certainly complicates the production of food.

The question arises: how to solve the problem of food self-sufficiency and security? In the region the natural and climatic conditions and interrelated resources are common (they are natural and they cannot be isolated by state and legal feature), and their rational use, giving the chance to ensure safe food security, is possible only with a concerted and joint effort of all five states.

Of course, food self-sufficiency and security of each country depends on economic opportunities and the efficient functioning of national economies, but the decisive natural factor for post-Soviet countries of Central Asia is water and the construction, upgrading, and maintenance of soil-reclamation and irrigation systems for proper operating and construction of reservoirs at the sources upstream in the mountains. In the mountains there is less evaporation, and salinization is impossible, whereas in hot steppes, deserts, and semi-desert areas of Kazakhstan, Turkmenistan and Uzbekistan, water is more evaporated and salted, and useful biochemical properties of water for irrigation are reduced. Also, search, drilling, and use of groundwater, improving water irrigation technologies, rationalization of structure of sowing areas for crops, and achievement of water-saving and more productive specialization of agriculture are the most important and indisputable objectives: national, joint inter-state, and region-wide.

In the future, in terms of global warming, the hot climate in post-Soviet Central Asia, and population growth, drinking water will become a problem as well. And mainly fresh and mineral waters of Kyrgyzstan and Tajikistan may be the source of addressing the needs of the population of post-Soviet Central Asia, and providing opportunities to export drinking water.

Caring for water resources of Kyrgyzstan and Tajikistan is caring for the life of the population of the whole post-Soviet Central Asia and its food security! Water is the central chain in the problem of food self-sufficiency and security.

Water is the most important hydropower resource. In post-Soviet Central Asia, Tajikistan and Kyrgyzstan have enormous hydropower resources in regard to its scale. In the Soviet Union they took second and third places respectively after the Russian Federation. The projects in Tajikistan and Kyrgyzstan planned to construct cascades of hydropower stations. In Kyrgyzstan 18 hydropower stations were to be built on the Naryn River. Only 6 stations were built and now function (Toktogul, Atbashi, Uch-Kurgan, Shamaldy-Say, Kurpsay, Taahkumyr), one more station (Kambarata-2) is being built, the construction of another (Kambarata-1) is expected. The construction of 6 hydropower stations was expected on the other river, Sary-Djaz. As was already mentioned, the cascade of hydropower stations was designed in Tajikistan as well.

If all these goals were performed, the electric power produced would fully satisfy not only the needs of the two countries, to the greatest degree, the needs of the whole post-Soviet Central Asia, and it would be exported. In Uzbekistan, Kazakhstan and Turkmenistan the number of Heat Electric Power Plants and State District Power Plants, based on coal, oil and gas, could be reduced, and it would be possible to use hydroelectric power. This is much cheaper and more environmentally friendly. It would be more pragmatic to use coal, oil and gas as fuel (fuel heaters and engine fuel) and raw material for chemical processing, etc.

Coordinating the complex pricing policies for electric power, oil, products of its processing, and gas, as well as the interrelating interests and cancelling needs by in-Central Asian interaction reduced prices, could provide a rational structure of a fuel and energy complex of post-Soviet Central Asia. If necessary, rather than confining it to national boundaries, this could go to the level of setting up interstate industrial complexes. Capabilities of each country should work not on generation of pressures and contradictions, but their removal and the harmonization of interests; their joint satisfaction.

A fuel and energy security (in terms of use of oil and gas) is a serious problem for Kyrgyzstan and Tajikistan. Not having such rich resources as in Kazakhstan, Turkmenistan and Uzbekistan; Kyrgyzstan and Tajikistan are extremely dependent on them. If the problems of food security, water for irrigation, achievement of a more economical and environmentally friendly power consumption and fuel consumption were solved in a complex and coordinated way, the dependence of the 5 countries upon each other would be interaction amortizable, and there would not be selfish manifestations, generated solely by narrow, selfish market desires.

National security

There is one more basis for coordination and creation of joint projects. It is connected with the fact that certain territorial zones of the countries are attached to each other, and there is the possibility of forming joint regional socio-economic communities, which consist of regions of two, and sometimes three or four countries. In the Fergana Valley, for example, Osh and Djalal-Abad oblasts of Kyrgyzstan, and Andijan oblast of Uzbekistan, represent one regional socio-economic formation, while Batken oblast of Kyrgyzstan, the Namangan and Fergana oblasts of Uzbekistan, as well as Khodjent oblast of Tajikistan represent another. There exist versatile daily economic and cultural-domestic communications of the population. Moreover, the population in these parts is ethnically mixed. For sustenance of the population it is important to keep the borders with each other open, not closed. Let the movement of the people not be blocked. It is a joint way to a better destiny.

Similar international regional communities can be formed in other places of the state borders: Kyrgyz-Kazakh, Kazakh-Uzbek, Uzbek-Tajik, Tajik-Turkmen-Uzbek, Kazakh-Turkmen-Uzbek. The internal borders between the countries of post-Soviet Central Asia should be open for people, and relevant border posts should be used to monitor observance of the rules and order of movement, and for protection against penetration of terrorist forces, but they should not be a ban for civil communication. In these regional formations the problem of providing the work force with jobs can be efficiently solved.

To ensure national security of each country of post-Soviet Central Asia from external threats it is extremely important to coordinate national efforts in this direction and to jointly pursue a policy of collective security of the whole post-Soviet Central Asia. In this regard the participation of most countries of post-Soviet Central Asia in the Collective Security Treaty Organization, which includes Armenia, Russia, Belarus, Kazakhstan, Kyrgyzstan, Moldova, Tajikistan, and Uzbekistan, is quite justified.

Transportation network

One more region-wide problem of post-Soviet Central Asia is the creation of a unified, technically advanced, high-capacity, high quality, and reliable region-wide transport network. Its creation would mean that there wouldn't be inter-state conflicts, misunderstandings, or mutual chicaneries due to it. On the basis of the international treaty, it should be assigned international status. Within such a region-wide unified transport system, new international transport lines (branches) will be revealed, which will link post-Soviet Central Asia with other countries and will have a significant economic value.

In particular, the construction of the railway, linking the Fergana Valley (in which parts of the territories of Kyrgyzstan are situated (three oblasts), Tajikistan (one oblast), Uzbekistan (three oblasts), and Naryn oblast of Kyrgyzstan with the Chinese People's Republic (Xinjiang-Uygur Autonomous Region) through Irkeshtam (Alai, Osh oblast) and Torugart (Naryn oblast)), would give a new impetus to the development of economic and trade relations of Kyrgyzstan, Tajikistan, and Uzbekistan with China, which has a very capacious market. There would emerge new export-oriented branches of industry: the development of mineral, fuel, and energy resources, setting up production of ferrous and nonferrous metals in Kyrgyzstan (in Naryn oblast), the production of agricultural processing and receiving food and nonfood products in the Fergana Valley in all three states. It is hard to overestimate the political, social, cultural and touristic value of this road.

Environmental issues

Protection, preservation and enhancement of the environment are the most important common problem of post-Soviet Central Asia. In one geographical region the peoples can install border posts and lines between each other according to the choice of state and legal way of life, but the natural and climatic conditions cannot deny each other and close the fences. They are a whole, created by nature, and they do not differ by national or state feature. And maintenance of natural habitat of one region should be a fairly common objective of all the states, situated in this region. If in one republic, measures are taken in this regard and are not taken in another, those that are not taken will certainly cause a backfiring in those places where measures were taken.

In post-Soviet Central Asia, inadequate economic activity that ignored its impact on the natural conditions, has resulted in, inter alia, the situation where the water basin of the Aral Sea has been lost, salted and dried, and dust winds sweep across the region. This adversely affects the climate, soil, economic activity, and human health. Nature is contaminated; clogged glaciers rapidly melt.

Central Asia is an amazing and uniquely beautiful region, with a variety of colour schemes and sharp contrasts: mountains with eternal glaciers and rocks famous in the world for peaks of six and seven thousand metres height that are, in some places, covered with magnificent rays and green forests, and in other places are hard and stony. The region is rich in mineral, fuel, and energy resources; it has high mountain pastures with an abundance of herbs and saturated with the scent of edelweiss; the purest medium and small lakes; while mountain rivers, large and small, nourish the valley with life-giving waters and are the major hydroelectric power resource and source of irrigation in the region. It has blooming valleys, the main land, where the most people live and which is the core of business; burning, scorching semi deserts and deserts, where human activities develop as well, and under which lie natural resources, which are worthy of economic attention.

With the acquisition of true state sovereignty, the formation of multiform economy (free, open and market), the natural resources of the region have become much more intensively developed and used than ever before.

Naturally, there arise problems of protecting the environment from air pollution; water and land degradation; deterioration of biochemical properties, and soil depletion; disappearance of grass cover and deforestation of pastures and mountains; reduction in water sources and desertification of fertile lands. All this may happen if we do not take into account what a production load the natural environment can have, and if the attitude to the development and use of natural resources is economically illiterate and barbaric.

In addition to the problems mentioned above, which are connected with the lives of people, we have to face natural disasters: earthquakes, snow avalanches and mountain stone landslides, floods and so on, which are also harmful to nature. Post-Soviet Central Asia is characterized by a high seismicity, a sharp continental climate, mountainous terrain, and rapid mountain rivers delivering water to the valleys, and the natural disasters mentioned above are peculiar to it.

Hence, the states should take measures for environmentally careful use of natural resources and create environmentally friendly production and pro-active organization of protective measures against natural disasters. The ecological element should take its strong, inalienable place in the economic mind and economic psychology of the society. Education and training should be started in childhood and carried on continuously throughout the whole life.

Every post-Soviet Central Asian country has positive experience in terms of protection of the environment; certain measures are outlined and taken. It makes no sense to confirm them. The following three problems are extremely important for ecological Central Asia.

Disposal of radioactive waste

The first problem is a safe disposal of radioactive and toxic wastes. Radioactive tailings of uranium ore mines are badly closed in Kazakhstan, Kyrgyzstan, Tajikistan and Uzbekistan. If some tailing breaks in, for example, one republic, it will immediately have a destructive influence on the territories of other countries and the population. Water and soil will be infected; there will be a threat to the life of the population in cities and villages. For example, if some radioactive tailing in southern Kyrgyzstan breaks and flows down the river, the nature and population of Uzbekistan will suffer more than Kyrgyzstan.

The reliability of disposal of radioactive and toxic wastes is vital for protecting the environment and ensuring public health security. Kyrgyzstan has, for example, 92 objects, which equates to a buried 457 million tons of toxic and radioactive wastes. International experts identify a number of factors that increase the risk of possible ecological catastrophe, and its neighbours, Uzbekistan, Tajikistan, Kazakhstan fall within this zone: activation of earthquakes, permanent erosion processes, long lack of control and restoration work at the tailings, the localization of most radioactive wastes in cross-border river basins, and therefore the pollution threatens the whole Central Asian region.

Such objects are sufficient in Kazakhstan, Tajikistan and Uzbekistan. And if some crucial situations arise in one republic, they will instantly cause a chain reaction in the other countries. Measures aimed at ensuring the safety of the tailings require considerable funds: financial and material. Not all the countries can cope with it properly, but the decision cannot be half-and-half or partial: there will be a threat to everyone. Therefore, there is no need to count each other's money and share, we should unite possibilities (as much as possible) and promote safe life for nature and the population of a unified region.

In general, ensuring safety of uranium tailings is a very costly problem, and aid from the international funds, financial institutions, and developed foreign states is inevitably necessary; Russia, primarily as a successor of the USSR. After all, the uranium in Central Asia was mined to ensure defence security of the USSR.

In the Arguments and Facts in Kyrgyzstan #29 2009, Irina Soboleva devoted her article to uranium tailings. The article is called Political Tails. Why does Europe need uranium dumps? Finally, she writes, the high-ranking officials realized that the problems of uranium tailings cannot be solved on one's own. And this revelation took place in Switzerland, where high delegations of these countries gathered. Were they worried only about ecology and mainland security, or did economic interests lead?

The problem of radioactive burial places scattered throughout Central Asia, has long ceased to be a problem of only this region. Time goes by, burial grounds fail, and the infection gets into the rivers, which, inter alia, have cross-border status, and they intoxicate the soil. The rate of human mortality from cancer diseases in these areas breaks all records.

The UN experts who study this problem argue that Kazakhstan has developed quite an effective regulatory basis, which regulates the safety of the population and protection of the environment. In Tajikistan, over the past 6-7 years, laws and other regulations were adopted, which allowed regulation of the situation. But still the laws should be improved. In particular, in this country there are standards and recommendations, but they are not approved yet, therefore they do not work and cannot help the processing plants of similar structure to make decisions on advisability of recycling the tails. The legislation of Uzbekistan is based only on three regulations, but they are rather efficient.

In Kyrgyzstan the situation leaves much to be desired. The main document, the Law on the tailings and mountain dumps, concerns only general issues of management of such objects. The standards of radiation and sanitary safety were actually copied from the Russian documents almost word for word, without taking into account local peculiarities. The regulation for engineering activities and restoration processes regarding the former uranium objects do not exist at all.

Another important standard, covering sanitary rules of liquidation, conservation and conversion of enterprises, and dealing with mining and processing of radioactive ores, was developed during the Soviet period, and no one reviewed it or other documents in relation to the realities of today. In connection with this, it is interesting where the money went that generous international donors allocated to addressing the problem of tailing across many years.

What is the real situation with radioactive wastes? In Kazakhstan 12 deposits of uranium require special attention. Two deposits, which account for nearly 60 million tons of waste, pose the most serious threat. In

Tajikistan the total amount of waste of the former uranium production is nearly 55 million tons. Uranium dumps in the areas of the cities Taboshara, Abdrasmana, and Degeyskoe have no elementary protective coating.

For over 40 years Uzbekistan was the main raw material and uranium base for the Soviet Union. Here in the areas of the Syr Darya and Amur Darya Rivers the largest amount of large deposits of uranium with a high content of this chemical element in the rock were found. The Union collapsed, and the strategic raw materials have not been demanded so far. But the tails are a reminder that grows more serious with every day.

The situation in Kyrgyzstan is as follows. The city of Mailuu-Suu has a leading position among the hazardous areas, which require close attention. Here the volume of the wastes considerably exceeds the volume of waste dumps, which limit them. A large proportion of uranium ore for two local processing plants were imported here from East Germany. Dumps are mostly uncultivated. Meanwhile, the region where Mailuu-Suu is, is in the zone of high seismicity. Earthquakes can reach magnitude 7-8 here. Because of the landslide activity there is a real threat of destruction of radioactive burial places, most of which are located on the banks of the Mailuu-Suu River.

Today, despite the falls in global stock and commodity markets, the price of uranium remains consistently high. Given the fact that the raw material from the tailings are right under your feet and there is no need to spend money specially on its transportation, the cost of uranium worked out of recycled raw materials, will be significantly lower than that which is produced from the imported ore. Instead, you can sell it for three times as much. There is one more aspect of the problem. Waste disposal of nuclear power stations costs so much money that it cannot be placed in line with drug trafficking or arms. Is the attention of the European politicians so close to the Central Asian region because of the tailings?

The second problem is the ecologically careful attitude to the Issyk-Kul Lake, the pearl of post-Soviet Asia, which is famous for sun, air and water, and which has become a favourite vacation spot for rehabilitation of people not only from Kyrgyzstan, but the whole of post-Soviet Central Asia and Russia as well. Today, the international relations of Kyrgyzstan (political, economic, trade, touristic, cultural, scientific, and educational, etc.) have expanded significantly, and Issyk-Kul attracts foreign countries as a place of recreation and tourism. New recreation centres are intensively built and continue to function, including hotels, cottages, and complexes with residential and medical buildings, restaurants and cafes, shopping and entertainment facilities. The inflow of people increases from year to year, and, hence, the load on the lake becomes harder. This unique lake is characterized by the fact that the water from the lake does not flow anywhere. The lake can, due to its biochemical properties, self-purify in a natural way only at a certain level of contamination, but if the lake is contaminated above this level, this contamination will accumulate and we may lose the Issyk-Kul Lake. In addition to the above, we should highlight one more circumstance, which is worth being concerned about. Actually, reliable purifying facilities are not set up around Issyk-Kul. And where does the sewage of all those recreation centres, which function at an increasing rate from year to year, go?! Loss of Issyk-Kul would be a loss for the whole of Central Asia, and for Kyrgyzstan it would be an ecological catastrophe. Everything can change for the worse in the nature around Issyk-Kul, which has already disappeared. The state cannot afford it. The past, present and future generations of people will not forgive it.

In the future, the availability of radioactive and toxic wastes, and unsafe disposal, as well as the possibility of extinction of large natural water basins of the Aral Sea, Balkhash Lake, and Issyk-Kul Lake, may pose one of the main threats to the national, broader regional security for post-Soviet Central Asia. One may say that the Aral Sea is considerably lost. God forbid, we cannot lose Balkhash and Issyk-Kul.

The third problem is that the natural disaster will destroy irrigation, hydropower facilities and transport systems. Water and electricity will no longer get to the neighbouring republic, cargo and passenger transportation from one country to the neighbouring one will be discontinued. It is impossible to build reliable ecological protection in one republic on one's own, in isolation. Only together can it be created in post-Soviet Central Asia as a whole.

THE KYRGYZSTAN ECONOMY AND ECONOMIC RELATIONS BETWEEN TURKEY AND KYRGYZSTAN

PROF. S. RIDVAN KARLUK[1]

A Brief History of Kyrgyzstan Republic and its Importance for Central Asia

Kyrgyz clans who left Hun dominion from 2nd century BC to 1st century BC, immigrated to Yenisei and Baikal areas in Central Asia. The Khaganate, the first Kyrgyz State which reigned from 6th century to 13th century AD, overthrew Uygur State and established their own state in 840. Kyrgyz, who then moved to the territories where they currently live, and adopted Islam during the Karahan era. They were under the dominion of Russia from 1862 and Soviets in 1919-1920 (Nadir Devlet, p.5).

Kyrgyzstan, during the Soviet era, was included as Kara Kyrgyz Autonomous Oblast within the Russian Soviet Federal Socialist Republic in the 1924 Constitution, then its name changed to Kyrgyz Autonomous Oblast and a republic was declared in 1936. With the Soviet Union being in the process of collapse, Kyrgyzstan, declared its sovereignty on 15th December 1990 and independence on 31st August 1991. It then joined the Commonwealth of Independent States (CIS) on 21st December 1991, together with four other Central Asian countries (Yeniçeri, p.13).

From the independence till 2005, the office of the President was occupied by Askar Akayev. As a result of protests that happened in the capital, Bishkek, on 24th March 2005, which were triggered by the insurgency movements in Osh city, south Kyrgyzstan, President Akayev left the country and opposition leader Kurmanbek Bakiyev was elected as President and Prime Minister (Değirmenci, p.5).

Kurmanbek Bakiyev was elected as President as a result of presidential elections held on 10th July 2005 and he assigned Feliks Kulov, who withdrew from presidential elections in Bakiyev's favour, as Prime Minister.

---

[1] Anadolu University, Eskişehir, Turkey.

Prime Minister Feliks Kulov and the Council of Ministers resigned on 19th December 2006. The Constitution was passed on 26th December 2006 and became effective on 16th January 2007.

Following enactment of the new constitution, Feliks Kulov was nominated by the President twice as the prime ministerial candidate, but the Parliament did not ratify such nomination. Despite it being mandatory for the Parliament to accept it if the same person is nominated thrice, the President nominated Azimbek İsabekov, Acting Minister of Agriculture, Water and Process Industry, to the Prime Ministry, and following ratification by the Parliament, İsabekov started his duty on 29th January 2007 (Karaağaçlı, p.11).

Upon this, the opposition declared that rallies be launched in spring 2007, under the leadership of Feliks Kulov. The President accepted the resignation of Prime Minister Azimbek İsabekov, for the purpose of lowering political tension, and nominated Almaz Atambaev, one of the leaders of the opposition to prime ministry and obtained ratification of the Parliament.

The Constitutional Court, which held a session on 14th September 2007 on request of the MPs, resolved that the Constitution of 29th December 2006, which was not submitted to referendum, was null and void on the grounds that the rights vested in the Kyrgyz people were being violated through the said constitution. Through a decision adopted by the President on 19th September 2007, it was decided that the constitutional amendment must be submitted to referendum on 21st October 2007.

During the referendum held on 21st October 2007, Constitutional amendment was adopted through 76% of the people's votes. As required by the Constitution, the President dismissed Almazbek Atambaev, since his tenure expired. Parliamentary elections were held on 16th December 2007, in accordance with the new constitution. Twelve parties were in the elections, those parties which exceeded 5% national threshold and 0.5% regional threshold, were Akyol, which was established under the leadership of President with 47% of the votes, Kyrgyzstan Communist Party with 5%, and Kyrgyzstan Social Democrat Party with 5%. Parties obtained 71, 11, and 8 seats respectively.

Akyol Party, which obtained the majority in the Parliament, nominated Igor Çudinov, The Minister of Industry, Energy and Fuel Resources, in the former government to the prime ministry, and Çudinov took office on 24th December 2007. Later, Daniyar Usenov was assigned in lieu of Çudinov, who served between 2007 and 2009.

Displeasure arose amongst the people due to resolutions adopted and increased corruption during that period. On 6th April 2010, opponent groups raided the governor's building and took the governor as hostage in Talas. On 7th April 2010, 50 thousand protesters gathered on the square before the Presidential Building (White House) and about 100 died in gunfire.

On the same date the White House was occupied by the protesters and President Bakiyev fled to Belarus. Roza Otunbaeva, who became Head of Temporary Government, announced on the evening of 7th April that they had taken power. On 11th April 2010, there were clashes between Kyrgyz and Uzbeks in the south of the country, which resulted in a death toll of several hundreds.

The constitution that was passed on 27th June 2010, was submitted to referendum, and 90.57% of the people voted yes for the constitution. Upon this result, a Parliamentary Republic was established in Kyrgyzstan. Roza Otunbaeva who was head of Temporary Government, was sworn in as transitional Interim President till 31st December 2011, on condition that she could not be re-elected. The date of the parliamentary elections was set on 10th October 2011.

88.5% of the Kyrgyz of the Commonwealth of Independent States, CIS, live in Kyrgyzstan. Remaining Kyrgyz are distributed amongst other CIS countries, mainly Uzbekistan and Tajikistan. According to the 1999 census, 69.9% of the population consist of Kyrgyz, 13.8% Uzbek, 12.5% Russian, 1.1% Dungan, 1.1% Uygur, and 5.7% other ethnic groups. 75% of the population is Moslem, and 20% is Russian Orthodox.

Official languages of Kyrgyzstan are Kyrgyz (64.7%) and Russian (12.5%). These are followed by Uzbek (13.6%).

The Turkish population (Ahıska or Akhaltsikhe and Crimean Turks) is about 35,700. The number of nationals of Republic of Turkey living in Kyrgyzstan is 6 thousand. During the era following independence, those Kyrgyz citizens of Russian and German origin started to leave the country.

Kyrgyzstan-Turkey Relations

Turkey was the first country that recognized the independence of the Kyrgyzstan Republic on 16th December 1991 and diplomatic relations were established on 29th January 1992 between the two nations. Embassies were opened mutually in line with the Memorandum of Understanding of 29th January 1992. Kyrgyzstan President Askar Akayev paid the first official visit to Turkey on 23rd December 1991 and several cooperation agreements were signed during that visit.

Economic and commercial relations which started by the virtue of Protocol On Economic and Commercial Cooperation, which was signed between Kyrgyzstan and Turkey on 29th May 1991 in Ankara, rapidly thrived and a Turkish-Kyrgyz Business Council was established on 25th December 1991. The Kyrgyzstan-Turkey Businessmen and Industrialists Union was established for the purpose of bringing industrialists and businessmen who are operating in Kyrgyzstan, and TICA's Bishkek Office was opened.

As a result of the developed economic relations after gaining its independence, the number of Turkish companies that invest in Kyrgyzstan rapidly grew. Turkish companies are mainly small and medium scale enterprises. These enterprises are engaged in hospitality, bakery, leatherwear, general contracting, and telecommunication sectors. Included amongst the investments they made in the country is a Coca-Cola factory and distribution companies, Bishkek, Osh highway rehabilitation project, installation of 3500-subscriber digital phone exchanges in Naryn and Talas cities, assembly and manufacture of TVs, leather and fur processing, and oil production facilities.

Prime Minister Recep Tayyip Erdoğan and State Minister Zafer Çağlayan paid an official visit to Kyrgyzstan between 1st and 2nd February 2011. During this visit, the Turkey, Kyrgyzstan Business Forum was held. Almazbek Atambaev, Prime Minister of Kyrgyzstan, held some meetings in Ankara on 28th April 2011 and attended Turkey, Kyrgyzstan Commerce and Investment Forum. As a result of that visit, Turkey cancelled USD 50 million of debt owed by Kyrgyzstan.

Atambaev, talked about the meeting he held with Prime Minister Recep Tayyip Erdoğan: "We applied pressure on Elder Brother Tayyip to give us money. 'He asked us why you are applying pressure on me?' And I told him 'We have no other elder brother'. Mr. Erdoğan cancelled USD 50 million of our debts." (Milliyet Daily, 28th April 2011). State Minister Ali Babacan explained that 100 treaties were signed between two countries, and that the mutual abolishment of visa practice is very important.

General State of Kyrgyz Economy

Kyrgyzstan, which is one of the Central Asian countries, is a small country with a population of 5.3 million. Annual population growth is 1.3%. Literacy rate is very high (98.7%). 23% of the population are graduates of higher educational institutions and 75.3% from secondary educational institutions. GNP in 2010 was 4.6 million USD, and per capita income is 846 USD in 2010. Its share in world trade is 0.02%. Kyrgyzstan has limited oil and natural gas reserves, which are able to meet only 12% of the local demand. Its coal sources are inadequate. Power generation is one of the basic industries in Kyrgyzstan. Power is generated in hydroelectric power plants and marketed to the consumers at cheaper rates.

People reacted a lot to a two-fold increase in power prices in 2009, constituting one of the reasons for revolt in 2010. The country has the third largest hydroelectric resources, following Russia and Tajikistan, amongst the CIS countries. It is estimated that a potential of 55,000 GWh per annum exists due to melting glaciers on Mount Tian Shan.

According to International Monetary Fund (IMF) data, the Kyrgyz economy exhibited a reasonable growth rate, except for 2010. Between 2000 and 2011, the growth rate was negative (-1.4%) only in 2010. The declining growth rate in Kyrgyzstan after 2007 is an outcome of global crisis. The IMF's 5% growth rate forecast for 2011 is an indicator that effects of the crisis started to fade out (IMF, Regional Economic Outlook).

Prices have recently shown a tendency to increase in Kyrgyzstan. This tendency was greatly contributed to by global crisis. The highest inflation rates since 1998 were experienced in 2008. The greatest effect from this was the boom in foodstuff prices, which reached almost 40%. The share of food prices in Kyrgyzstan in the inflation basket is about 58%.

The annual inflation rate of bread and pastry products in the country is about 62.6%, and that of animal fat and vegetable oil is about 49.3%. Inflation rate declined into single digits in 2009 and 2010.

The struggle against inflation is top priority to enable the economy to improve. The IMF forecasts a 15 to 18% increase in oil and food prices. The IMF's inflation anticipation for this year is about 10% (IMF, Public Information Notice).

Public financial balance as a fraction of GDP is always negative except in 2008. This indicates that the Kyrgyz economy is fragile. Decrease in public debt ratio to GNP is a positive development.

The fact that the current account balance as a fraction of GNP is progressively increasing is the one question which Kyrgyzstan must concentrate on. In a case where the crisis that emerged in some member states of The European Union spread to the entire globe, those countries with an international trade balance problem might be influenced by such a crisis much more quickly. The fact that the total gross foreign indebtedness as a fraction of GNP has a tendency to decline, is a positive development.

Table 1. Macroeconomic indicators of Kyrgyzstan

	2000-05	2006	2007	2008	2009	2010	2011
GDP Growth Rate (%)	4.1	3.1	8.5	7.6	2.9	-1.4	5.0
Consumer Price (%)	6.5	5.6	10.2	24.5	6.8	7.8	18.8
General Government Fiscal Balance (as % of GNP)	-5.6	-2.1	-0.3	0.0	-3.6	-6.5	-8.9
Total Gross Public Debt (as % of GNP)	103.7	72.5	56.8	48.5	58.0	62.6	59.5
Exports (USD Billion)	0.8	1.5	2.2	3.0	2.8	2.6	3.4
Imports (USD Billion)	0.9	2.3	3.2	4.7	3.7	4.1	5.2
Current Account Balance (USD Billion)	0.0	-0.1	0.0	-0.4	0.1	-0.3	-0.4
Current Account Balance (% of GNP)	-0.1	-3.1	-0.2	-8.1	2.0	-7.4	-8.7
Total Gross Foreign Indebtedness (as % of GNP)	107.1	77.7	60.2	45.1	58.2	68.3	63.6
Gross Official Reserves (USD Billion)	0.4	0.8	1.2	1.2	1.6	1.7	1.8

Source: IMF, Regional Economic Outlook, May 2011

6% of Kyrgyzstan comprises of forests and 4.2% of glaciers, and Tengri (Tian Shan) and Altai Range of mountains divide the country into separate valleys. Rivers, born on high mountains and thus having irregular and high flow rates are not suitable for transportation. Naryn, Tar, Kurshab, Talas, Alay, Chui and Kızıl Su are used for power generation and are the main rivers of the country.

Kyrgyzstan is a country rich in water sources. 90% of these sources are allocated to agriculture, 7% to industry, and the remaining 3% to miscellaneous areas, including consumption as potable water. The largest lake, out of almost 3000 lakes in the country, is Issyk-Kul, which is the second largest mountain lake in the world, with a surface area of 6202 km^2.

Of the workforce of about 2.2 million in Kyrgyzstan, 32.4% work in agriculture, 39.5% in services, and 12.5% in industry. The unemployment rate in 2010 was 8.4%, of which 52.7% were women. Long term unemployment rate in rural areas is about 70%. Minimum wage is SOM 600. Minimum wage for Bishkek and the surrounding area is 150-200 USD.

Table 2. Economic indicators of Kyrgyzstan economy

	2008	2009	2010
GDP (Som Million)	185,013.6	196,423.1	212,177.4
GDP (USD million, in market prices)	5,059.2	4,579.7	4,616.6
Real GDP Growth Rate (%)	7.6	2.9	-1.4
Per capita (GDP, USD)	968.4	888	864
Inflation rate (%)			
Consumer Price Index, (p.a, %)	24.5	6.8	7.8
Workforce (active population)	2,343,800	2,184,300	2,216,400
Unemployment rate (%)	11.2	10.3	8.4
Number of Workers Working Abroad	490,000	420,000	460,000
GDP Growth rates by sectors (%)			
Agriculture	0.7	7.4	-2.8
Industry	14.9	-6.4	9.8
Service	8.8	1.4	-4.7
International trade (USD Thousand)	5,699,000	4,475,900	5,265,500
Exports	1,641,500	1,439,000	2,027,800
Imports	4,057,000	3,036,900	3,237,700
Balance	-2,415,500	-1,597,900	-1,209,900
Share in Global Trade (%)	0.02	0.02	0.02
Share of Turkey in Total Figures of the Country			
Exports	2.7	2.5	1.83
Imports	2.2	2.4	2.61
Public Foreign Indebtedness (USD million)	2,127.9	2,475.6	2,615.7
Fixed Foreign Investments (USD thousand)	653,223.2	556,741.1	445,962.8
Emission Volume (SOM million)	30,559.8	35,738.7	
Selected Rates (%)			
Exports/Imports	40.4	47.4	62.0
Exports/GDP	32.4	31.4	43.0
Imports/GDP	80.2	66.3	70.0

Source: Kyrgyzstan National Statistics Institution and Kyrgyzstan Central Bank (Republic of Turkey, Bishkek Embassy)

Increased unemployment and lowered real income due to global crisis spread poverty in the country. As a result of increased economic instability, the first IMF loan was secured in 1994. Since it became a member of TWO on 20th December 1998, it is the first country amongst the Central Asian countries that assumed liberal international trade policies.

National currency was put into circulation, prices were allowed to be free, reforms were made in the agricultural sector and public assets were put into privatization process in 1993. As a result of these measures, a recovery took place in the economy after 1996.

The global crisis adversely influenced the Kyrgyz economy in and after 2008 (Günal, p. 29). Growth rate declined 2.9% in 2009 and became 1.4% in 2010. The IMF's estimated growth for 2011 is 5%. This estimate is an indicator that adverse effects of global crisis will progressively wear off.

In 2010, national income declined by 2.1%, excluding Kumtor gold mine production. When considered together with the mine's production, decline in the national income is 1.4%. As a result of reflection of global crisis on the country's economy, national income per capita declined by 2.7% in 2010 in comparison with previous year.

Table 3. Growth Rates of Caucasian and Central Asian economies

Growth rates in Caucasus and Central Asian Countries	**2009**	**2010**	**2011 (Forecast)**
Caucasus and Central Asia	3.7	6.6	5.7
Oil and Natural Gas Exporter Countries	4.9	7.1	5.8
Azerbaijan	9.3	5.0	2.8
Kazakhstan	1.2	7.0	5.9
Turkmenistan	6.1	9.2	9.0
Uzbekistan	8.1	8.5	7.0
Oil and Natural Gas Importer Countries	-3.5	4.0	5.2
Armenia	-14.2	2.6	4.6
Georgia	-3.8	6.4	5.5
Kyrgyzstan	2.9	-1.4	5.0
Tajikistan	3.9	6.5	5.8
Commonwealth of Independent States	-6.4	4.6	5.0
Russia	-7.8	4.0	4.8
China	9.2	10.3	9.6

Source: IMF, World Economic Outlook, country and IMF forecasts

Agriculture has a significant place in the Kyrgyz economy. 18.5% of the income generated in the country in 2010 originate from this sector. The surface area of the arable land to total surface area is 7%. Live stocking has a significant place in this sector. 55% of the agricultural production is realized through home enterprises.

The share of the manufacturing industry in national income is 15.97%. The most important sub-sector of the industrial production is the food processing sector. Food processing is also a sector which is the most attractive for foreign investment. 80% of the industrial production is production industry. 45.9% of the national income in 2010 originated from the service sector. Commerce, repair of automobiles and private appliances (16.1%), as well as transportation and communication (9.1%) are other important service sub-sectors.

Private enterprises are prominent in Kyrgyzstan. As of 1st January 2010, 24,500 companies were doing business in the country. Of these, 13.1% are state owned companies and the share of the private enterprises in the total is 69.4%. The companies are concentrated in Bishkek. A great majority of the companies are small enterprises. Shares of the medium and large scale enterprises are 14.4 and 6.8% respectively.

Foreign indebtedness, which was 2.48 billion USD in 2009, rose to 2.62 billion USD in 2010. Kyrgyzstan is amongst the 40 developing countries which are in the Heavily Indebted Poor Countries (HIPC) category (Alma Lucía Romer-Barrutieta, et. al, p.6). The high foreign indebtedness burden of Kyrgyzstan, which joined the World Bank in 1999, was restructured within the framework of Paris Club (Paris Club, p.6).

Kyrgyzstan, by giving due consideration to its high foreign indebtedness, joined in the CIS-7 initiative which was established by international creditor institutions in 2001, for the purpose of reforming financial structure of the new debts. A 2 billion USD Poverty Reduction Program covering the period between 2003 and 2010 was developed by the World Bank, IMF, and Asian Development Bank for Kyrgyzstan.

The banking system was re-regulated in Kyrgyzstan after independence. Of 22 commercial banks in the country, 15 are banks with foreign investment. Despite the fact that there are 10 banks, with more than half of the capital belonging to foreign investors, banking services are not developed. Cash based economy is prominent.

The amount of direct foreign investment (DPI) that flew into Kyrgyzstan after 1995 is USD 3,818 million. Of this amount, 32.3% is from CIS countries. In 2010, USD 446 million direct foreign investment entered into the country. Of this investment, 32.3% originated from CIS countries. Direct investment from CIS decreased by 20% in comparison with 2009. This was due to the political and social instability that took place in Kyrgyzstan in 2010.

The 7th April and 10th June 2010 events had very adverse effects on the economy. Due to such facts as inability to realize political stability for a long time, and borders with neighbouring countries, Kazakhstan and Uzbekistan, recession started in the economy and planned investments were either given up or deferred (Dikambaev, p.17).

Kyrgyzstan trades with countries of the region to a great extent. Its share in world trade is very little. Its exports depend on the importing performance of its neighbours. With decreased imports as a result of the devalued Ruble in the 1998 Russian crisis, as well as Kazakhstan's custom duties increase of 200% to decrease imports from Russia, Kyrgyz exports were adversely influenced.

The countries that are in the top ranks for imports of Kyrgyzstan are Russia (33.8%), People's Republic of China (21.9%), Kazakhstan (12.5%), USA (5.9%), and Uzbekistan (3.2%). The share of CIS countries in imports of the country is in the neighbourhood of about 56.5%. CIS countries are the most significant area of exports by Kyrgyzstan, with 36% of exports. Switzerland (19.1%), United Arab Emirates (14.9%), Russia (12.7%), and Kazakhstan (9%) are the countries which rank top in its exports.

Included in significant exported goods are precious metals (gold), non-organic chemicals, textile and ready-made apparels, vegetables, milk and dairy products, power, fruits, and cotton fibre.

Included in imports are mineral products such as kerosene and gasoline. These are followed by clothing and accessories, medicines, meat and meat products (winged), wheat, and natural gas.

Gold became the biggest export item of the country after Kumtor mine started producing gold. Gold represents an average 37% of the export revenues of the country, corresponding to 32% of the exports realized to non-CIS countries. Textile exports mainly comprise of ready-made clothing, which is mainly shipped to Russia.

Since Kyrgyzstan is a party to General System of Preferences which was established within the framework of General Agreement on Tariffs and Trade (GATT) and United Nations Conference on Trade and Development (UNCTAD), it benefits from unilateral preferences under GSP.

After free trade agreements it realized with CIS countries, it signed free trade agreements with the Russian Federation (March 1993), Armenia (October 1995), Moldova (November 1996), Ukraine (December 1997), Kazakhstan (November 1995), Uzbekistan (March 1997), Belarus (17th March 2000), Tajikistan (December 2001), and Azerbaijan (January 2004).

All CIS countries other than Turkmenistan apply a free trade regime to exports of Kyrgyzstan, and Kyrgyzstan to all products from CIS countries. The Trade and Economic Cooperation Agreement, which was made with Georgia in 1997, became effective on 6th January 2006. This agreement does not include a preferred regime clause.

Table 4. Kyrgyzstan's annual international trade by years according to the data by Kyrgyzstan Statistics Institution

(Thousand USD)	2008	2009	2010	Change (%)
Exports	1 641 500.00	1 439 000.00	2 027 800	21.2
Imports	4 057 500.00	3 036 900.00	3 237 700	6.5
Volume	5 699 000.00	4 475 900.00	5 265 500	11.7
Balance	-2 416 000.00	-1 597 900.00	-1 209 900	-25.0

Source: Kyrgyzstan National Statistics Institution (Republic of Turkey's Embassy to Bishkek)

(*) Kyrgyzstan Statistics Institution makes non-registered economy corrections on exports of agricultural products in July.

Economic and Commercial Relations with Turkey

Turkey is the first country that recognized the independence of Kyrgyzstan. A Protocol on Economic and Commercial Cooperation was signed in Ankara on 29th May 1991 for improving economic relations between Turkey and Kyrgyzstan.

The number of Turkish entrepreneurs who have an investment in excess of USD 1 million in Kyrgyzstan is 25. About 200 Turkish small and medium-sized enterprises (SME) are active in Kyrgyzstan. About 78 Kyrgyz invested companies are present in Turkey.

Turkey has investments in Kyrgyzstan exceeding USD 400 million. The share of Turkey in foreign investments in Kyrgyzstan is about 12%. Turkey is followed by such other important foreign investors as USA, Britain, Germany, South Korea, People's Republic of China, etc.

In addition to foodstuff investments, such as beverages, biscuits, candies, chocolates, etc., Turkish investments in the country include production of furniture, cleaning products, tea, flour, salt, sugar, paint, PVC and plastic pipes, construction materials, as well as operating shopping malls, general stores, banking, textile manufacturing, printing, tourism agency, educational institutions, and construction.

While commercial relations rapidly increased after independence, a decline was observed in 1998 and 1999. The main reason of this decline is the economic crisis that emerged in Far East Asia and deeply influenced the Russian Federation.

Kyrgyzstan has a share of 0.05% in the international trade of Turkey. The international trade of Turkey gave a surplus in bilateral trades according to data from both the Statistics Institution of Turkey (TÜİK) and Kyrgyzstan National Statistics Institution.

According to the Kyrgyzstan National Statistics Institute's data, Turkey is at 9th place in imports of Kyrgyzstan, after Russia, People's Republic of China, Kazakhstan, USA, Uzbekistan, Belarus, Germany, and Japan, while, Turkey is at 8th place in exports of Kyrgyzstan following Switzerland, United Arab Emirates, Russia, Kazakhstan, USA, Uzbekistan, and France.

International trade between Kyrgyzstan and Turkey started in 1992. International trade volume, which was USD 18 million in 1994, reached USD 41 million in 1995, and rose to USD 52 million in 1996. After 1997, international trade volume lost its rate of increase.

Due to the adverse effect of the 1998 Russian crisis on the Kyrgyzstan economy, international trade volume declined to USD 44 million in 1998 and to USD 27 million in 1999. The international trade volume increased in the following years and peaked at USD 239 million in 2008.

According to 2010 data from TÜİK, trade volume between Kyrgyzstan and Turkey is USD 160,125 million. A decline of 7.7% in exports of Turkey and 1.7% in exports of Kyrgyzstan were experienced this year.

This is because the workplaces were plundered as a result of revolts that happened in April and June of 2010 in Kyrgyzstan, global financial crisis, fleeing foreign investment from the country, decreased total demand due to social and economic instability, and increased oil product prices.

Imports of Turkey from Kyrgyzstan follow a fluctuating path. The imports, which were USD 3.94 million in 1994, rose to USD 7.9 million in 1997 and started to decline as of 1998 and were realized as USD 4.606 million in 1999 and USD 2.35 million in 2000. In the following years imports started increasing, and peaked at USD 47.9 million in 2008.

A similar trend is present in exports of Turkey to Kyrgyzstan. Exports which were USD 15 million in 1994, rose to USD 38 million in 1995 and to USD 47 million in 1996. They decreased in 1997 to USD 43 million, USD 23 million in 1999, USD 14 million in 2005, and increased again to peak at USD 191 million in 2008.

The products that Kyrgyzstan imports from Turkey are machinery, telecommunication equipment, fast food, motor vehicles, textiles, and apparel. Included in the products Kyrgyzstan exports to Turkey are leather, fur products, weaved raw materials, scrap copper, livestock, and animal products.

According to the data from the Information Centre of Undersecretary of International trade, while industrial products represent 99.2% of Turkey's exports to Kyrgyzstan, 84.1% of Turkey's imports represent agricultural products and 15.8% industrial products.

Table 5. Turkey Kyrgyzstan International trade According to Data of Kyrgyzstan National Statistics Institution

International trade	**2008**	**2009**	**2010**
Trade with Turkey (Thousand USD, National Statistics Institution*)	136,072	109,374	121,908
Imports of Turkey	45,001	36,654	37,209
Exports of Turkey	91,071	72,720	84,699
Balance	46,070	36,066	47,490

Source: Kyrgyzstan National Statistics Institution
* According to Kyrgyzstan National Statistics Institution data, international trade volume of Turkey and Kyrgyzstan was USD 122 million in 2010. Exports of Turkey to Kyrgyzstan is USD 84.6 million and exports USD 37.2 million.

Table 6. Turkey Kyrgyzstan International trade According to TÜİK data

Years	**Exports (FOB)**	**Change (%)**	**Imports (CIF)**	**Change (%)**	**Volume**	**Balance**
2000	20,572	-11.3	2,350	-15.5	22,922	18,222
2001	17,350	-15.7	6,350	168.4	23,657	11,043
2002	24,005	38.4	17,623	179.4	41,628	6,382
2003	40,862	70.2	10,906	38.1	51,768	29,956
2004	74,702	82.8	13,384	22.7	88,086	61,317
2005	89,530	19.8	14,113	5.4	103,643	75,417
2006	132,172	47.6	27,455	94.5	159,627	104,717
2007	181,311	37.2	45,020	64	226,331	136,291
2008	191,351	5.5	47,974	6.6	239,325	143,377
2009	140,002	-26.83	31,446	-34.45	171,448	108,556
2010	129,227	-7.7	30,899	-1.74	160,126	98,328

Source: TÜİK and Prime Ministry Public Diplomacy Coordinator's office

The most important items in Kyrgyzstan's exports to Turkey in 2010 are agricultural and animal products, reaching USD 25 million. First of all, walnuts and beans are the most important export items for Kyrgyzstan. Since demand for cotton increased in 2010, this item rose to 2nd place in 2010, while it was 4th place in 2009. The main reason is decreased cotton production due to flood disasters and adverse production conditions prevalent in India, Australia, and Pakistan, which are the main exporters of cotton.

Conclusions

With the collapse of the Soviet Union in 1991, the country became deprived of Soviet support and a decline was observed in private consumption, and public spending increased. As a result of the foregoing, between 1991 and 1995, national income dropped below half of its level in 1990. The 1998 Russian crisis and economic crisis experienced in global markets in 2007 greatly influenced the Kyrgyz economy.

Kyrgyzstan is a country which applied the most liberal decisions in terms of efforts to transition into a market economy after gaining its independence. It is the only country amongst the Central Asian countries that is a member of the World Trade Organization (WTO). Its WTO membership enabled Kyrgyzstan to start implementing international standards in international trade and investment fields.

The fact that growth is dependent on the demand from close neighbours and that the economy is open to foreign shocks, high inflation rates triggered by increased food and oil prices, decreased food and power consumption due to draught, power restrictions, all aggravated adverse effects of the crisis on the country's economy.

In spite of that, since Kyrgyzstan has not been fully integrated into international markets, effects of the crisis were felt less than in other countries.

Since the global crisis started in 2008, and slowed down the fast growth in construction industry of Kazakhstan, it caused recession in Kyrgyzstan which uses Kazakh capital as the driving force.

The fact that Kazakh banks, which have a significant place in Kyrgyz economy, were adversely influenced by the global crisis, was directly reflected in Kyrgyzstan. The fact that Kazakh banks, which hold more than half of the banking system, were having difficulties, had an adverse effect on Kyrgyz economy.

In spite of this, since the level to which the Kyrgyzstan banks are integrated into the global banks is not very high, the crisis had no devastating effect on the economy in comparison with other countries. The crisis was manifested as a 6.4% decline in Kyrgyzstan industry and 25.4% drop in its international trade in 2009.

Kyrgyzstan realized convertibility and liberalization of interest rates in spite of the crisis, but unemployment continued to be a major problem for the country.

In addition to adverse effects of the crisis, failure to solve structural problems in the economy, the large scale of off-the-books economy, problems the government experiences in securing adequate revenues, frequency of tax controls, failure of the social security system to operate better, and social unrest, all played an important role in increased poverty in the country. The poverty rate in Kyrgyzstan is 43%, and poor people are mostly those who make a living through stock breeding and farming in the regions outside Bishkek and Osh.

The decrease in the foreign currency transferred by workers who work in Kazakhstan and Russia, which were adversely influenced by the crisis, aggravated the effects of the crisis. Despite the fact that there was an increase in the foreign currency remitted from abroad in 2009, it failed to reach the level seen in 2008.

Kyrgyzstan has been a member of the IMF since 1993. During the past period the IMF extended support to Kyrgyzstan through various tools. Ex-Post Assessment (EPA) was completed in November 2004 and new EPA became valid between 2005 and 2010. The IMF finds the policies pursued and macroeconomic performance of the country during this period positive.

In spite of that, restructuring of the banking system of Kyrgyzstan and ensuring good governance are deemed as priorities by the IMF.

In spite of crisis, income targets were partially attained and foreign indebtedness was reduced. Monetary and flexible foreign exchange policies pursued during the global crisis ensured that foreign shocks of the crisis were fended off lightly. However structural reforms and the government's failure to ensure transparency in their dealings were criticized by the IMF.

Fundamental political priorities of Kyrgyzstan have been set as ensuring macroeconomic stability, forming a reasonable foreign indebtedness strategy, realization of adequate growth and structural reforms within the scope of Poverty Reduction and Growth Facility (PRGF) of the IMF.

The IMF's Board of Directors allocated resources to Kyrgyzstan on 20th July 2011 for three years within the scope of an Extended Credit Facility (ECF) to the amount of SDR 66.6 million (USD 106 million) and made a portion of the amount, SDR 9.514 million (USD 15.2 million), available.

This support program that the IMF extended to Kyrgyzstan shall eliminate the instability caused by domestic uprising in 2010 and ensure macroeconomic stability.

Kyrgyzstan has a very limited local market. Its central position in Central Asia, the fact that it adapted to free market conditions faster than other countries in the region, and existence of free trade zones, puts the country in a privileged position in market entry strategies for the region.

Kyrgyzstan is a neighbour to two fastest growing economies of the world; Kazakhstan and People's Republic of China. That is why it represents an attractive environment for the investors. In the event that economic and political stability are ensured in the country, it might get into a fast paced growth trend with its two neighbours and more quickly eliminate adverse effects of the crisis.

References

Karaağaçlı, 2010. "Instability in Kyrgyzstan", Wise Men Centre for Strategic Studies.

Romero-Barrutieta, 2011. Aleš Bulíř and José Daniel Rodríguez-Delgado, The Dynamic Implications of Debt Relief for Low-Income Countries, IMF Working Paper.

Dikambaev, 2009. "Effect of Global Economic Crisis on Kyrgyz Economy". Turkish Policy Quarterly.

BBC Turkish, "Medvedev Fears Kyrgyzstan become Talibanist" http://www.bbc.co.uk/turkce/haberler/2010/06/100618_medvedev_kyrgiz.shtml

Wise Men Centre for Strategic Studies, Instability in Kyrgyzstan. http://www.bilgesam.org/tr/index.php?option=com_content&view=article&id=715:krgzistanda-stikrarszlk&catid=83:analizler-ortaasya&Itemid=149

Wise Men Centre for Strategic Studies "Domestic and Foreign Dynamics of the Clashes in Kyrgyzstan.
http://www.bilgesam.org/tr/index.php?option=com_content&view=article&id=739:krgzistandaki-catmalarn-c-ve-d-dinamikleri&catid=83:analizler-ortaasya&Itemid=149,

Bishkek Embassy, Commercial Counsellor, 2010. General Economic Situation and Its Economic, Commercial Relations With Turkey. http://www.musavirlikler.gov.tr/upload/kır/rapor2010son.doc

Central Intelligence Agency, The World Factbook: Central Asia: Kyrgyzstan,
https://www.cia.gov/library/publications/the-world-factbook/geos/kg.html

Doing Business, Ease of Doing Business In Kyrgyz Republic, http://www.doingbusiness.org/data/exploreeconomies/kyrgyz-republic

International Monetary Fund, 2011. Press Release No. 11/245.

—. 2011. Executive Board of the International Monetary Fund, "Discussed the Ex Post Assessment of Longer-Term Program Engagement (EPA) with the Republic of Kyrgyzstan".

—. Caucasus, Central Asia Rebound, But Inflation Poses Risk, IMF Survey online, http://www.imf.org/external/pubs/ft/survey/so/2011/car042711b.htm

—. IMF Executive Board Discusses Ex Post Assessment of Longer-Term Program Engagement in the Kyrgyz Republic, http://www.imf.org/external/np/sec/pn/2011/pn1164.htm

—. IMF Executive Board Approves USUSD106 Million Extended Credit Facility Arrangement for the Kyrgyz Republic, http://www.imf.org/external/np/sec/pr/2011/pr11245.htm

—. Regional Economic Outlook Middle East and Central Asia, April 11, http://www.imf.org/external/pubs/ft/reo/2011/mcd/eng/pdf/mreo0411.pdf

—. IMF Working Paper, The Dynamic Implications of Debt Relief for Low-Income Countries, http://www.imf.org/external/pubs/ft/wp/2011/wp11157.pdf

Kyrgyzstan Republic National Statistics Committee, 2009. Kyrgyzstan Republic Socioeconomic Situation.

Kyrgyz National News Agency, www.kabar.kg/eng/

Library of Congress - Federal Research Division, 2007. Country Profile: Kyrgyzstan, http://lcweb2.loc.gov/frd/cs/profiles/Kyrgyzstan.pdf

Günal, 2010, "Kyrgyzstan Economy and Effects of Global Crisis", Twothousandtwentythree, Issue 109.

Milliyet, 2011. "Atambaev told "Elder Brother Tayyip, give us money" and Erdoğan cancelled a debt of USD 50 million". http://ekonomi.milliyet.com.tr/atambayev-tayyip-agabey-para-ver-dedi-erdogan-50-milyon-dolarlik-borcu-sildi/ekonomi/ekonomidetay/28.04.2011/1383380/default.htm

Devlet, 1993. Contemporary Turkish: Great Islamic History from Its Onset to Today. Çağ Publishing, Istanbul. National Bank of Kyrgyz Republic. www.nbkr.kg.

National Statistical Committee of Kyrgyz Republic, www.stat.kg

Yeniçeri 2010. "Process of Going from One Revolution to Another in Kyrgyzstan", Twothousandtwentythree, Issue 109.

Paris Club, 2010, Annual Report 2009.

Peyrouse, 2007. The Economic Aspects of the Chinese-Central Asia Rapprochement, Central Asia-Caucasus Institute & Silk Road Studies Program, A Joint Transatlantic Research and Policy Centre, Johns Hopkins University, Washington.

Karluk 2007. International Institutions, 6th Ed. Beta Basım Yayın A.Ş. (Co. Inc.) Istanbul.

Silk Road Paper, Economic Aspects of the Chinese - Central Asia Rapprochement, http://www.silkroadstudies.org/new/docs/Silkroadpapers/2007/0709China-Central_Asia.pdf

Republic of Turkey, Prime Ministry, Undersecretary of International trade, www.dtm.gov.tr.

Republic of Turkey, Undersecretary of International trade, Report on Basic Economic Characteristics of Kyrgyzstan. http://www.foreigntrade.gov.tr/dtmadmin/upload/ANL/YurtDisiMuteahhitDb/tmh/program/kirgizistan/EK-2.pdf

Republic of Turkey, Public Diplomacy Coordinator's Office, 2010. Turkey Supports The Vast Turkish Geography with Hundreds of Projects, Ankara.

The World Bank, Heavily Indebted Poor Countries (40 countries), http://web.worldbank.org/WBSITE/EXTERNAL/TOPICS/EXTDEBTDEPT/0,contentMDK:20260049~menuPK:528655~pagePK:64166689~piPK:64166646~theSitePK:469043,00.html

Turkish Policy Quarterly, http://www.turkishpolicy.com/

Turkish Science, 2005. Tulip Revolution in Kyrgyzstan, http://turkbilimi.com/?p=4038

Union of Turkish Republics, International Cooperation Platform. http://www.turkcumhuriyetleribirligi.com/index.php?option=com_content&task=view&id=12&Itemid=26

World Bank (various issues), World Development Indicators.

PERFORMANCE OF CENTRAL ASIAN ECONOMIES

ASST. PROF. FAHRI SOLAK[1] AND DR. ERCAN SARIDOĞAN[1]

Economic Structure

Azerbaijan

Azerbaijan's high economic growth during 2006-08 was attributable to large and growing oil exports, but some non-export sectors also featured double-digit growth, spurred by growth in the construction, banking, and real estate sectors. In 2009, economic growth remained above 9%, even as oil prices moderated and growth in the construction sector cooled. In 2010, economic growth slowed to 3.7%, although the impact of the global financial crisis was less severe than in many other countries in the region. The current global economic slowdown presents some challenges for the Azerbaijani economy as oil prices remain below their mid-2008 high, highlighting Azerbaijan's reliance on energy exports and its lacklustre attempts to diversify its economy. Pervasive public and private sector corruption and structural economic inefficiencies remain a drag on long-term growth, particularly in non-energy sectors. Long-term prospects will depend on world oil prices, the location of new oil and gas pipelines in the region, and Azerbaijan's ability to manage its energy wealth to promote sustainable growth in non-energy sectors of the economy and spur employment.

Kazakhstan

Kazakhstan's economy grew more than 9% per year from 2000 through 2007. Extractive industries, particularly hydrocarbons and mining, have been the engines of this growth. However, geographic limitations and decaying infrastructure present serious obstacles. At the end of 2007, global financial markets froze up and the loss of capital inflows to

---

[1] Marmara University, Istanbul, Turkey.

Kazakhstani banks caused a credit crunch. The subsequent sharp fall of oil and commodity prices in 2008 aggravated the economic situation, and Kazakhstan plunged into recession. While the global financial crisis took a significant toll on Kazakhstan's economy, it has rebounded well. In response to the crisis, Kazakhstan's government devalued the tenge (Kazakhstan's currency) to stabilize market pressures, and injected USD19 billion in economic stimulus. Rising commodity prices have helped revive Kazakhstan's economy, which registered 7% growth in 2010. Barring a dramatic decline in oil prices, strong growth is expected to continue in 2011. Despite solid macroeconomic indicators, the government realizes that its economy suffers from an overreliance on oil and extractive industries; the so-called "Dutch disease." In response, Kazakhstan has embarked on an ambitious diversification program, aimed at developing targeted sectors, like transport, pharmaceuticals, telecommunications, petrochemicals, and food processing.

When the banking sector of Kazakhstan's economy was hit by the US subprime crisis, the ‘fat years’ finished in 2007. The resulting credit crunch undermined the construction sector, one of the pillars of the booming Kazakh economy. Low prices for oil and metals, the main export commodities, were another serious blow that decreased budget revenues considerably. Stalled construction sites and closing mines generated the conditions for mounting social tensions. The government response was to open up the national oil fund and pump money into the economy. Around USD19 billion (or 14% of GDP) was invested in the construction, banking, agricultural and other sectors. The government also developed an action plan (‘roadmap’) to create employment opportunities. In addition, efforts were made to attract foreign investments. The largest infusion was the loan of USD10 billion from China to invest in energy and infrastructure projects. According to the government, all these measures, together with rising prices for export commodities (chiefly oil), led to an improvement in the prospects of the Kazakh economy (Kassenova 2010).

Kyrgyzstan

Kyrgyzstan is a poor, mountainous country with a dominant agricultural sector. Cotton, tobacco, wool, and meat are the main agricultural products, although only tobacco and cotton are exported in any quantity. Industrial exports include gold, mercury, uranium, natural gas, and electricity. The economy depends heavily on gold exports. Following independence, Kyrgyzstan was progressive in carrying out market reforms, such as an improved regulatory system and land reform. GDP grew about 8%

annually in 2007-08, partly due to higher gold prices internationally, but slowed to 2.3% in 2009. The overthrow of President Bakiev in April, 2010 and subsequent ethnic clashes left hundreds dead and damaged infrastructure. Shrinking trade and agricultural production, as well as political instability, caused GDP to contract by about 3.5% in 2010. The fiscal deficit widened to 11% of GDP, reflecting significant increases in crisis-related spending, including both rehabilitation of damaged infrastructure and bank recapitalization. Progress in reconstruction, fighting corruption, restructuring domestic industry, and attracting foreign aid and investment are key to future growth. The economic crisis affected the Kyrgyzstan economy negatively. The downturn in Russia and Kazakhstan, the main trade partners of Kyrgyzstan, has led to a plunge in industrial production (by about 20% in the first quarter of 2009). Remittances sent by Kyrgyz labour migrants from these two countries, which accounted for a third of GDP, also decreased by 40-50%. Thousands of migrants returned to Kyrgyzstan, adding to the levels of unemployment and the possibility of social tensions. As the most telling evidence of mismanagement and corruption, in Kyrgyzstan, where hydropower is among the major exports, there have been multiple energy crises. In addition to rising prices, the impoverished population has had to deal with regular power cuts.

Turkmenistan

Turkmenistan is largely a desert country with intensive agriculture in irrigated oases and sizeable gas and oil resources. The two largest crops are cotton, most of which is produced for export, and wheat, which is domestically consumed. Although agriculture accounts for roughly 10% of GDP, it continues to employ nearly half of the country's workforce. From 1998-2005, Turkmenistan suffered from the continued lack of adequate export routes for natural gas and from obligations on extensive short-term external debt. At the same time, however, total exports rose by an average of roughly 15% per year from 2003-08, largely because of higher international oil and gas prices. New pipelines to China and Iran, which began operation in early 2010, have given Turkmenistan additional export routes for its gas, although these new routes have not offset the sharp drop in export revenue since early 2009 from decreased gas exports to Russia. Overall prospects in the near future are discouraging because of widespread internal poverty, endemic corruption, a poor educational system, government misuse of oil and gas revenues, and Ashgabat's reluctance to adopt market-oriented reforms.

The isolation has not protected Turkmenistan from the impact of the global economic crisis. Falling prices and demand for its main export commodity, natural gas, have deprived the government of the lucrative revenues it had grown used to over the years. In April 2009, Russia (which buys most of Turkmenistan's gas) sharply reduced its imports. The government loosened some of its most heavily subsidized prices. Prices for basic foods are rising as well, up by 30% in 2008. In addition, foreign companies have cut the numbers of their local employees, especially in the construction sector, increasing the levels of unemployment. Despite its riches, there is no basis for sustainable growth of the country.

Uzbekistan

Uzbekistan is a dry, landlocked country; 11% of the land is intensely cultivated in irrigated river valleys. More than 60% of the population lives in densely populated rural communities. Export of hydrocarbons, including natural gas and petroleum, provided about 40% of foreign exchange earnings in 2009. Other major export earners include gold and cotton. Uzbekistan is now the world's second-largest cotton exporter and fifth largest producer. Potential investment by Russia and China in Uzbekistan's gas and oil industry, as well as increased cooperation with South Korea in the realm of civil aviation, may boost growth prospects. However, decreased demand for natural gas in Europe and Russia in the wake of the global financial crisis could reduce energy-related revenues in the short term. Although growth slowed in 2009-10, Uzbekistan has seen few other effects from the global economic downturn, primarily due to its relative isolation from the global financial markets.

Uzbekistan's industrial output has stagnated or fallen in the main sectors of the economy. The crisis has affected prices and demand for the country's leading export commodities: gas, metals, and cotton. The production of cars and buses is also falling due to the contraction of the Russian market. The welfare of the already impoverished population (26% of Uzbeks live below the poverty line) has been hit by a plunge in remittances from labour migrants, which have fallen by 30% over the last year.

Central Asian Economies by Numbers before and after the 2008 Global Crisis

For Central Asian economies, the 2008 global economic crisis caused decreasing exports of goods and services, declining economic growth, deteriorating fiscal and current account balance of the economies, and slightly increasing unemployment.

Table-1 shows the effects of the global economic crisis on the real GDP growth of Central Asian economies. The real GDP growth of the Azerbaijan economy decreased due to the negative effects of the global financial crisis. Although the real GDP growth of the Azerbaijan economy is 34.5% in 2006, unfortunately, the real GDP growth started declining by the year 2007 and began getting worse by 2009. In parallel, the real GDP growth of the Kazakhstan economy also started declining by the year 2007 and the deterioration of real GDP growth accelerated by 2008, and the worst of the real GDP growth was met by the year 2009. The real GDP growth in the other economies, Turkmenistan, Uzbekistan, and Kyrgyzstan, declined ultimately by the year 2009.

The main reason for the declining of the real GDP growth was the falling global demand for the export goods of these countries and deterioration of the credit mechanism in the global economy. It is projected by the IMF that the negative effects of the global economic crisis are decreasing over time.

Table 1. Real GDP Growth (*Annual Change; percent*)

	Average 2000-05	**2006**	**2007**	**2008**	**2009**	**2010**	**2011p**	**2012p**
Azerbaijan	11.3	34.5	25.0	10.8	9.3	5.0	0.2	7.1
Kazakhstan	10.3	10.7	8.9	3.2	1.2	7.3	6.5	5.6
Turkmenistan	16.6	11.0	11.1	14.7	6.1	9.2	9.9	7.2
Uzbekistan	5.1	7.5	9.5	9.0	8.1	8.5	7.1	7.0
Kyrgyzstan	4.1	3.1	8.5	7.6	2.9	1.4	7.0	6.0

Source: IMF, Regional Economic Outlook, Middle East and Central Asia, Oct. 2011, p.82 ; P:Projections

Table-2 shows nominal GDP of Central Asian economies. The global economic crisis negatively affected all the Central Asian economies except the Uzbekistan Economy.

Table 2. Nominal GDP, *(Billion USD)*

	Average 2000-05	2006	2007	2008	2009	2010	2011p	2012p
Azerbaijan	7.7	21.0	33.1	46.4	43.1	54.4	68.5	80.8
Kazakhstan	32.7	81.0	103.1	135.2	115.3	148.0	180.1	200.0
Turkmenistan	10.6	21.4	26.0	21.5	18.7	20.0	24.1	27.7
Uzbekistan	11.9	17.0	22.3	28.6	33.5	39.0	43.7	48.4
Kyrgyzstan	1.8	2.8	3.8	5.1	4.7	4.6	5.4	6.1

Source: IMF, Regional Economic Outlook, Middle East and Central Asia, Oct. 2011, p.83 ; P:Projections

Table-3 shows the unemployment rate in the Central Asian economies. The global economic crisis slightly negatively affected the unemployment rate in the Uzbekistan Economy and Kyrgyzstan Economy. On the other hand, the unemployment rate in the Azerbaijan economy and Kazakhstan Economy was not affected by the global economic crisis. The main reason for the unemployment rate in the Central Asian economies was the falling economic growth caused by deterioration of the global demand and credit mechanism in the global economy.

Table 3. Unemployment Rate *(Percent)*

	2005	2006	2007	2008	2009	2010	2011p	2012p
Azerbaijan	7.6	6.8	6.5	6.1	6	6	6	6
Kazakhstan	8.1	7.8	7.3	6.6	6.6	5.8	5.7	5.6
Kyrgyzstan	8.1	8.3	8.2	8.2	8.4	9.3	8.4	8.3
Turkmenistan	n/a	n/a	n/a	n/a	n/a	n/a	n/a	n/a
Uzbekistan	0.3	0.2	0.2	0.1	0.2	0.2	0.2	0.2

Source: IMF, World Economic Outlook Database, September 2011

Table-4 shows the consumer price inflation in the Central Asian economies. The global economic crisis directly affected the consumer price inflation in all of the Central Asian economies, except Uzbekistan's Economy. The consumer price inflation in the Uzbekistan Economy has a volatile structure. The main reason for decreasing consumer price inflation in the Central Asian economies is the falling domestic-global demand and falling commodity prices in the global economy.

Table 4. Consumer Price Inflation, ***(Year average; percent)***

	Average 2000-05	2006	2007	2008	2009	2010	2011p	2012p
Azerbaijan	4.1	8.4	16.6	20.8	1.5	5.7	9.3	10.3
Kazakhstan	8.2	8.6	10.8	17.2	7.4	7.4	8.9	7.9
Turkmenistan	8.4	8.2	6.3	14.5	-2.7	4.4	6.1	7.2
Uzbekistan	18.0	14.2	12.3	12.7	14.1	9.4	13.1	11.8
Kyrgyzstan	6.5	5.6	10.2	24.5	6.8	7.8	19.1	9.4

Source: IMF, Regional Economic Outlook, Middle East and Central Asia, Oct. 2011, p.86 ; P:Projections

Table-5 shows the broad money growth in the Central Asian economies. The monetary response to global economic crisis in the Central Asian economies varied by country. Although tightening monetary policy was implemented in the Azerbaijan economy, Kazakhstan economy and Turkmenistan economy in the year 2009, in order to eliminate the negative effects of the global economic crisis, expansionary monetary policy was implemented in these countries. On the other hand, the Uzbekistan economy and Kyrgyzstan economy have implemented expansionary monetary policy in order to eliminate the negative effects of the global economic crisis since 2009. Falling inflation rates in the Central Asian economies also helped the expansionary monetary policy.

Table 5. Broad Money Growth ***(Annual change; percent)***

	Average 2000-05	2006	2007	2008	2009	2010	2011p	2012p
Azerbaijan	28.8	86.4	72.4	25.5	16.6	21.9	23.6	19.9
Kazakhstan	40.7	78.1	25.9	35.4	17.9	15.7	14.5	14.0
Turkmenistan	32.4	55.9	72.2	62.8	10.9	43.4	42.9	36.0
Uzbekistan	41.0	37.8	46.9	38.7	40.8	52.4	27.7	27.4
Kyrgyzstan	22.1	51.6	33.3	9.8	20.9	21.1	20.9	19.7

Source: IMF, Regional Economic Outlook, Middle East and Central Asia, Oct. 2011, p.88 ; P:Projections ; Broad money (M5) is defined to include nonresident deposits.

Table-6 shows general government total expenditure and net lending in the Central Asian economies. The governments in the Central Asian economies, except Kazakhstan, have increased total expenditure and net lending in order to eliminate the negative effects of the global economic crisis since 2009. Another reason for expansionary fiscal policy is to decrease the deficiencies of the monetary policy implemented alone.

Table 6. General Government Total Expenditure and Net Lending *(Percent of GDP)*

	Average 2000-05	2006	2007	2008	2009	2010	2011p	2012p
Azerbaijan	24.0	27.4	25.9	31.1	34.8	30.8	32.0	31.0
Kazakhstan	22.3	20.2	24.6	26.9	23.5	22.5	22.8	22.9
Turkmenistan	20.2	14.9	13.4	10.9	14.5	15.6	18.2	16.8
Uzbekistan	34.4	29.0	30.4	30.0	33.6	34.4	36.6	35.9
Kyrgyzstan	27.7	31.1	28.9	29.2	36.1	38.1	43.1	40.4

Source: IMF, Regional Economic Outlook, Middle East and Central Asia, Oct. 2011, p. 93; P: Projections

Table-7 shows total government gross debt in the Central Asian economies. Increasing general government total expenditure and net lending in the Central Asian economies by the global economic crisis have led to an increase in total government gross debt in the Central Asian economies, except in Uzbekistan, for the years 2009 and 2010.

Table 7. Total Government Gross Debt *(Percent of GDP)*

	Average 2000-05	2006	2007	2008	2009	2010	2011p	2012p
Azerbaijan	20.9	10.2	8.6	7.3	12.1	10.8	10.7	10.0
Kazakhstan	16.3	6.7	5.9	6.7	10.2	10.7	12.9	13.0
Turkmenistan	19.5	3.3	2.4	2.8	2.6	11.8	20.5	26.8
Uzbekistan	43.5	21.3	15.8	12.7	11.0	10.0	12.6	14.0
Kyrgyzstan	103.7	72.5	56.8	48.5	58.0	62.6	55.2	54.6

Source: IMF, Regional Economic Outlook, Middle East and Central Asia, Oct. 2011, p. 94; P: Projections

Table-8 shows general government fiscal balance in the Central Asian economies. Increasing general government total expenditure and gross debt in the Central Asian economies due to the global economic crisis has led to the deterioration of the fiscal balance in the Central Asian economies. The budget surplus in the Central Asian economies decreased by the year 2009.

Table 8. General Government Fiscal Balance *(Percent of GDP)*

	Average 2000-05	2006	2007	2008	2009	2010	2011p	2012p
Azerbaijan	0.2	-0.2	2.6	20.3	7.2	15.3	9.8	10.1
Kazakhstan	2.4	7.2	4.7	1.1	-1.4	1.4	1.7	1.7
Turkmenistan	1.0	5.3	3.9	10.0	7.6	2.3	0.5	1.4
Uzbekistan	-0.6	5.4	5.2	10.7	3.1	4.8	3.3	4.6
Kyrgyzstan	-5.6	-2.1	-0.3	0.0	-3.5	-6.5	-8.4	-7.7

Source: IMF, Regional Economic Outlook, Middle East and Central Asia, Oct. 2011, p. 89; P: Projections

Table-9 shows exports of goods and services in the Central Asian economies. The global economic crisis significantly negatively affected the export of goods and services in the Central Asian economies because of the decreasing global demand by the year 2009. The negative effects of the global economic crisis on the exports of goods and services in the Central Asian economies led to a fall in economic growth, to an increase in unemployment and to deterioration of the fiscal and current account balance in the Central Asian economies.

Table 9. Exports of Goods and Services *(Billion USD)*

	Average 2000-05	2006	2007	2008	2009	2010	2011p	2012p
Azerbaijan	3.8	14.0	22.5	32.1	22.8	28.5	35.4	37.5
Kazakhstan	16.8	41.6	51.9	76.4	48.2	65.1	85.9	87.6
Turkmenistan	3.7	7.5	9.5	12.3	9.5	10.3	14.9	15.8
Uzbekistan	4.0	6.3	8.9	12.2	11.5	12.2	15.8	17.2
Kyrgyzstan	0.8	1.5	2.2	3.0	2.7	2.5	3.2	3.5

Source: IMF, Regional Economic Outlook, Middle East and Central Asia, Oct. 2011, p. 96; P: Projections

Table-10 shows imports of goods and services in the Central Asian economies. The global economic crisis negatively affected imports of goods and services in the Central Asian economies by the year 2009 because of falling economic activity and decreasing export revenue.

Table 10. Imports of Goods and Services *(Billion USD)*

	Average 2000-05	2006	2007	2008	2009	2010	2011p	2012p
Azerbaijan	4.2	8.1	9.4	11.5	9.9	10.5	16.7	18.0
Kazakhstan	14.8	32.9	45.0	49.6	39.0	43.3	47.5	51.5
Turkmenistan	3.1	3.6	4.9	7.8	11.3	10.9	13.5	14.0
Uzbekistan	3.5	5.4	8.1	11.4	11.7	11.0	14.0	15.4
Kyrgyzstan	0.9	2.3	3.2	4.7	3.7	3.9	5.1	5.6

Source: IMF, Regional Economic Outlook, Middle East and Central Asia, Oct. 2011, p. 97; P: Projections

Table-11 shows current account balance level in the Central Asian economies. The global economic crisis significantly negatively affected current account balance level in the Central Asian economies by the year 2009. The main reason for the deteriorating current account balance level in the Central Asian economies is decreasing exports of goods and services.

Table 11. Current Account Balance *(Billion USD)*

	Average 2000-05	2006	2007	2008	2009	2010	2011p	2012p
Azerbaijan	-0.9	3.7	9.0	16.5	10.2	15.0	15.5	15.6
Kazakhstan	-0.4	-2.0	-8.3	6.3	-4.4	4.3	10.7	9.2
Turkmenistan	0.4	3.4	4.0	3.6	-3.0	-2.3	-0.7	-0.7
Uzbekistan	0.5	1.6	1.6	2.5	0.7	2.6	3.5	3.6
Kyrgyzstan	0.0	-0.1	0.0	0.0	-0.4	-0.3	-0.4	-0.5

Source: IMF, Regional Economic Outlook, Middle East and Central Asia, Oct. 2011, p. 98; P: Projections

Table-12 shows current account balance/GDP ratio in the Central Asian economies. As mentioned in Table-11, the global economic crisis significantly negatively affected current account balance/GDP ratio in the Central Asian economies by the year 2009. It is important that current account balance/GDP ratio decreased despite the falling of GDP, which means current account balance decreased more than GDP. The main reason for the deteriorating current account balance/GDP ratio in the Central Asian economies is decreasing exports of goods and services.

Table 12. Current Account Balance ***(Percent of GDP)***

	Average 2000-05	2006	2007	2008	2009	2010	2011 p	2012 p
Azerbaijan	-12.2	27.3	17.6	35.5	23.6	27.7	22.7	19.3
Kazakhstan	-1.4	-2.5	-8.1	4.7	-3.8	2.9	5.9	4.6
Turkmenistan	4.1	15.7	15.5	16.5	-16.0	-11.7	-2.9	-2.6
Uzbekistan	3.8	9.1	7.3	8.7	2.2	6.7	8.0	7.4
Kyrgyzstan	-0.1	-3.1	-0.2	-8.1	0.7	-7.2	-7.7	-7.6

Source: IMF, Regional Economic Outlook, Middle East and Central Asia, Oct. 2011, p. 99; P: Projections

Table-14 shows gross official reserves in the Central Asian economies. The global economic crisis slightly negatively affected global credit mechanism because of a crisis of confidence. The monetary authorities tended to increase the official reserves kept. For this reason, gross official reserves in the Central Asian economies increased due to the global economic crisis. It is expected to increase the official reserves kept because of the ongoing global economic uncertainty.

Table 14. Gross Official Reserves ***(Billion USD)***

	Average 2000-05	2006	2007	2008	2009	2010	2011p	2012p
Azerbaijan	0.9	2.5	4.3	6.5	5.4	6.9	9.0	9.6
Kazakhstan	4.8	19.1	17.6	19.9	23.1	28.3	38.0	48.6
Turkmenistan	...	...	...	...	...	...	...	...
Uzbekistan	1.7	4.7	7.5	9.5	12.2	14.6	19.8	24.8
Kyrgyzstan	0.4	0.8	1.2	1.2	1.6	1.7	2.0	2.1

Source: IMF, Regional Economic Outlook, Middle East and Central Asia, Oct. 2011, p. 100; P: Projections

Table-15 shows total gross external debt in the Central Asian economies. The global economic crisis negatively affected total gross external debt in the Central Asian economies because of decreasing export revenues by the year 2009 (for Turkmenistan Economy by the year 2010). It is expected that there will be a decrease in total gross external debt for the Azerbaijan economy and Kazakhstan Economy by improving economic activity by the year 2012.

Table 15. Total Gross External Debt *(Percent of GDP)*

	Average 2000-05	2006	2007	2008	2009	2010	2011p	2012p
Azerbaijan	18.5	9.4	7.7	6.5	7.9	7.2	7.8	7.4
Kazakhstan	73.0	91.4	93.9	79.8	98.2	80.5	78.2	79.5
Turkmenistan	19.5	3.3	2.4	2.8	2.6	11.8	20.5	26.8
Uzbekistan	37.0	22.1	16.7	13.1	15.0	14.8	18.1	20.2
Kyrgyzstan	107.1	77.7	60.2	45.1	58.2	68.3	59.4	56.2

Source: IMF, Regional Economic Outlook, Middle East and Central Asia, Oct. 2011, p. 101; P: Projections

Table-16 shows capital adequacy ratios in the Central Asian economies. The global economic crisis significantly negatively affected global credit mechanisms because of the crisis of confidence. For this reason, the banking sector needed to increase their capital adequacy ratios. By the strong negative effect of the global economic crisis in December-2008, capital adequacy ratios in the Central Asian economies were increased, except for the Azerbaijan and Uzbekistan economies, but capital adequacy ratios in the Kazakhstan and Turkmenistan economies fell in December 2009. Due to the ongoing negative effects of the global economic crisis, capital adequacy ratios in the Central Asian economies, except Uzbekistan, are decreasing.

Table 16. Capital Adequacy Ratios (Percent of risk-weighted assets)

	Dec 2006	Dec 2007	Dec 2008	Dec 2009	Dec 2010	Mar 2011	Jun 2011
Azerbaijan	18.7	19.9	19.6	17.7	16.9	16.5	16.3
Kazakhstan	15.0	14.2	14.9	-8.2	17.9	17.8	18.8
Kyrgyzstan	28.5	31.0	32.6	33.5	30.4	30.4	28.2
Turkmenistan	25.3	15.9	30.9	16.5	17.2	14.9	...
Uzbekistan	...	23.2	23.2	23.4	23.4	...	...

Source: IMF, Regional Economic Outlook, Middle East and Central Asia, Oct. 2011, p. 102; P: Projections

Table-17 shows the return on assets in the Central Asian economies. The global economic crisis negatively affected the return on assets. In the Azerbaijan economy, the return on assets fell in December 2008. Although increasing the return on assets in December 2009, it has decreased since December 2010. In the Kazakhstan Economy, the return on assets started to fall in December 2008, after that it improved in December 2010. In the

Kyrgyzstan Economy, the return on assets started to fall from December 2008 to December 2010, before finally starting to improve in March 2011. In the Turkmenistan Economy, the return on assets started to fall from December 2009 to March 2011. In the Uzbekistan Economy, the return on assets fell in December-2009. As a result, the global economic crisis negatively affected the return on assets in the Central Asian economies.

Table 17. Return on Assets *(Percent)*

	Dec 2006	Dec 2007	Dec 2008	Dec 2009	Dec 2010	Mar 2011	Jun 2011
Azerbaijan	1.3	1.9	1.8	2.2	0.9	1.2	1.1
Kazakhstan	...	2.3	0.3	-24.1	12.5	...	...
Kyrgyzstan	3.4	4.4	3.8	2.5	1.1	2.5	2.7
Turkmenistan	5.4	4.1	4.3	3.6	3.6	2.9	...
Uzbekistan	...	2.4	8.9	7.4	7.7	...	...

Source: IMF, Regional Economic Outlook, Middle East and Central Asia, Oct. 2011, p. 103; P: Projections

Table-18 shows nonperforming loans in the Central Asian economies. The global economic crisis negatively affected nonperforming loans in the economies of the region. In the Azerbaijan economy, nonperforming loans started to increase from December 2008 to March 2011. In the Kazakhstan economy, nonperforming loans started to increase from December 2009 to June 2011. In the Kyrgyzstan economy, nonperforming loans started to increase from December 2009 to December 2011, remaining at high levels. In the Turkmenistan and Uzbekistan economies, nonperforming loans are not significantly affected.

Table 18. Nonperforming Loans *(Percent of total loans)*

	Dec 2006	Dec 2007	Dec 2008	Dec 2009	Dec 2010	Mar 2011	Jun 2011
Azerbaijan	6.6	3.0	3.3	3.5	4.7	5.2	5.0
Kazakhstan	...	...	5.2	21.2	23.8	25.3	26.3
Kyrgyzstan	6.2	5.3	5.3	8.2	15.8	13.8	12.3
Turkmenistan	0.6	0.4	0.1	0.1	0.1	0.1	...
Uzbekistan	...	2.6	3.0	1.2	1.0	...	...

Source: IMF, Regional Economic Outlook, Middle East and Central Asia, Oct. 2011, p. 104; P: Projections

Conclusion

Global economic crisis damaged macroeconomic fundamentals of economies across the world economy and had negative effects on economic growth, aggregate demand, supply, fiscal and current account balances, finance conditions, expectations, and welfare level.

In this study, we investigated the macroeconomic effects of global economic crisis on the Central Asian economies: Azerbaijan, Kazakhstan, Kyrgyzstan, Uzbekistan, and Turkmenistan.

We found the negative effects of the global economic crisis on the main macroeconomic variables as follows:

- The global economic crisis negatively affected the real GDP growth in the Central Asian economies. The real GDP growth in Azerbaijan, Kazakhstan and Kyrgyz economies showed the worst decreases among the Central Asian economies.
- The global economic crisis negatively affected the unemployment rate in the Central Asian economies. The unemployment rate in Kyrgyz economy had the worst increase among the Central Asian economies.
- The global economic crisis negatively affected general government fiscal balance in all the Central Asian economies (with the least negative effect in Azerbaijan).
- The global economic crisis negatively affected exports of goods and services in the Central Asian economies. The exports of goods and services in Azerbaijan and Kazakhstan had the worst decreases among the Central Asian economies.
- The global economic crisis negatively affected current account balance/GDP ratio in the Central Asian economies. The current account balance/GDP in Kazakhstan, Turkmenistan, and Kyrgyz economies displayed the worst decreases among the Central Asian economies.

The main result of the study is that the global economic crisis had important negative effects on the Central Asian economies. On the other hand, the effects of global economic crisis on the selected Central Asian economies varied by the economic structures, integration level into the world economy, and the foreign dependency level of the economies.

The main policy recommendation for the Central Asian economies is that it is vital to develop efficient global competitiveness-oriented economic policies in order to decrease their fragility to internal and external shocks, and to reduce foreign dependency. For this reason, Central Asian economies should transform their economies from a natural resource-based structure into a knowledge economy based structure by improving the policies and the strategies on human capital, education, information and communication technologies, research and development, science-technology-innovation, all crucial for global competition.

References

Bordo, M. D., Landon-Lane, J.S. (2010). "The Lessons from the Banking Panics in the United States in the 1930s for the Financial Crisis of 2007-2008" NBER Working Paper No. 16365

CIA, The World Factbook, Azerbaijan, CIA, Washington, D,C, htps://www.cia.gov/library/publications/the-world-factbook/geos/aj, html, Accessed: 11/01/2012

CIA, The World Factbook, Kazakhstan, CIA, Washington, D,C, htps://www,cia,gov/library/publications/the-world-factbook/geos/kz, html, Accessed: 11/01/2012

CIA, The World Factbook, Kyrgyzstan, CIA, Washington, D,C, htps://www,cia,gov/library/publications/the-world-actbook/geos/kg, html , Accessed: 11/01/2012

CIA, The World Factbook, Turkmenistan, CIA, Washington, D,C, https://www,cia,gov/library/publications/the-world-factbook/geos/tx, html Accessed: 11/01/2012

CIA, The World Factbook, Uzbekistan, CIA, Washington, D,C, htps://www.cia.gov/library/publications/the-world-factbook/geos/uz, html, Accessed: 11/01/2012

Claessens, Stijn., Tong, Hui., and Wei, Shang-Jin. (2011). "From the Financial Crisis to the Real Economy: Using Firm-level Data to Identify Transmission Channels" NBER Working Paper No. 17360,

Fisher, I. (1933). "'The Debt Deflation Theory of Great Depressions'", Econometrica, Vol. 1, No. 4 (Oct., 1933), pp. 337-357

Kassenova, N. (2009). "The Impact Of The Global Economic Crisis On Central Asia And its Implications For The EU Engagement" EUCAM Working Paper No.5, p. 5

Keeley, B. and Love, P. (2010). From Crisis to Recovery The Causes, Course and Consequences of the Great Recession, OECD

Minsky, H. P. (1992). "The Financial Instability Hypothesis" The Jerome Levy Economics Institute Of Bard College, Working Paper No. 74, Prepared For Handbook Of Radical Political Economy, Edited By Philip Arestis And Malcolm Sawyer, Edward Elgar: Aldershot, 1993.

Mishkin, F.S. (2010) "Over The Cliff: From The Subprime To The Global Financial Crisis" NBER Working Paper Series, Working Paper 16609

—. (2011). "Monetary Policy Strategy: Lessons From The Crisis" NBER Working Paper Series, Working Paper 16755

Reinhart, C. M. and Rogoff, K. S. (2008). "Is The 2007 U.S. Sub-Prime Financial Crisis So Different? An International Historical Comparison" NBER Working Paper 13761.

Sungur, N. and Sarıdoğan, E., (2010). "The Effects Of Global Economic Crisis On Turkish Manufacturing Industry", Marmara University The Journal of FEAS, Vol. XXIX, Iss.II, pp. 23-45.

CENTRAL ASIAN ECONOMIES AFTER THE 2008 GLOBAL CRISIS

ASSOC. PROF. MÜSLÜME NARIN[1] AND ASSOC. PROF. AKIN MARŞAP[2]

The liberalization movements and the innovations in the financial system applied in the world since the 1980s affected the world economies to a significant extent. The fact that it was easier to reach information with low cost, along with technological innovations, led to a more effective usage of information, and many financial products were developed according to risk and revenue expectations. The diversity in financial products gave rise to the expansion of the market by both extending the risk preferences and increasing the number of participants. Thus, the financial systems of all countries have become correlated, and US-based global markets were formed. Therefore, a problem experienced in a particular country affects all the markets in the global system, like the case during the global crisis. On the other hand, the extreme competition seen in the banking sector in recent years led to wrong decisions from time to time. The banking sector in the US has issued large quantities of low-quality mortgage credits in the last years. The problems in repaying these credits were the genesis of the financial crisis. The crisis, which started in the middle of 2007 in financial markets, expanded to the real estate sector in the second half of 2008, and spread to all developing countries. This crisis also affected Central Asian economies and Turkey. While the influence of the crisis on Turkey was felt dramatically, the effect was lower in the Central Asian economies.

Effects of the 2008 Global Crisis on the World Economy

The world economy faced the biggest crisis since the Great Depression of 1929. The problems which occurred in the US housing market in the

---

[1] Gazi University, Ankara, Turkey.
[2] Istanbul Aydın University, Istanbul, Turkey.

middle of 2007 increased gradually and they influenced the real sector after the financial markets in the second half of 2008. The crisis which started in the developed countries adopted a global dimension, expanding worldwide. The causes of the crisis can be listed as follows: the abundance of liquidity and the fall of the mortgage structures, extreme increases in the housing prices, the problems in securities and funding securities, a lack of transparency, the expansion of credit derivative markets, the inadequacy of efficiency of credit rating agencies, and the delay in the intervention of regulatory and supervisory agencies. The global crisis led to a fast decrease in the growth rates of all the countries in the world. Besides that, industrial production, trade volume, and fixed investment spending have fallen significantly. As a result, unemployment has risen.

Real GDP Growth: The growth rates have fallen worldwide due to the influence of the financial crisis on real economy. The growth rates, which started to fall worldwide in the last quarter of 2007, became negative in the third quarter of 2008 and hit rock bottom in the first quarter of 2009 with a 6.27% decrease. While this shrinking was 8.31% in the developed countries, it was 3.11% in the emerging and developing economies. However, a recovery process began worldwide in the second quarter of 2009 and the growth rates turned positive. The world economy grew about 5.1% on an annual basis due to the high growth rates in the Asian countries in the first quarter of 2010. The growth rate projections for 2011 and 2012 are expected to be 4.3% and 4.5% respectively (Table 1).

Industrial Production: Global benchmarks related to real economic activities decreased with the crisis and they began to recover in the second half of 2009. Global industrial production increased in the first quarter of 2010, and this growth reached double-digits. However, the industrial production both of countries with high income and of developing countries, which had a slight decrease and stagnation respectively in the second and third quarter of 2010, expanded more than 15% on an annual basis through the end of 2010. The industrial production started to drop in the first quarter of 2011 after this development. The industrial production in Japan dropped by about 15% in the first quarter of 2010 compared to 2009 and similar developments were observed in the countries such as the USA, Britain, Brazil and Mexico. The growth rate of industrial production exceeded the long-term growth trend in the rest of the world, except these countries. The industrial production, which fell in many countries in the last quarter of 2010, recovered in 2011 and increased (World Bank, 2011b: 18).

World Trade: The world trade volume, which was 7.2% in 2007, decreased to 3% in 2008, and shrank by 10.8% in 2009. The world trade volume, which began to increase starting with the second half of 2009, rose to 12.4% in 2010. It is expected to be 8.2% in 2011 and 6.7% in 2011 (Table 2).

Table 1. Real GDP Growth (annual change percent)

Countries	2004 (1)	2005 (1)	2006 (1)	2007 (1)	2008 (1)	2009 (2)	2010 (2)	Proj (2)	
								2011	2012
World Output	4.9	4.5	5.1	5.2	3.2	-0.5	5.1	4.3	4.5
Advanced Economies	3.2	2.6	3.0	2.7	0.9	-3.4	3.0	2.2	2.6
United States	3.6	2.9	2.8	2.0	1.1	-2.6	2.9	2.5	2.7
Euro Area	2.2	1.7	2.9	2.7	0.9	-4.1	1.8	2.0	1.7
Germany	1,2	0.8	3.0	2.5	1.3	-4.7	3.5	3.2	2.0
France	2.2	1.9	2.4	2.1	0.7	-2.6	1.4	2.1	1.9
Italy	1.5	0.7	2.0	1.6	-1.0	-5.2	1.3	1.0	1.3
Spain	3.3	3.6	3.9	3.7	1.2	-3.7	-0.1	0.8	1.6
Japan	2.7	1.9	2.0	2.4	-0.6	-6.3	4.0	-0.7	2.9
United Kingdom	2,8	2.1	2.8	3.0	0.7	-4.9	1.3	1.5	2.3
Canada	3.1	2.9	3.1	2.7	0.5	-2.8	3.2	2.9	2.6
Newly Industrialized Asian Economies	2.9	4.7	5.6	5.7	1.5	-0.7	8.4	5.1	4.5
Emerging and Developing Economies	7.5	7.1	8.0	8.3	6.1	2.8	7.4	6.6	6.4
Russia	7.2	6.4	7.7	8.1	5.6	-7.8	4.0	4.8	4,5
China	10.1	10.4	11.6	13.0	9.0	9.2	10.3	9.6	9.5
India	7.9	9.2	9.8	9.3	7.3	6.8	10.4	8.2	7.8
Brazil	5.7	3.2	4.0	5.7	5.1	-0.6	7.5	4.1	3,6
Mexico	4.0	3.2	5.1	3.3	1.3	-6.1	5.5	4.7	4.0
European Union	2.6	2.2	3.4	3.1	1.1	-4.1	1.8	2.0	2.1
Turkey (3)	9.4	8.4	6.9	4.7	0.7	-4.7	8.2	4.6	4.5

Source. (1) IMF, 2009: 189; (2) IMF, 2011a: 2, (3) IMF, 2011c: 185.

Table 2. World Trade (annual percent change)

		2004 (1)	2005 (1)	2006 (1)	2007 (1)	2008 (1)	2009 (2)	2010 (2)	Proj (2)	
									2011	2012
World Trade		10.7	7.7	9.2	7.2	3.3	-10.8	12.4	8.2	6.7
Import	Advanced Economies	9.3	6.4	7.6	4.7	0.4	-12.5	11.6	6.0	5.1
	Emerging and Developing Economies	16.0	12.2	13.2	14.0	10.9	-7.9	13.7	12.1	9.0
Export	Advanced Economies	9.1	6.2	8.5	6.1	1.8	-12.0	12.3	6.8	6.1
	Emerging and Developing Economies	14.2	10.8	10.9	9.5	6.0	-7.9	12.8	11.2	8.3

Source. (1) IMF, 2009: 189; (2) IMF, 2011a: 2.

Fixed Investment: Fixed investments also decreased in many regions. This decrease was 16.7% in Europe and Central Asia and 10.4% in Latin America and the Caribbean. The countries whose investments have decreased, who have had a close relationship with commercial and investment banks, and whose exports have fallen, were the ones directly affected by the financial crisis. The shrinking in the investments of some countries who had significant current account deficits was much higher. It has been observed that fixed investments were declining in developing countries as well in the third quarter of 2010. While the fixed investments dropped in Asia-Pacific, the Middle East, and North Africa, they increased in other regions. The fixed investments are expected to increase in some regions in 2011, 2012 and 2013, while decreasing in others (Table 3).

Table 3. Fixed Investment (annual percent change)

Countries	1998 2007	2008	2009	Est.	Forecast		
				2010	2011	2012	2013
East Asia and Pacific	9.3	9.1	19.2	11.9	11.0	9.2	9.9
Europe and Central Asia	8.8	6.6	-16.7	7.6	9.5	8.4	8.1
Latin America and the Caribbean	3.4	8.7	-10.4	11.9	7.0	7.8	6,7
Middle East and North Africa	6.0	7.7	1.0	-3.8	-2.4	3.4	5,9
South Asia	9.5	5.6	3.9	14.3	9.4	12.6	13.1

Source. World Bank, 2011a: 76, 81, 91, 102, 115 135.

Inflation: Both headline and core inflation started to increase worldwide with the global crisis. But the increase in inflation in 2007 and 2008 did not only result from the financial crisis, but also from the rises in the food and oil prices. Inflation rose rapidly, especially in the developing countries whose energy demand has been rising fast (IMF, 2010a: 31). Nevertheless, inflation expectations and low capacity usage rates are not expected to place pressure on inflation. The average inflation rate was 1.6% in developed economies in 2010 due to the increase in the energy prices and it is expected to be 2.2% in 2011, and 1.7% in 2012. The inflation rate, which rose to 6.2% in 2010 in emerging and developing countries, is expected to be 6.9% in 2011, and 5.3% in 2012 (IMF, 2011b: 187-191).

Unemployment Rates: Unemployment rates have significantly risen with the global crisis. The global unemployment rate, which had been declining since 2005, started to rise in 2008. However, it has been observed that there was a huge rise in the number of the unemployed in 2009 and it reached 205.2 million people. Therefore, 27.9 million people have become unemployed since 2007. The total number of unemployed people is predicted to be 205 million in 2010. Despite the fact that there has been a rapid recovery in the global economy since 2010, global unemployment has remained at a high rate. The number of unemployed people in the world in 2009 was 27.7 million more compared to the pre-crisis period in 2007 (ILO, 2011: 63).

Although the rise in the global unemployment rate stopped in 2010, regional predictions display the difference between developed and developing regions in a very specific way. The highest increase in unemployment rates was observed in developed economies and the European Union region between 2007 and 2009 (Table 4).

Table 4. Unemployment rate, world and regions (percent)

	2005	2006	2007	2008	2009	2010 Est.
World	6.2	5.9	5.6	5.7	6.3	6.2
Developed Economies and European Union	6.9	6.3	5.8	6.1	8.4	8.8
Central and South-Eastern Europe (non-EU) and CIS	9.4	9.3	8.6	8.6	10.4	9.6
East Asia	4.1	4.0	3.8	4.3	4.4	4.1
South-East Asia and the Pacific	6.3	6.0	5.4	5.3	5.2	5.1
South Asia	4.8	4.6	4.5	4.3	4.4	4.3
Latin America and the Caribbean	7.9	7.6	7.0	6.6	7.7	7.7
Middle East	11.2	10.7	10.5	10.2	10.3	10.3
North Africa	11.9	10.5	10.2	9.6	9.9	9.8
Sub-Saharan Africa	8.6	8.0	7.9	7.9	7.9	8.0

Source. ILO, 2011: 61.

Effects of the Global Crisis on Central Asian Economies

Central Asian economies, composed of Azerbaijan, Kazakhstan, Kyrgyzstan, Tajikistan, Turkmenistan, and Uzbekistan, who became independent after the Soviet Union was dissolved, have tended to grow rapidly since 2000. While the growth rates of these countries reached their peaks in 2008, these rates have fallen in 2009 due to the global crisis. Slight rises were recorded in inflation rates and current account deficits were observed in Kazakhstan and Turkmenistan, while current account surplus of other countries tended to decrease. Despite the global crisis, foreign capital inflow continued to enter to these countries.

Although they are not closed, the Central Asian economies have not been adequately integrated with the world economy. Oil and natural gas have been the main determinant of economic growth. While the black gold (oil) of the Caspian Sea has an important role for Kazakhstan, the blue gold (natural gas reserves) is significant for Turkmenistan and Uzbekistan (Emerson & Boonstra, 2010: 22). As the oil and natural gas prices rise in world markets, the macro-economic indicators and especially growth rates of these countries remain high. When the conditions decline, the macro-economic indicators of these countries deteriorate. The global crisis affected the economies of Central Asian economies as well as the world economy. The growth rates and inflation have decreased, public expenditures have risen and current account balances have had deficits, except for a few countries.

Real GDP Growth: The decline in GDP growth rates, which started with 2008, increasingly deepened in 2009. The decline of growth rates of especially Azerbaijan and Kyrgyzstan continued in 2010 as well, and the growth rates in other countries have risen in 2010 (Table 5).

Table 5. Real GDP Growth (annual change percent)

Countries	2006	2007	2008	2009	2010	Projections	
						2011	2012
Azerbaijan	34.5	25.0	10.8	9.3	5.0	0.2	7.1
Kazakhstan	10.7	8.9	3.2	1.2	7.3	6.5	5.6
Kyrgyzstan	3.1	8.5	7.6	2.9	-1.4	7.0	6.0
Tajikistan	7.0	7.8	7.9	3.9	6.5	6.0	6.0
Turkmenistan	11.0	11.1	14.7	6.1	9.2	9.9	7.2
Uzbekistan	7.5	9.5	9.0	8.1	8.5	7.1	7.0
Turkey*	6.9	4.7	0.7	-4.8	8.9	6.6	2.2

Source. IMF, 2011a: 79; *IMF, 2011b:182

While the non-oil growth rate of Azerbaijan and Kazakhstan, whose economies are significantly based on oil and natural gas, increased, it declined in Turkmenistan. What lay behind the rapid growth of Azerbaijan and Turkmenistan until 2008 was the rapidly increasing oil and natural gas prices. The decline in oil revenues due to a fall in oil and natural gas prices intensified the effect of the global crisis (Table 6).

Table 6. Oil and Non-Oil Real GDP Growth (annual change percent)

Non-Oil Real GDP Growth							
Countries	2006	2007	2008	2009	2010	Projections	
						2011	2012
Azerbaijan	12.1	11.3	15.7	3.0	7.6	8.9	6.2
Kazakhstan	10.8	9.1	3.2	0.5	6.9	6.6	6.0
Turkmenistan	11.6	10.7	18.6	14.8	8.8	8.0	7.5
Oil Real GDP Growth							
Azerbaijan	62.0	37.3	6.9	14.8	4.9	-8.1	8.2
Kazakhstan	9.9	6.9	2.8	7.1	10.2	6.1	2.1
Turkmenistan	8.6	12.6	-0.7	-35.5	12.9	25.3	5.2

Source. IMF, 2011a: 84.

Inflation: Inflation rates, which had risen until 2008, decreased in 2009, except for Uzbekistan. However, inflation is predicted to rise slightly in 2010 and 2011 (Table 7).

Table 7. Consumer Price Inflation (year average, percent)

Countries	2006	2007	2008	2009	2010	Projections	
						2011	2012
Azerbaijan	8.4	16.6	20.8	1.5	5.7	9.3	10.3
Kazakhstan	8.6	10.8	17.2	7.4	7.4	8.9	7.9
Kyrgyzstan	5.6	10.2	24.5	6.8	7.8	19.1	9.4
Tajikistan	10.0	13.2	20.4	6.5	6.5	13.6	10.0
Turkmenistan	8.2	6.3	14.5	-2.7	4.4	6.1	7.2
Uzbekistan	14.2	12.3	12.7	14.1	9.4	13.1	11.8
Turkey*	9.6	8.8	10.4	6.3	8.6	6.0	6.9

Source. IMF, 2011a: 79; *IMF, 2011b:188

General Government Fiscal Balances: General government fiscal balances have been affected by the global crisis in Central Asian economies. The ratio of government budget expenditures to GDP increased due to the rise in government expenditures and the decline in tax revenues (Table 8).

Table 8. General Government Fiscal Balance (Percent of GDP)

Countries	2006	2007	2008	2009	2010	Projections	
						2011	2012
Azerbaijan	-0.2	2.6	20.3	7.2	15.3	9.8	10.1
Kazakhstan	7.2	4.7	1.1	-1.4	1.4	1.7	1.7
Kyrgyzstan	-2.1	-0.3	0.0	-3.5	-6.5	-8.4	-7.7
Tajikistan	1.7	-5.5	-5.1	-5.2	-3.0	-4.9	-4.2
Turkmenistan	5.3	3.9	10.0	7.6	2.3	0.5	1.4
Uzbekistan	5.4	5.2	10.7	3.1	4.8	3.3	4.6
Turkey	-1.3	-1.8	-2.9	-6.2	-3.7	-1.4	-1.4

Source. IMF, 2011a: 79. IMF, 2011c: 5.

Current Account Balance: The significant decline in the exports of these countries led to current account deficits, except for Kyrgyzstan's economy. Current account balance tended to recover as of 2010, except for in Kyrgyzstan's economy (Table 9).

Table 9. Current Account Balance (Percent of GDP)

Countries	2006	2007	2008	2009	2010	Projections	
						2011	2012
Azerbaijan	17.6	27.3	35.5	23.6	27.7	22.7	19.3
Kazakhstan	-2.5	-8.1	4.7	-3.8	2.9	5.9	4.6
Kyrgyzstan	-3.1	-0.2	-8.1	0.7	-7.2	-7.7	-7.6
Tajikistan	-2.8	-8.6	-7.6	-5.9	2.1	-3.6	-6.7
Turkmenistan	15.7	15.5	16.5	-16.0	-11.7	-2.9	-2.6
Uzbekistan	9.1	7.3	8.7	2.2	6.7	8.0	7.4
Turkey*	-6.1	-5.9	-5.7	-2.3	-6.6	-10.3	-7.4

Source. IMF, 2011a: 79; *IMF, 2011b:198.

Unemployment: As the effect of the global crisis on the real sector of Central Asian economies was low, there has not been a rise in unemployment rates. Unemployment rates, on the contrary, decreased in these countries, except for Kyrgyzstan and Turkey (Table 10). As there are not any data about Turkmenistan and Tajikistan, they are not included in the evaluation.

Table 10. Unemployment rate (percent)

Countries	2006	2007	2008	2009	2010	Projections	
						2011	2012
Azerbaijan	6.8	6.5	6.1	6.0	6.0	6.0	6.0
Kazakhstan	7.8	7.3	6.6	6.6	5.8	5.7	5.6
Kyrgyzstan	8.3	8.2	8.2	8.4	9.3	8.4	8.3
Uzbekistan	0.2	0.2	0.1	0.2	0.2	0.2	0.2
Turkey	10.2	10.2	10.9	14.0	11.9	10.5	10.6

Source. IMF, 2011d.

Foreign direct investment: Despite the global crisis, Azerbaijan, Kazakhstan, Kyrgyzstan, Tajikistan, Turkmenistan, Uzbekistan, and Turkey, have 9.593, 81.352, 974, 915, 8.186, 4.460, and 181.910 million USD of foreign capital investment respectively, as of 2010. These investments have generally been made by developed countries. The investments made in Azerbaijan, Kazakhstan and Turkmenistan were mainly based on oil and natural gas (UNCTAD Stat, 2011). Foreign capital inflow to Kazakhstan and Kyrgyzstan has declined over the years, but it has increased in Azerbaijan, Uzbekistan and Turkmenistan (Table 11).

Table 11. Inward and outward foreign direct investment flows (USD at current prices, millions)

Inward foreign direct investment flows						
Countries	**2005**	**2006**	**2007**	**2008**	**2009**	**2010**
Azerbaijan	1.680	-584	-4.749	14	473	563
Kazakhstan	1.971	6.278	11.119	14.322	13.771	9.961
Kyrgyzstan	43	182	209	377	190	234
Tajikistan	54	339	360	376	16	45
Turkmenistan	418	731	856	1.277	3.867	2.083
Uzbekistan	192	174	705	711	711	822
Turkey	10.031	20.185	22.047	19.504	8.411	9.071
Outward foreign direct investment flows						
Azerbaijan	1.221	705	286	556	326	232
Kazakhstan	-146	-385	3.153	1.204	3.118	7.806
Turkey	1.064	924	2.106	2.549	1.553	1.780

Source. UNCTADSTAT, 2011.

Effects of the Global Crisis on Azerbaijan's Economy

Azerbaijan, whose economy is significantly dependent on oil export, had high rates of growth until 2008, and grew by 10.8% in 2008. Oil is the main source of export and budget revenues in Azerbaijan's economy. Thus, the fluctuation in oil prices affects the revenues and the economy of the country. But the investments in the energy sector and the rise of exports contribute positively to the country's economy. Oil prices, which had risen rapidly until 2008, led to a rapid growth of Azerbaijan's economy. But as the oil prices began to decline with the second half of 2008, the country's oil revenues decreased. This development intensified the effect of the global crisis on Azerbaijan's economy. However, Azerbaijan tried to expand its oil revenues by increasing its oil production. But the growth rate fell by 1.5% with the influence of the crisis and became 9.3% in 2009 (IMF, 2011a:79).

While private consumption expenditures declined significantly starting with 2008, public consumption expenditures increased with the influence of expansionary monetary policies, and they rose to 28.4% in 2009. It has been observed that both private and public consumption expenditures declined in 2010 and this decline is expected to go on in 2011 and 2012. Gross fixed investments declined in 2009 by 17% and they increased in 2010 (Rabobank Group, 2011a: 7).

Despite the significant decline in oil prices, Azerbaijan managed to maintain a strong external and fiscal position. Although its export fell considerably in 2009, the ratio of the current account surplus to GDP was 23.7%. This share rose to 30.7% with the increase in oil prices in 2010. The current account surplus is expected to decline slightly in 2011 and 2012, and it is predicted to be about 30% and 28%. Nevertheless it has a large trade volume and current account surplus, Azerbaijan's current account balance has a fragile structure. The export products of the country are not diverse, and oil products have the biggest share. For instance, the share of oil products was 93% of the total exports. Furthermore, 62% of Azerbaijan's export is to the European Union and the United States. Thus, Azerbaijan is significantly dependent on the EU and US economies (Rabobank Group, 2011a: 5).

In conclusion, the global crisis also affected Azerbaijan's economy. The economy shrank significantly due to the decrease in oil product prices, which has a significant share in its export and the drop in global demand.

Effects of the Global Crisis on Kazakhstan's Economy

Kazakhstan's economy grew at a rate of about 10% on average until 2007 on account of the increase in oil and metal prices. Kazakhstan was significantly affected by the sudden decrease in oil prices starting in July 2008 and the global crisis, and the growth rate fell to 3.2% in 2008 and 1.2% in 2009. The diminishing effects of the global crisis in 2010, the increase in oil prices and exports, and the positive developments in external demand conditions increased the growth rate, and the growth rate rose to 7% in 2010 (Rabobank Group, 2011b: 8).

The growth rate of Kazakhstan, which grew about 10% between 2000 and 2007, decreased in 2008 and 2009 with the influence of the global crisis. Kazakhstan's economy is dependent mainly on oil export, thus on oil revenues, like Azerbaijan (Kassenova, 2009:4). The drop in oil revenues, beginning from mid-2008, intensified the effect of the global crisis and the growth rate became 7.3% in 2010 (IMF, 2011a: 79).

Private consumption expenditures, which rose by 6.3% in 2008 with the influence of the global crisis, increased by 0.6% in 2009. Public consumption expenditures increased slightly instead of declining private consumption expenditures. Gross fixed investments fell significantly in 2009, but they have increased since 2010 (Rabobank Group, 2011b: 3).

Kazakhstan's exports, which started to decrease in 2008, shrank significantly in 2009. The same condition applied to its imports. The declining trade volume in 2009 led to a deficit in current account balance. There was a surplus of international trade in 2010 on account of the increase in exports. The international trade surplus is expected to rise in the coming years as well. Although the international trade increased, due to many foreign companies operating in Kazakhstan, service and revenue accounts have been controlled with significant deficits. The ratio of the current account deficit to GDP was 3.8% in 2009, the international trade recovered greatly in 2010 and it had a ratio of 3.7% surplus to its GDP. The ratio of the current account balance will be stable and about 4% to GDP in the coming years.

The money market interest rate decreased significantly starting from 2009. While it was 6.5% in 2008, it was 2.4% in 2009, and fell to 1.4% in 2010. It is expected to be about 3% by increasing slightly in 2011 and 2012. It decreased in 2009 and 2010 due to the fall in demand and commodity prices under the influence of the global crisis, but it is expected to increase starting with 2011.

Foreign capital investments dropped with the global crisis and while the ratio of foreign capital inflow to GDP was 11.3% in 2009, it decreased to 7.7% in 2010 (Rabobank Group, 2011b: 8). Foreign capital outflow increased rapidly in 2009. There was 3.118 million USD in 2009, and 7. 806 million USD capital outflow in 2010 (UNCTADSTAT, 2011).

Effects of the Global Crisis on Kyrgyzstan's Economy

Kyrgyzstan had a slow growth rate until 2006 and it grew at a rate of about 8.5% in 2007 and 2008. The global crisis, which affected the financial sector of Kyrgyzstan to a limited extent, influenced greatly the country's economy and led to a growth rate of 2.3% in 2009, and this rate shrank by 1.4% in 2010. However, the growth rate is predicted to be 7% and 6% in 2011 and 2012 respectively (IMF, 2011a:79). One of the reasons for Kyrgyzstan's declining economic development is the global crisis, and the other is the negative effect that the political and social instability created in the country. The widespread social and political instability between April-June 2010, looting, and periodically shutting borders down between Uzbekistan and Kazakhstan, had very serious effects on Kyrgyzstan's economy (IGEME, 2011: 5).

The decrease in the world commodity prices led to a noticeable fall in the inflation rate in 2009. While the inflation rate was 24.5% in 2008, it dropped to 6.8% in 2009. The upward movement in the commodity prices in 2010 caused pressure on inflation, and an inflation rate of 7.8% was recorded. The growth expectation in 2011 and the trend of depreciation in the national currency are predicted to raise the inflation rate.

Significant decreases were observed in foreign capital investments with the global crisis. While the ratio of foreign capital investments to GDP was 7.34% in 2008, it dropped to 4.14% in 2009. However, it started to increase again as of 2010 (IMF, 2011a: 79).

Effects of the Global Crisis on Tajikistan's Economy

The growth rates in Tajikistan also dropped with the influence of the global crisis. Tajikistan's economy grew at a rate of 7.9% in 2008 and the growth rate fell to 3.9% in 2009. However, it recovered starting from 2010, and the growth rate rose to 6.5%.

The inflation rates in Tajikistan dropped along with the rest of the world and the Central Asian economies due to the decrease in demand. The high inflation rate of 20.4% in 2008 dropped to 6.5% in 2009. But due to the increase in commodity prices, the inflation rate is predicted to rise in 2011.

There has been a significant decrease in the foreign capital investments with the global crisis. While the ratio of foreign capital investments to GDP was 12.1% in 2008, it dropped to 0.32% in 2009 (IMF, 2011a: 79; IMF, 2011e).

Effects of the Global Crisis on Turkmenistan's Economy

Turkmenistan, rich in natural gas, had tended to grow gradually since 2003, and it grew by 14.7% in 2008. However, the controversy with Russia over natural gas prices due to an explosion in the natural gas pipeline in April 2009, the halting of natural gas export, and the effects of the global crisis, led to a 6.1% decrease in the growth rate of Turkmenistan in 2009, and the country had a growth rate of 9.2% in 2010. It is predicted to have a growth rate of 9% in 2011 (IMF, 2011a: 79).

The inflation rates dropped considerably in 2009 due to shrinking demand and decrease in natural gas prices. While the inflation rate was 14.5% in 2008, it was -2.7% in 2009. But inflation rose to 4.4% in 2010 due to the increase in commodity prices.

Despite the global crisis, it has been observed that the share of gross investment and savings in GDP increased. The ratio of the public budget expenditures to GDP started to fall after 2008, and this rate was 2.3% in 2010. The current account balance started to have a deficit in 2009 and the increase in the current account deficit reached 16% of GDP in 2009. This process also continued in 2010. Foreign capital inflow rose until 2010 despite the crisis. While the ratio of foreign capital investments to GDP was 8.22% in 2008, it was 22.28% in 2009, and became 10.35% in 2010 by slightly dropping (IMF, 2011a: 79; IMF, 2011f).

In conclusion, Turkmenistan's economy was greatly affected by the global crisis and it went into a shrinking period. However, it began to recover starting from 2010.

Effects of the Global Crisis on Uzbekistan's Economy

Uzbekistan wasn't affected by the crisis much, and although there was a slight decrease in the growth rate, it grew by 8.1% in 2009 and 8.5% in 2010 (Rabobank Group, 2011c: 5). Uzbekistan's government implemented an anti-crisis program at the end of 2008 and in the beginning of 2009 in order to keep the growth rate at around 4% in the 2009-2012 period. As Uzbekistan has limited relations with global financial markets, there was no need for significant financial support to decrease the effects of the global crisis. But the efforts of the government were aimed at managing the risks in the financial sector, decreasing current account deficits and inflation, and achieving economic development in the long-term (World Bank, 2010b).

Uzbekistan, an important producer and exporter of energy, gold and cotton, contributed to the recovery of increasing prices of commodities and external balances (World Bank, 2011a: 87).

Uzbekistan's export kept increasing during the global crisis period, but its import fell slightly in 2009. Thus, international trade balance surplus continued. While the ratio of international trade balance surplus to GDP was 3.7% in 2008, it was 5.2% in 2009 and 10% in 2010. Although current account balance shrank slightly in 2009, it continued to have a surplus. While the ratio of the current account surplus to GDP was 14.5% in 2008, it was 10.9% and 14.9% in 2009 and 2010 respectively. The money market interest rate was fixed at 14%. However, it is predicted to be 12% in 2011 and 2012 (Rabobank Group, 2011c: 5). There weren't any changes in foreign capital investments with the global crisis, and they even increased in 2010 (UNCTADSTAT, 2011).

Effects of the Global Crisis on Turkey's Economy

Turkey entered a structural transformation and high growth period after the crisis in 2001. It grew at an annual average rate of about 7% during the five-year period of 2003-2007 after the revival in 2002.

However, Turkey's economy was greatly influenced by the 2008-2009 global crisis both commercially and financially. Thus, Turkey's economy, which grew at a rate of 0.7% in 2008, shrank at a rate of 4.8% in 2009. It achieved a 9% growth rate in 2010 thanks to consistent monetary and fiscal policies applied.

All macro indicators reached negative values in the first quarter of 2009, and export revenues fell by a third. Private sector investments were affected as well, and they dropped dramatically in the first of quarter of 2009. The inflation rate fell to 6.3% due to a lack of internal and external demand. Unlike other Central Asian economies, Turkey has had a continuous deficit in its current account balances. Foreign capital inflow increased in Turkey until 2007 and it dropped a little in 2008, but it reached nearly 7.7 billion USD in 2009, falling greatly due to the influence of the crisis (Rabobank Group, 2011d: 5).

Moreover, a cumulative total of about 19.2 million USD of foreign capital investments were made in 2000 in Turkey. In 2010, the cumulative total of this investment rose to 181.9 million USD. On the other hand, the cumulative total of the foreign capital investment that Turkey has made in other countries was 22.3 million USD (UNCTADSTAT, 2011). The unemployment rate, which has been over 10% for years, increased with the global crisis and rose to 14% in 2009. However, it fell to a rate of 12% in 2010. It is predicted to fall to the level of 10% again in 2011 and 2012 (IMF, 2011d). Turkey has had a deficit in its international trade and current account balance for years whose exports and imports have dropped along with the global crisis. While the ratio of current account deficit to GDP was 5.7% in 2008, it was 2.3% in 2009 and 6.5% in 2010. It has been observed that Turkey's foreign debts have been continuously increasing. The ratio of foreign debts to GDP rose to 41% in 2009, when the influences of the global crisis were deeply felt (Rabobank Group, 2011d: 5).

Conclusion

Central Asian economies, which had achieved a fast growth since 2000, have been influenced by 2008-2009 global crisis to different extents according to their economic structures and the level of integration with the world economy.

Azerbaijan's economy has been negatively influenced by the global crisis due to the decrease in external demand and oil prices. The oil prices which fell in the middle of 2008, decreased the export revenues of Azerbaijan and therefore the growth rate dropped compared to 2007. Besides this development, the shrinking demand, which was felt in world economies in 2009 under the influence of the global crisis, led to a gradual drop in the growth rate.

Kazakhstan's economy has also been negatively influenced by the global crisis, like Azerbaijan's economy, due to a drop in the oil and natural gas prices and the shrinking of internal and external demand. The economy recovered with the revival in demand and the increase in oil prices in 2010, and it has reached a high growth rate.

Kyrgyzstan's economy started to shrink in 2009 under the influence of political and social instability, along with the global crisis. This process intensified in 2010, and a negative growth rate was observed.

Tajikistan's economy was also negatively affected by the global crisis and the growth rate dropped in 2009. However, the economy started to develop in 2010, and it has achieved a consistent structure.

Turkmenistan's economy entered a shrinking process, especially due to a drop in natural gas exports, along with the decrease in external demand. On account of increases in prices and exports of natural gas, Turkmenistan's growth rate rose in 2010.

Uzbekistan's economy hasn't been affected by the global crisis as much as other Central Asian economies. It accomplished a high growth rate in 2010 by implementing an anti-crisis program in the beginning of 2009.

The effects of the global crisis were observed in Turkey in the last quarter of 2008 and they reached a great level in the last quarter of 2009. The growth rate turned negative. Turkey achieved a high growth rate in 2010 by implementing expansionary monetary, fiscal, and external trade policies starting from 2009.

In conclusion, Central Asian economies are significantly influenced by external shocks like other developing countries. It is vital for these countries to strengthen their economies to reduce their vulnerability to external shocks.

References

Cakman, Kemal (2009), "Night Owl of Minerva: The Formation to the Background of the Story for 2008 Crisis and Real and Artificial Soothsayer", Journal of Economic Comments, 46/532; 29-47, June 2009, http://kemalcakman.com/?sayfa=11, (15.12.2010).

Emerson, Michael & Jos Boonstra (2010), Into EurAsia Monitoring the EU's Central Asia Strategy, Centre For European Policy Studies (CEPS), Brussels & Madrid, February 2010, http://www.eucentralasia.eu/publications/eucam-publications/reports.html#c560, (25.12.2011).

ILO (International Labour Organization), (2011), Global Employment Trends 2011, The challenge of a jobs recovery, International Labour Organization, First published 2011, http://www.ilo.org/global/publications/books/WCMS_150443/lang--en/index.htm, (15.03.2011).

IMF (International Monetary Fund), (2011a), Regional Economic Outlook: Middle East and Central Asia, October 2011, http://www.imf.org/external/pubs/ft/reo/2011/mcd/eng/mreo1011.htm, (25.12.2011).

—. (2011b), World Economic Outlook: Slowing Growth, Rising Risks, September 2011, http://www.imf.org/external/pubs/ft/weo/2011/02/index.htm, (25.12.2011).

—. (2011c), Regional Economic Outlook: Europe, Navigating Stormy Waters, October 2011, http://www.imf.org/external/pubs/ft/reo/2011/eur/eng/ereo1011.htm, (25.12.2011).

—. (2011d), World Economic Outlook Data Base, http://www.imf.org/external/pubs/ft/weo/2011/02/weodata/download.aspx, (25.12.2011).

—. (2011e), IMF Executive Board Completes 2011 Article IV Consultation and Fourth Review Under ECF Arrangement for Tajikistan and Approves USUSD20.9 Million Disbursement, Press Release No. 11/168 May 11, 2011, http://www.imf.org/external/np/sec/pr/2011/pr11168.htm, (28.12.2011).

—. (2011f), IMF Executive Board Concludes 2011 Article IV Consultation with Turkmenistan, Public Information Notice (PIN) No. 11/161 December 20, 2011, http://www.imf.org/external/np/sec/pn/2011/pn11161.htm, (05.01.2012).

IGEME (Export Promotion Centre of Turkey), (2011), Kyrgyzstan Ülke Raporu, T.C. Başbakanlık, Dış Ticaret Müsteşarlığı, İhracatı Geliştirme Etüd Merkezi, Hazırlayan: Tuğrul Somuncuoğlu, Ankara-April 2011.

Kassenova, Nargis (2009), The impact of the global economic crisis on Central Asia and its implications for the EU engagement, working paper 05, EUCAM 2009, http://www.fride.org/publication/664/the-impact-of-the-global-economic-crisis-on-central-asia-and-its-implications-for-the-eu-engagement, (26.12.2011).

Rabobank Group (2011a), Azerbaijan (Country report), January 2011, http://www.rabobank.com/content/research/erd/international/eastern_europe_cis/europe_east.jsp, (31.12.2011).

—. (2011b), Kazakhstan (Country report), April 2011, http://www.rabobank.com/content/research/erd/international/eastern_europe_cis/europe_east.jsp, (31.12.2011).

—. (2011c), Uzbekistan (Update country report), September 2011, http://www.rabobank.com/content/research/erd/international/eastern_europe_cis/europe_east.jsp, (31.12.2011).

—. (2011d), Turkey (Update country report), November 2011, http://www.rabobank.com/content/research/erd/international/eastern_europe_cis/europe_east.jsp, (31.12.2011).

UNCTADSTAT (2011), Inward and outward foreign direct investment flows, annual, 1970-2010, http://unctadstat.unctad.org/ReportFolders/reportFolders.aspx, (15.12.2011).

World Bank (2010), Countries in Europe and Central Asia, http://web.worldbank.org/WBSITE/EXTERNAL/COUNTRIES/ECAEXT/0,contentMDK:21776903~menuPK:5026204~pagePK:146736~piPK:146830~theSitePK:258599,00.html, (10.12.2011).

—. (2011a), Global Economic Prospects: Maintaining progress amid turmoil, Volume 3, June 2011, http://web.worldbank.org/WBSITE/EXTERNAL/EXTDEC/EXTDECPROSPECTS/EXTGBLPROSPECTS/0,menuPK:615470~pagePK:64218926~piPK:64218953~theSitePK:612501,00.html, (25.012.2011).

—. (2011b), Global Economic Monitor, Developing Trends: July 2011, http://siteresources.worldbank.org/INTPROSPECTS/Resources/334934-1111002409131/829397-1308857322060/STRMG_Jul11.pdf, (25.12.2011).

PART II:

GROWTH AND DEVELOPMENT

AGRICULTURAL TRANSFORMATION AND FOOD SECURITY IN CENTRAL ASIA

DR. KAMILJON T. AKRAMOV[1]

Since the early 2000s, Central Asian countries have experienced strong economic growth. Prudent macroeconomic policies and structural reforms, together with a favourable external environment, which included a commodity boom and inflows of foreign direct investment and labour remittances, led to a strong recovery of output in the region. Farm restructuring, land reform, and individualization of the agricultural sector also helped to revitalize agricultural production. As a result, poverty declined sharply, and both macro and household level food security in the region improved significantly (Akramov, 2011). Nevertheless, the recent global food and financial crises have caused serious setbacks and shown that Central Asian countries are still vulnerable to external shocks. Since the global crises are external shocks, it is not surprising that countries in the region (mainly Kyrgyzstan and Tajikistan) that are more dependent on food imports and labour remittances have seen the highest increases in food prices and the sharpest falls in household welfare and food security.

Short-term policy responses to rising food prices by national governments in the region have varied according to whether a given country is a net food exporter or net food importer. The geography of wheat production and consumption, the most important item in the region's food consumption, is such that the capacity to export surplus production over domestic consumption is far more concentrated in Kazakhstan, while other countries of the region are net importers. The remoteness of the region, poor infrastructure, and other difficulties with access to global markets give Kazakhstan a unique position in the regional cereal market. It is one of the world's largest grain exporters and major exporter of wheat to its Central Asian neighbours, Kyrgyzstan, Tajikistan, Turkmenistan, and Uzbekistan. In this regard, the introduction of export restrictions on wheat in 2008 by the government of Kazakhstan created

[1] International Food Policy Research Institute, Washington, DC, USA.

additional problems for other countries of the region, who were already struggling with high food prices.

While the negative impact of the global food crisis was partially offset by increased remittance inflows in 2007 and 2008, the global financial crisis in 2008 led to a significant decline in international remittances. For example, compared with the preceding year, the inflow of international remittances in Tajikistan fell by more than 30% in 2009, negatively affecting both national and household incomes (World Bank, 2011a). As a result, food security both at macro and household levels significantly deteriorated. This study examines the impact of the recent food and financial crises on food security in the region using macro and household level data from international sources.

Economic Growth, Agricultural Transformation and Food Production

Economic growth

During the 1990s, Central Asian countries went through significant political and economic transformations that negatively impacted economic growth in the region (Figure 1). The evidence suggests that such negative growth rates were common in all transition countries due to liberalization of prices, inconsistent market reforms, and delays in building market and collective action institutions (Roselle and Swinnen, 2004). While all countries in the region observed continued decline in their domestic output, the magnitude (about 60%) of the collapse in Tajikistan's gross domestic product (GDP) was considerably larger than in its Central Asian neighbours, mainly due to political conflict during 1992-1997.

However, from the early 2000s until mid-2008, all Central Asian countries grew at significantly higher rates. A relatively stable political environment, prudent macroeconomic policies and structural reforms, together with a favourable external environment, which included a commodity boom and large inflows of foreign direct investment and labour remittances, led to a strong recovery of output in the region. International labour remittances were particularly important in maintaining high growth rates in Kyrgyzstan and Tajikistan, accounting for over 25% and 45% of their respective gross domestic product in 2008. Development assistance from multilateral and bilateral development partners, accounting for more than 10% of their respective gross national income, was also very important in these two countries (World Bank, 2011b).

While this growth was widely shared, differences in growth rates were noticeable among individual countries. For example, with average double digit growth rates in 2000-2008, the resource-rich Kazakhstan and Turkmenistan recorded significantly higher growth rates than other countries. However, it should be noted that other countries of the region also recorded decent average (more than 5%) growth rates over that period. As a result, aggregate output in all Central Asian countries, except Tajikistan, reached or surpassed its pre-transition level. Despite an impressive average growth rate of 8.6% in 2000-2008, Tajikistan's aggregate GDP has not reached its pre-transition level. While aggregate GDP in 2010 was only 85% of its 1990 level, per capita GDP was even lower at 64%.

High economic growth, particularly agricultural growth, together with strong inflows of labour remittances, led to significant poverty reduction in the region. However, poverty rates across the region are highly uneven. For example, the share of Kazakhstan's population living under the poverty line has dropped to single digits. In contrast, nearly half of Tajikistan's population still lives under the poverty line. Moreover, 17.5% of the country's population lives in extreme (food) poverty (Akramov and Shreedhar, 2012).

In this regard, international experience suggests that to further reduce poverty, Central Asian countries should raise productivity of agriculture through both market-based incentives and public support (World Bank, 2007; Ravallion 2008). Raising productivity of agriculture not only helps to increase household income and reduce poverty, it also improves domestic food availability by increasing food production. Central Asian countries have already made significant reforms concerning price liberalization, land use, and farm organization, which have created broad market-based incentives for farmers. As a result, the agricultural sector was an engine of economic recovery, especially in resource-poor countries such as Kyrgyzstan and Tajikistan (Akramov and Omuraliev 2009; Akramov and Shreedhar 2012).

Agricultural transformation

Prior to 1991, the agricultural sector in the region was dominated by large-scale inefficient socialist farms. The reasons for persistent inefficiency of collective farms are well documented in the literature and include soft budget constraints, excessive agency problems, and transaction costs. Therefore, the need for transition from a command economy based collective farming to a market based private farming system was necessary

(Lerman, et al., 2004). The transformation of the agricultural sector in the region began in the early 1990s and continues to the present day. The major elements of this transformation include:

(1) liberalization of prices and the removal of direct government intervention in agricultural decision-making;
(2) land reform and farm reorganization; and
(3) formation of market and collective-action institutions (Rozelle and Swinnen, 2004).

There are, however, important differences among individual countries in terms of the pace of transformation and the resulting farm structure. According to the World Bank's agrarian reform metric, Kyrgyzstan belongs to the advanced reformer group, with an average reform score of 7.2; this was significantly higher than those of its neighbours in Central Asia, which were rated as moderate (Kazakhstan, with an average score of 6.2) or slow (Tajikistan, 4.4 and Uzbekistan, 4.8) reformers (Csaki, et al, 2006).

In the beginning of the transition (1991-1992), Kyrgyzstan quickly liberalized its agricultural markets and prices, and, after four years (1995), started the distribution of agricultural land to farmers, giving them land use certificates for up to 99 years. These land use certificates granted five legal rights to individual farmers, namely the rights to transfer, exchange, sell, lease, and use the land certificate as collateral for credit. Later, in 1998, after a country-wide referendum, a constitutional amendment that allowed private land ownership was adopted. Currently, agricultural land may be owned by the state, by citizens of Kyrgyzstan who are at least 18 years old and have permanently resided in rural areas for at least two years, and by agricultural cooperatives. The agricultural land may be leased out, sold or donated, but it must be used exclusively for the purposes of agricultural production. The land shares and parcels may be traded for other land shares or parcels, but only within the boundaries of a given local government. Thus, although land reform is not yet complete, Kyrgyzstan has made significant progress in privatizing land and creating markets for agricultural land (Akramov and Omuraliev, 2009).

Other countries in the region have lagged in the implementation of agricultural reforms and generally still do not recognize private property rights to agricultural land, with some minor exceptions. Kazakhstan restricts private land ownership to small household plots of up to 0.2 hectares, whereas Uzbekistan and Tajikistan basically retain full state ownership of land (Lerman, et al, 2004). Overall, Kazakhstan has adopted the principle of state ownership of agricultural land with private use and transfer rights under long-term (up to 99-year) leases. Nevertheless, the government still seems to favour large agricultural enterprises, and very little (less than 10%) of the farmland is cultivated by individual farmers. The agricultural sector was neglected from the 1990s to the early 2000s, when the government introduced a price-support system for wheat and other agricultural products (Pomfret, 2008).

It is important to note that the pace of reform in Tajikistan has been slow. The land reform and farm restructuring are incomplete, and various characteristics of collective farming still remain there. Overall, land reform is restricted to reallocation of state-owned agricultural land among producers through the mechanism of land use rights. Land use rights can be transferred and individuals have the right to withdraw from the collective farm to establish private (dehkan) farms. In order to exercise this right, they needed to obtain approval from the farm chairman and the district government, and take on responsibility for a portion of the debt accrued by the former state or collective farm (Lerman and Sedik, 2008). In recent years, several government resolutions and legislations were passed to gradually reduce government intervention in land use and planning, as well as to ensure greater power to farmers in making production decisions. For instance, while the cotton debt crisis was resolved, a number of initiatives were passed under the "Freedom to Farm" bill through the Government Resolution No. 111 in 2007, which intended to reduce government intervention in farm activities. In addition, Tajikistan's Land Code and other land use and agriculture related laws have been amended numerous times. Overall, land reform is a high priority in the current reforms process, and the government has set goals to guarantee farmers freedom to make production decisions and accelerate farm restructuring by streamlining the allocation of land use certificates (Government of Tajikistan, 2011).

In Uzbekistan, the principle of exclusive state ownership of land, which does not allow private land ownership either by individuals or collectives, is in place. Currently, there are three types of farms in the country: corporate farms, peasant farms and household plots. The district governments allocate land to these three types of agricultural producers along with the right of inheritance, but without any rights to sell, transfer, or exchange. Despite restricted land reform, the farm structure in the country has gradually changed away from collective toward peasant farming (Lerman, 2008). This transformation took place step by step, and the government also gradually reduced price and market distortions in agriculture by introducing reforms aimed at reducing the negative incentives for farmers (Pomfret, 2008). Overall, Uzbekistan alternated between individualization and consolidation (optimization of farm sizes) policies, which led to a mixed farm structure, including both smallholders and medium-size farms.

Food security

Past studies suggest that agricultural reforms had strong positive impacts on agricultural production and food security in the region. First, the net effect of agricultural reforms was a dramatic shift in the distribution of agricultural land use in favour of private farms. In turn, changes in the distribution of agricultural land by farm type led to significant modifications in the structure of agricultural production. This impressive shift in the composition of agricultural production does not simply reflect the changes in the composition of land holdings across different farm types. The evidence suggests that private farms are significantly more productive than collective farms (Lerman, 2008; Akramov and Omuraliev, 2009; Akramov and Shreedhar, 2012). As a result, agricultural growth recovered and all Central Asian countries, except Kazakhstan, surpassed the pre-transition levels of agricultural output (Figure 2).

Second, agricultural reforms allowed farmers to improve their resource allocation based on market conditions and the profitability of particular crops. This led to more diverse production systems and substantial changes in cropping patterns by significantly increasing the land allocated to food crops (Lerman, 2008; Akramov and Omuraliev, 2009; Akramov and Shreedhar, 2012). Changes in land allocation led to considerable increases in grains, potato and vegetable outputs while production of cotton declined significantly. For example, in Tajikistan, the gross agricultural output in the grain sector, mainly wheat, has grown by more than 4 times during the transition period with an average annual growth rate of 7.7%. The annual growth rates of grain output have accelerated during the last decade with an average growth rate of more than 10%. Likewise, the potato output has tripled during this period with an average annual growth rate of 11.2%. This growth in grain and potato outputs is not solely due to changes in sown area. The grain and potato yields also increased considerably during the last decade, probably, due to increased allocation of irrigated land under these crops (Akramov and Shreedhar 2012). Finally, results from cross-section household surveys in Kyrgyzstan, Tajikistan and Uzbekistan suggest that agricultural reforms probably had a positive impact on household income by making more land available to rural households and giving decision-making power to individual farmers (Lerman, 2008; Lerman and Sedik, 2008).

Overall, the developments described above have led to significant improvements in food security in the region. On the one hand, agricultural reforms, by changing crop patterns in favour of food crops and increasing crop yields, have significantly increased domestic food availability. On the other hand, strong recovery of economic growth, together with increasing agricultural productivity and inflows of labour remittances, have substantially raised household income and, thus, improved economic access to food.

Global Food and Financial Crises and Food Security in Central Asia

On the eve of the global food and financial crises, most of the Central Asian countries, except Tajikistan, were food secure. However, the global crisis had a significantly negative impact on food security in the region, which was evident in declining food availability, rising domestic food prices, and growing numbers of food insecure people.

During 2007-11, Central Asian countries witnessed food price movements that closely echoed the price fluctuations in the international markets. The spike in domestic food price inflation in Central Asia was almost perfectly simultaneous with the surge in international food prices in 2007 (Figure 3). Reflecting the surge in global food prices, food price inflation in most of the region accelerated sharply and jumped into double digits during the second half of 2007, staying high through September 2008, when it started to decline, closely reflecting global food price trends. The escalation of domestic food price inflation was especially pronounced in Kyrgyzstan, where the food price index was up almost 40% on a year-on-year basis in October 2007, hit a peak of 48% in June 2008, and moderated to 20% in December 2008. The acceleration of food price inflation was less pronounced in Uzbekistan, where the government has pursued a policy of cereal self-sufficiency since the early 1990s, and has made extensive use of price controls.

Increasing global food prices even influenced Kazakhstan's domestic food market, one of the world's major exporters of high-quality grain. Kazakhstan's food price inflation reached double digits in August 2007 and then quickly accelerated to 25-26% on a year-on-year basis in the fourth quarter of 2007. Given surging global food prices and accelerating domestic inflation, the government felt that large, sudden increase in foreign demand might divert wheat from domestic markets and result in further increases in domestic food prices. This led to the Kazakh government's decisions initially to impose export tariffs on wheat in

February 2008, and later to enforce a temporary suspension on wheat exports in April 2008 (Mitra and Josling, 2009). Since Kazakhstan is the main supplier of wheat and wheat flour to other Central Asian countries, these trade restrictions likely had a negative impact on the availability of food and further raised domestic prices in these countries. For example, in the summer of 2008, prices of bread, wheat, and flour increased by more than 50% in Tajikistan (Akramov, 2011). Globally, Kazakhstan's decision to restrict wheat exports, echoing the moves of other wheat exporters (that is, Russia, Argentina, and Ukraine), caused international prices of high-quality wheat to surge by 25% in one day on February 25, 2007 (HIS 2008). Overall, international food prices might have increased by about 20% as a result of the temporary export restrictions (Ivanic and Martin, 2008).

The last several months of 2010 again witnessed rising prices of wheat and other staples, which were triggered by the drought in Russia in the summer of 2010 and lower grain production in various parts of the world. Some cereal exporters again responded through trade restrictions. For instance, Russia passed an embargo on wheat grain and flour exports in August 2010, which was extended through July 1, 2011 (USDA, 2010). As seen in 2007-08, rising international prices have been followed by rising food prices in Central Asia in key staples such as wheat and wheat flour. Notably, wheat prices in Tajikistan increased by approximately 30-40% (Akramov and Shreedhar, 2012).

Rising global food prices had negative impact on macro and household level food security in the region. The ratio of food imports to the total exports of goods and services, which reflects the relative cost of access to food available on the international markets, is often used to measure food security at the macro level (Diaz Bonilla et al. 2002; Ecker et al. 2010). This indicator reflects the fact that macro level food security is not equal to food self-sufficiency, and captures both the country's demand for food imports and its capacity to finance this demand using foreign exchange earnings generated by exports of goods and services. The higher the ratio of food imports to total exports, the less protected the country is in terms of macro level food security. In this regard, due to generally low dependence on food imports and strong export capacity, the resource-abundant countries of the region (Kazakhstan, Turkmenistan and Uzbekistan) are well protected from external shocks. They spend only about 2-5% of total export earnings to finance their food imports.

However, the impact of global food crisis was more pronounced in Central Asia's net food importers. Due to high dependence on food imports and weak export capacity, Kyrgyzstan and Tajikistan face enormous food security challenges. In 2005-2008, on average, Tajikistan and Kyrgyzstan used about 20% of their export earnings to finance food imports, which is about two times higher than the world average. The average value of this indicator for 178 countries around the world is approximately 9% (Ecker et al. 2010). This makes them highly vulnerable to possible periods of food insecurity arising from external shocks such as international price volatility and policy directives of their trade partners. In this regard, the ratio of food imports to total exports of Kyrgyzstan and Tajikistan has dropped significantly in recent years, exposing their vulnerability to rising global food prices. For example, during the last three years, about 35-40% of Tajikistan's export revenues were spent to finance its food purchases in international markets. Further, some argue that revenue from exports of goods and services does not truly represent the country's ability to finance its food imports (Akramov and Shreedhar, 2012). Other sources of foreign exchange, such as labour remittances, could also be important. This is especially true for countries like Tajikistan, where foreign exchange inflow from international remittances exceeds earning from exports of goods and services. Taking into account international remittances, in 2005-2008, on average, more than 12% of Tajikistan's total foreign exchange earnings were used to finance its food imports, which is still considerably higher than the world average. Moreover, this ratio declined even more in recent years as a result of the global food and financial crises. On the one hand, rising global food prices increased the costs of Tajikistan's food imports. On the other hand, global financial crisis led to lower international remittances because demand for Tajikistan's migrant labour in Russia and Kazakhstan plummeted. As a result of these two impacts, the ratio of food imports to foreign exchange earnings increased to over 20% in 2010 (Akramov and Shreedhar, 2012).

Further, rising food prices and deteriorating macro level food security eventually had a negative impact on food availability and access at the household level. According to USDA's annual food security assessments, in Kyrgyzstan, Turkmenistan, and Uzbekistan, food consumption for the lowest income quintile fell below the nutritional target in 2007. In Tajikistan, the most vulnerable country in the region, about 80% of the population fell below the nutritional target during the same time period. Overall, Tajikistan's 2007 distributional food gap — the amount of food needed to raise consumption in every income quintile to the minimum nutritional target — was estimated at 29 kilograms per person in grain equivalent (USDA, 2008).

The following analysis briefly examines the impact of the global financial crisis on the well-being and food security of households in

Central Asia using data from the 2010 EBRD, World Bank Life in Transition Survey II (LiTS). The LiTS was carried out in 29 transition countries and collected a host of socio-economic data about respondent households concerning the impact of the global economic crises on people's well-being. According to subjective measures, the impact of the crisis on all Central Asian households was enormous and pervasive. Nevertheless, the impact of the crisis was more pronounced in Tajikistan, which is more dependent on food imports and international labour remittances. For example, over 50% of households in Tajikistan reported that they were affected either "a great deal" or "a fair amount" compared to about 28% in Kazakhstan, 25% in Kyrgyzstan, and just 16% in Uzbekistan (EBRD, 2011). This subjective indicator of impact closely corresponds to objective indicators of shocks experienced by households. The survey results suggest that the majority of these households have been affected through the labour market and reduction in international remittances. For instance, the most important transmission channel of the crisis impact in Tajikistan has been distress in wage earnings: almost half of the affected households reported that they experienced reductions, delays, or suspensions in their wage earnings during the crisis. Nearly 42% of affected households in Tajikistan stated that either a head of household or another household member who lost his or her job during this period. A reduced inflow of international remittances was another important transmission channel in Tajikistan: about 38% of affected households reported that they had experienced significant reductions in flow of remittances during the crisis period. As a result, more than 50% of households in Tajikistan reported reducing staple food consumption, as compared to 35% in other Central Asian countries (Figure 4). This is not surprising, given that in Tajikistan, availability of public safety nets, including unemployment benefits, child support, and targeted social assistance, was among the lowest in transition countries. Thus, most affected households in Tajikistan were forced to rely on private safety nets, such as borrowing money from relatives and friends or to reduce their consumption of, mainly, staple food expenditures (Akramov and Shreedhar, 2012).

Constraints on improving food security in Central Asia

The brief overview of the region's agricultural reforms and growth provided above showed that land reform and individualization of agriculture led to the recovery of agricultural production and enhanced food security in the region. The evidence provided in this study also suggests that Central Asian countries, especially net food importers such as Kyrgyzstan and Tajikistan, still remain vulnerable to external shocks. Thus, a surge in domestic food prices and decline in inflow of international remittances closely associated with global food and financial crises, had a significant negative impact on macro and household level food security in the region. National governments in the region introduced various short-term policy measures to mitigate the negative impacts of rising food prices. These included reduced taxes and import duties on selected food grains (Kyrgyzstan and Tajikistan), targeted food subsidies for low income people (Kyrgyzstan), and subsidies for agricultural producers (Kyrgyzstan, Tajikistan and Uzbekistan) (ADB, 2008). Administrative price control measures and targeted social assistance programs have been in place for some time in Uzbekistan. In Tajikistan and Turkmenistan, governments also implemented measures to increase domestic grain production (USDA, 2008). However, the policy measures mentioned above cannot fully mitigate the negative effects of global food and financial crises on poor and vulnerable households.

Thus, an important policy challenge for the region is how to best position itself to respond to possible external shocks in the future. It is evident that the majority of Central Asians live in rural areas, and that agriculture employs a significant portion of labour forces and provides livelihood opportunities for most of the rural households in the region. Thus, increasing agricultural productivity is essential to improving the well-being of these households. Moreover, increasing agricultural productivity helps to increase domestic food production and reduces import dependence. The evidence suggests that there remain several constraints on achieving higher and sustained levels of agricultural growth and food production in the region. First, de-collectivization of agriculture significantly diminished the agency problem and significantly improved incentives for farmers throughout the region. Nevertheless, farmers in most of Central Asia still make their production decisions based on distorted prices, and are unable to benefit from higher international prices for their products, despite being exposed to higher input prices. Moreover, some governments in the region continue to intervene in farmers' cropping and marketing decision making (Lerman, 2008; Pomfret, 2008; Akramov and Shreedhar, 2012).

Second, transition to a market-based agriculture in Central Asia was accompanied by a significant decline in agricultural public expenditures, leading to a noticeable deterioration in the quality of rural infrastructure and the availability of agricultural services. This negative impact was perhaps most damaging for the irrigation infrastructure, a major component of the region's agricultural production. De-collectivization created an institutional vacuum because no organization was responsible for the operation and maintenance of the on-farm irrigation networks. This has led to poor upkeep of the existing infrastructure. The governments, supported by donors, tried to mitigate the problem by introducing an irrigation service fee and through establishment of water users associations (WUA). However, institutional reform in the irrigation sector was significantly slower than land reform, and irrigation facilities had already largely deteriorated by the time irrigation reforms were introduced. Moreover, the WUAs are still weak and financially unsustainable due to problems with the collection of service fees, incongruities between formal and informal rules, power abuse, rent seeking, information asymmetry, and distrust between community members (Akramov and Omuraliev, 2009).

Third, land reform and individualization of agriculture contributed to the fragmentation of land use. Due to their limited size, private smallholder farms cannot afford to purchase costly agricultural machinery. Without capital to replace and maintain existing equipment, the agricultural machinery fleet deteriorated in Central Asia, resulting in "de-mechanization" of the agricultural sector (World Bank, 2009). The recovery of agricultural production and strong growth suggests that negative impact so far has been offset by improvements in labour efforts and resource allocation. However, this may have important implications for agricultural productivity in the long run. In this regard, consolidation of land use is an important policy direction for Central Asian countries. The experience of market economies shows that leasing can play an important role in land consolidation (Lerman, et al., 2004). Further, the evidence suggests that small farmers can make use of scale economies by establishing trade and service cooperatives, which allows them to share the burden of capital expenditures by creating a machinery pool (Lerman, et al, 2004). The development of such cooperatives requires appropriate legal basis, and institutional reforms and promotion of service cooperatives may be a promising direction for fostering improvements in farmers' access to agricultural machinery and services. However, some Central Asian countries (for example, Uzbekistan) are leaning towards formal government-sponsored land consolidation programs based on enlargement of farm size by fiat, instead of the market-driven process. This may create significant problems for food security and poverty reduction because it may lead to the consolidation of agricultural land in the hands of a few well-connected and wealthy farmers, while many others may become landless.

Fourth, farmers need new services, such as agricultural advisory and marketing, to fully exploit the new economic paradigm of the market economy. Unfortunately, the agrarian reforms in Central Asia were inconsistent, and this dimension of the transition to market-based individual farming was mostly neglected during the earlier phases of transition. As a result, only a fraction of the region's individual farmers have access to such services. For example, in Kyrgyzstan, only one-fifth of farmers have access to advisory services and only 2-3% of farmers use marketing, information or legal services (Akramov and Omuraliev, 2009).

Further, international experience suggests that the countries that effectively manage the adverse effects of the crisis had social safety net programs in place to help cushion the negative impacts of external shocks. The available evidence shows that social protection policies in some Central Asian countries are very limited and only a few households can benefit from such programs (Akramov and Shreedhar, 2012). These countries, in collaboration with development partners, must continue efforts to develop effective social protection programs through the targeting of especially vulnerable groups with cash and food transfers, vouchers, and other such mechanisms. These programs can provide an essential safety net to needy households in reducing vulnerability to future food and economic crises that may arise.

Finally, remoteness of the region from major international ports lead to high transport costs, and the lengthy transit time needed for international shipments to and from Central Asia is a major constraint for achieving sustainable food security in the region. Thus, food security in the region can be significantly improved by enhancing regional cooperation and trade. This requires collaborative efforts from governments to remove existing trade barriers, such as tariffs and quantitative restrictions, as well as restrictions on the movements of goods and transport across borders and through territories of neighbouring countries. Some countries in the region have established, or are planning to establish, strategic grain reserves in reaction to global food crisis and the export bans and export taxes observed recently. In this regard, international experience suggests that an efficient food (grain) reserves policy should consider evidence-based solutions for stock management, potential linkages between strategic reserves and food markets, between strategic reserves and other food security and social safety programs. In addition, issues related to the impact of grain reserves on agricultural prices and interregional grain movement should be properly examined.

Conclusion

The recent global food and financial crises had significant negative impacts on macro and household level food security in Central Asia. These impacts are seen in rising domestic food prices, decreasing domestic food (cereal) availability, and declining inflow international remittances. The net effect of these developments was reduced food consumption, especially for the poor households. Short-term policy responses by national governments in the region varied according to whether the country is a net exporter or importer of food. The net importers faced additional problems with food security because some net exporters introduced temporary restrictions on cereal exports. The negative consequences of rising global food prices would have been more severe if the agricultural sector in the region had not been restructured during transition. The reform led to more diverse production systems and substantial changes in cropping patterns, with a significant increase in the land area devoted to food crops, such as wheat, vegetables, potatoes and fruits. This played an important role in improving food security by increasing per capita food availability.

Nevertheless, the recent surge in global food prices showed that Central Asian countries, especially Kyrgyzstan and Tajikistan, are still vulnerable to external shocks. In order to increase and sustain the agricultural growth rates and levels of food production, Central Asian countries need concerted efforts to remove remaining constraints in the sector. First and foremost, remaining distortions in agricultural markets and prices should be removed. Another essential problem is that transition to a market-based agriculture in Central Asia was accompanied by a significant decline in agricultural public expenditures, leading to a noticeable deterioration in irrigation infrastructure and availability of agricultural machinery and services. Thus, the governments and donors have to make collaborative efforts to address these shortcomings by channelling additional public resources to the sector, as well as by creating new market-based mechanisms. Further, additional reforms are needed with respect to property rights and institutional changes. These reforms should generate proper market-based incentives for agricultural land consolidation, and improve the market and collective action institutions, such as WUAs and cooperatives. Finally, the international experience suggests that, apart from increasing agricultural productivity and food production, long-term food security can be significantly improved by strengthening the public social safety net and enhancing regional cooperation and trade. Thus, Central Asian countries need to improve their social safety net and remove existing barriers on both regional and international movements of agricultural and food products.

References

Akramov, K. and N. Omuraliev, 2009. Institutional Change, Rural Services, and Agricultural Performance in Kyrgyzstan. Discussion Paper 175, Washington, DC: International Food Policy Research Institute.

Akramov K., 2011. International Food Prices, Agricultural Transformation, and Food Security in Central Asia, Development in Practice, 21 (4-5), p. 741.

Akramov, K. and G. Shreedhar, 2012. Economic Development, External Shocks, and Food Security in Central Asia. Discussion Paper, Washington, DC: International Food Policy Research Institute (forthcoming).

Asian Development Bank (ADB), 2008. Food Prices and Inflation in Developing Asia: Is Poverty Reduction Coming to an End? Manila, Philippines.

Diaz-Bonilla, E., M. Thomas., and S. Robinson, 2002. On Boxes, Contents, and Users: Food Security and the WTO Negotiations. Trade and Macroeconomics Division Discussion Paper 82. Washington D.C.: International Food Policy Research Institute.

Csaki, C., Kray, H. and S. Zorya, 2006. The Agrarian Economies of Central-Eastern Europe and the Commonwealth of Independent States: An Update on Status and Progress in 2005. World Bank ECSSD Working Paper 46, Washington D.C.

Ecker, O., Breisinger, C., McCool, C., Diao, X., Funes, J., and L. You, 2010. Assessing Food Security in Yemen:An Innovative Integrated, Cross-Sector, and Multilevel Approach. Discussion Paper 982. Washington D.C.: International Food Policy Research Institute.

European Bank for Reconstruction and Development (EBRD), 2011. *Life in Transition: After the Crisis*. London, UK.

Government of Tajikistan. (2011c). International Conference on Agrarian Reform. Conference Proceedings. Dushanbe: Government of the Republic of Tajikistan and Development Coordination Council.

HIS Global Insight, 2008. Wheat Prices Leap 25% as Kazakhstan Joins List of Countries Restricting Exports, http://www.ihsglobalinsight.com/SDA/SDADetail11647.htm

Ivanic, M. and Martin, W., 2008. Implications of higher global food prices for poverty in low-income countries, *Agricultural Economics 39 (Supplement), p 405.*

Lerman, Z., Csaki, C. and G. Feder, 2004. Agriculture in Transition: Land Policies and Evolving Farm Structures in Post-Soviet Countries, Lexington Books, Oxford, UK

Lerman, Z. and D. Sedik, 2008. The Economic Effects of Land Reform in Tajikistan. Report prepared for European Commission under the EC/FAO Food Security Programme.

Lerman, Z., 2008. Agricultural Development in Central Asia: A Survey of Uzbekistan, *Eurasian Geography and Economics,* 49(4), p. 481.

Mitra, S. and T. Josling., 2009. Agricultural Export Restrictions: Welfare Implications and Trade Disciplines, International Food and Agricultural Trade Policy Council Position Paper, Washington, D.C.

Pomfret, R., 2008. Kazakhstan, In Eds. Anderson, K. and J. Swinnen, Distortions to Agricultural Incentives in Europe's Transition Economies, Washington DC: World Bank.

Ravallion, M. 2008. Are There Lessons for Africa from China's Success against Poverty? *World Development,* 37 (2), p.303.

Rozelle, S. and J.F.M. Swinnen, 2004. Success and Failure of Reform: Insights from the Transition of Agriculture. *Journal of Economic Literature*, XLII (2), p404.

United States Department of Agriculture (USDA), 2008. Food Security Assessment 2007. *Agriculture and Trade Report GFA 19.* Washington, D.C.

—. 2010, Global Agricultural; Information Network Report RS 1039. Washington, D.C.

World Bank. 2007. World Development Report 2008: Agriculture for Development. Washington, D.C.: World Bank.

—. 2009. Farm Mechanization: A New Challenge for Agriculture in low and Middle Income ECA Countries. Washington, DC: World Bank.

—. 2011a. Tajikistan's Quest for Economic Growth: Stimulating Private Investment, Country Economic Memorandum. Washington, D.C.: World Bank.

—. 2011b. World Development Indicators database. Washington, D.C.: World Bank.

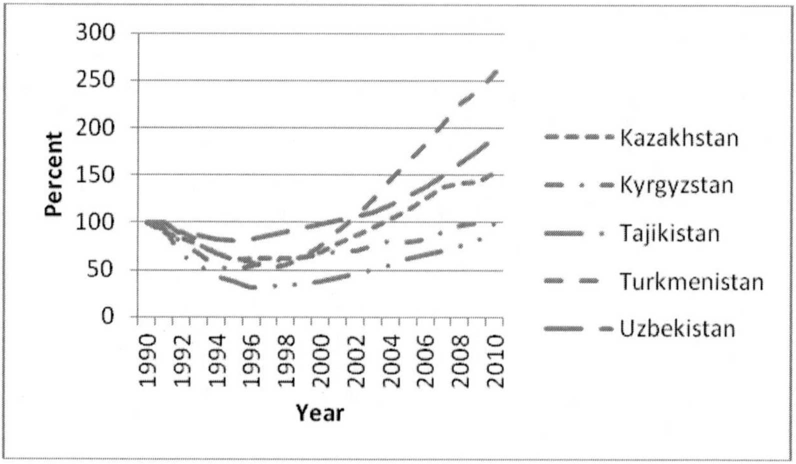

Figure 1. Cumulative economic growth in Central Asia, 1991-2010
Source: Author's representation using data from World Bank (2011b).

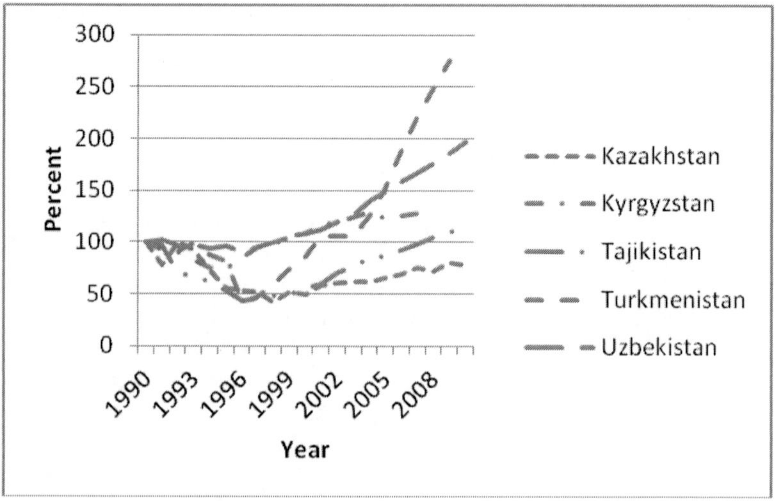

Figure 2. Cumulative agricultural growth in Central Asia, 1991-2010
Source: Author's representation using data from World Bank (2011b).

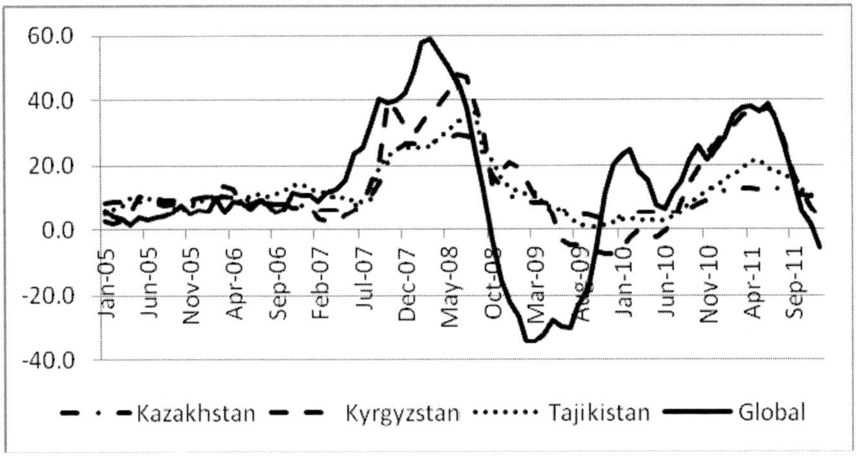

Figure 3. Twelve month growth rates of food prices in global markets and Central Asia (2005-2011)
Source: Author's representation using data from FAO and national statistical agencies of Kazakhstan, Kyrgyzstan and Tajikistan.
Note: Changes in global food prices measured using the FAO Food Price Index.

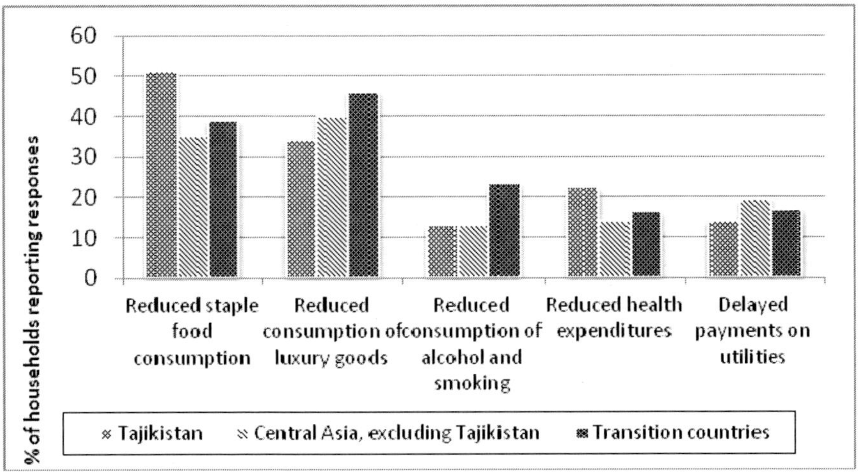

Figure 4. Household responses to the crisis in Central Asia
Source: Author's representation using data from EBRD (2011).
Note: Central Asia, excluding Tajikistan includes Kazakhstan, Kyrgyzstan, and Uzbekistan.

HUMAN DEVELOPMENT INDEX IN CENTRAL ASIAN COUNTRIES

ASST. PROF. VOLKAN ÖNGEL,[1]
ASST. PROF. İLYAS SÖZEN[1]
AND ASST. PROF. ALKAN ÇELIK[1]

Throughout history, economic development and growth have been amongst the most important goals of all governments. These prioritized targets have played an active role in the decisions and on the preferences of governors in political and economic areas. Until the 1970s, income growth was considered to be sufficient for a country's development. For many years, the concept of revenue growth, which was considered to be of equal standing as economic development, in the form of economics has now begun to change for various reasons. The expected economic growth rate is not achieved in various high-income level countries or low-income countries with relatively high development levels. Nowadays, economic development covers life expectancy at birth, literacy rate, reduction of gender discrimination, poverty reduction, equal distribution of income, as well as economic development.

After the collapse of the Soviet Union, the independent Central Asian countries, such as Kazakhstan, Turkmenistan, Uzbekistan, Tajikistan, and Kyrgyzstan, assessed economic development and growth as their priority policy. However, the countries that gained their freedom after the collapse of the Soviet Union, which already had independent economic and political structures, lack comparable conditions in terms of factors of production. While some countries (in particular Kazakhstan, Turkmenistan, and Uzbekistan) are rich in natural sources like gas, oil, and gold; others like Kyrgyzstan and Tajikistan do not benefit from these natural resources as much. For this reason, human capital has a great influence for achieving economic growth and development in the countries of the region.

The purpose of this study is to evaluate the status of human development index data in 2010, and the change of post-independence

[1] Beykent University, Istanbul, Turkey.

period year by year, through a periodic comparison between the rate of change in the Gross Domestic Product per capita (GDP-GDP) and the rate of change in Human Development Index (HDI-HDI). The analysis data concerning 5 Central Asian countries covers the years 1990-2010. This study is based on retrospective and illustrative library work. In conclusion it is shown that a high rate of GDP increases in Central Asian countries was not reflected in the human development index during the 20-year period.

Human Development Index

Development has been identified equally as economic growth over a long period in economic literature. For this reason, the best measure indicating economic performance, that also allows for cross-country comparison (such as between the rich and the poor, the developed and the developing), and similar classification with respect to national income per capita (GDP per capita), seems to be the human development index, as in the digital display (Jahan, 2004). However, in some countries reflecting high levels of economic development, political instability, rising unemployment rates, and inequalities in the distribution of income, have all begun to pose problems. In a variety of high-income countries, high crime rates and environmental issues have contributed to significant problems. Some middle-income countries were better in terms of human welfare, so these points, while creating a powerful basis for criticism regarding economic growth, did not reduce poverty or find solutions for a variety of social problems (Gürses, 2009).

Human development index (HDI-HDI) was first published by the United Nations Development Program (UNDP) Human Development Report Office in 1990. This index, which is published each year, contains a brief description of people's well-being, with no relation to national income (Kaya, 2008). Reactions related to the economic development at this time were intense. The first report was prepared by a team led by Pakistani economist Mahbub ul Haq (Gürses, 2009). This index, which measures levels of well-being of individuals living in the countries included, refers to the concept of human development. HDI indicators related to the basic approach, reflect the quality of human life in relation to their development, which would not be indicated with economic indicators only. A minimum income level is not sufficient for an individual to have a healthy and long life and meet the public sphere in the country they live. Revenue, at this point, is necessary but not sufficient for human development. It is important for an individual to be healthy and well-informed, as well as to have income. At this point the most important criterion is the capacity of national wealth to create development opportunities for individuals (Karabulut, et al. 2009). In other words, manufacturing of economic output depends on reunification of production factors (physical capital, human capital, labour, natural sources, etc.). Increase in human capital of individuals can provide a significant contribution to economic development. The appropriate environment must be given to people working for use of human capital. There is a waste of human capital unless the country's GDP growth per capita increases and uses the revenue parallel to the human capital (Karataş and Çankaya, 2010).

Human development index is generated using three sub-indices. These are the welfare, education, and health standards. Different distributions of these three criteria that contribute to the objectives of social development in general are obtained as follows (Demir, 2006).

- Welfare Standard: Resources to lead a life that corresponds to being satisfactory. The purchasing power of GDP per capita is obtained as a result of the calculation of parity. According to the standard index of prosperity, an increase of USD 1,000 in the GDP per capita affects 0.8% in 1998, 0.6% in 2000, 0.4% in 2005 and 0.3% in 2009.
- Education Standard: Measurement is done using two dimensional variables for education standards. These are literacy rate among adults and the average duration of education. In the sub-index of education standard, an increase in the adult literacy rate of 1% has an impact on HDI of 0.2%. Increase in the schooling rate of 1% has an impact on HDI of 0.1%.
- Health Standard: According to this sub-index, a long life is described as the health standard and measured by life expectancy at birth. A 1-year increase in life expectancy has an effect of 0.6% on HDI.

Education and health standards mentioned above are significant in terms of the quality of life. These elements improve the quality of an individual's life and can provide access to other wealth. Welfare standard has been added to the index in relation to the human success rate, depending on income level (Gürses, 2009). According to the human development index in 2010, which includes 169 countries, Norway occupies the first position as having the highest level of human development rate, with a value of 0.938. Barbados is at 42nd position, with a value of 0.788. The high level of human development index covers the countries between the Bahamas at 43rd, with a value of 0.784, and Tonga at 85th, with a value of 0.677. The average level of human development index covers the countries between Fiji at 86th, with a value of 0.669, and the Democratic Republic of Sao Tome and Principe at 127th, with a value of 0.488. The low level of human development index covers 42 countries between Kenya at 128th, with a value of 0.470, and Zimbabwe, ranked last, with a value of 0.140 (UNDP, 2010).

The literature review has mainly focused on the calculation criteria of HDI, with a number of additions and criticisms that stand out concerning the changes occurring in the index since 1990. Although there are various studies conducted on the basis of regions and countries, no studies seem to cover the Central Asian countries in their entirety. The only study focusing especially on the region is the article called "During the Period of after Cold War Human Development Performance of Transition Economies" by Mıhcı (Mıhcı 2011). According to Mıhcı (2011), who has taken all the countries of Commonwealth of Independent States, the development performance of developing countries is encouraging in relation to their income levels, although their HDI levels are relatively low.

HDI of Central Asian Countries by 2010

In the region of Central Asia, HDI values of Kazakhstan, Turkmenistan, Uzbekistan, Kyrgyzstan, and Tajikistan in 2010 are shown in Table 1.

As seen in Table 1, Kazakhstan is the country with the highest HDI value among these five Middle Asian countries. The index value of 0.714 in 2011 Human Development Index puts Kazakhstan in 66th position among 169 countries. Accordingly, Kazakhstan appears to be the only country with high HDI within the region. According to HDI 2010, four Central Asian countries have an average level of human development. Among these four countries, Turkmenistan is 87th, with an index value of 0.669; Uzbekistan is 102nd, with an HDI value of 0.617; Kyrgyzstan is 109th, with an index value of 0.598; and Tajikistan is 112th, with the lowest HDI value among the countries in the region: 0.580. Considering the differences among the countries in terms of the level of development of HDI values, the difference between Kazakhstan with the value of 0.714 and Tajikistan with the value of 0.580, is 0.134. The difference is almost equal to Zimbabwe's total HDI value in 2011. Evaluating these two countries considering the data from the sub-indices that form the human development index, the life expectancy at birth is 67.3 years in Tajikistan and 65.4 years in Kazakhstan. The 0.5-year average index difference in schooling rates between these two countries is mainly due to the value of GDP per capita.

Table 1: Human Development Indices in Central Asian Countries, 2010

World HDI Rank	Country	Human Development Index (HDI)	Life Expectancy at Birth	Schooling Average	GDP Per Capita*	GDP Per Capita Rank Minus HDI Rank	Non-income HDI Value
66	Kazakhstan	0.714	65.4	10.3	10,234	6	0.756
87	Turkmenistan	0.669	65.3	9.9	7,052	1	0.719
102	Uzbekistan	0.617	68.2	10.0	3,085	17	0.721
109	Kyrgyzstan	0.598	68.4	9.3	2,291	17	0.726
112	Tajikistan	0.580	67.3	9.8	2,020	22	0.709

* Purchasing Power Parity-US USD 2008

Source: Based on data in UNDP Human Development Report 2010, pp.143-147

When the sub-indices of life expectancy at birth for these 5 countries are examined, Turkmenistan has the lowest rate with 65.3 years, and Kyrgyzstan has the highest rate with 68.4 years. In terms of school attendance average, Kyrgyzstan is ranked last with 9.3 years, and Kazakhstan is ranked first with 10.3 years. Kazakhstan and Turkmenistan, the countries which have the highest HDI value in the region, have significantly higher GDP values than other countries, with USD10,234 and USD7,052 per person respectively. Uzbekistan, Kyrgyzstan, and Tajikistan, in Table 1, have the GDP values of USD3,085, USD2,291, and USD2,020 per capita respectively.

The conspicuous element for the countries in the region is that the HDI rankings of all the countries in the world are lower than the GDP per capita rankings. In GDP per capita in the world minus HDI section, Kazakhstan moves up 6 places, Turkmenistan 1, Uzbekistan and Kyrgyzstan 17, and Tajikistan 22. The key factor here suggests that either the revenue was not spent on human development, or the growth of national economies was provided by the export of natural sources rather than by human capital.

Table 2: Adjusted Human Development Index to Equity of Central Asian Countries, 2010

Human Development Index (HDI)		HDI Adjusted to Equity		
Country	**Value**	**Value in 2010**	**Loss Rate %**	**Change in 2010**
Kazakhstan	0.714	0.617	13.6	3
Turkmenistan	0.669	0.493	26.4	-12
Uzbekistan	0.617	0.521	15.7	17
Kyrgyzstan	0.598	0.508	15.1	15
Tajikistan	0.580	0.469	19.1	6

	Life Expectancy at Birth Adjusted to Equity		Education Index Adjusted to Equity		Income Index Adjusted to Equity	
	Value in 2010	**Loss Rate %**	**Value in 2010**	**Loss Rate %**	**Value in 2010**	**Loss Rate %**
Kazakhstan	0.595	17.2	0.753	5.3	0.525	17.6
Turkmenistan	0.520	27.5	0.647	10.2	0.355	38.7
Uzbekistan	0.565	25.9	0.672	1.4	0.372	17.9
Kyrgyzstan	0.601	21.6	0.611	11.1	0.357	12.2
Tajikistan	0.517	31.0	0.608	9.4	0.328	15.3

Source: Based on data in UNDP Human Development Report 2010, pp. 152-155.

The adjusted Human Development Index to equity of Central Asian countries is shown in Table 2. The HDI values adjusted to equity can be defined as an index that incorporates and adapts female-male discrimination into the Human Development Index. In this case, Turkmenistan, which ranks at 87, dropped 12 positions after losing values of HDI, and ranked at 99 in the world. In other countries, HDI values other than income show affirmative action applying to women. According to the HDI adjusted to equity, Kazakhstan goes up 3 places, Uzbekistan 17, Kyrgyzstan 15, and Tajikistan 6.

Human Development Indices in Central Asian Countries in 1990-2010 and Changes in Gross Domestic Product per Capita

20 years after the independence of Central Asian countries, changes have taken place in economic, political, and social areas. The changes in the human development indices of Central Asian countries between the years 1990-2010 are shown in Table 3.

Table 3: Changes in The Central Asian Countries' Human Development Index, 1990-2010

Country	**Values of Human Development Index**				
	1990	**1995**	**2000**	**2005**	**2010**
Kazakhstan	0.650	0.620	0.750	0.696	0.714
Turkmenistan	No Data	No Data	No Data	0.642	0.669
Uzbekistan	No Data	No Data	0.727	0.588	0.617
Kyrgyzstan	0.577	0.515	0.550	0.572	0.598
Tajikistan	0.592	0.501	0.493	0.550	0.580
	Changes in Total by Years				**2005-10**
	1990-2000	**2000-2005**	**2005-2010**	**2000-2010**	**Change in HDI Ranking**
Kazakhstan	0.100	-0.054	0.018	-0.036	-1
Turkmenistan	-	-	0.027	-	0
Uzbekistan	-	-0.139	0.029	-0.110	-1
Kyrgyzstan	-0.027	0.022	0.026	0.048	0
Tajikistan	-0.099	0.057	0.030	0.087	0

Source: Based on data in UNDP Human Development Report 2010, pp. 148-151.

With respect to the Human Development Indices of Central Asian countries given in Table 3 between the years 1990-2010, irregular changes are observed in all countries. The most significant data in the table show that all countries exhibit positive changes in HDI between 2005 and 2010. However, in terms of the HDI values of the countries mentioned, Kazakhstan and Uzbekistan fell 1 position, while Turkmenistan, Kyrgyzstan, and Tajikistan remained the same in the rankings between 2005 and 2010. Based on these data, the developments in Central Asian countries do not differ from those in other countries of the world; not even in the period of a regular increase in the HDI in all Central Asian countries.

Table 4: Gross Domestic Product of Central Asian Countries by Years, 2000-2010 (USD)

Country	Year			Changes by Years %		
	2000	2005	2010	2000-2005	2005-2010	2000-2010
Kazakhstan	4,792	8,704	12,236	81.64	40.58	155.34
Turkmenistan	NA	NA	7,500**	-	-	-
Uzbekistan*	1,447	1,911	2,875	32.07	50.44	98.69
Kyrgyzstan	1,338	1,742	2,246	30.19	28.93	67.86
Tajikistan*	886	1,413	1,840	59.48	30.22	107.67

Source: Asian Development Bank, Key Indicators for Asia and the Pacific 2011, p.162.
* Uzbekistan and Tajikistan's GDP per capita data have been updated by 2009.
**Based on data on the address www.cia.gov/library/publications/the-world-factbook/geos/tx.html (Date of Access: 05.09.2011).

Gross Domestic Product per capita data for Central Asian countries in 2000, 2005, and 2010 are shown in Table 4 above. Accordingly, between the years 2000-2010, income in Kazakhstan increased from USD4792 to USD12,236, an increase of 155.34%. The income increased in Tajikistan by 107.65%, in Uzbekistan by 98.69%, and in Kyrgyzstan by 67.86%. Therefore, the countries seem to be experiencing significant increases in revenues per capita in the 10-year period. The countries have experienced significant revenue changes in the 5-year period between the years 2005-2010 as well. GDP per capita has increased by 40.58% in Kazakhstan, 50.44% in Uzbekistan, 28.93 in Kyrgyzstan, and 30.22% in Tajikistan in this 5 year period. In order to observe the changes between the HDI and GDP per capita in Central Asian countries, the data shown in Table 3 and Table 4 can be evaluated together. According to this;

- The HDI value in Kazakhstan in 2000 was 0.750 and it decreased to 0.714 in 2010. The exchange in the index is approximately minus 5%. However, the revenue per capita in the country increased by 155.34% between the years 2000-2010.
- The HDI value in Uzbekistan in 2000 was 0.727 and it is calculated as 0.617 by 2010. This shows that the index value has decreased by approximately 13%. For the same period, income per capita in the country increased from USD1447 to USD2875. This indicates an increase of 98.69% for the income.
- An increase from 0.550 to 0.598, which is approximately 8%, was seen in Kyrgyzstan's HDI value between the years 2000-2010. However, income growth between 2000-2010 was calculated as 67.86%.
- In Tajikistan, which has the lowest income per capita and HDI value in the region, the HDI value of 0.493 in 2000 had risen to 0.580 by 2010. This change of approximately 22% is the highest rate seen in the region for this period. Between the years in question, the national income per capita of Tajikistan has increased from USD886 to USD1840, a change of 107.67%. This is the highest rate of change after Kazakhstan.

Conclusion

After the disintegration of the Soviet Union, economic development was one of the priority policy preference for the Central Asian countries Kazakhstan, Turkmenistan, Uzbekistan, and Tajikistan, with dissimilar natural resource potentials. In those countries that do not have equal conditions in terms of factors of production, it mainly appears that national income is dependent on natural resources and agricultural export. However, the development of a country being based only on GDP growth per capita, could theoretically amount to a waste of human capital, unless the increase in human capital parallels that in income. This seems to be the case in Central Asian countries such that growth of annuity economy contributes importantly to a country's development rate, although it does not contribute to the country's humanitarian development in the countries of this region.

It is certain that only Kazakhstan among the countries in the region was at the high human development index level, with a value 0.714, as a result of revision of the human development index in 2010. Kazakhstan, which ranks at 66 among 169 countries, is followed by Turkmenistan with a value of 0.669 at rank 87. The examination of the sub-indices of the human development index shows that these two countries have shorter life expectancy at birth. Kazakhstan and Turkmenistan's high HDI values based on high-income are due to the export of products such as oil and gas.

Uzbekistan ranks at 102 with a value of 0.617, Kyrgyzstan ranks at 109 with a value of 0.598, and Tajikistan ranks at 112 with a value of 0.580. Considering the GDP per capita in the world of the three countries ranking at lower levels according to the human development index values minus HDI rank order given, Uzbekistan and Kyrgyzstan display a change of 17, while Tajikistan has a 22 position change.

It can be observed that the human capital, which forms the foundation of less development countries, is deficient in the Central Asian countries, and this deficiency inhibits an increase in welfare. Another significant fact in these countries, except Turkmenistan, is that they have higher index values in terms of the HDI values adjusted to equity. This might be due to the absence of less-privileged status of women in the region in terms of human development and significant effects of positive gender discrimination. This feature of the region can be taken as a legacy of the Soviet System.

When the HDI values of the Central Asian countries in the post-independence period and the changes in GDP per capita and HDI value are examined, the resulting revenue increases throughout the region do not parallel those in the human development index. Income growth rates in the region were higher than those of the improvements in the human development index. As a result, high rates of GDP per capita increases in the 20-year period were not reflected in the human development index. Given that the experienced inadequacy has an effect on the growth of a country's economy, it is the primary obstacle to its development.

References

Jahan, 2004. "Measuring Human Development: Evolution of The Human Development Index", Journal of Social Studies-Dhaka, 2004. http://hdr.undp.org/en/media/Jahan_HDI.pdf .

Gürses, 2009. " 'Human Development' and Turkey, Balıkesir University, Journal of Institute of Social Sciences, Turkey, Volume:12, Issue:21, June 2009, pp.339-350.

Kaya, 2008. "Human Development Index (HDI) determines the wealth and the life standard beyond income", Eskişehir University Technology Research Centre, http://www.ogu.edu.tr/bduyuru.aspx?KID=1&DID=502 .

Karabulut and the others, 2009. "Human Development Level Analysis of Economic Development and Members States of Cooperation Organization in 2006" Journal of Economics and Administrative Sciences, Niğde University, 2009, Volume: 2, Issue: 2, pp.1-18.

Karataş and Çankaya, 2010. "A Study on Human Capital in the Process of Economic Development", Journal of Institute of Social Sciences, Mehmet Akif Ersoy University, Year:2, Issue: 3, 2010-Autumn, pp.29-55.

Demir, 2006. "The United Nations Programme's Human Development Index and Assessment in terms of Turkey", General Directorate of Social Sectors and Coordination, Ankara.

Mıhcı, 2011. "Human Development Performance of Transition Economies in The Post-Cold War Period", H.U. Journal of the Faculty of Economics and Administrative Sciences, Volume: 29, Issue: 1, 2011, pp.21-42.

United Nations Development Programme (UNDP), 2010. Human Development Report 2010, New York, November 2010.

CIA Factbook, www.cia.gov/library/publications/the-world-factbook/ geos/tx.html.

Asian Development Bank, 2011. Key Indicators for Asia and the Pacific 2011, 42th Edition, August 2011.

FOREIGN DIRECT INVESTMENTS IN CENTRAL ASIAN ECONOMIES

ASSOC. PROF. AHMET AY,[1]
ASST. PROF. İSMAIL KOÇAK[2]
AND ASST. PROF. CAN TANSEL TUĞCU[2]

One of the most important issues in the economic development of the least developed or developing countries is the providing of development financing. The sources include domestic and foreign sources that these countries are able to use for financing development. In fact, the insufficiency of domestic sources for these countries makes it imperative to resort to foreign sources. Foreign direct investments are the first among such foreign sources.

Foreign direct investment (FDI) is supposed to enhance the productivity of host countries and promotes economic development. The foreign direct investment (FDI) inflows into the developing countries have been an important factor during the growing period. The main reasons to attract FDI are boosting productivity, encouraging employment, stimulating innovation and technology transfer, and enchanging sustained economic growth. As a result, FDI improves the productivity of host countries and thus stimulates economic growth.

The importance of foreign capital cannot be denied in terms of the Central Asian economies, which gained independence with the collapse of the Soviet Union in 1991. Although some of these countries have abundant natural resources, foreign capital becomes essential for them as they lack sufficient domestic sources for processing and marketing of the natural resources; however, these countries are unable to draw enough foreign capital.

This study aims to display the relationship between foreign capital investments and GDP, openness, and inflation, which only betray the

[1] Selçuk University, Konya, Turkey.
[2] Nevsehir University, Nevşehir, Turkey.

market size, among many determinants of the foreign capital in the Central Asian economies.

FDI in the world and in Central Asian economies

During the period between 1990 and 2007, foreign capital inflows increased substantially due to stable growth of the world economy, liberalization ongoing in investment regimes, and wide scale internationalization strategy pursued by multinational companies (UNCTAD, 2009a:3), and had escalated from 207.6 billion USD in 1990 to 1970.9 billion USD in 2007, with an increase of about ten times. The increase in foreign capital inflows stopped in 2008 with the crisis that had begun in USA in 2007 and spread to the whole world afterwards, and the investments retreated to 1185.1 billion USD, declining 18% in the same year, and also 37% in 2009, then increasing to 1243.6 billion USD, a 5% increase, in 2010 (UNCTAD, 2011).

However, the foreign capital outflows had increased from 241.4 billion USD in 1990 to 2174.8 billion USD in 2007, declined to 1170.5 billion USD in 2009, a decrease of 39%, then increasing to 1323.3 billion US, a 13% increase, in 2010. The reduction in foreign capital outflows emanated from declining profits, increasing financial pressures, and re-channelling of dividends and credits from the subsidiaries to the headquarters of the multinational companies.

The effects of the global financial and economic crisis and its consequences on foreign capital flows are expected to continue, at least in the short term. According to the World Investment Report 2011, the industrial production and trade fell back to the pre-crisis figures in 2010, and the foreign capital investments are reported as to be still 15% below the average for the pre-crisis period, and are 37% below their peak in 2007 (UNCTAD, 2011:2).

The global financial and economic crisis that had begun in USA quickly developed and spread to the transition economies. The effects of the crisis show differences according to regions and countries. Global financial and economic crisis both decreases the investment capability of the firms as a result of the shrinkage in available sources of financing, and also affects the investment propensities of the firms through unfavourable economic and market expectations (UNCTAD, 2009a:19).

Table 1. Foreign Capital Inflow by Regions and Economies, 1990-2010 (Billion USD)

Foreign Capital Inflow					
	1990	**2007**	**2008**	**2009**	**2010**
World	207.6	1970.9	1744.1	1185.1	1243.6
Developed Countries	172.5	1306.8	965.1	602.8	601.9
Developing Countries	34.8	537.0	658.0	510.5	573.5
South East Europe/CIS	-	91.0	120.9	71.6	68.1
Foreign Capital Outflow					
	1990	**2007**	**2008**	**2009**	**2010**
World	241.4	2174.8	1910.5	1170.5	1323.3
Developed Countries	229.5	1829.0	1541.2	850.9	935.1
Developing Countries	11.9	294.1	308.8	270.7	327.5
South East Europe/CIS	-	51.5	60.3	48.8	60.5

Source: WIR 2011, s. 187-190, UNCTADSTAD, UNCTADStat-Table view-Inward and outward foreign direct investment flows, Annual, 1970-2010, http://unctadstad.unctad.org/TableViewer/tableView.aspx,

In terms of foreign capital inflows, the burden of the crisis fell mostly on the shoulders of the developed countries in 2008 and 2009. Compared to 172.5 billon USD foreign capital inflows to the developed countries in 1990, which accounted for 83% of the total foreign capital inflows, total capital inflows in 2008 and 2009 declined to 965.1 and 602.8 billion USD, by 55.3% and 50.9% respectively. And in the year 2010, it further decreased by 48.4% to 601.9 billion USD. This is the result of long term and deep problems that affected financial institutions, the deepening of the liquidity crisis in money and credit markets, and ultimately the recession (UNCTAD, 2009a:8). Concurrently, in the past 20 years, the share of developed countries in total foreign capital inflows fell below 50%.

Furthermore, the outflow of foreign capital from developed countries declined in 2008 and 2009. In 1990, 95% of the total foreign capital originated from the developed countries and was 229.5 billion USD. In 2008 and 2009, total capital outflow declined to 1541.2 billion USD and 850.9 billion USD, by 85.1% and 72.7%, respectively. For 2010, the ratio was 935.1 billion USD, with a 70.7% decrease.

The declines in stock exchanges lowered the market value of the assets of many parent companies and their subsidiaries, unfavourable expectations delayed the investment plans, and the increase in the cost of financing with borrowing contracted the investments financed with loans.

Although the situation is the same for the developing and transition economies, it is better than the developed countries. Compared to the 34.8 billion USD foreign capital that flowed to these countries, accounting for 16.8% of the total capital inflow, the capital inflow to these countries in 2008 and 2009 was 778.9 and 582.1 billion USD, accounting for 44.6% and 49.1% of the total capital inflow respectively. In 2010, this ratio was 641.6 billion USD, accounting for 51.5% of the total value. Consequently, despite being affected by the global crisis, an increase in foreign capital inflow occurred in 2008, contrary to the situation for developed countries, and foreign capital inflows declined to 25.2% in 2009. The current year is the end of the increase that has continuously prevailed for 6 years. The underlying reason for this is the positive and high growth rates, which are still observed across the developing countries (UNCTAD, 2009a:9).

If one considers the foreign capital outflow from developing countries and countries in transition, it can be observed that 11.9 billion USD of foreign capital flowed out from these countries in 1990, which accounted for only 5% of the total. In 2008 and 2009, total capital outflow was 369.1 billion USD and 319.5 billion USD, accounting for 85.1% and 72.7% of the total respectively. The capital outflow from these countries decreased by 23% in 2009. In 2010, this figure was 388 billion USD, accounting for 29.3% of the total value. Developing countries and transition economies were less affected from the global financial and economic crisis. As can be seen from Table 1, compared to 83% foreign capital inflow to the developed countries in 1990, the foreign capital outflow for them was 95% of the total. Over time, the ratios declined by 48.3% and 70.6% respectively, and it indicates that the mentioned countries increasingly exported capital. The foreign capital inflow to the developing countries increased 16 times from 1990 to 2007, compared to the 8.3 times increase of the foreign capital inflow to the developed countries for the same period.

As a result, the fact that the capital inflow to the developed countries declined from 83.0% to 48.3% and the increasing share of other countries from 16.8% to 51.5%, indicates that the latter has strengthened their global position. The underlying reasons for this success are high quality governance on every level, economic freedom for the firms on every level, presence of qualified manpower, presence of favourable conditions, and unique geographical characteristics (Kenisarin and Andrews-Speed, 2008: 302). Asia and China are the leaders of this success (UNCTAD, 2003a; 2003b; 2009b).

The increase of foreign capital inflows in favour of the developing countries and transition economies are expected to be maintained as of

2010, compared to the developed countries. This process has gained pace since 2007 as these countries took measures facilitating growth performance and foreign capital inflow, and due to their openness to international investments (UNCTAD, 2010:4).

Table 2. Foreign Capital Inflows and Outflows in Central Asian economies, 1995-2010 (Million USD and percent)

Foreign Capital Inflow/Outflow						
		1995-2005*	**2007**	**2008**	**2009**	**2010**
Azerbaijan	Inflow	1212	-4749	14	473	577
	Outflow	335	286	556	326	232
Kazakhstan	Inflow	1905	11119	14322	13771	9961
	Outflow	-99	3153	1204	3118	7806
Kyrgyzstan	Inflow	55	209	377	190	234
	Outflow	8	-	-	-	-
Tajikistan	Inflow	46	360	376	16	45
	Outflow	-	0	0	0	0
Turkmenistan	Inflow	201	856	1277	3867	2083
	Outflow	-	-0	0	0	0
Uzbekistan	Inflow	106	705	711	711	822
	Outflow	-	0	0	0	0
% of Total Fixed Capital Stock						
		1995-2005*	**2007**	**2008**	**2009**	**2010**
Azerbaijan	Inflow	54.3	67.1	0.2	6.1	5.8
	Outflow	17.1	4.0	6.1	4.1	2.4
Kazakhstan	Inflow	31.5	35.3	39.9	44.7	23.3
	Outflow	-1.6	10.0	3.3	10.1	18.3
Kyrgyzstan	Inflow	19.5	21.9	26.9	14.8	17.2
	Outflow	3.8	-	-	-	-
Tajikistan	Inflow	29.0	54.9	49.3	1.2	-3.4
	Outflow	-	0	0	0	-
Turkmenistan	Inflow	15.5	193.9	127.3	494.4	280.7
	Outflow	-	0	0	0	0
Uzbekistan	Inflow	2.9	14.8	13.2	10.6	10.3
	Outflow	-	0	0	0	0

Source: UNCTADSTAD, UNCTADStat-Table view-Inward and outward foreign direct investment flows, annual, 1970-2010, http://unctadstad.unctad.org/TableViewer/tableView.aspx,.

Annual average

Table 2 shows the foreign capital inflow and outflow data for Central Asian economies as of 1995. We do not have reliable data as these countries had not gained independence prior to 1992, and they had foreign capital inflows and outflows as part of the Russian Federation. The capital flows began to be observed in these countries once they together had gained independence after 1992. As these countries do not have sufficient capital accumulation, the capital outflows from them are not much, or are negligible. However, the reason for the minor amount of capital outflows lies not only in the scarcity of the capital, but also in the fact that the rule of the market economy has not been established fully and regulations regarding the capital movements have not enacted the existence of the controlled economy in these countries.

No substantial increase in foreign capital inflows is observed in these countries up to 2000s. For instance, the foreign capital inflow of Azerbaijan escalated from 130 million to 1392 million USD in 2002, and to 3285 million USD just after. However, this ratio even saw negative values in following years, and reached 473 million USD in 2009. Petroleum played a significant role in this increase in the early 2000s. This case applies approximately to the other countries and for Kazakhstan, where the increase in foreign capital inflows were apparent and higher. In the country, where 1200 million USD level had been preserved until the 2000s, the capital inflow with a level of 2836 million USD in 2001, increased to 4131 million USD in 2004, 6360 million USD in 2006, and 14322 million USD in 2008 (UNCTAD). Kazakhstan continues to be the most important country of the region in terms of foreign capital inflow. Another country that draws attention in terms of foreign capital inflows in recent years is Turkmenistan. Foreign capital inflow to the country has increased continuously since the 2000s, and reached 3867 million USD in 2008 and 2083 million USD in 2009. Foreign capital inflow to other countries was rather restricted.

The share of these countries in total foreign capital inflows does not exceed 1% for the period in question, even though they have abundant natural resources like natural gas and petroleum, and they are the established producers of some essential products like cotton. The share of the developing countries and transition economies for the same period increased from 16.8% to 51.5%. However, compared to the 2.5% share of Western Europe and North America in total petroleum reserves, Azerbaijan, Turkmenistan, Kazakhstan, and Uzbekistan together have 3.3% share in the total petroleum reserves of the world. In terms of world natural gas reserves, compared to the 7.1% share of North America and Western Europe in total reserves, Azerbaijan, Turkmenistan, Kazakhstan, and Uzbekistan together have 2.6% share in total natural gas reserves (OPEC, 2011:22-23). Moreover, Uzbekistan is ranked 4th among worldwide cotton producers, 10th among worldwide natural gas producers, and 8th among worldwide gold producers, so called three "gold" (Newman, 1999:554).

The largest part of the foreign capital inflows to these countries is investments in energy related to natural gas and petroleum. Particularly, the projects on energy lines for transmitting the energy sources in this region to the West are the determinants of capital inflows. In other words, the foreign capital flows to the region as “resource seeking”, because these countries have abundant natural resources and they are also on the route of the strategic petroleum or natural gas export pipelines. In this sense, the Baku-Ceyhan pipeline stands out as the most essential infrastructure project (Penev, 2007). Therefore, these countries are important raw material suppliers of the world economy. Foreign capital is mostly invested in raw material and mineral resource industries, construction of petroleum and natural gas pipelines, and telecommunication and market infrastructure, etc. (Komarov, 2002:371).

UNCTAD (2003b:16-22) indicated that there are basically four types of FDI that can be distinguished; a) resource-seeking, b) market-seeking, c) efficiency-seeking, d) strategic asset-seeking, and in this context the best choices for countries in the initial stages of development are usually resource-based and labour intensive, export-oriented FDI. For example, early 2000 FDI concentrated in the oil and gas sector, which accounted for 65% of the cumulative total FDI (UNCTAD, 20003b:72).

It is suggested that inflow of the foreign capital to these countries, mostly as investments in natural resource industries, would be accompanied by some problems. For example, Barry (2009) concludes that the region had gained more welfare because of the total production efficiency of the foreign investments in the energy sector and the improvement in trade terms, but also notes that it is not a healthy indicator. For instance it has been found that the foreign investments in the natural gas industry of Uzbekistan had resulted in distortion of the trade balance. He further indicates that the increase in the natural gas and petroleum export in Central Asia resulted in contraction of the export among all the other industries. Similarly, asserting that along with efficiency and total output increase in the natural gas and petroleum industry, the same indicators decreased in other industries, Barry diagnoses this phenomenon as the Dutch disease. For this reason, Barry advises the Central Asian countries to pursue a balanced approach for development (Barry, 2009).

Lee, et al. (2010) reach a similar conclusion. In their studies they indicate this as resource seeking. The direct foreign capital has little effect on the economic growth and competitiveness of the host country, and the direct foreign capital invested in manufacturing is not the same. For this reason they assert that whether these two sectors will be sufficient to ensure economic development is dubious (Lee, et al., 2010).

Despite the above mentioned issues, foreign capital investments play an important role in economic development for these countries. First of all, even if resource seeking, the natural gas and petroleum industries require a high level of investments, are very costly, and the resources of Central Asian economies are limited. Moreover, the foreign capital which flows into these countries decreased the share of the government in the capital stock along with reforms, while it increased the share of the private sector and increased the contribution of their fixed capital investments. As can be seen from Table 2, the foreign capital amount received as a fraction of the total capital stock varies from 44.7% in Kazakhstan to 494.4% in Turkmenistan. Therefore, foreign capital is important for these countries.

If so, why don't the Central Asian economies draw a sufficient amount of foreign capital?

The study carried out by Blazer Foundation revealed nine determinants of foreign capital appeal in post-Soviet states. The three most important of these determinants are the liberalization and deregulation of economic activities, predictable legal framework, and improvements in institutions and public administration. The other six determinants are removing the barriers to the international capital and trade, promoting the financial sector, decreasing the level of corruption, minimizing political risk, building image through advertising of the country, and rationalizing the investment incentives (Kenisarin and Andrews-Speed, 2008:303).

Penev points to the mitigation of investments risks, speeding up of transition process, and development of an environment favourable for investments, as the most important factors for attracting FDI. In this context, Penev notes that Central Asian countries have a strong development potential because of their abundance of energy and natural resources, educated manpower, technological infrastructure, and strategic position. Despite this potential, high investment risk, underdeveloped institutional and physical infrastructure due to languid institutional reforms, bad governance and corruption, weak regional cooperation, small domestic market and low purchasing power, all restrict the foreign capital inflow to these countries (Penev, 2007).

As Kaynak et al. note, even if corruption affects the foreign investments, it is not a main deterrent factor; the most serious problems are the ineffectiveness of the local labour force, excessive bureaucracy, graft, and different habits (Kaynak et. al., 2006).

Literature

There is a very comprehensive literature in terms of the relationship between foreign capital, and generally the foreign capital countenance economic growth through both direct investments and efficiency increase.

With the advent of endogenous growth theories, Barro (1991), Barro and Sala-i-Martin (1995), Lucas (1988), and Grossman and Helpman (1991) made it more plausible to include FDI as one of the determinants of long run economic growth. FDI promotes economic growth in a capital scarce economy by increasing volume as well as efficiency of physical investment (De Mello, 1997; Al-Iriani and Al-Shamsi, 2007; Adhıkary, 2011).

There are many empirical studies examining the impact of FDI and they found that FDI inflows positively influence economic growth through the technology transfer and spillover effect (Borenztein, et al., 1998; Khaliq and Noy, 2007, Kotrajaras, 2010).

However, besides many empirical studies that support the relationship between FDI and growth, several empirical studies have found insignificant or no relationship between FDI and growth. Mencinger (2003), Carkovic and Levine (2002), and Ozturk (2007) found no significant effect for economic growth, or a negative causal relationship with growth.

In this case, the inflow of the foreign capital to a certain country becomes important. Therefore, analysis of the elements which promote foreign capital inflow to a country or attractive elements in terms of drawing foreign capital becomes essential. All together, there are many elements that promote foreign capital inflow to a country, and some of them, like the market size, the openness of the economy, the price stability, and the foreign capital inflow among them, constitute the subject of this research (vast literature has been formed on this topic, see Kenisarin and Andrews-Speed, 2008).

Many studies have arrived at a conclusion that the market size is important for attracting foreign capital to a country. For instance, Shatz and Veneables (2000) and Torrisi et al. (2008) emphasize the importance of market size, whereas Fung et al. (2002) found that absolute value of gross domestic product is important, while Billington (1999) found that growth has an important positive effect on foreign capital inflow. The importance of market size or market growth for attracting foreign capital has been also considered by Root and Ahmed (1979), Kravis and Lipsey (1982), Barrell and Pain (1996), Milner and Pentecost (1996), Janicki and Wunnava (2004), Vogiatzoglou (2007), and Benassy, Quere et al. (2007). Al Nasser (2007) shows that macroeconomic instability affected foreign capital inflow besides basic macroeconomic factors like market size and growth rate in 19 Latin America and Asia countries, whereas Schneider and Frey (1985) point out the balance of payments as an important economic parameter in addition to real per capita gross domestic product.

The degree of market size, openness, and inflation, are also likely to influence the flows of international capital in terms of risk-return relationship. Schmitz and Bieri (1972), Root and Ahmed (1979), Kravis and Lipsey (1982), Bajo-Rubio & Sosvilla-Rivero (1994), Barrel & Pain (1996), Brouwer, Paap &Viaene (2008); there is a long list of studies reporting positive associations between market size and FDI. Chakrakarti (2001) reports positive associations between market size and FDI (see Mangır et al. 2010).

Openness and FDI attractiveness are also important factors, as several economic studies show that the level of a country's openness will increase FDI. Root and Ahmed (1979), Balasubramanyam et. al. (1996), Chakrabarti (2001), and Mangır et. al. (2010) supported evidence to indicate that export-promoting trade and investment strategies attract inflows of foreign capital (Lan, 2006).

The market size or the market growth is not an exclusive determinant for an economy. Addison and Heshmati (2003) have found that openness to trade is an important determinant particularly for Latin American countries, while Asiedu (2002) detected that it is important for developing countries, and both found that FDI is relatively higher in countries where trade is significant. Janicki and Wunnava (2004) and Bevan and Estrin (2004) have found that openness of trade is important, and trade and investment are complements of each other. Al Nasser (2007), Akhter (1993), and Torrisi et al. (2008) have arrived at a similar conclusion and concluded that openness is important for drawing foreign capital.

Baniak et al. (2005) conclude that macroeconomic instability decreases foreign capital inflow in their study, in which they explain the factors that determine foreign capital inflow to transition economies, and indicate that increasing transparency related to the legal structure of the country affects the foreign capital decisions, along with the macroeconomic stability. Naude and Krugell (2007), Ramcharran (1999, 2000), and Akhter (1993) indicate that political instability affects the economic activities negatively and for this reason it is important for foreign capital as well.

Additionally, many other factors that affect foreign capital inflow have been analysed. For instance, Janicki and Wunnava (2004) and Barrell and Pain (1996) point to labour force costs as an important factor in investment decisions, whereas Rodriguez and Pallas (2008) emphasize the importance of the difference between productivity of the labour force and its cost, as it is a key to explaining the foreign capital. Miyamoto (2003), Noorbakhsh et al. (2001), and Saggi (2002) emphasize the role of human capital.

Wang and Wong (2004) indicate that FDI promotes economic growth only when host countries have an adequate level of human capital, by using data from 12 Asian economies over the period 1987-1997 (Lan, 2006:10).

Hartman (1984) and Wei (2000) specify that the effect on the foreign capital host country's tax policy is complex, but foreign capital decisions are affected by changes in tax policy. Baniak et al (2005) and Benassy-Quere et al. (2007) indicate that the amount of time and the complexity that are necessary for bureaucratic operations affect the expected utility from the profit, and consequently affect foreign capital decisions. Loree and Guisinger (1995), Wheeler and Mody (1992), and Addison and Heshmati (2003) have found that the developed communication and transportation infrastructure have a positive effect on foreign capital inflow. Groh and Vich (2009) emphasize that the economic activities, legal and political environment, business environment, and infrastructure are the basic determinants of the foreign capital inflow.

While the theories on FDI present a much broader set of FDI determinants including the main economic factors, we use market size, openness, and inflation rate, due to the nature of our objective and the availability of data.

Model and Data

The function which estimates the coefficients of determinants of foreign direct investment in countries considered is as follows:

$$\ln FDI_{i,t} = \ln A_{i,t} + \beta \ln GDP_{i,t} + \delta \ln OPEN_{i,t} + \phi \ln INF_{i,t} + \varepsilon_{i,t}$$

where FDI represents foreign direct investment, A represents the constant, GDP represents income, OPEN represents the degree of openness to international trade, INF represents inflation, ϵ represents the error term, t represents time trend, and i represents the cross sections. All variables in the function are in logarithmic form.

For the analysis, inward flow of foreign direct investments in USD at current prices and exchange rates in millions is the proxy for foreign direct investment; the income is proxy by gross domestic product, which is measured by USD at current prices and exchange rates in millions; the degree of openness to international trade is proxy by the rate of exports plus imports, which are measured by USD at current prices and exchange rates in millions to GDP; and inflation is proxy by consumer price index, which is measured by annual price change.

The study is based on annual panel data covering the time period 1997-2010. The data for FDI, GDP and OPEN was downloaded from UNCTADStat database, and the data for INF was derived from Statistical Database System of Asian Development Bank.

Methodology

In order to estimate the function, linear panel data estimation techniques were chosen. The estimation of linear panel equations is conducted by the ordinary least squares (OLS), the fixed-effects model (FEM), or the random-effects model (REM). However, since the OLS cannot capture the unobservable effects, which are one of the most important properties of panel data, FEM or REM is generally utilized for the estimation. But before the estimation, the existence of unit root in the data set should be searched. In this regard, Levin, Lin Chu (LLC) (2002) and Im, Peseran and Shin (IPS) (2003) unit root tests were executed on the data.

At first glance, the REM seems to be the proper choice for the estimation, because this study covers cross sections which are randomly selected (Baltagi, 2005: 12-15). However, the REM requires no correlation between unobservable effects and explanatory variables. In order to determine whether there exists correlation or not, this study employs Hausman (1978) and Hausman-Taylor (1981) test statistic (i.e. Hausman test). This test shows the estimator of REM (FGLS - Feasible Generalized Least Squares) is unbiased and consistent under the null of no correlation between unobservable effects and explanatory variables.

Either REM or FEM covers two unobservable effects which should be taken into account. These effects are called group and time effects. This study utilizes Breusch and Pagan (1980) LM statistics in order to prove the existence of group and time effects (Green, 2003: 298-299). LM_1 and LM_2 statistics test the significance of group effects under the null of no group effects and the significance of time effects under the null of no time effects, respectively.

The diagnostics of the study is composed of checking whether serial correlation, multicollinearity, and heteroscedasticity exist in the data. For this purpose, Baltagi-Li (1995) test for serial correlation (SC), VIF (Variance inflation factor) for multicollinearity, and Green (2003) test for heteroscedasticity (LM_h) were used.

Results

Panel Unit Root

Stationarity of the data is checked by LLC (2002) and IPS (2003) tests, which are often used in panel data studies. According to Table 3, which displays the findings, although there are some variables that are level stationary and there is only one variable that is not difference stationary in intercept and the trend option, all variables are difference stationary under the intercept option.

Table 3. Unit root test results

	Variables	Tests			
Level		LLC	prob	IPS	prob
Intercept	lnFDI	3.371	(0.99)	4.329	(0.99)
	LnGDP	0.692	(0.75)	4.227	(0.99)
	LnOPEN	-3.686	(0.00)	-2.171	(0.01)
	LnINF	-1.315	(0.09)	-2.375	(0.00)
Intercept and trend	lnFDI	-0.127	(0.44)	0.023	(0.50)
	LnGDP	-3.389	(0.00)	-0.692	(0.24)
	LnOPEN	-1.284	(0.09)	1.431	(0.92)
	LnINF	-2.602	(0.00)	-2.363	(0.00)
Difference					
Intercept	lnFDI	-1.609	(0.05)	-2.558	(0.00)
	LnGDP	-3.646	(0.00)	-2.831	(0.00)
	LnOPEN	-2.485	(0.00)	-3.240	(0.00)
	LnINF	-7.903	(0.04)	-8.733	(0.00)
Intercept and trend	lnFDI	-1.891	(0.02)	-1.574	(0.05)
	LnGDP	-1.639	(0.05)	-1.210	(0.11)
	LnOPEN	-5.084	(0.00)	-4.030	(0.00)
	LnINF	-11.536	(0.00)	-7.949	(0.00)

Estimation and the Diagnostics

Table 4 shows estimation results and the diagnostics. Estimation results reveal that all variables except the constant in the estimated function are statistically significant, and GDP and OPEN have positive impact on FDI, whereas INF has a negative one. According to the findings, income is the dynamic that has the strongest positive impact on foreign direct investment. 1% increase in GDP increases FDI by 0.937%. The second positive impact stems from the degree of openness to international trade. 1% increase in OPEN increases FDI by 0.433%. However, inflation is the dynamic that negatively affects FDI. In this regard, 1% increase in INF decreases FDI by 0.023%.

According to the diagnostics, there is no serial correlation, multicollinearity, or heteroscedasticity in the data. Furthermore, the Hausman test statistic proved that there is no correlation between unobserved individual effects and explanatory variables, supporting the REM is the right choice. On the other hand, Breusch and Pagan's (1980) LM statistics indicated that there exists only a group effect in the estimated function.

Table 4. Diagnostics and estimation results (Dependent variable: lnFDI)

Independent Variables	Coefficients
lnA	0.149 (0.92)
lnGDP	0.937 (0.00)
lnOPEN	0.433 (0.04)
lnINF	-0.023 (0.03)
lnFDI=0.149*lnA + 0.937*lnGDP + 0.433*lnOPEN - 0.023*lnINF+ε	
Diagnostic checking	**Statistics**
Hausman	0.90 (0.82)
LM_1	180.05 (0.00)
LM_2	-1.76 (0.96)
Baltagi-Li (SC)	0.47 (0.49)
VIF	1.23 (0.81)
Green (LM_h)	21.06 (0.02)

* Numbers in parentheses are *p-values*.

Conclusion

The primary limitation of economic development, that is the ultimate goal of both the underdeveloped and developing countries, is the insufficiency of adequate resources for financing development. For this reason, countries which aim for economic development need a number of domestic and foreign sources for financing. In the case of failure of internal resources, referring to foreign sources is inevitable. In this context, foreign direct investment appears to be the most effective source of funding. This state of affairs has a similar significance in terms of the study sample; Central Asian countries. In this study, at first in terms of the direct foreign capital investments, withdrawal potentials of the Central Asian economies and their current situations are evaluated with the data; and then these data are analysed in light of the econometric model and tests. In the first part, the Central Asian economies reveal the development trend of foreign direct investments over the years. In the literature other major studies on the subject have been given, and their similar and discrete points with the findings of this study have been revealed.

For the analysis, inward flow of foreign direct investments in the USD at current prices and exchange rates in millions is the proxy for foreign direct investment; the income is proxy by gross domestic product, which is measured by USD at current prices and exchange rates in millions; the degree of openness to international trade is proxy by the rate of exports plus imports, which are measured by USD at current prices and exchange rates in millions to GDP; and inflation is proxy by consumer price index, which is measured by annual price change.

In order to estimate the considered function, linear panel data estimation techniques were chosen. The estimation of linear panel equations is conducted by the ordinary least squares (OLS), the fixed-effects model (FEM), or the random-effects model (REM).

The diagnostics of the study is composed of checking whether serial correlation, multicollinearity and heteroscedasticity exist in the data. For this purpose, Baltagi-Li (1995) test for serial correlation (SC), VIF (Variance inflation factor) for multicollinearity, and Green (2003) test for heteroscedasticity (LM_h) were used.

Stationarity of the data is checked by LLC (2002) and IPS (2003) tests, which are often used in panel data studies. According to Unit root test results, which reveal the findings, although there are some variables that are level stationary and there is only one variable that is not difference stationary in intercept and the trend option, all variables are difference stationary under the intercept option.

Estimation results reveal that all variables except the constant in the estimated function are statistically significant, and GDP and OPEN have positive impact on FDI, whereas INF has negative one. According to the findings, income is the dynamic that has the strongest positive impact on foreign direct investment. 1% increase in GDP increases FDI by 0.937%. The second positive impact stems from the degree of openness to international trade. 1% increase in OPEN increases FDI by 0.433%. However, inflation is the dynamic that negatively affects FDI. In this regard, 1% increase in INF decreases FDI by 0.023%.

According to the diagnostics, there is no serial correlation, multicollinearity, or heteroscedasticity in the data. Furthermore, the Hausman test statistic proved that there is no correlation between unobserved individual effects and explanatory variables, supporting the idea that REM is the right choice. On the other hand, Breusch and Pagan's (1980) LM statistics indicated that there exists only a group effect in the estimated function.

References

Addison, T. and Heshmati, A. (2003), "The New Global Determinants of FDI Flows to Developing Countries: The Importance of ICT and Democratization", UNU-WIDER Research Paper DP 2003/45.

Adhikary, B. K. (2011)," FDI, Trade Openness, Capital Formation, and Economic Growth in Bangladesh: A Linkage Analysis", International Journal of Business and Management, Vol. 6, No. 1, pp. 16-28.

Akhter, S. H. (1993), "Foreign Direct Investment in Developing Countries: The Openess Hypothesis and Policy Implication", The International Journal, Vol. 7, Issue 6, pp.655-672.

Al Nasser, O. M. (2007), "The determinants of the U.S. Foreign Direct Investment: Does the Region Matter?", Global Economic Review, Vol. 30, Issue 1, pp.107-119.

Al-Iriani M. and Al-Shamsi F.(2007), " Foreign Direct Investment and Economic Growth in the GCC Countries: A Causality Investigation Using Heterogeneous Panel Analysis", Discussion Papers, www.luc.edu/orgs/meea/volume9/.../Al-Iriani%20-%20paper.doc (03.02.2010)

Asiedu, E. (2002), "On the Determinants of Direct Investment to Developing Countries: Is Africa Different?", World Development, Vol. 30, pp. 107-119.

Balasubramanyam, V. N., Salisu, M. and Sapsford, D. (1996). "Foreign Direct Investment and Growth in EP and IS Countries", The Economic Journal, Vol. 106, No. 434, pp. 92-105.

Baltagi, B. (2005). Econometric Analysis of Panel Data. (3rd ed.). UK: John Wiley-Sons Ltd.

Baltagi, B. H. & Li, Q. (1995), "Testing AR(1) Against MA(1) Disturbances in an Error Component Model", Journal of Econometrics, Vol. 68, Issue 1, pp. 133–151.

Baniak, A., Cukrowski, J. and Herczynski, J. (2005), "On the Determinants of Foreign Direct Investment in Transition Economies", Problems of Economic Transition, Vol. 48, Issue 2, pp. 6-28.

Baro, R. J. and Sala-I-Martin, X. (1995), Economic Growth, Cambridge MA: McGraw-Hill.

Barrel, R. and Pain, N. (1996), "An Econometric Analysis of U.S. Foreign Direct Investment", The Review of Economics and Statistic, Vol. 78, No.2, pp.200-207.

Barry, M. P.(2009), "Foreign Direct Investments in Central Asian Energy: A CGE Model ", Eurasian Journal of Business and Economics, Vol. 2, Issues 3, pp. 35-54.

Benassy, Quere, A., Coupet, M. and Mayer, T. (2007), "Institutional Determinants of Foreign Direct Investment", World Economy, Vol. 30, Issue 5, pp.764-782.

Bevan, A. A. and Estrin, S. (2004), "The Determinants of Foreign Direct Investment into European Transition Economies", Journal of Comparative Economics, Vol. 32, Issue 4, pp. 775-787.

Billington, N. (1999), "The Location of Foreign Direct Investment: An Empirical Analysis", Applied Economics, Vol. 31, Issue 1, pp. 65-76.

Borenztein, E., De Gregorio, J. and Lee, J.-W. (1998), "How Does Foreign Direct Investment Affect Economic Growth", Journal of International Economics, Vol. 45, pp. 115-135.

Breush, T. S. and Pagan, A. R. (1980), "The Lagrange Multiplier Test and Its Applications to Model Selection In Econometrics", Review of Economics Studies, Vol. 47, pp. 239-253.

Carkovic, M. and Levine, R. (2002), "Does Foreign Direct Investment Accelerate Economic Growth", World Bank Conference, http://www.iie.com/publications/chapters_preview/3810/08iie3810.pdf (12.12.2010)

Chakrabarti, A. (2001) , "The Determinants of Foreign Direct Investment: Sensitivity Analysis of Cross Country Regressions", Kyklos, Vol. 54, pp.89-114.

De Mello, L.R.(1997), "foreign Direct Investment in developing Countries and growth: A Selective Survey", Journal of development Studies, Vol. 34, pp.1-34.

Fung, K. C., Iizaka, H. and Parker, S. (2002), "Determinants of U.S. and Japanese Direct Investment in China", Journal of Comparative Economics, Vol. 30, Issue 3, pp.567-578.

Green, W. H. (2003), Econometric Analysis, (5th ed.), New Jersey, Prentice Hall.

Groh, A. P. and Wich, M. (2009) "A Composite Measure to Determine a Host Country's Attractiveness for Foreign Direct Investment", IESE Business School Working Paper 833.

Hartman, D. G. (1984), "Tax Policy and Foreign Direct Investment in the United States", National Tax Journal, Vol. 37, No. 4, pp. 475-487.

Hausman, J. A. (1978), "Specification Tests in Econometrics", Econometrica, Vol. 43, pp. 727-738.

Hausman, J. A. and Taylor, W. E. (1981), "Panel Data and Unobservable Individual Effects", Econometrica, Vol. 49, pp. 1377-1398.

Im, K. S., Pesaran, M. H. and Shin, Y. (2003), "Testing for Unit Roots in Heterogeneous Panels", Journal of Econometrics, Vol. 115, Issue 1, pp. 53-74.

Janicki, H. P. and Wunnava, P.V. (2004), "Determinants of Foreign Direct Investment: Empirical Evidence from EU Accession Candidates", Applied Economics, Vol. 36, Issue 5, pp. 505-509.

Kaynak, E., Yalcin, S. and Tatoglu, E. (2006), "A Comparative Study of Foreign Direct Investment Activities in Georgia and Kyrgyz Republic", Multinational Business Review, Vol.14, No. 3, pp. 29-52.

Kenisarin, M. M. and Andrews-Speed, P. (2008), "Foreign Direct Investment in Countries of the Former Soviet Union: Relationship to Governance, Economic Freedom and Corruption Perception", Communist and Post-Communist Studies, Vol. 41, pp. 301-316.

Khaliq, A. and Noy, I. (2007), "Foreign Direct Investment and Economic Growth: Empirical Evidence from Sectoral Data in Indonesia", http://www.economics.hawaii.edu/research/workingpapers/WP_07-26.pdf

Komarov, V. (2002), "Investment in the CIS", Society and Economy, Vol. 24, Issue 3, pp. 363-379..

Kotrajaras, P. (2010), "Impact of Foreign Direct Investment on Economic Development: Comparative Study among Selected East Asian Countries", http://www.internationalconference.com.my/proceeding/icber2010_proceeding/PAPER_190_ForeignDirectInvestment.pdf

Kravis, I. B. and Lipsey, R. E. (1982), "The Location of Overseas Production and Production for Export by Multinational Firms", Journal of International Economics, Vol. 12, No. ¾, pp. 201-223.

Lan, N. P. (2006), " Foreign Direct Investment and Its Lınkage to Economic Growth in Vietnam: A Provincial Level Analysis", https://editorialexpress.com/cgibin/conference/download.cgi?db_name =ESAM07&paper_id=24

Lee, J.-W., Baimukhamedova, G. and Akhmetova, S. (2010), "Foreign Direct Investment, Exchange Rate, and Their Roles in Economic Growth of Developing Countries: Empirical Evidence from Kazakhstan", Journal of International Business Research, Volume 9, No. 2, pp-75-92.

Levin, A., Lin, C.-F and Chu, J. (2002), "Unit Root Tests in Panel Data: Asymptotic and Finite Sample Properties", Journal of Econometrics, Vol. 108, Issue 1, pp. 1-24.

Liu, X., Wang C. and Wie, Y. (2001), 'Causal Links between Foreign Direct Investment and Trade in China', China Economic Review, Vol. 12, Issue 2-3, pp. 190-202.

Loree, D. and Guisinger, S. E. (1995), "Policy and Non-policy Determinants of U. S. Equity Foreign Direct Investment", Journal of International Business Studies, Vol. 26, Issue 2, pp. 281-299.

Lucas, R. E. (1988), "On the Mechanics of Economic Development", Journal of Monetary Economics, Vol.22, pp. 3-42.

Mangır, F., AY, A., SARAÇ, T. B., "The impact of FDI on a country's prospects for sustainable development: A Comparison of Turkey and Poland", Paper presented to Tenth International Conference on Current Issues of Sustainable Development -Governance and Institutional Change, the Opole University, May 18th-20th, 2010, Opole-Poland.

Mencinger, J. (2003), "Does Foreign Direct Investment Always Enhance Economic Growth?", Kyklos, Vol. 56, Issue 4, pp.491-508.

Milner, C. and Pentecost, E. (1996), "Locational Advantage and US Foreign Direct Investment in UK Manufacturing", Applied Economics, Vol. 28, Issue 5, pp. 605-615.

Miyamoto, K. (2003), "Human Capital Formation and Foreign Direct Investment in Developing Countries", OECD Working Paper No. 211.

Naude, W. A. and Krugell, W. F. (2007), "Investigating Geography and Institutions as Determinants of Foreign Direct Investment in Africa Using Panel Data", Applied Economics, Vol. 39, Issue 10, pp.1223-1233.

Newman, A. (1999), "Investing in Uzbekistan: A Rough Ride on the Silk Road", Law & Policy in International Business, Vol. 30, pp. 553-567.

Noorbakhsh, F., Paloni, A. and Youssef, A. (2001), "Human Capital and FDI Inflows to Developing Countries: New Empirical Evidence", World Development, Vol. 29, Issue 9, pp. 1593-1610.

OPEC (2011), Annual Statistic Bulletin, 2010/2011 Edition.

Öztürk, I. (2007), "Foreıgn Dırect Investment - Growth Nexus: A Revıew of the Recent Literature", International Journal of Applied Econometrics and Quantitative Studies, Vol. 4, No. 2, pp.79-98.

Penev, S. (2007), "Investment Climate and Foreign Direct Investment Trends in the South Caucasus and Central Asia", South East European Journal of Economics and Business, Vol. 2, No. 1, pp. 31-40.

Ramcharran, H. (1999), "Foreign Direct Investment and Country Risk: Further Empirical Evidence" Global Economic Review, Vol. 28, Issue 3, pp.49-59.

—. (2000), "Foreign Direct Investment in Central and Eastern Europe: An Analysis of Regulatory and Country Risk Factors", American Business Review, Vol. 18, Issue 2, pp.1-8.

Rodriguez , X. A. and Pallas, J. (2008), "Determinants of Foreign Direct Investment in Spain", Applied Economics, Vol. 40, Issue 19, pp. 2443-2450.

Root, F. R. and Ahmed, A. A. (1979), "Empirical Determinants of manufacturing Direct Foreign Investment in Developing Countries", Economic Development and Cultural Change, Vol. 27, No. 4, pp. 751-776.

Saggi, K. (2002), "Trade, Foreign Direct Investment, and International Technology Transfer: A Survey", The World bank Research Observer, Vol. 17, No. 2, pp. 191-235. .

Schneider, F. and Frey, B. S. (1985), "Economic and political determinants of Foreign Direct Investment", World Development, Vol. 13, No. 2, pp. 161-175.

Shatz, H. J. and Venables, A. J. (2000), "The Geography of International Investment", The World Bank, Policy Research Working Paper No. 2338.

Torrisi, C. R., Delaunay, C. J., Kocia, A. and Lubieniecka, M. (2008), FDI in Central Europe: Determinants and Policy Implication", Journal of International Finance and Economics, Vol. 8, No. 4, pp. 136-147.

UNCTAD (2009), Assessing the Impact of the Current Financial and Economic Crisis on Global FDI Flows, UN, New York and Geneva.

—. (2003), World Investment Directory, UN, New York.

—. (2003), Foreign Direct Investment in Central Asian Caucasian Economies: Policies and Issues, UN, New York and Geneva.

—. (2009), Investment Brief, 2009, www.unctad.org.

—. (2010), World Investment Report 2010, Investing in a Low-Carbon Economy, UN, New York and Geneva.
—. (2011), World Investment Report 2011, Non-Equity Modes of International Production and Development, UN, New York and Geneva.
—. www.unctad.org/wir,
—. www.unctad.org/fdistatistics,
UNCTADSTAD, UnctadStad-Table view-Inward and outward foreign direct investment flows, Annual, 1970-2010, http://unctadstad.unctad.org/TableViewer/tableView.aspx,
Vogiatzoglou, K. (2007), "Vertical Specialization and New determinants of FDI: Evidence from South and East Asia", Global Economic Review, Vol. 36, No. 3, pp.245-266.
Wei, S. (2000), "How Taxing is Corruption on International Investors?", The Review of Economics and Statistics, Vol. 82, No. 1, pp.1-11.
Wheeler, D. and Mody, A. (1992), "International Investment Location Decision: The Case of U.S. Firms", Journal of International Economics, Vol. 33, No. 1-2, pp. 57-67.

CORPORATE RESTRUCTURING, ECONOMIC GROWTH AND HUMAN DEVELOPMENT INDEX IN CENTRAL ASIAN ECONOMIES

ASSOC. PROF. GÜNSELI MINE GERNI,[1] ASST. PROF. MUSTAFA ERSUNGUR,[2] DILEK ÖZDEMIR[2] AND PROF. ÖMER SELÇUK EMSEN[2]

Inward-looking and interventionist strategies, which emerged due to the debt crises of the 1980s and balance of payment crises in the aftermath, were replaced by export-oriented industrialization strategies under the influence of the success stories of outward-looking and liberal regimes. In this strategy, the exchange rate regime, which is to feed export income and capital inflow, was fundamental. Among the applications in question, commercial and financial investment and their immediate liberalization were regarded as a fundamental prescription for crises as they ensure indirect integration with the world economy (Akyüz, 1999). On the other side, it is worth noting that after the period of growth that the socialist bloc experienced initially, it moved to a stable level, and there were partially liberal policy searches among the bloc. In the Soviet Union, which attracted attention with its success of growth, the average growth rate between 1928 and 1984 was 4.3-4.8%, the closest follower to this rate was Japan with 4.5% growth rate between 1874-1984. It is easily noticed that this success of the Socialist planning began to fall down in 1975 and started to stagnate in the 1980s. The growth rates in 1976-1980, 1981-1985, and 1986-1990 were 3.7%, 3.2%, and 1.3%, respectively (Kuşkay, 2001: 8-9). Therefore, the signals of stagnation or even of collapse for the Soviet Union appeared in the 1960s when the high growth rate fell by half.

[1] Marmara University, Istanbul, Turkey.
[2] Atatürk University, Erzurum, Istanbul.

The system, which exhibited high growth performance until the 1960s, underwent a non-stop stagnation in growth for two consecutive decades (Campos, 2001: 664). Kuznets, who claims that sustainability of growth can be defined as the increase of per capita income and productivity, also argues that this is only possible with continuous structural change (Ofer, 1987: 1769). The prescription proposed for the world in general and the Soviet Union in particular is that stagnation can be overcome by social dynamics. The system, of which political, economic and social structure were made untouchable with revolution(s), kept up with the era with (socialist) revolution or went ahead of it, then it began to fall behind, which emerged as the fundamental problem. The fundamental determinants of growth in social dynamics are structural transformations, which contain continuous mobility in them. These structural transformations are based on liberal policy applications, which maintain their own internal dynamics and movements in political, economic, socio-cultural fields.

With the notion that the liberal and democratic structures are the basis of transformation, this structure is considered to be based on institutions and on being corporate. In this framework, in 1998, the World Bank described the institutions as the power mechanisms that shaping the attitudes of individuals and organizations in society with formal and informal rules. While official institutions have law, regulations and contracts; unofficial institutions have trust, ethics, and political norms. Organizations include political (legislation, political parties, state institutions, and justice), economic (private companies, unions, and vocational institutions), and social (non-governmental institutions and schools) dimensions. When defined in line with corporate growth literature, institutions are elements that dominate any kind of politics. In this definition, top level juristic regulations that ensure equality of opportunity, including property rights and education, by providing balance of powers, are emphasized (Fischer and Sahay, 2004: 5-6). This comprehensive definition of corporate restructuring can be said to be the main feeder of the component of entrepreneurialism, which is the locomotive power of growth. It is obvious that the components of initiative, which continuously increase social income by creating investment and employment opportunities, develop in liberalization-based environments.

In this respect, unlike the Mercantilist approach, which regards precious metals and physical money as the source of wealth, A. Smith regards the production powers of nations as the source of wealth, and leaves initiatives to entrepreneurs. Therefore, A. Smith claims that wealth of the nations is going to increase with the removal of limitations in regard to the front of personal initiatives. Thus, economic liberalism requires the diminishing role of the state in free trade and economy (Güran, 1991: 119-120).

While the source of wealth shaped in Smith's thinking has taken its place in new growth theories of present economic growth literature by maturing more with the evolution of economics and managerial sciences, it is handled with good governance in management literature. Yet, the common component of growth/development and management literature is governance quality. There is a consensus on the six dimensions of governance indicators (Kaufman, et al., 2002: 254-255). Explanations on these variables are given below briefly (T.C. Ministry of Finance, 2003):

i. Responsibility/accountability: This includes civil liberties and political rights, which are the indicators of political process. These indicators measure the distance of government from the citizens participating in elections. Also, it includes the measurement of freedom of press and is a reflection of the responsibilities of press for authority.
ii. Political stability and lack of violence/terrorism: These consist of indicators like destabilizing government with violence and unconstitutional acts or overthrowing it.
iii. Efficiency of government: This consists of the quality of public services, qualifications of bureaucracy, adequacy of civil services and their efficiency, reliability of political responsibilities of the government.
iv. Quality in regulations: This focuses on politics, and includes measurement of policies that are not pro-market, such as price controls or inadequate bank controls, and burdens brought by excessive regulations in international trade and business development.
v. Superiority of law: This is the indicator that measures how citizens should obey social rules. It consists of degree of repetition of crimes, efficiency of judges, and applicability of contracts. On the other hand, this indicator measures success of a society where property rights are protected with economic and social interactions in a fair and foreseen environment.
vi. Control of corruption: This measures the perception of corruption, which is conventionally defined as the exercise of official powers against public interest or the abuse of public office for private gains, the existence of the figures who have revealed corruption and objects should be taken into consideration.

In addition to the classification based on the six components by the World Bank, corporate restructuring should be handled within the liberalization index on transition economies created by the European Bank for Reconstruction and Development (EBRD). Therefore, in EBRD index, including corporate restructuring, there are nine components, which are big-scale privatization, small-scale privatization, corporate restructuring, price liberalization, trade and forex system, competition policy, banking reforms, and interest liberalization, exchange rate markets and non-banking financial institutions, and general infrastructure reforms.

In this study, the relationships between growth-development and corporate restructuring in Central Asian economies to liberal-market orientation are targeted to be researched. These economies are in a transition period from socialist-planning structure in which any kinds of initiative and prosperity rights were preserved under state monopoly, and individualism was blocked for 71 years.

Literature Survey and Model Rationality

When the literature regarding the relationships between corporate restructuring and economic growth is studied, we find that some studies include nine components of EBRD liberalization index and some of them as corporate restructuring. On the other hand, some studies utilize governance indicators prepared by the World Bank and are used as corporate restructuring variables. Studies equating corporate restructuring to democratization take the political rights and civil freedom index values prepared by Freedom House into consideration.

The study of Radulescu and Barlow (2002) comes in the first place among research which reveals that corporate restructuring values in EBRD Index together with large-scale privatization, governance features and price liberalization have negative effects on growth initially, and then have a delayed positive effect. In this study, it is argued that liberalization applications contributed to the fall of inflation and there was an indirect negative relationship between inflation and growth. Similarly, Lawson and Wang (2004) find that price liberalization and corporate reforms have a negative effect on growth initially, and the negative effects start in 1991 and continue until 1995 (Falcetti, et al., 2006: 425-425).

In the study of the relationships between growth and corporate structures in the period of 1989-2007, they find that corporate structure, given by the total value of EBRD index in growth performance, had a positive effect on 25 transition economies out of 29. On the other hand, the longer the transition period is, the shorter the transition recession; and negative effects of U-shaped growth are weak as well (Cerović and Nojković, 2009: 7-31).

In Berg, et al. (1999), inward liberalization (price liberalization and trade monopolies) as structural reform index, outward liberalization index (quota, commercial restrictions, and exchange rate restrictions), and the relationships between private sector index (privatization and financial liberalization) and macroeconomic variables are studied. Findings show that countries that accelerate liberal policies recover from the deep effects of transition recession more rapidly than the others (Berg, et al., 1999: 20-21). While the importance of the institutional construction is emphasized in the search of economic development dynamics in transition economies, the World Bank governance indicators are used. In this framework, horizontal cross-sectional analyses are conducted and it was found that the number of years under socialism and the role of natural resources in institutional construction are the main factor of institutional construction. It has been observed that economies that are natural resource-based and that spent many years under socialism, failed to build institutions compatible with market economies. In the analyses, a strong causality relationship is found between per capita GDP income and components of corporate development (institutionalization) (Beck and Laeven, 2006: 157-186). Literature review and application results show that political stability has positive effect on growth (Brunetti and Weder, 1995).

The importance of institutionalization as the determinant of growth and foreign direct investments for 25 transition economies between 1990 and 1998 are investigated by Grogan and Moers (2001). According to the estimated results, it has been revealed that public institutions in particular are significant for foreign investments and growth. Also, a strong causality relationship from institutionalization to economic growth, but a weak causality relationship towards FDI, is found. Barro (1996: 1-27) in his study on growth and democracy in about 100 countries between 1960 and 1990, uses political freedom indices. The findings show that superiority of law, free market, a lower share of public expenditures, and human capital elements have positive effects on growth. He also found that political freedoms are affected by the improvements in health and education conditions as the indicators of life standards.

In literature searches, ensuring recovery in terms of liberalization index in general and restructuring values in particular, as well as governance indicators, are the signs showing that a transition period will be undergone softly. Undergoing a transition period softly indicates that recession in transition will be less and shorter, and a high or hyperinflation period triggered by instability will disappear. The economic reflections of recovery in these quality values are positive. Figure1 briefly summarizes the features of central planning and transition economies.

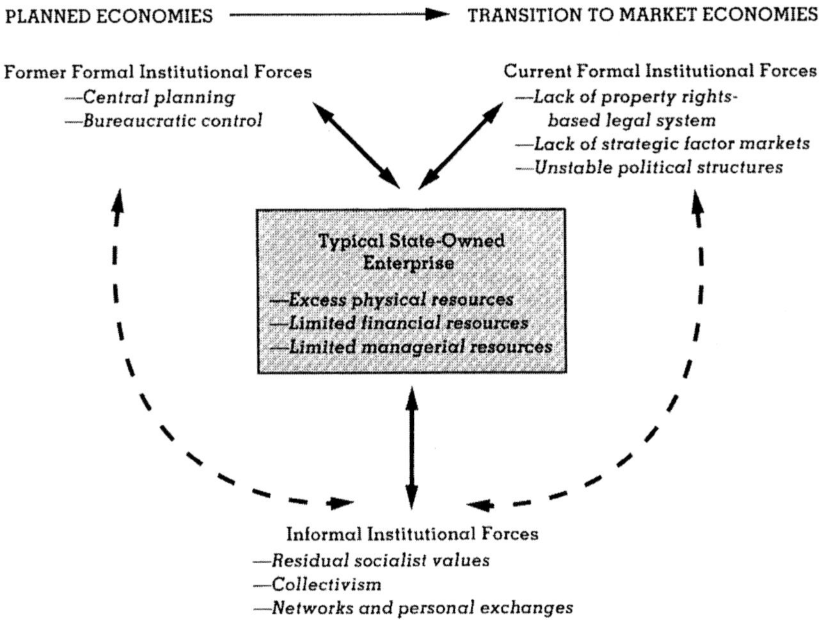

Figure 1: Interactions of Foundation and Institutions in Old-planning Economies
Source: Peng and Heath, 1996: 501.

In the literature, although the six governance indicators of the World Bank refer to the corporate quality, when corporate restructuring indicators prepared by the EBRD are considered, it is claimed that recoveries in these two components feed economic development, and similarly, the economic development process causes recoveries in these quality indicators. In other words, it can be said that there is a mutual causality relationship between corporate restructuring and governance indicators, and the level of economic development (real GDP from the World Bank data and/or human development index from UNDP data).

In this study, apart from handling corporate restructuring in liberalization index, governance indicators by the World Bank as the determinants of corporate restructuring, openness ratio and political rights, and the civil freedom index values prepared by the Freedom House will be discussed. While political rights reflect the distance in the level of democratization, civil rights reflect individual rights and freedom, as well as being described as the ground to be able to invest. Similarly, openness ratio of economy, which is formed through using the WB data, indicates the existence of liberal structures. Although the innovation dimension is not felt, the imitation dimension provides the country's initiative with movement.

Model and Results

Thus, in compliance with the literature, the model in this study can be constructed as follows:

$$RE_{t,i} = F(CL_{t,i}; PR_{t,i}; INST_{t,i}; OPEN_{t,i}) + \varepsilon_i \qquad (1)$$

T in model number 1 refers to time; i is used for countries. RE represents restructuring indicator and is used as a dependent variable; CL denotes civil liberties; PR political rights; INT governance indicators; OPEN the openness ratio of the economy. The relationships between real GDP (real Y) and/or human development indicators (HDI) from the RE value estimated with equation 1 will then be investigated. This is expressed in equation 2.

$$Real\ Y_{t,i}\ or\ Y_{t,i} = F(RE_{t,i}) + \varepsilon_i \qquad (2)$$

Thus, a causality relationship between new-estimation corporate restructuring values to be obtained from the first estimation in equation number 2 and HDI indicators prepared by real GDP values as the indicators of economic growth and UNDP will be studied.

This study investigates the relationships between corporate restructuring, and economic growth in Central Asian economies (Azerbaijan, Kazakhstan, Kyrgyzstan, and Turkmenistan) from some transition economies has been formed by equations 1 and 2. In the model (1), considering that restructuring (RE) variable is dependent, civil liberties (CL) which is considered to elaborate on this dependant, political rights (PL), governance indicators (INST), and openness (OPEN) ratio have been used.

The analyses will be conducted by using 7 variables in 5 transition economies between 1991 and 2008, it is necessary to make unit root examinations regarding these variables. Results are expressed in Table 1.

Table 1: Unit Root Examinations

		Levin, Lin & Chu t	Breitung t-stat	Im, Pesaran and Shin W-stat	ADF - Fisher Chi-square	PP - Fisher Chi-square	Hadri Z-stat
HDI	Level	-5.028[(a)]	-0.533	-0.551	16.435[(c)]	18.524[(b)]	3.882[(a)]
Real Y	Level	-2.932[(a)]	2.085	-0.483	19.590[(b)]	29.121[(a)]	5.208[(a)]
RE	Level	-1.4e15[(a)]	0.019	-4.9e12[(a)]	7.105	8.265	7.297[(a)]
CL	Level	-4.586[(a)]	-0.333	-0.817	11.449[(c)]	18.66[(a)]	5.339[(a)]
PR	Level	-2.611[(a)]	0.198	-0.277	2.801	11.422[(a)]	4.537[(a)]
INST	Level	0.015	-3.247[(a)]	1.253	3.945	3.001	6.350[(a)]
	1st diff	-10.865[(a)]	-1.537[(c)]	-1.892[(b)]	30.758[(a)]	28.150[(a)]	6.6457[(a)]
OPEN	Level	-9.080	0.652	-1.884[(b)]	29.137[(a)]	8.208	7.778[(a)]

Note: Probabilities calculated (by) using the asymptotic chi-square distribution of Fisher's tests, other tests show asymptotic normality distribution. (a) shows significance at the 1% level, (b) 5% level, and (c) 10% level.

According to the variable-related unit root tests examination results, while six variables, except for INST, are stable in their level values, the INST variable has been observed to be stable in the 1st difference. Thus, 1st differences of INST variable are taken to form the variable D(INST) in the estimation process for the first model and estimation processes has been started for the common consistency and randomly-efficient models. Both F test and Hausman tests indicate the consistency of fixed-effect variable. Similarly, "The fixed effects model is an appropriate specification if we are focusing on a specific set of N firms etc" (Baltagi, 2008: 14). The fixed effect estimation results and t statistics are as below.

$$RE_{it} = 1.4817 + 0.2313CL + 0.0123PR + 0.0076D(INST) + 0.0313OPEN$$

(2.142) (1.050) (0.122) (0.101) (0.254)

R^2=0.887 F=35.531 D.W.= 1.085

It is observed that 4 variables bear significance in terms of t values given in the parentheses. Thus, in the CL, PR, INST and OPEN variables, which are thought to explain RE, significance has not been observed in terms of statistics. For this reason, instead of investigating real GDP and/or human development index to be regarded as the measurement of economic development, namely relationships between HDI values and estimated RE, relationships between real GDP and/or HDI values and current RE values and/or INST values have been investigated. In order to do so, causality tests have been conducted, and results are shown in Table 2.

Table 2: Results of Granger Causality Test

H_0 Hypothesis		Lags to Include: 1		Lags to Include: 2		Lags to Include: 3	
	# Obs	F-Stat	Prob.	F-Stat	Prob	F-Stat	Prob
HDI does not Granger Cause RE.	45	0.2535	0.6172	0.5942	0.5574	1.2262	0.3186
RE does not Granger Cause HDI.		3.5854	0.0651	3.8685	0.0303	2.8012	0.0581
Real Y does not Granger Cause RE.	45	0.0515	0.8215	0.2237	0.8006	0.1625	0.9206
RE does not Granger Cause Real Y.		0.2661	0.6086	0.2018	0.8182	0.5749	0.6362
D(INST) does not Granger Cause RE.	45	0.2565	0.6155	0.1794	0.8366	0.0845	0.9678
RE does not Granger Cause D(INST).		0.0653	0.7996	1.1360	0.3345	0.4574	0.7146
Real Y does not Granger Cause D(INST).	45	2.5179	0.1211	2.0841	0.1421	0.6267	0.6051
D(INST) does not Granger Cause Real Y.		0.9061	0.3473	2.6337	0.0884	0.9980	0.4115
HDI does not Granger Cause D(INST).	45	2.1899	0.1474	0.2537	0.7776	0.7569	0.5297
D(INST) does not Granger Cause HDI.		1.8176	0.1858	0.2583	0.7741	0.7522	0.5323
Real Y does not Granger Cause HDI.	45	0.0831	0.7746	0.1673	0.8466	0.8840	0.4614
HDI does not Granger Cause Real Y.		3.2297	0.0795	0.9936	0.3804	0.4122	0.7455

In the examination of causality, one way causality has only been detected in three variables. In causality examination, while real GDP value is affected at the 10% level by the 1st lag of HDI, and 10% level by the 2nd lag of D(INST); HDI is affected at the 10% level by the 1st lag, 5% by the 2nd lag, and 10% by the 3rd lag. The summary of these relationships is as shown in Figure 2.

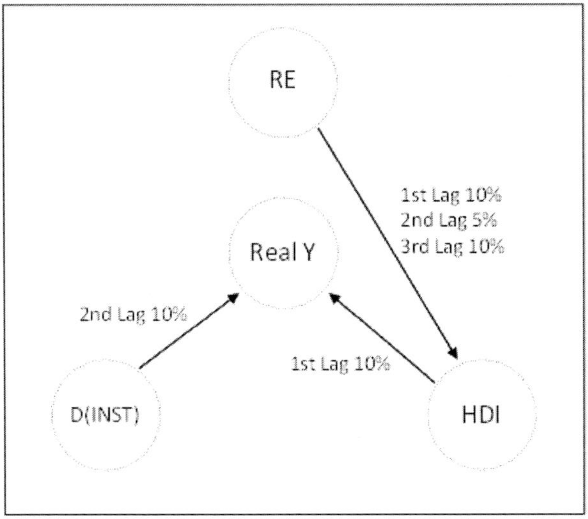

Figure 2: Causality between Variables

General Evaluation and Conclusion

The emergence of tendencies to explain growth structures of countries with different arguments apart from standard growth theories are a result of the inability of the two basic production factors, capital and labour, to explain economic growth. It is observed that in countries that tend to move from socialist planning to market economy as the economic structure, the effects of capital and labour show significant changes. At this point, theoretical economic growth and development patterns that standard input components will give the same output, have been questioned. As a result of the questionings, the thoughts that production and/or economic growth structures are affected by other quantitative elements apart from two quantitative elements, capital and labour, began to be modelled as a result of the developments in mathematical economics. With these developments, liberalization indexes, which contain a quality dimension in growth and restructuring were attempted to be explained with the aid of the indicators of civil liberties, political freedom scores, and quality of governance.

In this study, focusing on the relationships between liberalization-democratization-good governance elements and economic growth rates, it was found out that recoveries in these variables affect economic growth. The aim of this study was to investigate the effects of good governance elements, and liberalization-democratization on economic growth in

Central Asian economies, which have been deprived of corporate structure because they have just celebrated 20 years of their political independence.

Although findings do not prove strong relationships as in the literature, it is worth noticing the existence of causality relationships from restructuring, in particular human development and good governance as indicators to economic growth in the long-run. As a result, for the Central Asian economies, of which most of the current growth is based on agriculture and underground resources, to reach a stable and trustable economic system could be possible with the developments in institutionalization, and accordingly with human development.

References

Akyuz, Yilmaz (1999), "Enterprise Restructuring and Economic Growth", Factors of Economic Growth in Ukraine, pp: 41-47. (Http://Ta.Swap-Rural.Org.Ua/Files/Library/200910301404270.Fostering%20Sustainable%20Growth%20in%20Ukraine%20(IEA).Pdf). (July 2011).

Baltagi, H. H. (2008) Econometric Analysis of Panel Data, John Wiley &Sons, Ltd, UK.

Barro, Robert J. (1996), "Democracy and Growth", Journal of Economic Growth, 1: 1-27.

Beck, Thorsten and Luc Laeven (2006), "Institution Building and Growth in Transition Economies", Journal of Economic Growth, 11: 157-186.

Berg, Andrew, Eduardo Borensztein, Ranta Sahay and Jeromin Zettelmeyer, The evolution of Output in Transition Economies: Explaining the Differences, Working Paper No. 99/73. IMF, Washington, DC., 1999.

Brunetti, Aymo and Beatrice Weder (1995), "Political Sources of Growth: A Critical Note on Measurement", Public Choice, 82: 125-134.

Campos, Nauro F. (2001), "Will the Future Be Better Tomorrow? The Growth Prospects of Transition Economies Revisited", Journal of Comparative Economics, 29: 663-676.

Cerović, B and A. Nojković (2009), "Transition and Growth: What was Taught and What Happened", Economic Annals, Volume LIV (183): 7-31.

Efendic, Adnan, Geoff Pugh, and Nick Adnett, Institutions and Economic Performance: System GMM Modelling of Institutional Effects in Transition, 2010, http://www.riinvestinstitute.org/pdf/Efendic_et_al.pdf (July 2001).

Falcetti, Elisabetta, Tatiana Lysenko, and Peter Sanfey (2006), "Reforms and Growth in Transition: Re-Examining the Evidence", Journal of Comparative Economics, 34(3): 421-445.

Fischer, Stanley and Ranta Sahay, Transition Economies: The Role of Institutions and Initial Conditions, IMF mimeo, Washington DC, 2004.

Grogan, Louise and Luc Moers (2001), "Growth Empirics with Institutional Measures for Transition Countries", Economic Systems, 25: 323–344.

Güran, Tevfik, İktisat Tarihi, Acar Matbaacılık Yayıncılık, İstanbul, 1991.

Kaufman, Daniel, Aart Kraay and Mossimo Mastruzzi (2002), "Governance Matters III: Governance Indicators for 1996, 1998, 2000, and 2002", The World Bank Economic Review, 18(2): 253-287.

Kaufman, Daniel, Aart Kraay and Mossimo Mastruzzi, Governance Matters VIII: Aggregate and Individual Governance Indicators 1996–2008, The World Bank, Policy Research Working Paper 4978, 2009.

Kuşkay, S. Yılmaz, Sovyet-Tipi Ekonomilerin Merkezi Plandan Serbest Piyasaya Geçiş Deneyimi (1989-2000): Türkiye ve Diğer Gelişmekte Olan Ülkelere Dersler, Atatürk University (Unpublished PhD Dissertation), Erzurum, 2001.

Lawson, Colin, Wang, Haifeng, Economic Transition in Central and Eastern Europe and the former Soviet Union: Which Policies Worked?, Mimeo. Department of Economics and International Development, University of Bath, 2004.

Ofer, Gur (1987), "Soviet Economic Growth: 1928-1985", Journal of Economic Literature, 25(4): 1767-1833.

Peng, Mike W. and Peggy Sue Heath (1996), "The Growth of the Firm in Planned Economies in Transition: Institutions, Organizations, and Strategic Choice", The Academy of Management Review, 21(2): 492-528.

Radulescu, Roxana and David Barlow (2002), "The Relationship between Policies and Growth in Transition Countries", Economics of Transition, 10(3): 719–745.

T.C. Maliye Bakanlığı, İyi Yönetişimin Temel Unsurları, Ministry of Finance of Turkish Republic, General Directorate of European Union and Foreign Relations, Ankara, 2003.

PART III:

INTERNATIONAL TRADE

RELATIONSHIPS BETWEEN ECONOMIC GROWTH AND INTERNATIONAL TRADE IN CENTRAL ASIAN ECONOMIES

PROF. CEVAT GERNI,[1]
ASSOC. PROF. MUSTAFA KEMAL DEĞER,[2]
PROF. ÖMER SELCUK EMSEN[3]
AND PROF. SELAHATTIN SARI[1]

The classical economists are behind the basis of the argument that free trade will increase prosperity and economic growth. In this respect, classical economists claim that free trade is the driving force behind economic growth (Baharom et. al, 2008: 1-2). According to classical economists, it is hard to support large-scale production that will provide high and sustainable growth in economies with limited domestic markets. Therefore, it will be useful for these types of economies to provide productions based on dynamic comparative advantages under free trade. It is generally agreed that in order to achieve this goal, international trade regime which will help economy merge with the international framework and resource allocation that will occur accordingly are the basic dynamics. Therefore, the natural aim of this strategy is to provide industrialization and development and it is suggested that the necessary dynamism for this purpose will be possible only by constructing an economic structure based on foreign demand rather than the domestic one. Only in this way, import-substitution policies can be transformed into export-based industrialization policies and more competitive sectors can be supported (Çelebi, 1991: 33; Tussie and Aggio, 2005: 89). This argument, generally suggested against close economy and thus import-substitution strategies, forms the basis of the liberal economic idea. With the downturn of the perception of national development in the late 1970s and the collapse of the Eastern block at the

[1] Beykent University, Istanbul, Turkey.
[2] Karadeniz Technical University, Trabzon, Turkey.
[3] Atatürk University, Erzurum, Turkey.

end of the 1980s, the benefits of expanding abroad based on the classical view, started to become a hot topic on the agenda again. For this reason, while strategically outward and export-oriented models were being implemented, it became necessary to have a certain level of development for these implementations in the last quarter of the 20th century (Han and Kaya, 2006: 245; Sun and Parikh, 2001: 187-188).

On the other hand, forming the basis of the opposing view against liberal understanding, List suggests that free trade is beneficial for countries at the same level of development; while it does not have a useful effect for countries at different levels of development. In this respect, List also claims that England, the first country where the Industrial Revolution took place, gained from free trade; but it was relatively unfavourable for less developed countries, which were trying to keep up with England (Chang, 2004:20).

As opposed to the pro and con views on free international trade which were briefly summarized above, 'New (Endogenous) Growth Theories', particularly the ones emerged in the 1980s, free trade began to be modelled and to be empirically tested. It is often claimed that countries with internal development models stressing the significance of advancement of technology as a driving force of long term economic growth will reach more consistent and higher development levels as compared to international trade oriented countries (Grossman and Helpman, 1990: 796). However, in order to achieve a higher growth performance, it is claimed that this alone would not be enough and it is important that such efforts be supported through convenient, modern policies, such as educational, infrastructural, financial and microeconomic policies (Tussie and Aggio, 2005: 89). From this perspective, it is agreed that international trade is a necessary condition but is not sufficient, and this insufficiency should be handled primarily with political liberalization.

After the 1970s, Far East Asian economies, which are considered to be a good example for the success of export-oriented and thus export-based industrialization strategy, were presented as a de-facto global development model by the IMF as well (Palley, 2002: 2). Among primary factors for this transformation of the world economy, which began in the 1970s, are the growth differences between open economies and closed economies. That is, the growth rate of some closed economies such as USSR in the time periods 1950-1980 and 1981-1988 were 4.9% and 2% respectively, and it was 1.3% in 1986-1990. However, the growth rates in countries such as Japan and South Korea with open economies were 8.9% and 6.4% respectively (Kuşkay, 2001: 9). From a different point of view, while the growth rates in globalized countries were 2.0% in the 1970s, 3.5% in the

1980s and 5% in the 1990s, the growth rates in closed countries were 3.3%, 0.8%, and 1.4% respectively (Dollar and Kraay, 2001: 2). Among several reasons behind the shift from economic growth to the stagnation and bottleneck, the most significant ones are cumbersome planning, inability in developing new methods, inefficient productivity, and inability to establish a transition from extensive growth to intensive growth.

Therefore this study aims to investigate the relationships between international trade and economic growth in Central Asian economies that switched from command economy to market economy when they gained their economic and political independence after 1991.

Literature Review on Trade Openness and Economic Growth

There is a quite extensive literature about the empirical relationships between international trade and economic growth. However, most of the research on this issue basically focuses on the export side of international trade; there is limited investigation on the effects of import on economic growth. While some of the studies dealing with empirical relationships between exports and economic growth support the idea of export-led growth, others do not find meaningful relationship between exports and economic growth. Some studies even suggest that export had negative effects on economic growth (for further literature see: Ahmad and Kwan, 1991; Edwards, 1993; Ghartey, 1993; Love, 1994; Giles and Williams, 2000; Medina-Smith, 2001; Subasat, 2002; Abou-Stait, 2005).

In addition, stressing the qualities and varieties of exported products, some studies claim that export-led growth only occurs in countries at a certain level of industrialization (Subasat, 2002). According to this hypothesis, called *minimum development level*, a country should have some certain level of industrialization and development so that exports can provide positive externality and productivity effects on domestic economy. In other words, varying impact of exports on different countries and regions depends on economic development levels of those countries. This impact also includes a dynamic interaction process between structural transformation of economies and economic development (Sun and Parikh, 2001: 188). Therefore, it is generally agreed that export-led development occurs in less developed countries and developing countries only if they have a certain level of industrialization and if they have achieved necessary structural economic transformations (Giles and Williams, 2000; Santos-Paulıno, 2005; Emsen and Değer, 2007).

On the other hand, although there are different findings of different studies dealing with the effects of exports on economic growth, the majority of the findings suggest that particularly the imports of intermediate and capital goods urge economic growth (Gerni et. al., 2008). In general, when the literature about the relationships between international trade and economic growth are considered, it is logical to state that the reasons behind the varying effects of imports and exports on economic growth are basically a result of different characteristics of subject countries.

In the current study, the relationships between import, export and economic growth in the Central Asian economies, which gained their independencies in political terms after the fall of the USSR in 1991, will be examined. When the current structure of Central Asian economies is considered, it is obvious that they have insufficiencies in either political or socio-economic terms. Therefore, the literature review was basically structured by the studies dealing with the issues in developing countries summarized in Table 1.

Table 1. Literature Review on Trade Openness and Economic Growth in Developing Countries.

Author(s)	Countries and Sample Period	Method	Evidences
Yucel (2009)	Turkey (1998-2001)	Co-integration and Causality Tests	OPEN → GDP
Gries, et. al (2009)	16 Sub-Saharan Africa Countries (1960-2004)	Causality Tests	Short Run: Cameroon, Cote d'Ivoire and Nigeria OPEN → GDP, Ethiopia, Senegal, Sierra Leone and Togo OPEN →GDP, Long Run: Nigeria : OPEN → GDP Rwanda: OPEN → GDP
Awokuse (2008)	Argentina (1993-2002), Colombia (1994-2002) and Peru (1990-2002)	Causality Tests	Colombia and Peru: M → X Argentina and Colombia M → GDP Peru: M → GDP

Maneschiöld (2008)	Argentina, Brazil and Mexico (1993-2006)	Co-integration and Causality Tests	Argentina and Mexico: X and GDP co-integrated Argentina and Brazil: X ⟶ GDP Before NAFTA Mexico: X ⟶ GDP After NAFTA Mexico: X ⟶ GDP
Baharom et al. (2008)	Malaysia (1975-2005)	Time Series Regression Analysis	Short and Long Run: (+)
Gerni et. al. (2008)	Turkey (1980-2006)	Regression Analyses and Causality Tests	Annual Data: (+) X ⟶ GDP M ⟶ GDP Monthly Data: X ⟶ GDP M ⟶ GDP X ⟶ M

Musonda (2007)	Zambia (1970-2003)	Co-integration Test and Error Correction Model	X and GDP co-integrated (+)
Kingsley. et al. (2004)	Nigeria (1980-2002)	Co-integration Tests	OPEN and GDP not co-integrated
Ibrahim (2002)	Hong Kong, South Korea, Malaysia, Philippines, Singapore and Thailand (1964-1993)	Time Series Regression Analysis	Hong Kong: (+), Malaysia: (+) South Korea: (+), Singapore: (+) Philippines: (0), Thailand: (+)
Vohra (2001)	India, Pakistan, Philippines, Malaysia and Thailand (1973-1993)	Co-integration Tests and Regression Analysis	India: (0) Pakistan: (+) Philippines: (+), Malaysia: (+) Thailand: (+)
Sun and Parikh (2001)	29 Regions in China. (1985-1995)	Panel Data Regression Analysis	(+)
Medina-Smith (2001)	Costa Rica (1950-1997)	Time Series Regression Analysis	(+)

Lawrence and Weinstein (1999)	South Korea (1964-1985)	Time Series Regression Analysis	(+)
Fosu (1990)	28 African Countries (1960-1980)	Cross-Countries Regression Analysis	(+)

Notes: X stands for export, M for import, GDP for Gross Domestic Product, and OPEN ((export + import) / GDP) for trade openness degree, (+) refers that export or trade openness is a significant positive determinant of economic growth while (0) refers to statistically insignificant relationship.

As is clearly seen in Table 1, the results of several studies for developing countries are in favour of export-led growth. However, there are also some other findings that do not support this idea.

Data and Methodology

Based on the literature on relationships between international trade and economic growth, this study investigates the relations of real exports (RX), real imports (RM), and real Gross Domestic Product (RGDP) in five Central Asian economies (Azerbaijan, Kazakhstan, Kyrgyzstan, Turkmenistan, and Uzbekistan) in the transition period via causality tests. Although the main purpose of the study is to investigate the relationships between exports and economic growth, both the relationship between imports and economic growth and relationship between import and export in these countries will also be handled.

For this purpose, in addition to the Granger causality test, dynamic panel method causality tests are also used. The data of these countries for the time period of 1991-2008 was obtained from the website of the World Bank, World Development Indicators.

Empirical Findings

Before the relationships between exports and growth, imports and growth, and exports and imports are determined via causality tests, a unit root test developed by Levin, Lin and Chu (2003) is applied to find out whether the variables include a unit root. Table 2 shows the unit root test results of the values of variables, which are transformed to logarithmic form in their constant and trended structures. Results in Table 2 show that all level values of variables are stationary.

Table 2. Levin, Lin and Chu Unit Root Test Results (Individual Intercept and Trend)

Variables	Statistics	Probability
LRX	-1.432	0.076
LRM	-1.914	0.028
LRGDP	-7.409	0.000

Descriptive Statistics and Correlation Coefficients

Table 3 summarizes descriptive statistics calculated based on real gross domestic product (RGDP), real export (RX), and real import (RM) values in the Central Asian countries.

Table 3. Descriptive Statistics

Variables	RGDP	RX	RM
Mean	10.031	4.528	4.109
Median	7.062	2.975	3.078
Maximum	37.269	21.322	16.729
Minimum	1.043	0.307	0.442
Standard Deviation	8.698	4.556	3.633
Observations	92	92	92

The average production level in these five Central Asian economies for the time period 1991-2008 is 10 billion USD, based on 2000 prices, but there is a high standard deviation of GDP by about 8.7 billion USD, which indicates that there is a significant difference between the production levels of these countries and shows that their economies are not homogenous. For example, while Kazakhstan was the country to have had the highest production level, with 17.2 billion USD in 2008, Kyrgyzstan was the last country in the order, with the smallest production level of 1.04 billion USD in 1995. On the other hand, it is seen that these five countries realized about 4.5 billion USD import and 4.1 billion USD export on the average. In addition to this, Kazakhstan was first in both the value of exports at 21.3 billion USD in 2008 and the value of imports at 16.7 billion USD in 1992. On the other hand, while Kyrgyzstan was the country with the lowest export value, with 307 million USD in 1995, it was also the country with the lowest import value with 442 million USD imports in 1994 and 1995. Besides, standard deviation values of either imports or exports variables were found rather high, which indicates that this country type has quite heterogenic foreign economic structure.

In the light of these descriptive data, correlation coefficients and probability values depicting simple relationships among these three variables are presented in Table 4.

Table 4. Correlation Coefficients of the Variables

Variables	LRGDP	LRX	LRM
LRGDP	1.000		
LRX	0.938 (0.000)	1.000	
LRM	0.932 (0.000)	0.951 (0.000)	1.000

There is a positive and quite high relationship between real exports, real imports, and real product level in Central Asian economies. Correlation coefficients illustrating simple relationships between two variables are quite significant in terms of reflecting the relations between exports and growth, imports and growth, and establishing meaningful relations between imports and exports. Figure 1 shows high correlation relations among these variables. Although Figure 1 indicates that import and export rates show more volatility compared to GDP level, it also shows that all the variables follow similar trends.

Causality Test Analysis

It is now essential to illustrate the causal side of this high relation. Therefore, causality test results will be discussed in order to determine the reason for this high correlation level between these variables. Granger causality test, which gives the direction of causality between two variables as a result of Walt test, will be used first for the determination of causal relations between economic growth and imports, economic growth and exports, and between imports and exports in Central Asian economies.

$$Y_{it} = \alpha_0 + \sum_{l=1}^{m} \alpha_{lt} Y_{it-1} + \sum_{l=1}^{m} \delta ltX_{it-1} + e_{it} \text{ (i=1,...,N; t=1,...,T and m=2)}$$

(1)

Equation (1) is utilized for this purpose, where Y represents dependent variable, X represents explanatory variable, i represents cross-sectional units, t represents time, and m represents lag length. Granger causality test results are presented in Table 5.

There is a unidirectional causal relationship running from LRGDP to both LRM and LRX. This causal relation from economic growth to exports in Central Asian economies, as Awokuse (2008) also states, is a model of growth-led exports. Therefore, this result shows that export performance in Central Asian economies do not have a stimulus impact on economic growth which is consistent with the hypothesis of minimum development level. According to this hypothesis, countries should reach a certain level of industrialization and development in order that exports can stimulate economic growth by causing productivity and external effects of export.

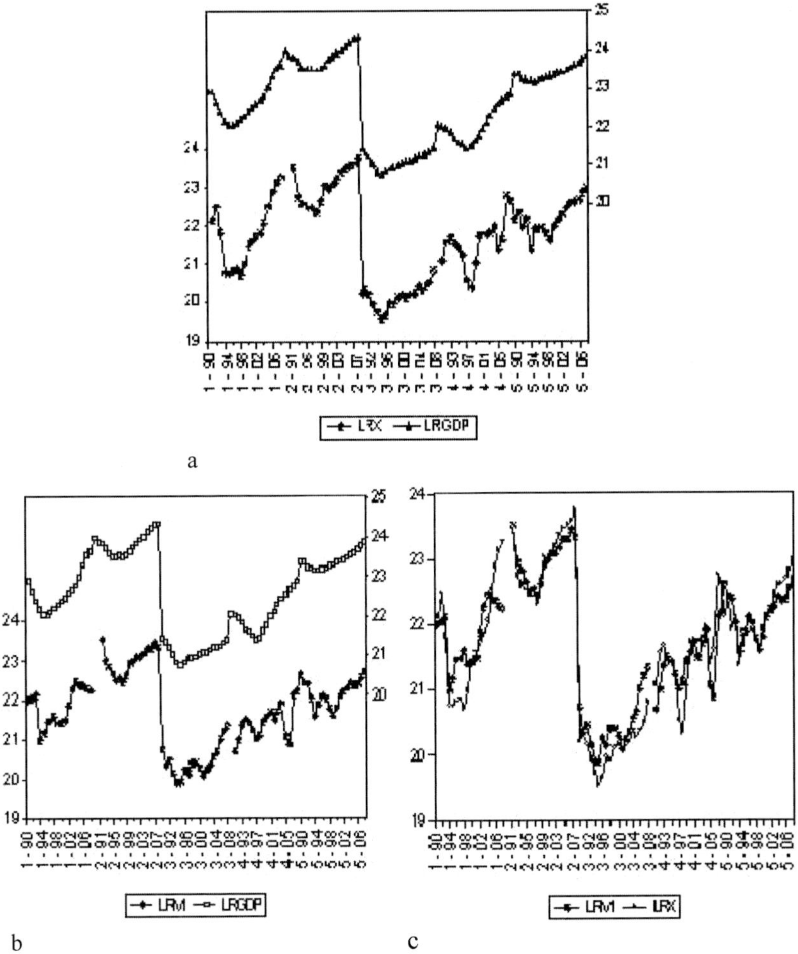

Figure 1. GDP, Import and Export Levels of Central Asian economies (1990-2008)

Table 5. Granger Causality Test Results

Null Hypothesis	Observations	F-Statistic	Probability
LRX does not Granger Cause LRGDP	82	1.390	0.255
LRGDP does not Granger Cause LRX		18.893	0.000
LRM does not Granger Cause LRGDP	82	0.453	0.638
LRGDP does not Granger Cause LRM		8.486	0.001
LRM does not Granger Cause LRX	82	0.705	0.497
LRX does not Granger Cause LRM		3.480	0.036

The fact that the industrialization level of the five Central Asian countries is insufficient, and that most of the exported productions of these countries, such as petrol, natural gas, agriculture and mining, are basically composed of primary goods, might be seen as the possible reasons why exports do not have an effective role on economic growth in the Central Asian economies.

Similarly, a unidirectional causal relationship running from output level (RGDP) to imports suggests that the import levels of these countries, particularly the consumer goods imports, will change in parallel with the increase in production level. The reason why these changes in imports do not cause growth effects might be because they are basically dependent on consumer goods imports rather than investment goods imports.

Finally, another finding is that there is a unidirectional causality from exports to imports. Exports carried out in these Central Asian economies directly have stimulus effects on imports. In other words, foreign currency that flows into the country from primary goods exports leaves the country after it has stimulus impact on imports. This situation suggests that imports are composed of consumer and luxury consumer goods rather than of investment and intermediate goods. However, this situation might also suggest that there is another positive impact of imports on the growth of exports in parallel with the developments in the export potentials.

In addition to the traditional Granger causality analysis, another causality analysis test developed by Holtz-Eakin et al. (1988) is also used. In this method, causal relations between the dependent variable Y and the explanatory variables X are determined based on the equation given below (Holtz-Eakin et. al., 1988: 1373).

$$Y_{it} = \alpha_{0t} + \sum_{l=1}^{m} \alpha_{lt} Y_{it-l} + \sum_{l=1}^{m} \delta_{lt} X_{it-l} + \psi f_i + u_{it} \text{ (i=1,...,N; t=1,...,T)}$$

(2)

Again, i represents cross-section units reaching up N, t represents time term up to T, and *fi* represents impacts, which are peculiar to cross-section units and time-invariant. In order to remove these fixed effects (*fi*) peculiar to cross-section units, equation (3) is obtained by taking the difference of both sides of equation (2) (Holtz-Eakin, et al., 1988: 1373).

$$\Delta Y_{it} = \sum_{l=1}^{m} \alpha_l \Delta Y_{it-l} + \sum_{l=1}^{m} \delta_l \Delta X_{it-l} + \Delta u_{it} \qquad (3)$$

In Equation (3), since ΔY_{it-l} is linked to Δu_{it} there is a need for the use of instrumental variables method. Thus, equation (3) is predicted using generalized method of moments (GMM), following Arellano and Bond (1991). Causality relations between variables are determined with Wald test, which is adapted into estimation coefficients belonging to independent variables obtained with GMM.

Table 6. Dynamic Panel Data Causality Test Results

Explanatory Variables	ΔLX	ΔLGDP	ΔLM	ΔLGDP	ΔLX	ΔLM
ΔLGDP (-1)	1.692[c]	1.773[a]	0.959	1.636[a]	-----	-----
ΔLGDP (-2)	-0.300	-0.911[a]	-0.230	-0.719[a]	-----	-----
ΔLX (-1)	0.370	0.028	-----	-----	1.089[b]	0.337
ΔLX (-2)	-0.439[a]	0.007	-----	-----	-0.326	-0.088
ΔLM (-1)	-----	-----	0.462	-0.019	-0.303	0.345
ΔLM (-2)	-----	-----	-0.434[a]	-0.020	0.093	-0.286
J Statistics	1.949	1.477	3.368	2.997	3.894	3.826
Sargan Test (Probability)	0.583	0.688	0.338	0.392	0.273	0.281
Wald Test ($\chi 2$ Statistics)	6.847[b]	0.231	2.71	0.68	0.881	0.757
# Obs	72		72		72	

Table 6 summarizes regression coefficients obtained by estimating the equation (3) and Wald test results, which give the direction of causality. Sargan test results showed that instrumental variables in all of the estimated equations were meaningful. GMM results point out only a unidirectional causal relationship from economic growth to exports. Any other meaningful relation among other variables could not be found. This result shows that there is consistency with the hypotheses of growth-led export and minimum development level, and also indicates that export in Central Asian economies can only be efficient on economic growth when these countries reach up to a certain level of industrialization and development.

Conclusion and Evaluation

Relationships between exports and economic growth have a very old history dating back to Mercantilism, even earlier than the classical economics. As opposed to Mercantilism, the classical deals not only with exports, but also with imports as well. Therefore, the classical school gives priority to liberalism, which brings prosperity. Different from the classical school, the Keynesian school permits intervention in certain conditions, which provided efficient solutions for the 1929 Great Depression. It also brought some devaluation implementations to compensate for shrinkages in the world trade.

Following World War II, along with positive economic growth in Asia and the decline of growth in Iron Curtain countries, a bipolar structure supporting both liberalism and interventionism caused the classical school to regain significance. After the collapse of the Berlin Wall and the Iron Curtain, liberal views have become dominant in the world. Therefore, relations between outward orientation and economic growth are included in growth models.

This study investigated the relationships between exports, imports and economic growth of Central Asian economies on the way of liberal economic policies after the collapse of the USSR. It was found that there is a unidirectional causality running from economic growth to exports. This result suggests consistency with the growth-led export and minimum development level hypotheses in the literature. That is, according to the growth-led export model, these countries will be able to export as they grow; however, according to minimum development level hypothesis, exports will help economic growth in these Central Asian economies only after they reach a certain level of development and industrialization. In economies that could not yet reach a certain level of development with no matured level of production, exports do not give rise to imports, but only transform the country to a consumer heaven by stimulating the consumption patterns. In a structure with increasingly rising imports, inability to finance it by export revenues that are real income resources, gives rise to both corruption in trade lines and boosts the external debts to very high levels in a short time.

However, it is obvious that the notion of growth-led export in Central Asian economies, together with the liberalization implementations, will stimulate the recognition process of foreign marketing through learning by experience in the long term. For this reason, depending on the world experiences, it can be suggested that maintenance of liberalization implementations will stimulate international trade based growth. Here, it is necessary to state that short-term policies should not be far from the world realities. In other words, rather than anti-liberal policies, particularly in the countries with small economies, in contrast to low-income, low-saving, low investment spiral, monetary policies will be more efficient. For this reason, restriction of the imports of luxury goods through consumer taxes, as Asian Tigers did, might lead to both an increase in saving and accordingly may compensate for the external debt crisis.

References

Abou-Stait, Fouad, 2005. "Are Exports the Engine of Economic Growth? Application of Cointegration and Causality Analysis for Egypt, 1977-2003", African Development Bank, Economic Research Working Paper Series, No: 76.

Ahmad Jaleel and Andy C. C. Kwan, 1991. "Causality between Export and Economic Growth: Empirical Evidence from Africa", Economics Letters, 37(3): 243-248.

Arellano, Manuel and Stephen Bond, 1991. "Some Tests of Specification for Panel Data: Monte Carlo Evidence and an Application to Employment Equations", Review of Economic Studies, 58,(2): 277-297.

Awokuse, Titur O., 2008. "Trade Openness and Economic Growth: Is Growth Export-led or Import-led", Applied Economics, 40: 161-173.

Baharom, A. H., M. S. Habibullah and R. Royfaizal, 2008. "The Relationship between Trade Openness, Foreign Direct Investment and Growth: Case of Malaysia", Munich Personal RePEc Archive, MPRA Paper No. 11928: 1-10.

Chang, Ha-Joon, 2004. Kalkınma Reçetelerinin Gerçek Yüzü, (Çev. Tuba Akıncılar Onmuş), İletişim Yayınları, İstanbul.

Çelebi, Işın, 1991. Dışa Açık Büyüme ve Türkiye, e Yayınları, İstanbul.

Dollar, David and Aart Kraay, 2001. "Growth Is Good for the Poor", Policy Research Working Paper, World Bank, Washington D.C.

Edwards, Sebastian, 1993. "Openness, Trade Liberalization, and Growth in Developing Countries", Journal of Economic Literature", XXXI: 1358-1393.

Emsen, Ö. Selçuk and M. Kemal Değer, 2007. "İktisadi ve Siyasal Liberalizasyon ve Ekonomik Büyüme İlişkileri: Geçiş Ekonomileri Üzerine Panel Veri Analizi", Atatürk Üniversitesi İİBF Fakültesi Dergisi, 21(2): 161-195:

Fosu, Augustin Kwasi, 1990. "Exports Economic Growth: The African Case", World Development, 18 (6): 831-835.

Gerni, Cevat, O. Selcuk Emsen and M. Kemal Deger, 2008. "İthalata Dayalı İhracat ve Ekonomik Büyüme: 1980-2006 Türkiye Deneyimi", 2. Ulusal İktisat Kongresi, 20-22 Şubat 2008, Dokuz Eylül Üniversitesi, İzmir, Türkiye.

Ghartey, Edward E., 1993. "Causal Relationship between Exports and Economic Growth: Some Empirical Evidence in Taiwan, Japan and the U.S.", Applied Economics, 25(9): 1145-1152.

Giles, Judith A. and Cara L. Williams, 2000. "Export-led Growth: A Survey of the Empirical Literature and Some Noncausality Results Part 1", Journal of International Trade and Economic Development, 9(3): 261-337.

Gries, Thomas, Manfred Kraft and Daniel Meierrieks, 2009. "Linkages Between Financial Deepening, Trade Openness, and Economic Development: Causality Evidence from Sub-Saharan Africa", World Development, 37(12). 1849-1860.

Grossman, Gene M. and Elhanan Helpman, 1990. "Comparative Advantage and Long Run Growth", The American Economic Review, 80(4): 796-815.

Han, Ergül and A. Ayşen Kaya, 2006. Kalkınma Ekonomisi Teori ve Politika, Nobel Yayın Dağıtım, Ankara.

Holtz-Eakin, Doudlas, Whitney Newey and Harvey S. Rosen, 1988. "Estimating Vector Autoregressions with Panel Data", Econometrica, 56(6): 1371–1395.

Ibrahim, Izani, 2002. "On Exports and Economic Growth", Journal Pengurusan, 21: 3-18.

Kingsley, O. Kanayo, O. George Okechukwu and Adenuga Adeniyi, 2004. "Is 'Trade' Openness Valid for Nigeria's Long-Run Growth: A Cointegration Approach?", On the Design of Trade Policy Reforms in Nigeria, Central Bank of Nigeria, December 2004: 1-21.

Kuşkay, Sıtkı Yılmaz, 2001. Sovyet-tipi Ekonomilerin Merkezi Plandan Serbest Piyasaya Geçiş Deneyimi, Yayımlanmamış Doktora Tezi, Atatürk Üniversitesi Sosyal Bilimler Enstitüsü, Erzurum.

Lawrence, Robert Z. and David E. Weinstein, 1999. Trade and Growth: Import-led or Export-led? Evidence from Japan and Korea, NBER Working Paper Series, 7264.

Levin, A., C. F. Lin and C. Chu, 2002. "Unit Root Tests in Panel Data: Asymptotic and Finite-Sample Properties", Journal of Econometrics, 108(1): 1–24.

Love, Jim, 1994. "Engines of Growth: The Export and Government Sectors", World Economy, 17(2): 203-218.

Maneschiöld, Per-Ola, 2008. "A Note on the Export-Led Growth Hypothesis: A Time Series Approach", Cuadernos de Economia, 45: 293-302.

Medina-Smith, Emilio J., 2001. "Is The Export-Led Growth Hypothesis Valid For Developing Countries? A Case Study of Costa Rica", Policy Issues in International Trade and Commodities Study Series No. 7, New York.

Musonda, Ireen, 2007. "Is Economic Growth Led by Exports in Zambia", Workshop on Sector-Led Growth in Africa and Implications for Development, November 7-9: 1-21 (http://www.unidep.org/Release3/Conferences/Afea_2007/IDEP-AFEA-07-09.pdf) (June 2010).

Palley, Thomas I., 2002. "Export-Led Growth: Evidence of Developing Country Crowding-out", Open Society Institute, Washington, DC 20036: 1-28 (http://www.thomaspalley.com/docs/articles/economic_development/crowding_out.pdf) (June 2010).

Santos-Paulino, Amelia U., 2005. "Trade Liberalisation and Economic Performance: Theory and Evidence for Developing Countries", World Economy, 28: 783-821.

Sun, Haishun and Asho Parikh, 2001. "Exports, Inward Foreign Direct Investment (FDI) and Regional Economic Growth in China", Regional Studies, 35(3): 187-196.

Tussie, Diana and Carlos Aggio, 2005. "Economic and Social Impacts of Trade Liberalization", Coping with Trade Reforms: A Developing-Country Perspective on the WTO Industrial Tariff Negotiations, (http://192.91.247.38/tab/events/namastudy/fullreport-version14nov-p106-119.pdf) (June 2010).

Vohra, Rubina, 2001. "Export and Economic Growth: Further Time Series Evidence from Less-Developed Countries", IAER, 7(3): 345-350.

Yucel, Fatih, 2009. "Causal Relationships between Financial Development, Trade Openness and Economic Growth: The Case of Turkey", Journal of Social Sciences, 5(1): 33-42.

Trade Patterns between Turkey and Central Asian Countries

Asst. Prof. Abdüllatif Çeviker,[1]
Asst. Prof. Hanifi Murat Mutlu[2]
and İsmail Taş[3]

Central Asian countries attract the attention of the entire world as both a supply and a consumption market. Especially the natural resources and the logistic importance of the region make commerce with these countries highly desirable. Many countries including Turkey develop and implement comprehensive policies to improve economic relations with the region. The purpose of this study is to analyse the size and technological concentration of commerce between Turkey and Central Asia, who have close ties with each other in terms of history, culture, and geographical position.

The total credit amount that Turkey has issued for the countries of the region through Eximbank is about 1 billion USD. Besides this, Turkish International Cooperation and Development agency (TİKA) was established to provide technical assistance for Central Asian countries. The trade volume of Turkey with these countries amounts to about 6.5 billion USD, and investments of Turkish companies in the region are over 4.7 billion USD as of 2010. Total value of the project executed by Turkish contracting companies in the region is approximately 30 billion USD. Up to two thousand Turkish companies operate in the region (Ministry of Foreign Affairs of the Republic of Turkey Turkey´s Relations With Central Asian Republics).

Turkey has made significant contributions to the admission of the countries of the region into the international community. Turkey has undertaken a leading role in the membership of Central Asian countries to

[1] Istanbul Medeniyet University, Istanbul, Turkey
[2] Gaziantep University, Gaziantep, Turkey
[3] Tunceli University, Tunceli, Turkey

the UN, IMF, the World Bank, and similar organizations. Moreover, Turkey has provided professional support for these countries to transition into the free market economy and border trade, and to develop free zones. Certain Turkish state banks have established joint banks in Central Asia so as to develop modern banking services (Taşağıl, 2004). International trade relations made up between Central Asian countries and Turkey as from 1992 have increasingly developed in the subsequent years. However, considering the available potential, the current progress is far from satisfying (Solak, 2003).

The most important subject for Turkey-Central Asian countries is energy. The increasing prominence of energy resources of the Caspian Basin, primarily with Kazakhstan and Azerbaijan in the 2000s, started to act as a new driving force in relations between Turkey and the region (Kılıç, 2009). Turkey, being a prominent energy importer and a safe destination in terms of geographical conditions, possesses a high level of attraction for Central Asia (Gömeç, 2007).

Kyrgyzstan, Uzbekistan, Kazakhstan, Turkmenistan and Tajikistan, among the 15 new states after the disintegration of the Soviet Union in 1991, are listed in the definition of widely accepted Central Asian countries. Apart from not being included in this definition, Azerbaijan, with a significant position in the foreign affairs of Turkey, is studied within the Central Asian countries group. With an aim to investigate the size and technological concentration of commercial relations between Turkey and the region, analyses were made by classifying the data obtained from United Nations International Trade Database according to their technological concentration. Results of the analysis will convey at which technological level these countries import or export products. Therefore, it will be possible to make a comparison between Turkey and Central Asian countries in terms of technological level in international trade. In addition, this comparison analysis will be an important starting point for decision makers directing the international trade performance. This is because, while the exports of technology intensive products furnish information on the current technological level of a country, the import levels are expected to provide data on the potential growth level. As technology imports are used as a vital factor in the growth of a country by developing countries, production structures established as technologically intensive prepare a regular, solid and sustainable infrastructure. Technology intensive products rapidly develop, provide a high level of return, and first and foremost, they create their own demand. They have substantial externality in exploring new abilities and know-how. For these reasons, this approach towards commercial relations of Turkey with the region from the technological perspective will both reveal the current level of Turkey and provide information on the development potential of the countries in the region in the future.

Central Asian Economies

In countries that obtained their independence following the disintegration of the USSR, there occurred a transition from the central planning economy into the free market economy. The term *transition economies,* indicating a new economic restructuring, entered into the economic literature at the end of the 1980s to define Central and Eastern Europe, the Baltic States, and the former Soviet Union members (Bal, 2003). Transition from the planned economic model into the free market economy is basically the formation of a corporate framework including deregulation in the market, efficiency in resource distribution, dependence of the macroeconomic sustainability to the market powers, privatizations for economic productivity, strict budget discipline, proprietary rights, and the rule of law (Ardor, 2006). The successful integration of the transition economies into the world economies would be for the benefit of all countries and these countries face a high level of harmonization cost; yet advantages of being in a larger and more competitive global market outweigh for these countries (Wang, 1996). When the general characteristics of the transition economies are concerned, low level of technology and industrialization, low level of productivity against high level of agricultural population, lack of ethical norms, and low level of accountability are among the basic properties (Ramazanoðlu and Acar, 2005).

Economic recession and downturn in the transition economies occurred at different levels and with differing effects from 1990. In average 9.5% contraction was experienced in almost all transition economies between 1990-1993 when the economic recession was the deepest and the wildest. Although fruits of the structural reforms started to be picked after 1997, the Russian financial crisis had a negative effect on economic activities of Central Asian and Eastern Asian countries (Ağcakaya, 2009). Russia being the biggest trade partner of Central Asian countries even after the disintegration of USSR increased the severity of this effect.

In general, Central Asian countries have a comparable superiority in cotton, natural gas and petroleum products and certain dominance in investment goods. Apart from petroleum and natural gas reserves, other less known metals of the region are gold, zinc and uranium. Central Asia is the second biggest cotton producer of the world and provides high quality fruits and vegetables. Central Asian countries have not been able to diversify international trade. Exports of Central Asian countries focus on certain goods in terms of commodity composition. For example, the share of raw petroleum of 42.6% within the total exports of Azerbaijan in 1999 increased to 62.7% in 2004. These rates were 39.3% in 1999 and 56.8% in 2004. The share of gold and raw cotton within the total exports of Kyrgyzstan was 45.4% in 1999 and 46.2% in 2004. Although Uzbekistan tried to encourage exports of manufactured goods, the 67.7% share of gold, cotton fibre, and natural gas within total exports in 1999 decreased to 64.1% in 2004 (Asian Development Bank, 2006).

Economic performance experience of Kazakhstan and Kyrgyzstan, highly effective in creating market guided economy, at the beginning of 2000 caused disappointment, yet they were the countries that came out of the transition recession. Both countries were affected substantially by the Russian crisis in 1998. The biggest cotton manufacturers of the USSR, Uzbekistan and Turkmenistan were more cautious in reforms. Uzbekistan that benefited from the high cotton prices at the beginning of the 1990s was the country that delivered the best performance among the Central Asian countries and had relatively small decrease in GDP and reasonable social indications. Turkmenistan showed a negative economic performance due to an unproductive domestic market and autocratic leadership structure that considered reforms invaluable despite its cotton and gas exports income (Pomfret, 2005).

Azerbaijan delivered high growth rates as a result of increasing foreign investment in its economy since 1996, contractionary fiscal and monetary policies and low inflation rates and macroeconomic stability was provided substantially. The annual average 10.2% GDP increase between 2000 and 2004 increased to 26.4% in 2005 and to 34.5% in 2006, and reached 25% in 2007. The average inflation rate of 2% between 2000 and 2003 started to increase as of 2003. In 2008, GDP increased 11 times when compared to that of 1998. Azerbaijan had the highest growth rate among the Central Asian countries in 2008 with 10.8%.

Kazakhstan reached double-digit growth rates in 2000s. The economy of Kazakhstan delivered negative growth almost always between 1990 and 1998. A decrease in GDP in Kazakhstan in 1999 was a result of the Asian economic crisis and the decrease in prices of exported goods of the country, mainly petroleum, gas, and colour metals. However, the Kazakhstan economy accelerated its economic development after 2000; GDP which was 26 billion USD in 1990, reached 78.0 billion USD in 2006, and 133 billion USD in 2008.

Cotton production of Uzbekistan meets 50% of the needs of USSR, and it has certain advantages in meat, milk, egg, silk production, and fruit growing. It is a known fact that the Red Sand Desert covering a substantial part of the country has highly rich natural gas, gold, and uranium reserves. The annual 100 ton capacity gold mine of Uzbekistan whets the appetite of other countries, because this amount is a lot more than the generation of the biggest gold mines of the world. Besides this, there are uranium reserves in Uzbekistan that are being processed but not declared in exact amounts, as it is a strategic substance (Akdiş, 1999).

Kyrgyzstan was the first country to adopt low trade barriers and trade policy and to become a member to the World Trade Organization from the former Soviet Russia (Pomfret, 2005). With the strict monetary policy implemented in Kyrgyzstan, the inflation rate of 700% in 1993 and 200% in 1994 recessed back to 10% in the middle of 1998. However, very rapid increases occurred in prices and exchange due to the Russian crisis that emerged in August in 1998 (Hatipağaoğlu, 2002).

Analysis of Commercial Relations between Turkey and Central Asia

Size of International trade between Turkey and Central Asia

While the trade from Turkey towards Central Asian countries varied between 560 and 610 million USD between 1999 and 2002, it reached approximately 900 million USD after 2003, and amounted to 3.9 billion USD in 2008 after a rapid increase. The trade from Central Asian countries towards Turkey, on the other hand, varied between 461 and 496 million USD between 1999 and 2002, and amounted to 3.9 billion USD in 2008, developing in parallel with the trade in the reverse direction. Turkey increased its exports to Central Asia by 7 times and imports by 8.5 times during the period.

The proportional weight of Central Asian countries within the total import volume of Turkey was 1.13% in 1999 and almost doubled, reached 2.19% in ten years. This indicates that the share of Central Asia increased substantially as a supply market in the concerned period. The proportional share increase in exports was not as high as in imports.

Table 1. Trade between Turkey and Central Asian economies (USD)

	Export	Import	Balance
1999	560,030,580	461,236,537	98,794,043
2000	547,941,632	644,390,204	-96,448,572
2001	544,944,863	296,131,598	248,813,265
2002	610,114,733	496,054,364	114,060,369
2003	905,930,591	679,420,315	226,510,276
2004	1,209,180,549	992,715,184	216,465,365
2005	1,410,542,797	1,296,410,534	114,132,263
2006	2,017,664,837	2,067,608,570	-49,943,733
2007	2,970,779,467	2,646,909,048	323,870,419
2008	3,906,368,610	3,911,059,927	-4,691,317

Table 2. Mutual shares of trade between Turkey and Central Asian economies (1999-2008)

	Share of Central Asia within total international trade of Turkey %		Share of Turkey within total international trade of Central Asia %	
	Import	Export	Import	Export
1999	1.13	2.18	5.49	3.73
2000	1.19	2.08	4.80	3.75
2001	0.72	1.83	4.06	1.69
2002	0.97	1.77	4.48	2.69
2003	0.98	1.97	5.21	2.87
2004	1.03	1.96	4.92	3.01
2005	1.13	1.98	4.74	2.81
2006	1.49	2.40	5.22	3.15
2007	1.65	2.79	5.74	3.21
2008	2.19	2.97	6.00	3.47

When commercial relations are analysed from the perspective of Central Asia, the rate of imports from Turkey within the total imports of Central Asian countries was 5.49% in 1999. This rate showed a downward trend until the mid 2000s, however, it increased regularly and reached 6% later on. The rate of exports to Turkey within the total exports of Central Asian countries was around 3.2%, except for 2001, in which year a serious economic crisis occurred in Turkey.

Technological Concentration of International Trade between Turkey and Central Asia

Technological concentration is focused on the structural analysis of international trade between Turkey and Central Asia. Both Turkey and Central Asian countries are among developing countries. Analysis of technological structure of international trade has important results for countries in the developing countries category. As is known, technological development is one of the most important engines of long term economic growth. While new products, new production methods, or new markets are created with technological development, increase occurs in output per unit input. Almost all economic views accept that technological development plays an important role in the growth process (Archibugil and Michie, 1998). On the other hand, another widely acknowledged growth resource is exports. When technological development and exports are considered together as growth engines, technological concentration of the structure of exports inevitably draws attention around the problem of economic growth of countries.

When the effect of the exports structure on the economic growth rate is considered, the positive effect of an export structure comprised of high technology intensive products is higher than that of low technology intensive structure. First of all, it is necessary to underline that sectors in which product and process innovations are frequently encountered generally experience more demand than technologically stable sectors (Lall 2000). This perspective should be effective in evaluation of the fact that the most dynamic outputs of world trade are information and communication technologies products. In these markets, where innovative sectors have a high level of demand potential, the probability of encountering new rivals is low in contrast to low technology product markets. Because new rivals are always ready as human capital, financial capital, and other resources required for production, these fields are not relatively lacking in technological abilities. Producers not willing to encounter new rivals also require a low price policy and naturally low profit margin. In contrast, producers in technology intensive product markets are more resistant to the potential threat of new rivals. Besides market integration, there are difficulties deriving from intellectual property rights and the need for high quality labour in the technology intensive product market; producers adapt to changes in the demand structure with flexible production for an advantage against the current players. On the other hand, advanced technology production/export structure has certain external advantages: high potential of creating domestic innovation and provision of productivity in sectors in which production is realised using low technology with innovative complementary methods, can be listed among them.

Advanced technology advantage of a country, in other words specialty in international market puts a positive effect on international trade of that country (Archibugil and Michie, 1998). When the effect mechanism between specialty level or innovation and performance is considered, three connections come to the forefront: A process innovation associated with production method decreases cost and provides a significant competition advantage for the producer. As minor innovations in the product subject to commerce increase quality, it elevates the level of demand in both domestic and foreign markets and improves customer satisfaction. Major innovations, on the other hand, provide monopoly and thus, extraordinary profit for the producer even in the short run. When all these reasons are considered, it can be concluded that the export structure in which advanced technology is determinant increases competition power in international markets, and may put an effect on growth through different channels.

The classification arranged by Sanjaya Lall (2000) based on classification attempts made by Pavit (1984) and OECD (1994) is implemented in the study. The diagram arranged according to SITC-2 is given in Table 1.

Figures 1 and 2, arranged based on the data set in Table 2, indicate the structure and change of trade between Turkey and Central Asia in terms of technical density. The share of primary products of Turkey among the exports to Central Asian countries was 4.9% between 1999 and 2008. The average share of these products among imports from Central Asia was 72.4% in the same period. The most imported primary products by Turkey from Central Asia were copper and raw petroleum. Resource based products constitute 17.2% of Turkish exports. The major exports items of Turkey in this field are sugar and wood commodities. Resource based product imports of Turkey from Central Asia had a share of 11.7% and the biggest import items in this share were scrap iron and mineral oil. It can be observed that low technology products form a relatively important product group within the exports of Turkey to Central Asia. While Turkey makes 33.6% of its exports in this field, imports remain at 11% in the same group. The biggest exports items of Turkey were rug-carpet and wire, the most exported products were yarn and cotton textile. Medium technology products constituted the biggest part of Turkish exports, with 38.6%. Imports were 4.6%. While the biggest export items of Turkey were polymerized products and white goods, again polymerized products played a significant role within the medium technology imports of Turkey from Central Asia. Despite requiring further research, it can be concluded that intra-industry trade is present between the parties of the trade in polymerized products. Products in the high technology group constituted 5.6% of Turkish exports and their imports remained at 0.1%. The biggest export items of Turkey in high technology products were telecommunication devices and pharmaceutical products, and import items in this group were measurement devices and telecommunication devices.

Table 1: International trade Technological Classification SITC 2, Digit 3

Tech.	SITC 2 Code
Primary Product	001,011,022,025,034,036,041,042,043,044,045,054,057,071,072,074, 075,081,091,121,211,212,222,223, 232,244,245,246,261,263,268,271,273,274,277,278, 291,292,322,333,341,681,682,683,684,685,686,687,
Research Based	012,014,023,024,035,037,046,047,048,056,058,061,062,073,098,111, 112,122,133,247,248,251,264,265,269,281,282,286,287,288,289, 323,334,335,411,423,424,431,511,514,515,516,522,523,531,532,551, 592,621,625,628,633,634,635,641,661,662,663,664, 667,688,689
Low Tech	611,612,613,651,652,654,655,656,657,658,659,831,842,843,844,845, 846,847,848,851,642,665,666,673, 674,675,676,677,679,691, 692,693,694,695,696,697,699,821,893,894,895,897,898,899
Medium Tech	266,267,512,513,533,553,554,562,572,582,583,584,585,591,598,653, 671,672,678,711,713,714,721,722,723,724,725,726,727,728, 736,737,741,742,743,744,745,749,762,763,772,773,775,781,782,783, 784,785,786,791,793,812,872,873,882,884,885,951
High Tech	716,718,751,752,759,761,764,771,774,776,778,524,541,712,792, 871,874,881

Table 2: Technological Composition of International trade between Central Asia and Turkey

Technological concentration of international trade between Central Asia and Turkey (million USD)					
	Primary Based	Resource Based	Low Tech	Medium Tech	High Tech
	TURKEY EXPORT				
1999	41.8	136.5	182.8	163.1	35.9
2000	31.3	121.6	172.7	180.1	42.2
2001	32.4	123.2	146.6	194.1	48.8
2002	42.3	126.0	195.8	208.9	37.2
2003	49.8	165.8	293.3	344.0	53.1
2004	60.8	195.6	428.9	451.8	72.0
2005	80.0	230.8	509.3	514.2	76.2
2006	100.2	304.4	672.2	829.2	111.8
2007	122.6	449.7	1008.0	1234.0	156.5
2008	165.6	672.4	1329.1	1546.7	192.5
	TURKEY IMPORT				
1999	380.6	16.2	46.9	17.1	0.4
2000	475.5	66.0	70.3	32.0	0.6
2001	185.1	54.8	41.5	12.4	2.3
2002	333.2	52.2	77.3	32.7	0.7
2003	417.1	86.3	130.1	40.3	5.6
2004	642.4	105.6	159.2	83.8	1.8
2005	885.3	166.7	180.5	63.1	0.7
2006	1479.0	208.2	258.0	120.2	2.1
2007	1998.9	279.2	290.2	77.8	0.7
2008	2972.8	547.6	244.1	146.2	0.3
Technological concentration of international trade between Central Asia & Turkey (%)					
	Primary Based	Resource Based	Low Tech	Medium Tech	High Tech
	TURKEY EXPORT				
1999	7.5	24.4	32.6	29.1	6.4
2000	5.7	22.2	31.5	32.9	7.7
2001	5.9	22.6	26.9	35.6	8.9
2002	6.9	20.6	32.1	34.2	6.1
2003	5.5	18.3	32.4	38.0	5.9
2004	5.0	16.2	35.5	37.4	6.0
2005	5.7	16.4	36.1	36.5	5.4
2006	5.0	15.1	33.3	41.1	5.5
2007	4.1	15.1	33.9	41.5	5.3
2008	4.2	17.2	34.0	39.6	4.9
Mean	4.9	17.2	33.6	38.6	5.6

	TURKEY IMPORT				
1999	82.5	3.5	10.2	3.7	0.1
2000	73.8	10.2	10.9	5.0	0.1
2001	62.5	18.5	14.0	4.2	0.8
2002	67.2	10.5	15.6	6.6	0.1
2003	61.4	12.7	19.1	5.9	0.8
2004	64.7	10.6	16.0	8.4	0.2
2005	68.3	12.9	13.9	4.9	0.1
2006	71.5	10.1	12.5	5.8	0.1
2007	75.5	10.5	11.0	2.9	0.0
2008	76.0	14.0	6.2	3.7	0.0
Mean	72.4	11.7	11.1	4.6	0.1

*Data obtained from Comtrade.

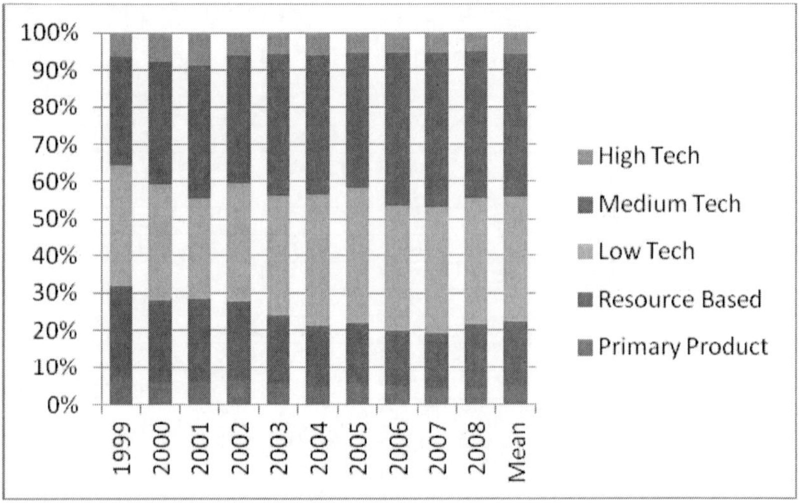

Figure 1. Composition of Trade from Turkey towards Central Asia

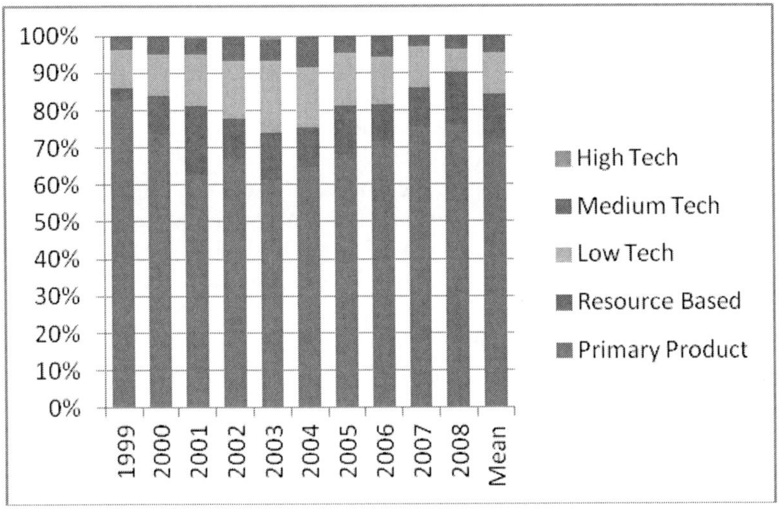

Figure 2. Composition of Trade from Central Asia towards Turkey

Conclusion

Results of the study aiming to review the size and characteristics of trade between Turkey and Central Asia may be evaluated under three main titles. First of all, generally considering the volume of international trade between Turkey and Central Asian countries, mutual proportional shares and results of their changes, trade between Turkey and Central Asia for the concerned period maintains a balanced increasing progress, yet the relative importance of the trade partners against each other was not equal. The share of Central Asian countries in the total imports of Turkey was 2.19% in 2008, and the share of Turkey in the total imports of these countries was 6%. This indicates that Turkey holds importance about 3 times more than Central Asia as a supply market. Although this inequality decreased at a certain level from 1999 until 2008, it is considered as a hindrance against the development of the commercial relation in a sustainable manner.

Secondly, considering the structural change of exports of Turkey to Central Asia from the technological concentration perspective, the resource based product group contracted by 7.2% from the beginning until the end of the period 1999-2008, yet the medium technology group increased by 10.5%. On the other hand, it is interesting that the proportional weight of primary products among others supplied by Central Asian countries to the Turkish market decreased by 6.5%, and the resource based product group increased by 10.5%. In general terms, while Turkey improved its expertise in the medium technology field and developed a competitive power against Central Asia, Central Asian countries increased their competitive power in the resource based product group against Turkey.

Thirdly, one of the most interesting results on the primary product group of the analyses conducted based on the classification of the international trade products in terms of technological concentration, is the substantial share in imports of Turkey. In a technology based comparison on the structure of international trade, as raw material products do not have a significant importance, findings on raw material trade flows should be evaluated in other studies. However, it can be concluded at this point that trade between Turkey and Central Asia is partially similar to the structure of trade between developed countries and developing countries.

Although capital, scale, and skill factors in production of effort intensive and simple resource based products provide an advantage, as the important thing is the presence of raw material, the factors affecting competition here would be the process technology used in the preparation of the natural resource, as well as its presence and transportation costs. Therefore, it can be stated that competition advantage in products in this group is identified by external factors. At this point, trade between Turkey and other countries is identified by geographical locations.

Low technology products, textile, clothing, soil based products and simple commodities are stable and have a character with a high level of worldwide spread. As the necessary capital for production in this technology group is generally low, the cost determinant factor is the price of the labour force. Naturally, the most important element in competition on price differentiation basis is the general level of prices. As these markets generally have low preventions against market entry, profitability levels of players are maintained at low levels on purpose. It can be observed that the industry group is effective on brand and design factors on profitability level (Lall, 2000). While a substantial amount of Turkish exports in the low technology group can be construed as controlling prices under pressure to have a sustainable competition advantage, it should rather focus on other elements such as brand design. The most exported product in this field, rug-carpet, confirms that the design factor is used by Turkish manufacturers. However, it should be kept in mind that Turkey can always encounter new rivals in the low technology product markets. The best strategy to follow at this point would be to supply resources for cost cutting innovations instead of counting on price advantage to provide competition power in price, and to make investments in the brand and design duo. Nevertheless, the most important thing in the end is to develop the sector towards medium and high technology.

Another important export product group of Turkey is the medium technology products. The medium technology group acts as the heart of the industry in mature economies and needs complicated production management (Lall, 2000). A trained labour force and serious economic resources are needed in this technology group for intensive research and development activities and a long learning process. It embodies certain market entry hindrances and important profit potential at the same time. Sometimes intensive effort production can be in question in the medium technology group, but it is hard for production to reach world standards and play a leading role this way, so it cannot reach significant levels in the economy of the country. Turkey makes a substantial amount of its exports in this group as white household goods. However, considering the low value added and high transportation cost of this group, it creates a negative condition in terms of exports profitability. Development of Turkey in the medium technology group would allow the technological infrastructure to convey itself to the production of high technology products.

High technology products constitute a rapidly changing technology group in which research and development costs are very high. A complex technological infrastructure, high level of technical skill, and a national innovation system that provides and plans close interaction among companies and between companies, universities, and research institutes, are required for production in this group. Moreover, effort intensive product may be required in the final montage of certain products, such as electronics, and production of output in low cost production areas with a high level of weighted rates provides economic saving. Such products, for creating different production costs, lead the international integration system due to differentiation in the production process. High technology products apart from electronics (aircraft, sensitive devices, pharmaceutical equipment) last in economies with a high level of skill and technology, and a wide supplier network (Lall, 2000). At this point, it should be analysed in detail what Turkey exports as high technology products. The biggest export items of Turkey in this group are telecommunication devices. However comparative analyses also covering the sub-groups are required for accurate findings in this concern.

References

Ağcakaya, 2009. "Geçiş Ekonomilerinden Orta Asya Türk Cumhuriyetleri'nde Bütçe Yönetimi Ve Mali Disiplin Sorunu" *Akademik Bakış*, 16

Akdiş, 1999. "Orta Asya Türk Cumhuriyetleri İle Ekonomik Sosyal Kültürel İlişkiler-Bölgeye Yabancı İlgisi Ve Beklentiler" Dış Ticaret Dergisi, 14/4.

Akmeşe ve Çetin, 2009. "2008 Dünya Ekonomik Krizinin Türkiye Ekonomisi Ve Türk-Azeri Ekonomik İlişkileri Üzerindeki Etkileri" *Journal of Azerbaijani Studies,* 12, p 55

Archibugil ve Michie, 1998. "Technical Change, Growth and Trade: New Departures in Institutional Economics" *Journal of Economic Survey,* 12, no 3

Ardor, 2006. "Türk Cumhuriyetlerinin Bölge Ekonomisiyle Bütünleşmesi", *Gazi Üniversitesi İ.İ.B.F. Dergis,* 8/2 sf. 35-52

Asian Development Bank, 2006. " Central Asia, Increasing Gains from Trade Through Regional Cooperation in Trade Policy, Transport, and Customs Transit"

Bal, 2003. "Uluslararası Ticaret ve Geçiş Ekonomileri: Kyrgyzstan Örneği" *Sosyal Bilimler Dergisi,* 7, sf.137-162

Hatipağaoğlu, 2002. "Merkezi Planlamanın Çöküşünden Dönüşüme: Kyrgyzstan'da Ne Oldu", *DTM Dergisi*, 1

Havrylyshyn and Wolf, 1999. Determinants of Growth in Transition Countries", *Finance and Development*, 36, no 2,

Kılıç, 2009. "Türkiye, Türk Dünyası İlişkileri: 1991-2009", Uluslarası Stratejik Araştırmalar Kurum,

Krumm, 2007. "Central Asia The Struggle for Power, Energy and Human Rights" *Friedrich-Ebert-Stiftung*

Lall, 2000. "The Technological Structure and Performance of Developing Country Manufactured Exports, 1985-98" *Oxford Development Studies, 28,*

Pavitt, 1984. "Sectoral Patterns of Technical Change: Towards A Taxonomy And A Theory", *Research Policy",* 13, p. 343–373.

Pomfret, 2005. "Trade Policies in Central Asia after EU Enlargement and before Russian WTO Accession: Regionalism and Integration into The World Economy", *Economic Systems,* 29, p 32–58

Ramazanoğlu and Acar, 2005 "Bir Geçiş Ekonomisi Örneği Olarak Kyrgyzstan: Siyasi, Ekonomik Ve Toplumsal Yanaşımlar", *Review Of Social, Economic & Business Studies,* 7/8, sf 385-402

Solak, 2003. "Türkiye Orta Asya Cumhuriyetleri Dış Tcaret İlişkilerinin Gelişimi", *Marmara Üniversitesi İ.İ.B.F Dergisi*, 18/1

Srholec, 2006. "High-Tech Exports From Developing Countries: A Symptom Of Technology Spurts Or Statistical İllusion?" 143, issue 2, p 227–255,

Star, 2004. "Central Asia in The Global Economy" *Asian Development Bank*

Wang, 1996. "Integrating Transition Economies into the Global Economy", *Finance Development*, 33, no 3, p19–22.

Ministry of Foreign Affairs of the Republic of Turkey Turkey´s Relations With Central Asian Republics http://www.mfa.gov.tr

Gömeç, 2007, "An Evaluation About The Turkey And Turkish Republics Relations" *The Journal Of International Social Research*, 1/1 Fall 2007

Taşağıl, 2004, Türkiye'nin Orta Asya Türk Cumhuriyetleri ile İlişkilerinin Dünü, Bugünü ve Yarını, *Stratejik Araştırmalar Dergisi,* Yıl: 2,: 3, Şubat 2004. Prof. Dr. Ahmet

INTRA-INDUSTRY TRADE BETWEEN TURKEY AND THE CENTRAL ASIAN COUNTRIES

DR. MURAT OZAN BAŞKOL[1]

International trade theory analyses the reasons for trade between primary and manufactured goods. However, a significant portion of trade, especially between industrialized countries, is in the form of two-way trade in products belonging to the same industry, namely, intra-industry trade. A study carried out by the OECD shows that the share of intra-industry trade within total manufactured goods was 77% in France, 76.2% in Canada, 73.7% in England, and 68.5% in the USA (OECD, 2002).

The aim of this study is to examine the intra-industry trade between Turkey and the Central Asian countries. The period 1992-2009 will be analysed using the Grubel-Lloyd index at the level of SITC 3-digit trade data obtained from the Turkish Statistical Institute (TURKSTAT) database.

Intra-industry Trade and its Measurement

Intra-industry trade is the simultaneous export and import of goods belonging to the same industry. The phenomenon of intra-industry trade has received increasing attention since Verdoorn (1960) and Balassa (1966) found evidence of increasing intra-industry trade following the customs union formation in Europe (Lee and Lee, 1993). Since then, theoretical and empirical interest in intra-industry trade has grown. While one group of economists developed theoretical models for intra-industry trade, a second group concentrated on the measurement and empirical determinants of intra-industry trade.

Grubel and Lloyd (1975) provide a theoretical view on intra-industry trade and also develop a measurement method of intra-industry trade. The theoretical literature on intra-industry trade was developed rapidly in the late 1970s by the contributions of A. Dixit and J. Stiglitz and K. Lancester.

---

[1] Uludağ University, Bursa, Turkey

For a comprehensive survey of the literature on intra-industry trade, see Greenaway and Milner (1986, 1987) and Greenaway (1987). These studies offered insights into alternative ways of handling preference for diversity, called *love of variety*, and scale economies in a general equilibrium framework and were applied to an open economy setting by P. Krugman and K. Lancester, respectively.

For the measurement of intra-industry trade, the body of empirical research uses the index proposed by Grubel and Lloyd, which calculates intra-industry trade as a fraction of a country's total international trade. The Grubel-Lloyd (G-L) index is formulated as:

$$B_j = \frac{X_j + M_j - \left|X_j - M_j\right|}{X_j + M_j} \times 100$$

Here X_j and M_j represent the exports and imports of the same industry j, respectively. B_j is the intra-industry trade index for industry j with a value between 0 and 100. B_j is equal to 100 if all trade in industry j is intra-industry trade, i.e. $X_j = M_j$, and it is equal to 0 if all trade in industry j is inter-industry trade, i.e. either $X_j = 0$ or $M_j = 0$.

To obtain the average level of intra-industry trade for a country, Grubel and Lloyd proposed calculating a weighted average, using as weights the relative size of exports plus imports of each industry in the total value of exports plus imports of the set of n industries (Grubel and Lloyd, 1975). The formula is:

$$\bar{B}_j = \frac{\sum_{j=1}^{n}\left(X_j + M_j\right) - \sum_{j=1}^{n}\left|X_j - M_j\right|}{\sum_{j=1}^{n}\left(X_j + M_j\right)}$$

The most important issue observed in the measurement of intra-industry trade regards the choice of the aggregation level. Categorical aggregation exists when international trade data indicate the simultaneous export and import by a single country of goods with different production functions (Gray, 1979). J. M. Finger (1975), R. Lipsey (1976), and Paul B. W. Rayment (1976) argue that almost all measured intra-industry trade is purely a statistical artefact brought about by "categorical aggregation". According to them, at an extremely fine level of disaggregation, there will be no intra-industry trade.

The aggregation level ranges from one to five depending on the number of stages based on product classification, where the highest aggregation level is a 1-digit and the lowest aggregation level is a 5-digit aggregation. The reduction in the number of stages in product classification causes an increase in the aggregation level, and increasing the number of stages in product classification causes a decrease. If the chemical industry (SITC 5) is defined as 2-digit, it is possible to make an analysis for 7 sub-sectors, whereas if it is defined as 3-digit, it is possible to make an analysis for 33 sub-sectors. If intra-industry trade is calculated with 2-digit trade statistics, G-L index value would be higher than it should be. For this reason, in calculating the G-L index, the basic issue is the choice of the aggregation level at which the study is conducted.

Structure of International Trade between Turkey and the Central Asian Countries

The volume of international trade between Turkey and the Central Asian countries has been increasing. While the volume of international trade between Turkey and the Central Asian countries was 274.6 million USD in 1992, it reached 6.3 billion USD in 2009. Despite this increase, the share of these countries in total exports and total imports is still small. In 1992, the share of the Central Asian countries in Turkey's total exports was 1.3% in 1992, rising to 3.3% in 2009. The share of these countries in Turkey's total imports rose from 0.4% in 1992 to 2.0% in 2009.

Table 2 and Table 3 present the sectoral distribution of exports and imports between Turkey and the Central Asian countries. In this distribution, manufactured goods (6), and machinery and transport equipment (7), are the main exports, whereas mineral fuels (2), lubricants (3), and manufactured goods (6), are the main imports. The share of manufactured goods in total exports rose from 4% in 1992 to 32.3% in 2009. The export share of the machinery and transport equipment sector was 27.8% in 2009.

The share of manufactured goods Turkey imports from the Central Asian countries has been increasing (14.7% in 1992, 40.4% in 2009). The share of mineral fuels, lubricants, and related materials, and of manufactured goods classified as material in total import is 50.3% and 38.5% in 2009, respectively.

Table 1: Turkey's International trade with the Central Asian countries (million USD)

	Export				Import			
	0-4	5-8	Total	%	0-4	5-8	Total	%
1992	117.8	67.6	185.4	1,3	76.2	13.0	89.2	0,4
1993	165.9	284.5	450.4	2,9	149.5	40.4	189.9	0,6
1994	110.6	318.9	429.5	2,4	155.9	33.7	189.6	0,8
1995	203.3	341.8	545.1	2,5	190.4	96.8	287.2	0,8
1996	267.1	480.1	747.3	3,2	181.4	122.6	304.0	0,7
1997	271.7	636.1	907.8	3,5	193.5	205.9	399.4	0,8
1998	224.0	610.9	834.9	3,1	229.9	219.0	448.9	1,0
1999	147.6	426.0	573.6	2,2	284.3	172.9	457.2	1,1
2000	126.7	445.7	572.4	2,1	393.0	235.0	628.0	1,2
2001	116.8	440.4	557.3	1,8	154.3	128.1	282.5	0,7
2002	111.1	508.2	619.3	1,7	211.0	256.7	467.7	0,9
2003	121.1	777.9	899.1	1,9	274.9	348.3	623.3	0,9
2004	143.2	1.051.0	1194.3	1,9	365.7	579.8	945.6	1,0
2005	165.5	1.243.7	1409.2	1,9	463.4	804.0	1267.4	1,1
2006	190.4	1791.2	1981.6	2,3	582.9	1384.4	1967.4	1,4
2007	238.3	2636.1	2874.5	2,7	1009.8	1659.4	2669.2	1,6
2008	314.8	3434.6	3749.4	2,8	2391.6	1886.8	4278.5	2,1
2009	283.0	3114.0	3397.0	3,3	1708.0	1165.0	2.874.0	2,0

Table 2: Sectoral distribution of exports of Turkey to the Central Asian countries (%)

	0	1	2	3	4	**0-4**	5	6	7	8	**5-8**
1992	60.0	1.0	0	0	3.0	**64.0**	8.0	4.0	17.0	7.0	**36.0**
1993	35.0	1.0	0.2	0.5	0.9	**37.6**	11.4	7.0	31.0	13.0	**62.4**
1994	21.0	2.0	0	1.0	2.0	**26.0**	8.0	15.0	29.0	22.0	**74.0**
1995	31.0	3.0	0.2	0.2	2.1	**36.5**	8.4	17.4	17.9	19.6	**63.5**
1996	28.0	4.0	0	2.0	2.0	**36.0**	10.0	21.0	21.0	12.0	**64.0**
1997	24.0	2.0	1.0	1.0	2.0	**30.0**	11.0	27.0	22.0	10.0	**70.0**
1998	20.0	2.0	1.0	2.0	2.0	**27.0**	12.0	25.0	25.0	11.0	**73.0**
1999	20.0	1.0	0	2.0	1.0	**24.0**	12.0	26.0	22.0	16.0	**76.0**
2000	15.0	1.0	1.0	4.0	1.0	**22.0**	14.0	28.0	23.0	13.0	**78.0**
2001	15.0	0.2	1.1	4.1	0.1	**20.5**	14.3	27.0	27.5	10.7	**79.5**
2002	13.0	0.3	1.3	3.0	0.3	**17.9**	16.1	32.0	21.8	12.2	**82.1**
2003	10.0	0.3	1.1	2.0	0.1	**13.5**	14.3	30.8	26.5	14.9	**86.5**
2004	9.0	0.6	1.1	1.2	0.1	**12.0**	13.8	32.7	26.4	15.1	**88.0**
2005	8.0	1.0	1.0	2.0	0	**12.0**	15.6	31.1	24.3	17.0	**88.0**
2006	7.0	0.6	1.1	1.2	0.1	**10.0**	14.0	30.2	30.1	15.7	**90.0**
2007	6.0	0.4	0.9	1.0	0.1	**8.4**	13.1	30.4	32.5	15.6	**91.6**
2008	6.0	0.3	0.9	1.4	0	**8.6**	13.2	34.2	29.1	15.0	**91.4**
2009	6.0	0.3	1.4	1.0	0	**8.7**	15.0	32.3	27.8	16.2	**91.3**

Table 3: Sectoral distribution of imports of Turkey from the Central Asian countries (%)

	0	1	2	3	4	**0-4**	5	6	7	8	**5-8**
1992	0.3	0	82.6	1.7	0.7	**85.3**	1.3	12.8	0.5	0	**14.7**
1993	2.0	0	72.0	4.0	0	**78.0**	4.5	17.0	0.3	0.2	**22.0**
1994	1.0	0	81.0	0	0	**82.0**	4.0	14.0	0	0	**18.0**
1995	1.0	0	65.6	0	0	**66.6**	2.0	31.0	0.3	0.1	**33.4**
1996	0	0	57.8	1.5	0	**59.3**	3.2	36.5	0.6	0.4	**40.7**
1997	0.2	0	46.4	1.7	0.2	**48.5**	3.0	47.3	1.0	0.2	**51.5**
1998	3.0	0	33.0	15.0	0	**51.0**	2.0	46.0	1.0	0.1	**49.0**
1999	1.0	0	20.0	41.0	0	**62.0**	2.0	35.0	1.0	0	**38.0**
2000	3.0	0	24.0	35.0	0	**62.0**	1.0	36.0	1.0	0	**38.0**
2001	4.0	0	33.0	18.0	0	**55.0**	1.0	40.0	3.0	1.0	**45.0**
2002	10	0	20.0	15.0	0	**45.0**	6.0	48.0	1.0	0	**55.0**
2003	15	0	12.0	18.0	0	**45.0**	5.0	48.0	1.0	1.1	**55.0**
2004	5.0	0	12.3	21.3	0	**38.6**	7.0	53.4	0.6	0.4	**61.4**
2005	3.0	0	6.3	27.2	0	**36.5**	4.6	58.2	0.3	0.4	**63.5**
2006	3.0	0.6	7.5	18.7	0	**29.8**	3.4	65.9	0.3	0.6	**70.2**
2007	9.0	0	6.6	22.2	0	**37.8**	2.3	59.4	0.2	0.3	**62.2**
2008	12	0	3.4	40.6	0	**56.0**	2.8	41.0	0.1	0.1	**44.0**
2009	4.0	0.2	5.1	50.3	0	**59.6**	1.6	38.5	0.2	0.1	**40.4**

Share of Intra-industry Trade in Turkey's International Trade

Despite the increasing number of studies on intra-industry trade in Turkey in recent years, there is still need of further research that examines the intra-industry trade of Turkey. Doğaner-Gönel (2001a), Lohrman (2002), Erlat and Erlat (2003), Koçyiğit and Şen (2007), and Başkol (2009) calculated the share of intra-industry trade in Turkey's total trade. The studies by Doğaner-Gönel (2001b) and Kaya and G. Atış (2007) are exemplary of studies that examine Turkey's intra-industry trade at the sectoral level. Table 4 presents some selected studies on intra-industry trade of Turkey. In addition, the following studies could also be examined: Schüler (1995), Kösekahyaoğlu (2002), Çepni ve Köse (2003) and Türkcan (2005).

Table 4: Selected studies on intra-industry trade of Turkey

Authors	Period, Measurement, Aggregation Level	Country Groups	Main results
Gönel (2001a)	1992-1997, G-L, Adjusted G-L and Aquino Index SITC 2 digit	EU & Central Asian economies	Share of Turkey's intra-industry trade with Central Asian economies is relative low when compared to EU
Gönel (2001b)	1990-1997,G-L Index and MIIT Index, Textile Industry (SITC 3 digit)	World	Rising intra-industry trade in the textile industry due to trade liberalization and the formation of the customs union with the EU
Lohrman (2002)	1991;1995;1999, G-L Index, MIIT, HIIT and VIIT measures, SITC 3 digit, industries 5 to 8	EU	GL index shows an increase in intra-industry trade during the 1990s for Turkey vis-`a-vis the EU
Erlat and Erlat (2003)	1969-1999, G-L Index, MIIT, SITC 3 digit	World	Although the share of intra-industry trade has increased post-1980 period, Turkey's international trade structure still has inter-industry nature
Kaya and Gacaner Atış (2007)	1990-2005, G-L Index, MIIT, Chemical Industry (SITC 5 digit)	EU, Russia, Ukraine and China	Although the share of intra-industry trade of the chemical sector has increased, Turkey's trade in the chemical sector still has inter-industry nature.
Koçyiğit and Şen (2007)	1992-2005, G-L and Adjusted G-L Index (SITC 2 digit)	EU	Turkey's trade with the EU also becoming in nature intra-industry trade
Başkol (2009)	1969-2009, G-L Index SITC 3 digit, industries 5 to 8	World	Although the share of intra-industry trade has increased, Turkey's international trade structure still is inter-industry nature. Intra-industry trade is important in manufactured goods as well as machinery and transport equipment sectors

As seen in Table 4, the research by Gönel is important for our purposes as it analyses the intra-industry trade between Turkey and Central Asia. They note that the share of Turkey's intra-industry trade with Central Asian countries is much lower compared to the EU. The G-L index value for the Central Asian countries is calculated as 3.3% in 1992 and 6.3% in 1997, while for the European Union it is 26.9% in 1992 and 27.2% in 1997 (Gönel, 2001b).

Table 5: Intra-Industry Index Values for Turkey's Trade with the World

1992	26.9
1993	25.6
1994	28.5
1995	28.1
1996	29.6
1997	30.4
1998	32.6
1999	36
2000	33.5
2001	38.2
2002	34.6
2003	36.6
2004	38.5
2005	39.7
2006	39.4
2007	40.6
2008	41.7
2009	42.1

The intra-industry trade index for Turkey reached 42.1% in 2009, which was 26.9% in 1992 (Table 5). Although the share of intra-industry trade has increased, it could be stated that Turkey's international trade structure is still of inter-industry nature.

The extent of intra-industry trade is typically much higher in manufactured goods because these products are more likely to benefit from larger economies of scale in production (OECD, 2002). Turkey's G-L index at the sectoral level demonstrates that intra-industry trade is significant in manufactured goods, as well as machinery and transport equipment sectors. The G-L index of manufactured goods rose from 2.0% in 1969 to 10.5% in 2009 (Başkol, 2009). As seen in Table 6, the share of machinery and transport equipment sectors was 5.6% in 1992, which reached 15.8% in 2009.

Table 6: Sectoral G-L Index for Turkey's International trade (%)

	0	1	2	3	4	**0-4**	5	6	7	8	**5-8**	**0-8**
1992	1.5	0.9	1.3	1.2	1.1	**6.0**	3.3	10.5	5.6	1.5	**20.9**	**26.9**
1993	1.8	0.7	1.5	0.8	0.5	**5.2**	2.6	10.5	5.3	1.9	**20.3**	**25.6**
1994	1.2	0.6	1.5	1.2	0.6	**5.2**	3.2	12.6	5.9	1.7	**23.4**	**28.5**
1995	1.3	0.6	1.4	1.0	0.8	**5.2**	2.7	11.8	6.4	2.0	**22.9**	**28.1**
1996	1.2	0.9	1.6	0.8	0.5	**5.0**	2.5	11.7	7.6	2.8	**24.6**	**29.6**
1997	1.2	1.1	1.4	0.5	0.5	**4.7**	2.5	12.8	7.3	3.0	**25.7**	**30.4**
1998	1.6	0.9	1.4	0.7	0.5	**5.2**	2.7	12.7	8.8	3.2	**27.5**	**32.6**
1999	1.7	0.9	1.4	1.0	0.7	**5.8**	3.0	11.9	12.2	3.1	**30.2**	**36.0**
2000	1.4	0.9	1.2	0.8	0.2	**4.5**	2.7	11.5	11.7	3.1	**28.9**	**33.5**
2001	1.2	0.8	1.3	1.2	0.5	**5.0**	3.3	12.7	13.9	3.2	**33.2**	**38.2**
2002	1.0	0.5	1.2	1.6	0.2	**4.5**	3.1	11.8	11.8	3.4	**30.1**	**34.6**
2003	1.0	0.4	1.2	1.7	0.4	**4.7**	2.9	11.3	12.9	4.8	**31.9**	**36.6**
2004	0.9	0.3	1.1	1.7	0.3	**4.3**	2.8	11.1	17.3	3.0	**34.2**	**38.5**
2005	1.0	0.3	1.0	2.7	0.4	**5.4**	2.7	11.0	16.9	3.3	**34.3**	**39.7**
2006	1.0	0.3	1.1	3.1	0.3	**5.7**	2.9	11.1	15.2	3.6	**33.7**	**39.4**
2007	1.0	0.3	1.0	3.6	0.2	**6.0**	2.9	11.0	15.9	3.9	**34.6**	**40.6**
2008	1.1	0.3	0.8	4.5	0.2	**6.9**	3.1	10.8	14.6	3.9	**34.8**	**41.7**
2009	1.5	0.4	0.9	3.1	0.3	6.1	3.5	10.5	15.8	4.5	**34.4**	**42.1**

Importance of Intra-Industry Trade between Turkey and the Central Asian Countries

This study calculates intra-industry trade between Turkey and the Central Asian countries for the period 1992-2009 by using the G-L index at SITC (Rev 3.) 3-digit international trade data obtained from the TURKSTAT database.

The share of Turkey's intra-industry trade with the Central Asian countries is relatively low, compared to the share with the world (G-L index 42.1% in 2009) and with the EU (G-L index 41.0% in 2009). Although the share of intra-industry trade has increased between Turkey and the Central Asian countries (the G-L Index value of 1.7% in 1992 reached 6.3% in 2009), Turkey's trade with the Central Asian countries has predominantly an inter-industry structure in nature.

Table 7: G-L Index Values for Turkey's Trade with the Central Asian countries

1992	1.7
1993	2.7
1994	4.0
1995	2.1
1996	4.0
1997	3.1
1998	3.0
1999	3.9
2000	4.7
2001	6.2
2002	4.7
2003	7.4
2004	6.7
2005	6.9
2006	6.0
2007	5.3
2008	5.9
2009	6.3

Table 8: Sectoral G-L Index for Turkey's Trade with the Central Asian countries

	0	1	2	3	4	**0-4**	5	6	7	8	**5-8**	**0-8**
1992	0.1	0	0	0	0.5	**0.6**	0.3	0.6	0.2	0	**1.1**	**1.7**
1993	0.5	0	0.1	0.7	0	**1.3**	0.1	1.2	0.1	0	**1.4**	**2.7**
1994	0.7	0	0	0.1	0	**0.8**	0.2	2.9	0.1	0	**3.2**	**4.0**
1995	0.3	0	0	0	0	**0.3**	0.3	1.3	0.2	0	**1.8**	**2.1**
1996	0.2	0	0.1	0.9	0	**1.2**	0.2	2.1	0.3	0.2	**2.8**	**4.0**
1997	0.1	0	0.1	0.3	0	**0.5**	0.1	2.0	0.4	0.1	**2.6**	**3.1**
1998	0.1	0	0.1	0.3	0	**0.5**	0.1	1.8	0.5	0.1	**2.5**	**3.0**
1999	0.2	0	0.1	0.5	0	**0.8**	0.3	2.2	0.6	0	**3.1**	**3.9**
2000	0.7	0	0.1	0.5	0.3	**1.6**	0.1	2.2	0.7	0.1	**3.1**	**4.7**
2001	1.0	0	0.2	0.5	0	**1.7**	0.2	2.1	1.8	0.4	**4.5**	**6.2**
2002	0.5	0	0.1	0.5	0	**1.1**	0.6	2.3	0.5	0.2	**3.6**	**4.7**
2003	0.8	0	0.1	0.6	0	**1.5**	0.7	3.7	0.9	0.6	**5.9**	**7.4**
2004	0.3	0	0	1.8	0	**2.1**	0.7	3.0	0.5	0.4	**4.6**	**6.7**
2005	0.3	0	0.2	1.7	0	**2.2**	0.8	3.3	0.3	0.3	**4.7**	**6.9**
2006	0.5	0	0.1	1.2	0	**1.8**	0.6	2.6	0.4	0.6	**4.2**	**6.0**
2007	0.5	0	0.1	1.0	0	**1.6**	0.8	2.3	0.2	0.4	**3.7**	**5.3**
2008	0.4	0	0.1	1.3	0	**1.8**	0.7	3.1	0.1	0.2	**4.1**	**5.9**
2009	0.7	0	0.1	1.1	0	**1.9**	0.8	3.2	0.2	0.2	**5.9**	**6.3**

The G-L index between Turkey and the Central Asian countries at the sectoral level shows that intra-industry trade of manufactured goods, although not significantly high, is higher than that of primary goods, as expected. The G-L index rose from 1.1% in 1992 to 5.9% in 2009 in manufactured goods. The share of manufactured goods was 0.6% in 1992, and 3.2% in 2009 (Table 8). On the other hand, intra-industry trade is at a negligible level in the sectors of chemicals and related products (SITC 5), machinery and transport equipment (SITC 7) and miscellaneous manufactured articles (SITC 8).

Table 9: Distribution of the GL Index in Turkey's Trade with the Central Asian countries

	GL≥0.75	0.75>GL≥0.50	0.50>GL≥0.25	GL<0.25
1992	5	3	8	165
1993	3	8	5	205
1994	4	5	7	215
1995	3	9	12	210
1996	3	7	12	225
1997	3	6	14	226
1998	5	5	9	235
1999	6	6	14	218
2000	7	5	14	224
2001	8	4	18	208
2002	7	4	14	215
2003	6	9	14	213
2004	4	9	8	224
2005	5	6	14	223
2006	7	7	13	221
2007	6	6	12	224
2008	7	5	11	230
2009	6	3	13	226

The distribution of sectors for each year was classified as the number of sectors that fall into one of the following four intervals: G-L ≥ 0.75; 0.75 > G-L ≥ 0.50; 0,50 > G-L ≥ 0.25; and G-L < 0.25. It is easily noticeable from Table 9 that Turkey's international trade with the Central Asian countries is predominantly of an inter-industry structure in nature. When the sectors with a G-L index lower than 0.25 are considered to be primarily involved in inter-industry trade (Erlat and Erlat, 2003), then their number is almost always greater than 90% each year.

Table 10 presents the sectors with the highest G-L index in Turkey's trade with the Central Asian countries for the sub-periods 1992-1997, 1998-2003, and 2004-2009.

In the sub-period 1992-1997, the highest G-L index is cotton fabrics, woven sector (SITC 531) where the G-L level is 67.8%, followed by aluminium (SITC 684) where the G-L level is 49.2%. In the sub-period 1998-2003, intensive intra-industry trade is observed in knitted or crocheted fabrics (SITC 655), machine tools for working metal, sintered metal carbides or cermets, without removing material (SITC 733), metal salts and peroxy salts, of inorganic acids (SITC 523) and aluminium (SITC 684).

In the sub-period 2004-2009, the highest G-L index is observed in salts and peroxy salts, of inorganic acids (SITC 523) where the G-L level is 65.1%, followed by other plastics, in primary forms (SITC 575), where the G-L level is 63.5%.

In the sub-period 2004-2009, intensive intra-industry trade is observed as well in flat-rolled products of iron or non-alloy steel, clad, plated or coated (SITC 674), knitted or crocheted fabrics (SITC 655), aluminium (SITC 684), and arms and ammunition (SITC 891) sectors.

Table 10: Sectors which have the highest G-L index in Turkey's trade with the Central Asian countries

1992-1997		1998-2003		2004-2009	
SITC	GL Index	SITC	GL Index	SITC	GL Index
652	67.8	655	68.7	523	65.1
684	49.2	733	56.2	575	63.5
611	43.6	523	53.1	674	56.3
651	37.4	684	51.4	655	55.3
574	35.2	891	47.6	684	53.1
654	32.8	674	47.4	891	50.3

Conclusion

The primary finding of this study is that Turkey's international trade with the Central Asian countries is primarily of *inter-industry* nature, despite the increases in intra-industry trade.

The conclusions of this study are summarized as follows:

1. Although the share of intra-industry trade has increased, Turkey's international trade structure is still of inter-industry nature. Intra-industry trade index for Turkey reached 42.1% in 2009, while it was 26.9% in 1992.

2. From Turkey's G-L index at the sectoral level, it is seen that intra-industry trade is important in manufactured goods, as well as machinery and transport equipment sectors.

3. Although the share of intra-industry trade has increased between Turkey and the Central Asian countries (the G-L Index value of 1.7% in 1992 reached 6.3% in 2009), Turkey's trade with the Central Asian countries has a predominantly inter-industry structure.

4. If the sectors with a G-L index lower than 0.25 are considered to be primarily involved in inter-industry trade (Erlat and Erlat, 2003), then their number is almost always greater than 90% each year. This is another indicator that shows that the trade between Turkey and the Central Asian countries is characterized as inter-industrial in nature.

5. In terms of the G-L index between Turkey and the Central Asian countries at the sectoral level, it is seen that the share of manufactured goods rose to 3.2% in 2009 from 0.6% in 1992. Intra-industry trade is at a negligible level in the sectors of chemicals and related products, machinery and transport equipment, and miscellaneous manufactured articles (SITC 8).

References

Başkol, Murat Ozan, 2009. "Türkiye'nin Endüstri-içi Ticaretinin Analizi", Uludağ Üniversitesi İİBF Dergisi, Cilt: 28, Sayı :2

Çepni, Elif and Nezir Köse (2003). "Intra-Industry Trade Patterns of Turkey: A Panel Study", G.U.I.I.B.F. Dergisi V:5 No:3

Erlat Güzin and Haluk Erlat, 2003. "Measuring Intra-Industry Trade and Marginal Intra-Industry Trade", Russian and East European Finance and Trade,Vol:39, No:6

Finger, J. Micheal, 1975. "Trade Overlap and Intra-Industry Trade", Economic Inquiry, V:XIII, No:4

Gönel, Feride Doğaner, 2001a. "Tekstil sektöründe endüstri-içi ticareti" Dış Ticaret Dergisi, Yıl:6, Sayı:21

—. 2001b. "How Important Is Intra-Industry Trade Between Turkey and Its Trading Partners: A Comparison Between the European Union and Central Asia Central Asian economies", Russian and East European Finance and Trade,Vol:37,No:4

Gray, Peter,1979. "Intra-Industry Trade: The Effects of Different Levels of Data Aggregation" içinde Herbert Giersh, On The Economics of Intra-Industry Trade, Tübingen:Mohr

Greenaway, David "The new theories of Intra-Industry Trade" Bulletin of Economic Research, 1987, Vol:39:2

Greenaway, David and Chris Milner, 1986. The Economics of Intra-Industry Trade, Oxford:Basil Blackwell

Greenaway, David and Chris Milner, "Intra-Industry Trade: Current Perspectives and Unresolved Issues", Review of World Economics, 123(1):39-57, March 1987

Grubel Herbert and Peter J.Lloyd, (1975) Intra-Industry Trade: The Theory and Measurement of International Trade in Differentiated Products, London:MacMillan

Kaya, Ayşen Ayten and Aydanur Gacener Atış, 2007. "Türkiye Kimya Sanayi Endüstri-içi Ticaretinin Statik ve Dinamik Analizi: Avrupa Birliði Üye ve Aday Ülkeleri, Rusya Federasyonu,Ukrayna ve Çin", Ege Akademik Bakýþ,V:7(1)

Koçyiğit, Ali and Ali Şen, 2007. "The Extent Of Intra-Industry Trade Between Turkey and The European Union: The Impact Of Customs Union", Journal of Economic and Social Research, Vol. 9, No. 2

Kösekahyaoğlu, Levent (2002), "Does Trade Liberalization Matter?: An Analysis of Intra-Industry Trade for Turkey and the EU", Marmara Journal of European Studies 10(1)

Lee, Hyun-Hoon and Yonng-Youn Lee, 1993. "Intra-Industry Trade in Manufactures: The Case of Korea", Weltwirtschaftliches Archiv, V:129,No:1

Lipsey, Robert E., 1976. "Review of Grubel H.G. and Lloyd P.J. "Intra-Industry Trade (1975)", Journal of International Economics,Vol:6, No:3

Lohrmann, Astrid.-Marina, 2002. "A dynamic analysis of Turkey's trade with the European Union in the 1990s." Russian and East European Finance and Trade,V:38, No:2

OECD, 2002. "Intra-Industry and Intra-Firm Trade and the Internationalisation of Production" OECD Economic Outlook , No:71

Rayment, Paul B.W, 1976. " The Homogeneity of Manufacturing Industries with Respect to factor Intensity: the case of UK", Oxford Bulletin of Economics and Statistics,V:38(3)

Schüler, Martin Kurt (1995) "The Path of Intra-Industry Trade Expansion: The Cases of Spain and Turkey." METU Studies in Development, V:22,No:1,

Türkcan, Kemal (2005), "Determinants of Intra-Industry Trade in Final Goods and Intermediate goods between Turkey and selected OECD countries", Ekonometri ve Istatistik Dergisi, Issue: 1

PART IV:

ECONOMIC INTEGRATION

Perspectives on Kyrgyzstan's and Tajikistan's Membership to Common Economic Space of Belarus, Kazakhstan and Russia

Prof. Jusup Pirimbaev,[1]
Dr. Kamalbek Karymshakov[1]
and Dr. Junus Ganiev[1]

Creation of the Commonwealth of Independent States (CIS) was the starting point for the regional integration process in post USSR space. However, the CIS format was unable to launch effective regional integration process because of the post communist economic reforms, varying paths of political transition, adoption of different trade regimes, and deterioration of the traditional economic links between CIS countries. Search for the viable integration form among CIS countries resulted in several bilateral and regional agreements on trade and economic cooperation.

Thus, Customs Union between Kazakhstan, Belarus and Russia was formed in 1995 with accession of Kyrgyzstan in 1996 and Tajikistan in 1999. But member countries were less effective in implementation of the agreement. Therefore, another agreement on creation of the Eurasian Economic Community (EurAsEC) was signed by Belarus, Kazakhstan, Kyrgyzstan, Russia and Tajikistan and came into force in May 2001. Armenia, Moldova and Ukraine have the status of observers. In 2006, Uzbekistan's accession to the organization was ratified, but Uzbekistan suspended participation in the EurAsEC in 2008. The EurAsEC envisages completion of a free trade zone, creating a unified customs tariff and unified system of non tariff regulations; implementation of customs union; and, then, common economic space. Therefore, it implies eventual economic integration among member countries through free trade, free

[1] Kyrgyzstan-Turkey Manas University, Bishkek, Kyrgyzstan

capital and labour force movement, and forming a common financial market and energy market.

The next stage in economic integration in post-Soviet space became the formation of the EurAsEC Custom Union, resolution of which was adopted by the heads of six Community states at a EurAsEC Interstate Council Meeting in 2007. It was noted that initially the Custom Union would be formed by three countries, Belarus, Kazakhstan and Russia (BKR) and in perspective open for other EurAsEC members as well. The Customs Code came into effect on 6 July 2010. The Custom Union envisages common customs territory, in which goods exchanged in mutual trade are exempt from customs duties. Along with this, parties apply a common external tariff and other unified measures for regulation of goods trading with third countries. The Customs Union Commission is established as a unified regulatory body of the Customs Union. The Commission's resolutions have an obligatory nature. The vote of Russia in the Commission is 57%, while Kazakhstan and Belarus have 21.5% each.

Formation of the Common Economic Space (CES), that started to function on 1 January 2012 and is envisaged to start for fully fledged functioning from July 2012, is the next step for integration of Belarus, Kazakhstan and Russia. Common Economic Space relies on four basic principles: free trade of goods, free trade of services, free movement of capital, and free movement of labour. CES envisages conduction of coordinated macroeconomic policy (fiscal, monetary, finance etc), development of unified transport, energy, and information systems, application of common rules of competition, and uniform rules for subsidizing producers. To ensure efficient functioning of the Customs Union and Common Economic Space, presidents of the three countries on 18 November 2011 signed the Treaty establishing the Eurasian Economic Commission as the single supranational authority of the Customs Union and Common Economic Space.

There have been some other initiatives for regional integration in the post-Soviet space. These include, among others: GUUAM - between Georgia, Ukraine, Uzbekistan, Azerbaijan and Moldova; and Central Asia Cooperation Organization established by four Central Asian countries (Kazakhstan, Kyrgyzstan, Tajikistan and Uzbekistan). Nevertheless, up to now these attempts did not result in a de facto integration processes.

Therefore, the EurAsEC and eventual formation of the Customs Union and the Common Economic Space became a case of effective implementation of regional integration processes in post-Soviet space. The leading role of Belarus, Kazakhstan and Russia, with their potential for industrial production and relatively large total population, represents for other CIS countries potential benefits in becoming a member of this integration process.

From the beginning of the Custom Union, Kyrgyzstan has been considered as the most likely member. Its membership in perspectives is conceived to open membership opportunities for Tajikistan. The question of joining CES in both countries provoked debates on benefits and losses of membership. Given their trade and migration relationship with CES countries, membership is likely to significantly improve their economic performance. Although, if we consider current differences in economic structure then it may cause negative consequences as well.

Importance of CES of Belarus, Kazakhstan and Russia for Kyrgyzstan and Tajikistan

Although after the collapse of the USSR external trade orientation of most of the former USSR countries has considerably changed, the current structure of external trade of Kyrgyzstan and Tajikistan has important ties with the economies of Belarus, Kazakhstan and Russia (BKR). However the significance of BKR for these two countries is beyond the trade dynamics, and includes labour migration issues and investment activities as well.

Trade

Formally the trade regime in both Kyrgyzstan and Tajikistan is liberal; although, Kyrgyzstan is considered more liberal, since it was first among CIS countries to become a WTO member in 1998. Attempts to form free trade within CIS and, eventually, within the EurAsEC were not effectively implemented. However, instead of the multilateral agreements, bilateral trade agreements appeared as the basis for development of trade cooperation among CIS countries. Kyrgyzstan signed bilateral free trade agreements with Russia in 1993, with Armenia in 1994, with Kazakhstan and Moldova in 1995, and with Ukraine and Uzbekistan in 1998. Tajikistan signed bilateral free trade agreements with Russia and Armenia in 1994, with Kyrgyzstan and Uzbekistan in 1996, with Belarus in 1998, and with Ukraine in 2001.

Table 1. Major Merchandise Export and Import Items of Kyrgyzstan in Trade with Belarus, Kazakhstan and Russia

	1996 - 2000	2001- 2005	2006- 2010
Export (in percent of total):			
BKR	35.6	33.4	45.2
excluding export of gold	44.7	46	50.3
Other CIS	19.8	11.3	18.3
ROW	44.6	55.3	36.5
Export to Belarus (in percent of total)	1.5	0.6	0.3
Export to Kazakhstan (in percent of total), of which:	12.2	12.2	16.7
Food and live animals	*17.4*	*18.9*	*27.9*
Mineral fuels, lubricants and related materials	*27.7*	*17.4*	*20.9*
Manufactured goods	*19.2*	*31.4*	*26.2*
Machinery and transport equipment	*16.1*	*12.3*	*9.8*
Export to Russia (in percent of total), of which:	21.9	20.6	28.1
Food and live animals	*24.4*	*13.2*	*31.3*
Crude materials, inedible, except fuels	*9.5*	*27.0*	*10.5*
Manufactured goods	*10.2*	*8.5*	*8.1*
Machinery and transport equipment	*15.3*	*14.5*	*6.8*
Miscellaneous manufactured articles	*5.1*	*10.9*	*32.1*
Import (in percent of total):			
BKR	34.7	46.3	46.9
Other CIS	17.3	11.7	6.7
ROW	48	41.9	46.4
Import from Belarus (in percent of total), of which:	0.9	0.8	1.4
Import from Kazakhstan (in percent of total), of which:	*11.5*	*19.9*	*10.4*
Food and live animals	*17.5*	*16.2*	*34.6*
Beverages and tobacco	*4.0*	*7.6*	*10.3*
Mineral fuels, lubricants and related materials	*52.1*	*51.3*	*22.2*
Import from Russia (in percent of total), of which:	22.3	25.7	35.2
Mineral fuels, lubricants and related materials	*20.9*	*28.1*	*36.7*
Manufactured goods	*23.0*	*24.5*	*10.6*
Commodities and transactions, n.e.s.	*0.0*	*0.0*	*24.1*

Source: UNCTAD

BKR have a significant share in exports of goods from Kyrgyzstan, more than 45% on average (see Table 1). According to export data given in Table 2, BKR are not the major export destination economies for Tajikistan. BKR and other CIS countries together make up just more than 16% of total exports, which seems to suggest that Tajikistan's trade direction is highly oriented to other non-CIS countries. But if one excludes the major items in the export of both Kyrgyzstan and Tajikistan, which are gold and aluminium respectively, then the share of BKR is higher. Among BKR countries, trade performances with Belarus in the case of both Kyrgyzstan and Tajikistan have not yet achieved considerable volumes.

The majority of export items of Kyrgyzstan to economies of BKR consist of agricultural products and manufactured goods. A large portion of exported goods to Russia and Kazakhstan from Kyrgyzstan are fruits and vegetables, cotton, clothing and textile fabrics, meat and milk products, bituminous minerals and electric current. Similarly, the major goods exported from Tajikistan to Russia and Kazakhstan are fruit and vegetables, cotton, and cotton fabrics, wool and electric current. A considerable portion of imports of both of these countries consists of food and mineral fuels. Such composition of export and import of Tajikistan and Kyrgyzstan is quite expected given their economic structure: under the dominance of raw materials in exports and weak manufacturing sector in the economy, agricultural products obtain an important role in the economy. Along with this, absence of large oil resources makes both countries depend heavily on the import of petroleum.

In analysis of trade performance of Kyrgyzstan and Tajikistan, especially of the former, one should take into consideration the scope of informal trade as well. Because of the weak monitoring capacity and corruption in the borders, official statistics underestimate the actual trade volume. Vashakmadze, Kaminski and Mironova (2011) argue that informal trade is an important channel of international trade in Central Asia. They define non-standard trade as being carried out by small traders subject to simplified procedures of imports, or as smuggled and, therefore, difficult to assess. Two groups of products move through this channel: consumer goods imported mainly from China, and locally produced agricultural and industrial foods including clothing. According to their estimation, Kyrgyz exports through non-standard channel are larger than total exports. Moreover, re-exports accounted for more than 80% of non-standard goods. With the same share, economies of the BKR represent destination of export of goods through non-standard trade in 2006-2010. A large share of re-export in Kyrgyzstan is related to the re-export of Chinese goods through Kyrgyzstan to other economies of the region. Kaminski and

Table 2. Major Merchandise Export and Import Items of Tajikistan in Trade with Belarus, Kazakhstan and Russia

	1996-2000	2001-2005	2006-2010
Export (in percent of total):			
BKR	36.3	23.1	9.6
excluding export of aluminium	31.9	26.9	19.8
Other CIS	11.5	8.4	6.1
ROW	52.3	68.6	84.3
Export to Belarus (in percent of total)	0.6	0.3	0.4
Export to Kazakhstan (in percent of total), of which:	2.0	1.1	1.5
Food and live animals	*5.5*	*26.2*	*21.1*
Mineral fuels, lubricants and related materials	*16.8*	*25.0*	*26.4*
Chemicals and related products, n.e.s.	*59.3*	*26.0*	*18.6*
Manufactured goods	*7.0*	*10.9*	*17.0*
Machinery and transport equipment	*9.1*	*9.3*	*12.4*
Export to Russia (in percent of total), of which:	33.7	21.6	7.7
Food and live animals	*23.1*	*26.4*	*32.1*
Crude materials, inedible, except fuels	*9.3*	*21.8*	*27.9*
Manufactured goods	*51.1*	*38.7*	*21.0*
Machinery and transport equipment	*11.1*	*9.9*	*15.1*
Import (in percent of total):			
BKR	29.8	32.0	36.4
Other CIS	41.8	32.3	15.5
ROW	28.4	35.7	48.0
Import from Belarus (in percent of total)	0.9	0.8	1.2
Import from Kazakhstan (in percent of total), of which:	10.8	12.1	9.7
Food and live animals	*57.9*	*46.1*	*47.3*
Mineral fuels, lubricants and related materials	*24.1*	*28.2*	*28.5*
Chemicals and related products, n.e.s.	*10.1*	*7.6*	*6.7*
Import from Russia (in percent of total), of which:	18.1	19.1	25.5
Food and live animals	*10.2*	*9.9*	*11.9*
Crude materials, inedible, except fuels	*12.3*	*12.7*	*16.7*
Mineral fuels, lubricants and related materials	*12.6*	*15.9*	*25.5*
Chemicals and related products, n.e.s.	*19.5*	*17.5*	*10.0*
Manufactured goods	*16.9*	*16.4*	*15.8*
Machinery and transport equipment	*21.3*	*21.2*	*15.1*

Source: UNCTAD

Raballand (2009) show that through bazaars Kyrgyzstan became the window for further Chinese export expansion in the region. An enormous part of the goods imported to Kyrgyzstan from China was unofficially re-exported to other countries.

Therefore the informal trade volume, the scope of which is difficult to estimate, is important for getting knowledge about actual trade flows. Libman and Vinokurov (2010), assessing the regional trade integration among Central Asian countries, use mirror statistics in order to involve the informal trade as well. Results show that inclusion of informal trade in trade indicators increases the level of regionalization in Central Asia and is strongly related to the re-exports of Chinese bazaar goods through Kyrgyzstan. Thus, the large scope of informal trade, dominance of agricultural products, raw materials and some other manufactured goods, such as cotton and textile products, in exports to BKR and prevalence of petroleum in imports from BKR are basic features of the trade relation of these economies. These features suggest that access to BKR markets has important welfare implications for Kyrgyzstan and Tajikistan.

Changes in customs regulation of Russia and Kazakhstan in 2010 showed the importance of the Kyrgyzstan and Tajikistan economy to trade with CES economies. After political upheaval in Kyrgyzstan in April 2010, Kazakhstan closed borders with Kyrgyzstan till the end of May. Along with this, within the Customs Union regulation Kazakhstan tightened administration at the border. Estimations made by Beshimov, Abdykaimov and Sultanalieva (2010) showed that during these two months (April and May) wholesale trade decreased by 30% of market turnover, dairy production reduced by 40%, in the clothing industry informal exporters of garments suffered. These estimations show the extent to which the markets of Kazakhstan and Russia are important for Kyrgyzstan exports. They also state that in a broader sense, functioning of Customs Union did not seriously influence official trade turnover in 2010, but rather its impact on informal trade was significant.

Another fact which shows the sensitivity of Kyrgyzstan and Tajikistan to trade with Russia was Russia's imposition of an export duty for light oil export for Kyrgyzstan and Tajikistan in 2010. However, shortly after, it was cancelled for Kyrgyzstan, and for Tajikistan the rate of duty was slightly decreased in 2011. In Tajikistan it brought about increases in prices of essential consumer goods and services. Thus, in imports of oil both economies depend on Russia and a rise in price of strategic goods is extremely challenging for low income countries with possible social tensions.

Migration

Post-Soviet economic performance of Kyrgyzstan and Tajikistan resulted in large scale unemployment and increasing poverty level. According to the UN statistics for 2010, GDP per capita level in Kyrgyzstan was 862 USD, in Tajikistan 816 USD, whereas in Russia it was 10,351 USD, in Kazakhstan 9,167 USD, and in Belarus 5,702 USD. These consequences, along with growing demand for labour force in Russia and Kazakhstan, served as motivations for migration. Indeed, the CIS countries are interconnected by numerous migration flows and can be characterized by historical ties, geographical proximity, "transparent" borders (visa-free movements), common transport infrastructure, psychological easiness to moving (language, former common territory) etc. (Iwinski, 2008, p.8).

There is no exact data on migrants from Kyrgyzstan and Tajikistan, since most of them stay abroad illegal, especially in Russia. Nevertheless, according to Kyrgyzstan officials, approximately 600,000 migrants work abroad (Murzaeva, 2011). However, according to unofficial evaluations the number of migrants is up to one million. If one relies on official data and uses as the benchmark for the economically active population in Kyrgyzstan of 2.5 million (UNCTAD database), then the share of migrants in the total economically active population of Kyrgyzstan accounts for about 25%. The number of migrants from Tajikistan to Russia in 2011 was more than 740,000 (Devonaev, 2012). If one compares it with the number of the economically active population, 2.8 million (UNCTAD database), then about 28% of them work abroad. And moreover, if to take into account the underestimation issue in migration statistics in these economies, then its actual rate may be higher.

For migrants from both countries, the principal destination is Russia. According to Jones, Black and Skeldon (2007, p.10), the principal destination of Tajik migrants is Russia (83%), followed by Kazakhstan (14%) and Kyrgyzstan (2%). Within the Russian Federation, the most common destination is Moscow. According to unofficial statistics, there might be over one million Tajiks residing in Moscow, although Tajik migration is also quite widely distributed across other parts of Russia.

Most migrants are employed in low skilled sectors. Olimova and Bosc (2003, p.36) identify four main types of labour migration from Tajikistan:

i. *Hired workers*, migrants who are hired by state (or private) enterprises on a permanent basis and under some form of contract (formal or informal)
ii. *Construction workers*, migrants who are engaged in a state-run or private construction enterprise under some form of contract,

normally on a seasonal basis for 9 months of the year from spring until autumn;

iii. *Shuttle traders*, or *shopping tourists*, who earn money by buying goods in one region and selling them in another;

iv. *Agricultural workers*, rural Tajiks migrating to southern Russia and Kyrgyzstan to work on private farms as tenant farmers during the agricultural season.

Kyrgyz migrants are also employed in similar sectors, and the two main sectors of employment are construction (45%) and trade (30.4%) (Sulaimanova 2005, Asian Development Bank 2008).

Table 3 shows that the size of remittances in Kyrgyzstan and Tajikistan is significant for these economies. In 2010 remittances accounted for more than 27% of GDP of Kyrgyzstan, while in Tajikistan it accounted for almost 40% of GDP. Given the possible large volume of transfers in cash and in kind, estimation of the precise volume of remittances is difficult (Jones, Black and Skeldon, 2007, p.10; IMF, 2006, 6). However, the recent tendencies of enlarged banking services on money transfers and reductions in their costs allows us to assume that official estimations based on banking system transactions may approximate the real volume.

Table 3. Migrant workers' remittances to Kyrgyzstan and Tajikistan In percent of GDP (2002-2010)

	2002	2003	2004	2005	2006	2007	2008	2009	2010
Kyrgyzstan	2.29	4.07	8.53	13.09	16.98	18.80	23.98	21.15	27.63
Tajikistan	6.43	9.40	12.14	20.18	36.00	45.46	49.29	35.12	39.97

Source: World Bank, World Development Indicators Database.

Dependence of Kyrgyzstan and Tajikistan on Russia's and, to a lesser extent, on Kazakhstan's labour markets is obvious. These two destination economies are major sources of migrant remittances. With a less developed social insurance system, low income level, and small capacity of domestic labour markets, large scale labour migration and remittances have become conducive to alleviating unemployment and poverty issues in Kyrgyzstan and Tajikistan.

Investment activities

One of the factors for successful economic integration is the bottom-up process driven by private sector actors. Presence of private corporations in different countries contributes to increase in demand for integration process. In Kyrgyzstan and Tajikistan, investment activities of Russia and Kazakhstan account for at least half of the total and have an even higher share during the favourable period for economic growth, while Belarus capital is insignificant (see Table 4 and Table 5). The 2008 global crisis and continuing sluggish tendency in the world economy seems to have a slight negative impact on investment expansion of the CES economies.

Table 4. FDI inflows to Kyrgyzstan

	2005	2006	2007	2008	2009	2010
Total	210.31	335.59	436.82	866.20	660.95	666.09
Russia	8.13	19.79	13.35	36.18	44.91	97.37
Kazakhstan	40.34	136.84	182.71	360.97	213.05	41.32
Belarus	0.59	0.30	0.86	3.34	0.75	0.07
in percent						
Russia	3.87	5.90	3.06	4.18	6.79	14.62
Kazakhstan	19.18	40.78	41.83	41.67	32.23	6.20
Belarus	0.28	0.09	0.20	0.39	0.11	0.01

Source: National Statistical Committee of Kyrgyz Republic

Table 5. FDI inflows to Tajikistan

	2004	2005	2006	2007	2008	2009
Total	22.00	51.70	385.20	388.40	716.70	76.90
Russia	0.30	2.80	231.70	160.20	566.80	18.50
Kazakhstan	0.00	0.00	2.40	10.90	36.20	26.00
in percent						
Russia	1.36	5.42	60.15	41.25	79.08	24.06
Kazakhstan	0.00	0.00	0.62	2.81	5.05	33.81

Source: National Bank of Tajikistan, 2010.

According to official statistics, Russia and Kazakhstan are important investors in both economies. However, it should be noted that official statistics do not fully reflect the actual foreign investment flow, since offshore schemes and informal channels are important ways of investment in these economies. Although in the two countries the concentration of foreign direct investment (FDI) by their countries of origin is different.

Data on FDI inflow to Kyrgyzstan show that Kazakhstan is the leader in investment activities. In particular, its dominance clearly appeared in 2006-2008 years. The main sectors of Kazakhstan investment in Kyrgyzstan are the banking sector, where the share of Kazakh capital in the Kyrgyz banking sector reaches almost 30%. Along with this, tourism, mining, construction, real estate, cement and slate plants are sectors with participation of Kazakh capital. Also within the recently established Kyrgyzstan-Kazakhstan Joint Investment Fund with authorized capital of 100 million USD, Kazakhstan officials declared their interest in mining, tourism, and light industry sectors.

Russian investments play the leading role in the FDI inflow to Tajikistan. The main sectors of Russian investment in Tajikistan are hydro power, oil and gas, telecommunication and construction. Kazakhstan investments in Tajikistan started to become active in recent years and in forming analogous Joint Investment Fund with Tajikistan showed its intention to expand in this economy.

Development of strategic sectors of Kyrgyzstan and Tajikistan economies such as energy, mining, and infrastructure requires large inflow of foreign capital. But it is a quite difficult task under the unfavourable investment environment conditions. Declaration of Russian and Kazakh officials about their interest to invest in energy sectors, construction of Kambar Ata hydro power in Kyrgyzstan and Rogun hydro power in Tajikistan, mining and other possible projects in manufacturing, gives an opportunity for Kyrgyzstan and Tajikistan officials to accelerate economic growth performance.

Opportunities and Challenges

Membership of Kyrgyzstan and Tajikistan to the integration processes of Belarus, Kazakhstan and Russia has both opportunities and challenges. Evaluation of this perspective is also difficult because of the still ongoing process of integration and possible changes in the future. Necessary administrative and trade regulative changes are not yet complete. Moreover, membership of Russia to the World Trade Organization (WTO), which is expected to be completed in 2012, may bring about amendments to conditions of the CES membership.

Debates on pros and cons of membership underline different arguments as potential benefits, as well as significant welfare losses. Currently, there is no large number of empirical studies forecasting possible positive and negative effects of membership to CES. Although Tumbarello (2005, p.17-18), analysing the welfare implications of implementation of Eurasian Economic Community Customs Union, states that Kazakhstan, Kyrgyzstan and Tajikistan will incur welfare losses, because a decrease in consumer surplus will only partially be offset by tariff revenues, whereas there will be small welfare gains for Belarus and Russia. Results of her simulations on implementation of Customs Union after WTO accession of these countries, except Kyrgyzstan, compared to the first scenario show larger welfare gains for Belarus and Russia, and smaller losses in consumer surplus for Kazakhstan, Kyrgyzstan and Tajikistan. Estimations by Ulgen and Levent (2011) show that with accession of Kyrgyzstan to Customs Union of BKR, trade may increase by 8.8% and employment rate by 2.5%.

Undoubtedly, complete assessment of economic consequences of the integration process in Kyrgyzstan and Tajikistan is a complex task given the difference in social and economic structure of these economies from the CES economies.

Potential benefits of membership

Advantages of free trade: Primary expected positive effect of the CES membership is an opportunity to have access to a large market with more than 170 million people. Free trade within the CES gives an opportunity to increase production of goods and services. This argument is very reasonable if one considers the small domestic market of Kyrgyzstan and Tajikistan. Free trade may be reflected in legalization of the informal trade volume, and moreover an increase of production volume. In particular, this argument is firmly related to agricultural production and textile products, which are important for these economies in terms of export potentials and employment. According to Ulgen and Levent (2011), in the case of Kyrgyzstan membership, trade volume is estimated to increase by 8.8%, and employment by 2.5%. Another advantage is that elimination of import and export duties within the CES allows for non-tax import of petroleum, to which Kyrgyzstan and Tajikistan economies are very sensitive.

New perspectives for FDI inflow: Geographical location, acceptance of common standards of regulative measures over business, common transport networks, and transparency of borders within the CES may have considerable positive influences over FDI attraction. Envisaged adoption of common standards on different aspects over conducting business within the CES will create transparency for foreign investors and will give them opportunity to operate within the CES without barriers. Therefore, accession to the CES of BKR would help Kyrgyzstan and Tajikistan to address the issue of attracting foreign investment, in particular to large and strategic sectors, such as hydro power constructions.

Removal of restrictions on migration: Most of the migrants from Kyrgyzstan and Tajikistan work in Russia illegally. Removal of restrictions would contribute to solving the acute problem of protection of migrants' rights in Russia and in Kazakhstan. Moreover, with free movement of labour, workers would get plenty of opportunities to use their professional skills in a larger labour market and, eventually, this process would alleviate the unemployment problem in Kyrgyzstan and Tajikistan. Use of a common language (Russian), similarity of education systems, and higher rate of wage in Russia and in Kazakhstan may facilitate intensive migration from Kyrgyzstan and Tajikistan to other CES economies.

Administrative efficiency and higher quality standards: Some studies conclude that existence of an external anchor, such as membership to the European Union, for post-Soviet economies facilitates institutional development in these economies, which is one of the important factors for their economic performance. Di Tomasso, Raiser and Weeks (2007); and Drautzburg, Melnykovska and Schweickert (2008) discuss the importance of an external anchor for institutional development in transition economies. Similarly, the CES if not as an anchor, but at least as an organization of integration process, obligates member countries to commit different measures ranging from strengthening border monitoring to standardization of transportation norms. Acceptance of these standards and obligation to implement them and removal of custom control within the CES will be conducive to an increase in transparency and reduction of corrupt behaviour, especially in customs. Since the increase of administrative efficiency is not primary objective of the CES, we can mention it as an indirect positive effect. Additionally, administrative efficiency on borders, and application of common standards on sanitary, veterinary and phytosanitary controls will contribute to achieving international standards of quality.

Challenges

Adjustment to the CES custom regulations: The primary concern of Kyrgyzstan and Tajikistan in membership to the CES is related to the necessary adjustments to custom regulations applied commonly by the CES countries. This regulation policy includes necessary adjustments to the CET line applied by the CES, and other non-tariff regulative measures, including strengthening of border monitoring, anti-dumping and compensatory measures, technical regulation, and sanitary, veterinary and phytosanitary controls.

Currently, adjustment to CET line applied by the CES economies implies an increase of tariffs of both Kyrgyzstan and Tajikistan. The average tariff of the CES is about 10%, while in Tajikistan it is 7.6%

meaning that with the membership to the CES it will increase by 3% (Karimov, 2011). Similarly, for Kyrgyzstan the average tariff is about 5%, which means an increase of tariffs by almost twofold on average. But, if one considers membership of Kyrgyzstan to WTO, then correspondence to the CET line is relatively difficult. It will require a revision by Kyrgyzstan of its WTO commitments. Pavlov (2011, p. 22) shows that 30% of Kyrgyzstan tariffs coincide with CES tariffs, and 21% of tariffs can be equalized to CES tariffs without revision of WTO commitments, whereas 46.8% of tariffs do not coincide. However, he also states that in the case of membership of the CES countries to WTO, a smaller number of tariffs should be changed by Kyrgyzstan. According to some Kyrgyzstan officials, change of tariffs and revision of WTO commitments by Kyrgyzstan may bring about obligatory compensatory payments to other WTO members, which may range from 1 billion to 1.5 billion USD, while some experts argue that within WTO member countries make arrangements through negotiations.

Along with tariff changes, requirement of correspondence to other regulative measures necessitates significant administrative and financial resources for Kyrgyzstan and Tajikistan. Non correspondence to technical standards and other sanitary norms may not guarantee access to the CES market, even under full membership to CES.

Policy implications of increased prices on imported goods: Consequences of tariff increases and strengthening of border monitoring will be reflected on imported goods from non-CIS countries. This may reduce the government's budget income from customs duties. Imports of Kyrgyzstan and Tajikistan goods for basic needs, such as food and textile, and machinery from non-CIS countries, especially from China, are significant from a consumer standpoint. Increasing the price of importing goods will have the potential to considerably decrease consumer surplus and may provoke inflationary pressure, which is undesirable in low income countries because of social and political concerns. Moreover, given the current economic structure of Kyrgyzstan, elimination of re-export of Chinese goods may have a serious negative impact on the employment level reflected in bazaars' trading activities. According to the World Bank (2009, p.12), the share of employment by "Dordoi" (Bishkek, Kyrgyzstan) bazaar in total employment in the region is 8%, while "Korvon" (Dushanbe, Tajikistan) bazaar has a share of employment at 7%. Membership to the CES necessitates change of the re-export nature of Kyrgyzstan economy, which causes at least short term costs in terms of the increased unemployment. Given the importance of the BKR market as re-export destination, the argument on the negative effect of elimination of re-export activities is important even in the case of non-membership to the CES. Therefore, it does not matter whether these two economies, especially Kyrgyzstan, access the CES or not; necessity of increasing export of goods manufactured in domestic market, and not those imported from outside, remains crucial.

Loss of competitiveness: Potential benefits in the form of access to the large market of the CES, opportunity for scale economies, and potential for foreign investment inflow, do not imply an automatic increase of domestic production. Even the case of the protectionist trade policy and acceptance of the common conditions of competition within the CES brings about critical importance of competitiveness of the economy. Although, according to Vashakmadze, Kaminski and Mironova (2011), as long as Belarus, Kazakhstan and Russia do not revoke free trade agreements with the CIS countries, CIS countries will be competitive compared to the non-CIS countries in Custom Unions market. Therefore, even though Kyrgyzstan and Tajikistan are not members of the CES, they gain a certain level of competitiveness compared to non-CIS countries.

For Kyrgyzstan and Tajikistan, liberal trade relations with non-CIS countries are important in terms of the low cost machinery and raw material for manufacturing. For instance, in the clothing industry of Kyrgyzstan, imports from Turkey and China are used as raw materials. In the case of an increase of tariffs, one may assume an increase of costs and hence, textile products becoming uncompetitive in the CES market.

Increase of competitiveness of Kyrgyzstan and Tajikistan requires substantial measures aimed at improving the investment environment. One may include these primary measures in the list: property rights security, combating corruption, decrease of overwhelming government regulations of the private sector, etc. But, development of competitive potentials may require structural measures in sectors of the economy. For instance, the agricultural sector is dominant in the economic structure of Kyrgyzstan and Tajikistan. But this sector has structural issues that may seriously restrain its competitiveness. In both countries processing of agricultural products is underdeveloped, while agriculture in Kyrgyzstan is represented by small size farmers. Therefore, although this sector seems to have potential to expand, given the more developed agricultural product processing industries of the CES economies, it may not be competitive in the CES market.

Conclusions

Integration process of the BKR is not completed yet and perspectives of membership to the CES of BKR for Kyrgyzstan and Tajikistan have both opportunities and challenges. Indeed, the main positive effects are obvious: a large market, increase of FDI inflow, legalization of migration, and employment-generating effects. However, in the short term there might be negative effects in terms of inflationary pressure and loss of employment-generating sectors, even though the recent Kazakhstan experience suggest that countries may, for some period, take different tariff preferences for non-CES trade. Moreover, implementation of these potential benefits depends on the ability of the economies to respond to new conditions. To completely benefit from opportunities, sectors of the economy may need structural changes, including modernization.

Taking into consideration possible negative effects and benefits, the optimal decision for Kyrgyzstan and Tajikistan, in particular for the former, would be joining the CES after its member countries join WTO. In this case, concerns of Kyrgyzstan and Tajikistan about their trade relations with non-CES countries would be mitigated. However, it should be pointed out that the negative effect of the CES on Kyrgyzstan and Tajikistan may occur even in the case of non-membership. One may argue that trade relations of Kyrgyzstan and Tajikistan with the CES countries will not change even in the case of non-membership due to free trade agreements with these countries signed before. Nevertheless, existence of these agreements does not guarantee the application by CES countries of trade restrictions such as veterinary and phytosanitary controls. This concern may also serve as a factor for accession to CES. So the right question for debate would not be "what are the benefits and losses of membership?", but rather "what are the benefits and losses of joining, and their extent in the case of non-membership?".

In evaluation of potential accession of Kyrgyzstan and Tajikistan to the CES, it is important to take into account interdependence of these countries. Without Kyrgyzstan, the membership of Tajikistan seems less likely because of the geographical location. Membership of Uzbekistan in the future would facilitate economic performance of these economies because of geographical location and existing transportation network.

Despite the large economic potentials, heterogeneity of political powers, creation of over state government bodies for the implementation of economic union, and political concerns about national independence after membership may be the major political obstacles towards CES integration.

References

Asian Development Bank, 2008. "Remittances and Poverty in Central Asia and South Caucasus (Kyrgyz Republic)". http://www.edrc.am/WP/Rem&Poverty_in_Central_Asia.pdf, 10/01/12

Beshimov, A., Abdykaimov, O., and Sultanalieva, S., 2010. "Economic consequences of the Customs Union for the Kyrgyz Republic - Phase II" Final Report Prepared for the Ministry of Economic Regulation, November 30.

Devonaev, 2012. Bolee 750 tys. Tadjiskih Trudovyh Migrantov Vyehali v RF v 2011 Godu. http://vecherka.tj/news/bolee-750-ty-s-tadzhikskih-trudovy-h-migrantov-vy-ehali-v-rf-v-2011-godu/

Di Tomasso, M., M. Raiser and M.Weeks., 2007. "Home Grown or Imported? Initial Conditions, External Anchors and the Determinants of Institutional Reform in the Transition Economies", The Economic Journal, 117, 858–881.

Drautzburg, T., I. Melnykovska and R. Schweickert, 2008. "Determinants of Institutional Change in Transition Countries: Does Membership in International Institutions Matter?", Kiel Working Papers 1421.

Iwinski, T., 2008. "Migration and mobility in the Eurasian region, Prospects for the Future", Parliamentary Assembly Council of Europe. http://assembly.coe.int/Documents/WorkingDocs/Doc08/EDOC11747.pdf

Jones, L., Black R. and Skeldon R. (2007). Migration and Poverty Reduction in Tajikistan. Institute for Development Studies, Working Paper C11.
http://www.migrationdrc.org/publications/working_papers/WP-C11.pdf, 10/01/12

Kaminski and Raballand, 2009. Entrepot for Chinese Consumer Goods in Central Asia: The Puzzle of Re-Export through Kyrgyz Bazaars, Eurasian Geography and Economics, 50 (5) pp.581-590.

Karimov, B., "Tadjikistan i Tamojennyi Soyuz: Plyusy i Minusy", http://news.tj/ru/newspaper/article/tadzhikistan-i-tamozhennyi-soyuz-plyusy-i-minusy

Libman and Vinokurov, 2010. "Is It Really Different? Patterns of Regionalisation in the Post-Soviet Central Asia", Frankfurt School Working Paper Series, No 155.

Murzaeva, 2011. "Mintruda Kyrgyzstana: Bol'shinstvo Trudovyh Migrantov-Kyrgyzstantsev na Rodiny Ne Vozvrash'aiutsia", http://www.pr.kg/news/kg/2011/07/08/20388/

National Bank of Tajikistan, 2010. "Otchet o Sostoianii Chastnogo Negarantirovannogo Vneshnogo Dolga I Inostrannyh Investitsiy Respubliki Tadjikistan za 2009 god"

Olimova, S. and Bosc I., 2003. "Labour Migration from Tajikistan", International Organization for Migration. ww.iom.int/.../Tajik_study_oct_03.pdf, 10/01/12

Pavlov, A., 2011. Otsenka Ekonomicheskogo Effekta Prisoedinenia Kyrgyzskoi Respubliki k Tamojennomu Soyuzu. Evraziyskaia Ekonomicheskaia Integratsia, 4 (13), pp. 18-29.

Sulaimanova, S., 2005. "Labor Migration from the Kyrgyz Republic", World Bank, Unpublished Report.

Tumbarello, P., 2005. "Regional Trade Integration and WTO Accession: Which Is the Right Sequencing? An Application to the CIS" IMF Working Paper, May 2005, WP/05/94

Ulgen, F., and Levent, H., 2011. "Ekonomicheskiie Posledstvia Vstupleniia Kyrgyzstana v Tamojennyi Soiuz Belarusi, Kazahstana i Rossii (TSBKR): Analiz Effekta" presented at Vstuplenie Kyrgyzstana v Tamojennyi Soiuz Belarusi, Kazahstana i Rossii: vygody i riski , 23 November, 2011, Bishkek.

Vashakmadze E, Kaminski, B., and Mironova , Y., 2011. "Customs Union Between Belarus, Kazakhstan and Russia: Potential Impact on Kyrgyzstan and Tajikistan", World Bank.

World Bank, 2009. "Bazaars and Trade Integration in CAREC Countries"

STRUCTURAL CHANGES IN THE KYRGYZ ECONOMY

ASST. PROF. TUNCER ÖZDIL[1] AND AINURA TURDALIEVA[1]

Introduction

National economy is the system of established manufacturing process and of economic sectors formed in the development process, with mutual dependence relations with each other. Therefore, one of the main objectives of economic policies in developing countries is implementing structural changes to enhance economic development. Globalization has accelerated structural changes in Kyrgyzstan as well as all over the world. Despite the fact that the concept of economic structure is broad, the structural change explained by the different approaches in the research is important in reflecting different aspects of the country's economic structure and in determining economic plans and policies.

For this purpose, input-output tables prepared by the Kyrgyz National Statistics Committee for the period 2005-2009 were used to examine changes in the structure of economic production by industrial interdependence; changes in production techniques; the intermediate product effectiveness; and total efficiency coefficients, in order to inform about structural changes in the economy and make some contribution to policy and plan-making processes.

This research is based on analysis of 34-sector input-output tables prepared by Kyrgyz National Statistics Committee as a source of data for the years 2005 to 2009. For the study, structural changes were calculated and compared by industrial interdependence with the production techniques, intermediate production usage coefficients on sectoral and macro-level. Thereby, technical results were obtained for the explanation of positive and negative aspects of production in Kyrgyzstan on sector basis, allowing recommendations to be made.

[1] Kyrgyzstan-Turkey Manas University

Structural Change in Input-Output Analysis

Inter-industrial flow of goods and services are multilateral and have a complex structure. For the planning of the national economy, first and foremost, there is need to recognize the structure of the economy and to know the relationship between industries. Input-output analysis, with the help of mathematical and statistical techniques, is a model for examining this inter-industrial relationship. It is the data sum of the specific structural features that defines the economic system and the technique that defines and explains system's behaviour during a specific interval of time (Todaro, 1987). The analysis based on the assumption that any country's economy can be divided between homogeneous or similar goods-producing industries and interactions of these industries with each other and the economy has mathematical expression. The models of input-output analysis are widely used in different areas to analyse the consistency of sectoral planning in order to test foreign trade theories, form human resource planning to regional planning, from structural change to inter-industrial interdependency. The main advantage of the input-output analysis is in its simplicity and possibility to view together the various relations between production, consumption, foreign trade in the whole economy, and also on the sectors level, and to give an opportunity for applicability high techniques.

An important element of the economic structure is the mutual dependencies between sectors resulting in production. There isn't any isolated or dependent sector in the economy; all sectors are interdependent that take place in the production process. Interdependencies between economic sectors are due to purchases of goods and services. This mutual exchange of goods and services is referred to shortly as industrial interdependence (Aydoğuş, 1999). The industrial interdependence occurs in two ways: first, one sector, for its own production, needs and demands intermediate product from the others. This effect is known as a backward linkage. Second, the sector poses its own output as intermediate product to another production sector. This effect is defined as forward linkage. In this context, industrial interdependence analysis made by backward and forward linkages is widely used in determining a key sector and investment priorities in the economy, also in both the inter-industrial production structure and seasonal/country comparison is emerging as an indispensable technique.

In input-output models, production structure comparison generally covers topics such as industrial interdependence, production techniques, and basic intermediate product usage. Particularly, in the comparison of countries, production structure appears to be different geographically, in terms of level of development, and in socio-cultural characteristics. One of the reasons for these differences arises from the principles and from the period of preparation. Undoubtedly, effects of number of sectors and their contents, aggregation, economy-wide inflationary effects caused by theoretical hypothesis of input-output analysis, in seasonal comparison, are thought to be very little or no (Aydoğuş, 1999).

As the main element of production structure, the industrial interdependence comparison is based on the comparison of the sectoral connection effects. This comparison can be made by direct, total forward and backward linkage effects, also a commonly used indicator developed by Santhanam and Patil, the dependency ratio coefficient. The dependency ratio for any *"j"* sector, b_j

$$b_j = \frac{\left[\frac{1}{2}\left(\sum_i x_{ij} + \sum_j x_{ij}\right)\right] / \sum_j x_{ij}}{x_j \big/ \sum_j x_j}$$

This definition of the term is, in the denominator, the *j* sector output to total output rate, in the numerator, the ratio of industry total intermediate product to total uses, the term in the share of intermediate inputs in total intermediate demand of the sector, with the average of the total output produced by the output of the sector, which represents the proportion of total intermediate demand (Aydoğduş, 1999). The bigger the value of this coefficient, the more important the dependence of the economy on this sector. In periodic comparisons, increases and decreases in sectoral dependence coefficients allow the study of changes in dependency during the period.

In input-output analysis, sectoral production techniques in the narrow sense, is represented by the technology (coefficient) matrix columns. In economics, in two different *r* and *s* periods, *j* sector production techniques can be compared as following coefficients:

$$PT_j^{rs} = \frac{\sum_i \left|a_{ij}^r - a_{ij}^s\right|}{(1/2)\sum_i \left(a_{ij}^r + a_{ij}^s\right)}$$

In other words, PT_j^{rs} is defined as the ratio/relation in two periods, the sum of the absolute values of differences of *j* sector input coefficients to the arithmetic average of same coefficients. PT_j^{rs} is pure coefficient and can take values between 0 and 2 (Aydoğduş, 1999). If there is no change between the periods and the technical coefficients have the same meaning, the absolute difference in denominator is equal to 0, in this case, coefficient will be equalled to 0. This means there is no change in the production technology during the period. If technical coefficients have changed thoroughly because of 1/2 in the denominator, the result will be maximum two. This means that there is a lot of change. If the coefficient is close to 0, there will be small change; if coefficient is close to 2, the change will be bigger. Generally, if it is larger than a 0.80 rate, it will be indicated as a large change.

In various periods, degrees of efficiency in intermediate product usage are compared as follows:

$$IU_i^{rs} = \frac{\sum_j a_{ij}^r x_j^s}{\sum_j a_{ij}^s X_j^s}$$

IU_i^{rs} means the degree of similarity of i product in r and s periods, X_j^s is the second or the last period production vector. The term in the numerator means how much an intermediate product in the r period needed for the s period for i good production, the term in the denominator means how much the i is needed as an intermediate product for the same production (production vector) (Aydoğduş, 1999). Here, there is a natural ratio. If the ratio result is equal to 1, it means that there is no difference in intermediate product usage and no change in efficiency of intermediate product usage in the sector during the period. If the ratio result is less than 1, it is interpreted that during the period, intermediate product usage is reduced, and efficiency and productivity of the intermediate product usage is increased in the sector, and vice-versa.

Production techniques comparison in two different periods M and N can be calculated by a more holistic and meaningful indicator, inverse matrices and final demand vectors as follows.

$$T_i^{MN} = \frac{\left(\sum_j r_{ij}^M F_{0j}\right)}{\left(\sum_j r_{ij}^N F_{0j}\right)}$$

Here, the term in the numerator, and indicates the total i good amount in order to meet F_0 final demand vector in M period, the term in the dominator indicates total *i* good amount in order to meet the same demand vector in *N* period (Aydoğduş, 1999). Naturally, if the coefficient is equal to 1, it means there is no change in the total intermediate product usage and absence of any technical progress; if the coefficient is less than 1, it means that the same production is realized due to less use of intermediate product and increased effectiveness in the economy in general; if the coefficient is bigger than 1, it means that for the same demand more intermediate product was needed and ceteris paribus, reduced effectiveness in the current period.

It is natural that the changing in elements of the country's economic structure changes the whole economic structure. Therefore the analysis of given elements are important in economic policy making and implementation.

Structural Change in the Kyrgyzstan Economy during 2005-2009

The analysis of structural change in the Kyrgyzstan economy was made by the use of input-output tables prepared by Kyrgyz National Statistics Committee for the years 2005 and 2009. After obtaining independence in 1991, intersectoral analyses by input-output techniques were initiated in 1994 by the National Statistics Committee. Before the collapse period, as a republic of the Soviet Union, in Kyrgyzstan input-output tables were prepared for the years 1966 and 1972, and it is known that the information obtained from these tables is used in the republic's macroeconomic planning (Koychuev, 1983). However, due to the lack of financial resources after the collapse and broken relations with the other republics, the changes in socio-economic structure of society have emerged as disruptions in this research.

The base table of input-output analysis, reflecting goods and service flow between economic sectors, was made for 1998-2003 and published for the first time only in 2003. The first table prepared for 2003 consisted of 91 sectors. This work was then developed in the joint project supported by the World Bank to further enhance it. Within the bounds of this project, economic sectors scope classification was made according to ISIC product and activity classification, and from 2005 these tables were prepared on a regular basis for each year. The 2009 input-output table is the latest table for the current period.

Our research is based on the identity, in terms and numbers, of the sectors of the input-output table for the years 2005 and 2009. Every table contains 34 sectors and is prepared on current prices. The export is thought of as an element of final demand and a column-vector in II. While imports are not decomposed into competitive or complementary, imports are accepted as competitive imports, and the sectoral imports are placed in the final demand components as a source of supply with the minus (-) value column vector. In the given research, the calculations were made on net values, taking into account the above issues.

Industrial relations in the Kyrgyzstan's economy in 2005-2009 years

To measure the industrial relations of the Kyrgyzstan economy for 2005 and 2009, input-output tables for the years for 2005 and 2009 were used in order to calculate dependency ratio (b_j), and to compare production techniques (Table 1) on the basis of absolute difference of technical coefficients, to calculate total efficiency in the intermediate product usage, and to analyse changes in sectoral intermediate product usage; as well as the inverse matrix by Leontieff and the final demand vectors and their comparisons (Table 2).

Ratio of sectoral dependency and effectiveness of production in the Kyrgyzstan economy

For the economy of Kyrgyzstan in 2005 and 2009 input-output tables were used, as well as a production efficiency coefficient which was calculated with the help of sectoral dependency ratios. Results are shown in Table 1. Sectoral dependency coefficients were calculated on sectoral direct backward and forward linkage effects. If the coefficient is close to zero, it means less sectoral dependence on the economy; if it is bigger than 1, it means that the given sector is dependent upon the economy. The calculated coefficients for the given two periods show how close to each other they are, and how little their dependency is. The calculated dependency coefficients and developments for the years 2005 and 2009 are given in Table 1. In general, dependence coefficients of all sectors except agriculture and relevant industries were quite big. For a better view of the sectoral change in the dependence coefficient during the period, coefficients of 2009 were proportioned to 2005 coefficients. The given ratios of the dependency coefficients were greater than 1, especially in the agricultural sector, consisting of five sub-sectors: 01. agriculture, hunting and forestry, 02. Fishing, 03. Coal, crude petroleum and natural gas, 04. Mining ferrous and non-ferrous metals ores 05. Other mining and quarrying.

The dependence of sectors on the economy has increased during that period. The sectoral dependency increases and there is a ratio bigger than 1 in the manufacturing industry, consisting of 19 sub-sectors: 06. manufacture of food products, beverages and tobacco, 09. manufacture of pulp, paper and paper products; publishing and printing, 10. manufacture of coke, refined petroleum products; manufacture of chemicals, chemical products, rubber and plastic products 11. manufacture of other non-metallic mineral products, 14. manufacture of machinery and equipment, 16. electricity generation, 17. gas fuel mains distribution services, 18. steam and hot water supply, 19 water collection, purification and distribution services. There is a reduction in sectoral dependency in an important part of the service sectors (Table 1).

Input-output analysis of each column shows the sectoral intermediate product usage that could be taken as the production function, defining the technology and production relation in a given sector. Here, production technique coefficients are calculated by proportioning the absolute differences technique coefficients for each sector to the average of coefficients. The coefficient takes a value between 0 and 2. If it is equal to 0, it means the absence of technological change in the given period; the highest level of the coefficient (when equal to 2) shows a greater change in technology. Generally greater than 0.8 is considered to be important. In general, results are found that indicate the absence of technological change in the economy among the production sectors: 2. fishing, 11. manufacture of other non-metallic mineral products, 20. construction, 23. maintenance and repair of motor vehicles, motorcycles and personal, household goods, 26. communication, each having the coefficient close to or above 0.8 (Table 1).

Total efficiency in intermediate product usage in Kyrgyzstan economy

In the input-output analysis approach, the comparison of direct intermediate product usage is made by multiplying the technical coefficient matrix that shows the use of intermediate product per unit production, by the production vector of the compared years, and the obtained results are compared with each other. Intermediate product usage is calculated directly, or for holistic and macro-level comparison by the Leontief inverse matrices and final demand vectors. The result achieved from both methods is expected to be identical. However, intermediate product usage calculated with the help of inverse matrices is more important than the other in finding the total direct and indirect impact. The results obtained are given in Table 2.

Calculation of the total efficient coefficients is based on finding the answer to the question: what would be 2009's sectoral production (here, final demand vector of 2009), if the technology of 2005 was used? In the comparison of the production with the same demands as 2009, the difference between 2005 and 2009 production could be caused by the usage of intermediate product. In the case of a decrease in the sectoral production, it is thought that the final demand is met by little quantity of intermediate product. If production value is larger than previously, it is technically caused by rising of intermediate product usage. But this explanation is not economically rational, and a result is not compatible with theoretical expectations. If technological wear does not occur in the given period of time, it should be investigated. What came first in this case, were the theoretical assumptions of input-output analysis and differences in the development of the table. The reliability of results achieved by input-output tables needed a proper check, and a strong national accounting system and a production recording system should be developed in detail. In addition, there are limiting factors caused by analyses assumptions. These are, briefly, price changes which are not reflected in input-output tables, the lack of the appropriate deflators on sub-sector base, sectors coverage, and the import division into complementary and competitive imports. Of course, all of them are research issues here. But this research does not examine the impact of all limitations that follow from the theoretical assumptions of input-output analysis and economic conditions on the obtained results. It is thought that the results in the tables reflect the most accurate and significant results.

For the period of 2005-2009, sectoral production was calculated by a total productivity approach. Total productivity was achieved from multiplying 2009's final demand vector and 2005's reverse matrix; this was then proportioned with 2009's production, and compared. All results are given in Table 2.

According to Table 2, the ratio results in some sectors are greater than in 1. As noted above, if we do not take into account limitations that follow from the analysis technique and disadvantages that arose from the pricing process, the given ratio explained as intermediate product usage in these sectors increased, and the technology wore off during the period. According to the results, in agriculture and agriculture based industries ratio is greater than 1. In addition, intermediate product usage decreased and increased effectiveness in 5 sub-sectors of agriculture: 01. agriculture, hunting and forestry, 02. Fishing, 03. Coal, crude petroleum and natural gas, 04. Mining ferrous and non-ferrous metals ores 05. Other mining and quarrying.

Intermediate product usage has decreased in manufacturing, consisting of 14 sub-sectors: 06. manufacture of food products, beverages and tobacco, 09. manufacture of pulp, paper and paper products; publishing and printing, 10. manufacture of coke, refined petroleum products; manufacture of chemicals, chemical products, rubber and plastic products, 11. manufacture of other non-metallic mineral products, 14. manufacture of machinery and equipment, 16. electricity generation, 18. steam and hot water supply, 19. water collection, purification and distribution services. In general economy, intermediate product usage has decreased in 19 of 34 sectors in the given period.

Of course, the results obtained here should be treated with caution. As mentioned previously, in the analysis technique used, limitations arose from the table preparation period, sector coverage, price increases, some constraints such as lack of accounting, and recording system, all of which can affect the reliability of the conclusions reached here. However, there are results obtained from analyses of similar studies on economic structure based on the production statistics of the Kyrgyzstani economy, and they are close to the noticed conclusions. In these studies, the industrial production capacity rates fell, the sectoral structure is far from ensuring the efficiency in the 2005-2009 period, and cost increases in industry are stated as the most important problem for the Kyrgyzstan economy. (Экономическая политика социально-экономического развития Кыргызской республики на долгосрочный период до 2025 г.2007; Национальный Статистический Комитет КР. 2010).

Conclusion

The limitations proceeded by the table preparation period and theoretical assumptions from the period have emerged in the structural changes analyses of the Kyrgyzstan economy through the Input-Output tables approach. Also, there were some results encountered that are not compatible with the theoretical expectations. In fact, each of these results can be examined as a separate subject of research. However, this aspect of the subject and their effects on the obtained results are not examined here. Information in the table assumed that the given results reflect accurate and reliable information.

Despite all this, input-output analysis is the mathematical model reflecting the relations of each sector in the economic system. However, in order that the input-output tables give reliable results, a country must have proper and healthy national accounting; and the production recording system should be developed in detail. In addition, there are some limiting factors that followed from the analysis assumptions. These are, briefly: the price changes in the period are not reflected in the tables, the lack of appropriate deflators on a sub-sector basis, sector coverage, and import division on complementary and competing imports. All of these influence the reliability of results obtained with the input-output approach, and allow interesting results for the macroeconomic planning to be achieved.

The general appraisal of the obtained results is that they are compatible with each other. This study analyses different approaches examining structural change on a sector base, and in many sectors the received coefficients are consistent with each other. In other words, effective and non effective sectors are compatible with their coefficients. For example:

05. Other mining and quarrying;

07. Manufacture of textile and textile products, manufacture of leather and leather products,

10. Manufacture of coke, refined petroleum products; manufacture of chemicals, chemical products, rubber and plastic products,

13. Manufacture fabricated metal products,

11. Manufacture of other non-metallic mineral products,

12. Manufacture of basic metal,

21. Wholesale trade,

23. Maintenance and repair of motor vehicles, motorcycles and personal and household goods,

26. Communication,

30. Education,

32. Sewage and refuse disposal, sanitation and similar activities

In these sectors, all coefficients support each other. In other sectors, the difference between the coefficients is not much.

The production techniques comparison was made on the basis of the technical coefficients between the two periods, in 19 sub-sectors of agriculture and manufacturing industries, except for 4 sectors:

02. Fishing;

11. Manufacture of other non-metallic mineral products;

17. Gas fuel mains distribution services,

05. Other mining and quarrying

In these sectors there has been very little change in production techniques. In other words, the calculated coefficients are lower than 0.8 and range from 0.692 to 0.314.

Like other countries in the world economy, Kyrgyzstan is a country undergoing a rapid change. In macroeconomic planning this characteristic must be taken into account. For this reason, input-output tables must be prepared periodically for macroeconomic planning of the Kyrgyzstan economy.

References

Aydoğuş O., Girdi-Çıktı Modellerine Giriş, Gazi Kitabevi Ankara, 1999.

Bocutoğlu, E., Girdi – Çıktı Analizine Giriş, Karadeniz Üniversitesi İktisadi ve İdari Bilimler Fakültesi Ders Notları, Yayın No:23, Trabzon, 1985

Chenery H.B, Clark P.E, Endüstrilerarası İktisat, (Çev. Cemil Çınar), ODTÜ, Ankara, 1965.

Kepenek Y. Türkiye İmalat Sanayiinin Üretim Yapısı (1963-1973), Ankara ODTÜ, 1977.

Kepenek Y., Türk İmalat Sanayiinin Üretim Yapısı, Friedrich Ebert Vakfı Araştırma Sonuçları, İstanbul, 1991.

Korum U., Input Output Analizi, Sevinç Matbaası, Ankara, 1963.

Korum U., Türk İmalat Sanayi ve İthal İkamesi : Bir Değerlendirme, Ankara Üniversitesi Siyasal Bilgiler Fakültesi Yayınları No:408, Ankara,1977.

Koyçuyev T., SSCB Ülkerinde Dengeli Ekonomik Büyüme Özelliklerinin Analizi ve Teorik Problemler, Doktora Tezi, Moskova İktisat Enstitüsü, Moskova-1983.

Miernyk W.H., The Elements of Input Output Analysis, Random House, West Virginia University, 2 Printing, 1966.

Öney E. , İktisadi Planlama, 3. Baskı, A.Ü.S.B.F. Yayın No:526, Ankara, 1983.

Todaro M.P., Kalkınma Planlaması (Modeller ve Yöntemler), (Çev. Orhan Sezgin), İstanbul, 1987.

Национальный статистический комитет КР. Межотраслевой баланс производства и использования товаров и услуг КР за 2005, 2009 гг.

Экономическая политика социально-экономического развития Кыргызской республики на долгосрочный период до 2025 г.: Том I.-Б.: ЦЭС при МЭРиТ КР, 2007, -368 с.

Нацинальный Статистический Комитет КР. Промышленность КР за 2005-2009. Годовая публикация. Бишкек 2010.

Table 1. Industrial relationship and production efficiency (2005-2009)

	Sectors	Industrial relationship (bj)		Ratio (b_{09}/b_{05})	
		2005	**2009**		Produc. Tech.
01	Agriculture, hunting and forestry	3.49	3.54	1.01	0.680
02	Fishing	115,480.68	27,960.96	0.24	1.219
03	Coal, petroleum and natural gas	142.39	214.29	1.50	0.543
04	Mining ferrous and non-ferrous metals ores	2,680.44	1,714.33	0.64	0.475
05	Other mining and quarrying	706.69	995.93	1.41	0.764
06	Manufacture of food products, beverages and tobacco	22.77	26.16	1.15	0.437
07	Manufacture of textile and textile products, manufacture of leather and leather products	80.30	71.10	0.89	0.486
08	Manufacture wood and wood products	1,088.59	703.26	0.65	0.533
09	Manufacture of pulp, paper and paper products; publishing and printing	177.94	233.38	1.31	0.498
10	Manufacture of coke, refined petroleum products; manufacture of chemicals, chemical products, rubber and plastic products	44.16	58.45	1.32	0.645
11	Manufacture of other non-metallic mineral products	39.95	71.53	1.79	0.796
12	Manufacture of basic metals	13.51	9.65	0.71	0.570
13	Manufacture fabricated metal products	244.12	219.80	0.90	0.314
14	Manufacture of machinery and equipment	56.28	105.34	1.87	0.545
15	Other manufacturing	85,243.50	512.02	0.01	0.537
16	Electricity generation	36.50	81.94	2.25	0.692
17	Gas fuel mains distribution services	86.63	281.36	3.25	0.942
18	Steam and hot water supply	179.22	319.20	1.78	0.572
19	Water collection, purification and distribution services	503.31	593.29	1.18	0.605
20	Construction	38.77	14.49	0.37	0.814
21	Wholesale trade	56.68	47.00	0.83	0.596
22	Retail trade	9.36	9.46	1.01	0.619
23	Maintenance and repair of motor vehicles, motorcycles and personal and household goods	57.23	120.85	2.11	0.819
24	Hotels and restaurants	94.28	71.67	0.76	0.569

25	Transport and storage	23.68	24.61	1.04	0.481
26	Communication	31.02	43.72	1.41	0.864
27	Financial intermediation	47.84	38.64	0.81	0.377
28	Real estate, renting and business activities	31.58	26.31	0.83	0.729
29	Public administration and defence; compulsory social security	81.57	29,051.82	356.15	0.597
30	Education	889.47	297.86	0.33	0.627
31	Health and social work	692.09	355.73	0.51	0.744
32	Sewage and refuse disposal, sanitation and similar activities	1,093.04	2,670.99	2.44	1.066
33	Activities of membership organizations; recreational, cultural and sporting activities	327.25	230.50	0.70	1.130
34	Other service activities	10,524.41	302.94	0.03	0.811

Source: Calculated on Input-output tables prepared by the Kyrgyz National Statistics Committee for the period 2005-2009

Table 2. Total efficiency in intermediate product usage (2005-2009)

	Sectors	Efficiency		Ratio (X_{09}/X_{05})
		$X_{2009-09}$	$X_{2005-09}$	
01	Agriculture, hunting and forestry	233,347	121,521	1.92
02	Fishing	26	17	1.55
03	Coal, petroleum and natural gas	6,503	34,596	0.19
04	Mining ferrous and non-ferrous metals ores	443	449	0.99
05	Other mining and quarrying	834	4,370	0.19
06	Manufacture of food products, beverages and tobacco	44,222	46,745	0.95
07	Manufacture of textile and textile products, manufacture of leather and leather products	30,529	20,281	1.51
08	Manufacture wood and wood products	8,863	4,556	1.95
09	Manufacture of pulp, paper and paper products; publishing and printing	6,316	11,733	0.54
10	Manufacture of coke, refined petroleum products; manufacture of chemicals, chemical products, rubber and plastic products	91,871	107,455	0.85
11	Manufacture of other non-metallic mineral products	11,481	23,865	0.48
12	Manufacture of basic metals	64,436	47,420	1.36
13	Manufacture fabricated metal products	9,093	8,733	1.04
14	Manufacture of machinery and equipment	21,860	40,493	0.54

15	Other manufacturing	2,581	1,407	1.83
16	Electricity generation	9,702	20,997	0.46
17	Gas fuel mains distribution services	8,111	7,030	1.15
18	Steam and hot water supply	2,232	3,353	0.67
19	Water collection, purification and distribution services	856	1,116	0.77
20	Construction	47,802	35,143	1.36
21	Wholesale trade	13,336	8,669	1.54
22	Retail trade	67,603	55,300	1.22
23	Maintenance and repair of motor vehicles, motorcycles and personal and household goods	5,296	8,875	0.60
24	Hotels and restaurants	9,784	7,604	1.29
25	Transport and storage	57,667	62,590	0.92
26	Communication	19,953	29,631	0.67
27	Financial intermediation	16,047	23,370	0.69
28	Real estate, renting and business activities	20,845	28,935	0.72
29	Public administration and defence; compulsory social security	22,058	24,365	0.91
30	Education	12,373	12,205	1.01
31	Health and social work	7,931	7,865	1.01
32	Sewage and refuse disposal, sanitation and similar activities	201	517	0.39
33	Activities of membership organizations; recreational, cultural and sporting activities	5,230	5,309	0.99
34	Other service activities	2,280	1,650	1.38

Source: Calculated on Input-output tables prepared by the Kyrgyz National Statistics Committee for the period 2005-2009

EXTERNAL DEPENDENCE OF KAZAKHSTAN ECONOMY

ASST. PROF. DR. TUNCER ÖZDIL,[1]
AINURA TURDALIEVA[1]
AND ZAMIRA OSKONBAEVA[1]

Introduction

In the process of globalization the economy of developed and developing countries is ensuring economic development, and the countries try to be open to outward development. However, the process of opening up for some countries may lead to negative consequences by increasing their external dependency. In this research a trial is carried out to investigate the structure of foreign trade and external dependency of an economy though the input-output analysis approach.

The inverse import matrix will be calculated by using foreign trade flows coefficients, with the help of input-output tables prepared for the period of 2006-2009, and consequently the import quantities necessary to meet final demand and their changes during the period will be examined. According to the results obtained, the potential impact of Kazakhstan's foreign trade structure on both Kyrgyzstan and other Central Asian Turkish Republics will be discussed.

Economy and Foreign Trade of Kazakhstan

Kazakhstan is a Central Asian country with a population of 16.2 million and with rich oil deposits and natural gas. It gained its independence after the collapse of the USSR in the early 1990s. The country's income per capita in 2009 was 7,257 USD. Total exports were 43.196 million USD, while imports were 28.408 million USD. Export-import ratio was 152%. Annual inflation was 6.2%; the foreign debt to GDP ratio with inter-firm debt obligations was 104.1%; without taking

[1] Kyrgyzstan-Turkey Manas University

into account an inter-firm debt obligation the ratio of external debt was 58.8%. In 2009, annual real GDP growth rate was 3.3%. The significant part of the imports of Kazakhstan consists of intermediate and investment goods related to industry. In 2008, total share of imports of consumer goods in the country was 19%, intermediate goods 43.1%, and investment goods 37% (Agency of the Republic of Kazakhstan on Statistics). For the same year, according to the distribution of the imports of goods, automotive and spare parts have the highest share, at 35%, which was followed by the metallurgical industry and products at 26.8%, the chemical industry at 12.1%, and mining at 9.6%. The share of animal product imports and wood forest products belonging to the agricultural sector was 11.4%. Considering the distribution of imports by country groups, in 2008, among the ten countries Russia attracts attention with a share of 13.8%. This list followed up with China, Germany and Ukraine. Turkey, with a share of 1%, ranked eighth among the other ten countries. Considering the geographical distribution of imports by country groups, European countries have a share of 47.1%, CIS countries of 26.2%, and Asian countries of 22.3%.

In 2009, the volume of Russia's imports have a share of 30.3% in total, China 15.9%, Ukraine 9.1%, Germany 7.6%, U.S. 6.1%, Italy 3.8%, United Kingdom 2.3%, and Japan 2.3% (Balance of payment and external debt of Kazakhstan for 2009).

According to the structure of Kazakhstan current foreign trade, a significant portion of the total imports consist of investment and intermediate goods. Imports of raw material cannot even be met by the exports. As a result, an increase that has occurred in the exports has been reflected in imports, and this growth became the question of the external deficit. The current account deficit problem, as well as the rampant imports of raw materials, decreases the volume of domestic producers' production of intermediate goods. As a result, the growth of country export has been reflected in the production and employment process of other countries. Today's condition of the mutual dependence of the world economy, of course, makes the complete elimination of dependence on foreign trade impossible. However, keeping a large portion of the revenue from production at home, as well as further increase in employment, investment and domestic value added by increasing the share of local content of products, requires the withdrawal of this dependence to the lowest possible levels (Ozdil, 2011). For this purpose, it is important to determine the industries that have high effects of forward and backward links, and to ensure the development of these sectors. This is because using industries with high forward link impacts as input to other sectors leads to reduction of dependence on outside sources; on the other hand, having industries with high effects of back-link in need of input from other sectors leads to stimulation and recovery of economy. To rescue sectors from dependency, measures will be determined on a sectoral basis (Ozdil, 2009). This study examines the change in external dependence of Kazakhstan's economy and the potential impact on regional economies.

External Dependency by Input-Output Analysis Approach

Input-Output Analysis is a model which examines the relationships between industries via mathematical and statistical techniques. It could be described as a sum of the data that defines the specific structural features of an economic system and as an analytical technique that could impact and explain the system's behaviour during the specific interval of time (Todaro, 1987). The analysis is based on the division of any country's economy between homogeneous or similar goods-producing industries and on the mathematical expression of these industries' interactions with each other and the economy.

The input-output analysis approach is based on the manufacturing sector. If a particular commodity is being produced by only one sector, outputs of the sectors cannot be substituted with each other. This analysis applies to the economy in terms of the long run equilibrium position (Protect, 1963). The input-output table generated by Leontief considers the production activities only, whereas consumption is considered as a result. In assessing production, the economy is divided into two sections. The first is where production takes place and the latter is where production is used as the final demand. Columns of input-output tables, which are used as a basic estimation method in the sectoral planning of a country, indicate inputs, and rows indicate outputs. In the generated input-output table, the row and column sums are equal to each other. The difference between total production of a sector with an intermediate consumption, is defined as an added value. The sum of final demand of rows is equal to the sum of value added of columns. This shows us the general balance of an input-output table (Kepenek, 1977). As an economic method of analysis in input-output analysis, the product of any industry is considered as a commodity demanded in the final consumption and as an input used in its own production and other industry products. It is a trial to examine interdependence between the various sectors of the economy. For this purpose on the generated inter-industry flow table, sectors are located twice in rows and columns, on the one hand as consuming sectors; on the other hand as producing sectors. Thus, it can be seen how the shared production is being used by the sectors in the economy at a certain period. Rows and columns of the input-output flow table include important information for the sectors. Each columns give definite information about input composition of production of the sector, while the rows give the composition of demand (Miernyk, 1996).

Production of a sector increases, as well as in the final demand, but in addition to this, demand for extra intermediate input stimulates the production of other sectors. Stimulated production sectors are stimulated by the production of other sectors through the intermediate input demand. This cyclical interaction indicates that the initial stimulation has an impact on the entire economy. For these reasons, the effects of backward-link at least take the value 1. The values greater than 1 show the degree of excitation on the additional production (Senesen, 2005).

In an inter-industry flow table the import may take place in two ways, as import-competing or complementary (Chenery, 1965). Complementary imports take place in the 1st quadrant, as used as imported inputs in the production of its own sector. According to different assumptions, the inclusion of exports and imports in the model can be seen in the different approaches. In general, the real exports of goods and services, is assumed only as domestic investment and the consumption demand component of final demand, which are located as a vector column in the 2nd quadrant of the table. Imports may take place in different places according to competing or complementary imports. Complementary imports take place in the 1st quadrant among input coefficients. Competing import is assumed as a foreign source of supply and it could be included into the model based on different approaches. However, it is difficult to make an exact distinction between the complementary and the competing imports, and the followed standard approach is the assumption that the imported goods are fully competitive in the production and in the final use of domestic production. According to this extreme assumption, imports are treated as a fully competitive source of supply and are located as a column vector with minus (-) among final demand components. In this case, all the analysis is done via the net values (Aydoğuş, 1999).

One of the ways of using these tables is to predict the import requirements and the effects of certain changes in final demand on the balance of payments (Thirlwall, 1990). From these tables, the structure of imports and the exchange of intermediate inputs of domestic and international industries with each other can be worked out. For this case it is sensible to use a special import matrix. In this matrix domestic intermediate inputs have been located, as well as imports used by domestic industries. Import matrix as a derived tool, by adding into domestic input-output table, has the function of a different industry (Fleissner, 1993).

Import inverse matrix, which is used to measure an economy's dependence on imports, is one of the supporting techniques derived from the input-output model. Import inverse matrix for any year is obtained by multiplying the input coefficients matrix of import with the inverse matrix of domestic input coefficients. R shows import inverse matrix, $A_{m,}$ import input coefficient matrix, A_d domestic input coefficients matrix. Import inverse matrix indicating the imported inputs flows is shown below:

$$R = A_m (I - A_d)^{-1}$$

(Bocutoğlu, 1990). Below are the column totals of the import inverse matrix:

$$R_j = \sum_{j=1}^{n} r_{,j} (j = 1,2,3,...).$$

R_j shows the sum of import requirements to the outcomes of all industries when final demand for goods of j industry increase by one unit. In other words, it shows the sum of the imported inputs that must be purchased by all industries in order to increase the production of j industry by one unit. An increase in the value of the column totals in a given period of time indicates an increased dependence on imports of the industry in terms of input. The column totals are defined as the industry's backward link on imports.

Row totals of the import inverse matrix, are shown below:

$$R_{,i} = \sum_{i=1}^{n} r_i (i = 1,2,3,...)$$

R_i shows the forward-link effects of import. It shows the need for imported goods of industrial production of i industry to meet the growth in the demand when the final demand for goods of all industries increases by one unit. These totals are forward link effects of imports.

So, with the help of rows and columns inverse matrix by finding direct and indirect imports, this will have achieved the import values created in the sector and economy when final demand for any sector increases by one unit.

Examination of Dependence of Foreign Kazakhstan's Economy by Input-Output Analysis Approach

Due to its natural resources and economic wealth, Kazakhstan has an important place among Turkish republics of Central Asia, as well as the geography where it is situated. Positive or negative developments in the national economy, psychological factors of economic markets, and the multiplier accelerate mechanisms affect all countries of the region. With the impact of globalization, today when economic integration is on the agenda, it is impossible to eliminate dependence. It is important at least to decrease dependency or to know the results of increases in dependency. This study investigates the possible potential effects of external dependency on the economies of Central Asian countries and the economies of the region, by examining the external dependency of Kazakhstan, which is active and has an important role in the region.

Aim of the Study Method and Data Sources

The purpose of this study is to determine import of dependency by direct and indirect effects in inter-industry using intermediate inputs in Kazakhstan, and to investigate the change during the period 2006-2009. Final demand, which is composed of autonomic items that affect the dependency on imports, are excluded from the scope of the study. Also, competing imports are not included in the analysis.

The basic data source used in the study are the input-output tables of Kazakhstan for the period of research, prepared by Kazakhstan Statistics Agency. Input-output tables were published on a regular basis during the post-independence period in Kazakhstan, since 1999 every year except 2001 and 2002. The last published table is from 2009. In the tables for the earlier year 2005 there is flow table no inter–sectoral imported inputs use. The included table was for the first time published in 2005 and later subsequent years. Input-output tables were prepared as a 61-sector table in 2005. From 2006 tables are prepared as 59-sector tables, therefore to ensure homogeneity in terms of number of the sectors in the study table of 2005 has not been analysed. Analysis was carried out using tables for the years 2006, 2008 and 2009.

Industries in which the relative share in total imports and in general economy is very small because of comments and the ease calculation, have been reduced to 50 sectors. According to the notations of International Industrial Sector Classification (ISIC), sector contents were examined. In all the tables, except for the year 2007, the economic production sectors' name, contents and orders were the same. The table of 2007 was excluded from the analysis because the minor differences could make misleading results.

In addition, it was assumed that there are no problems such as impact of inflation and sector contents, which arise from both theoretical assumptions of IO tables and the methods of preparation of the table; because of these problems existing in all of the tables, it was assumed that they have no impact on the results comparisons.

Using the tables prepared for the years 2006, 2008, and 2009, it was calculated that:

- ($\mathbf{A}_d$) domestic technical coefficient matrix with the help domestic inputs uses over 50 sectors
- ($\mathbf{A}_m$) imported intermediate input matrix with the help of inter-sectoral imported intermediate inputs' uses

Through multiplying ($\mathbf{I}$-$\mathbf{A}_d$), obtained by taking the difference of the domestic technical coefficients matrix from the unit matrix, by imported intermediate input matrix ($\mathbf{A}_m$) the value ($\mathbf{R}$) was obtained. By taking the row and column totals of the matrix, the direct and indirect demands in the imported inputs use were obtained, which equals the total effect of the forward and back-link. Results are shown in table 1 and table 2.

Effects of backward links in the imported intermediate input uses of Kazakhstan's Economy

The sum of elements of any column *j* with the import inverse matrix shows the amount of increase in the imported commodities of all industries when final demand for commodities produced in the specified sector increases by one unit. In other words, sectors with high backward link effects, by requiring intermediate inputs from other sectors, stimulate and revive the economy (Ersungur, 2009). Backward link coefficients of imports are calculated for the period of research on Kazakhstan's economy, and the importance order table was obtained by descending the coefficients, which shows relative position of the sectors, given in Table 1.

During the period, the total backward link effect decreased in 2008, but again in comparison with 2006 it increased by 14% in 2009. In some sectors the rate change of coefficients has negatively shown the reduction in dependency. It has revealed the growth in dependency in 29 sectors out of 50 sectors during the period. The first seven sectors numbered from 01 to 07 create the agriculture and agro-based industries. 25 sectors, numbered from 08 to 32, create the manufacturing industry; the rest of the sectors are service sectors. Accordingly, it has been revealed that there is growth in the use of imported intermediate inputs in 4 sectors of agriculture out of 7 sub-sectors; in manufacturing in 14 sectors out of 25 sub-sectors; and in service in 11 sectors out of 18 sub-sectors (Table 1).

The first ten sectors with the highest use of imported intermediate inputs in 2009 are sub-sectors of manufacturing:

17. Chemical industry
18. Manufacture of chemical and plastic raw materials
29. Products are not included in other classifications
15. Issue and publishing, recorded media pl.
10. Textile products
09. Tobacco products
13. Timber and the production of wood joinery
49. Research and development services
27. Motor vehicles, trailers and semi-trailers
25. Radio, television and communication equipments and devices

When the manufacturing industry, in which there is an increased dependence on imports, considered together with the relative positions in the following sectors during the period, growth was revealed in the use of imported intermediate inputs and these sectors came forward significantly in the ranking of importance.

09. Tobacco products
10. Textile products
13. Timber and the production of wood joinery
17. Chemical industry
24. Manufacture of electrical machinery and apparatus
25. Radio, television and communication
27. Motor vehicles, trailers and semi-trailers sectors

In the other hand, in sub-sectors of the manufacturing industry, with the reduction of imported intermediate input use, it has been seen to have declined towards the back in the ranking of importance. For example:

08. Food products and beverages
15. Issue and publishing recorded media pl.
16. Furnace coke and refined petroleum products.
20. Metallurgical industry.

That is, with the reduction of using imported intermediate inputs, relative importance also declined (Table 1). This feature also could be applied to the service industry of sub-sectors.

Despite the increased propensity to import in the back link effects of uses of imported intermediate inputs, there was no change in the order of importance nor an appearance of decline. Despite the growth in the use of imported intermediate inputs, the following sectors declined 2 steps back:

01. Agriculture, hunting and related services
14. Production of paper and cardboard and paper products
have not been changed the relative importance. In the sub-sectors
11. Clothing, processing and dyeing of fur
19. Other non-metallic mineral products
22. Production of machinery and equipment

In the service sectors, such as 35. wholesale trade and commission trade declined 1 step back, and 42. communication, 2 steps back. In 43. financial intermediation, there was no change. There is a 2 step decline in 45. financial intermediation and insurance related processing industries (Table 1). In other words, despite the increase in the use of intermediate inputs, it has not changed the relative importance in the total imported intermediate inputs, and it has created the impression of some economic problems specific to the sector.

Effects of forward links in the imported intermediate inputs used in the Economy of Kazakhstan

The draft totals of the reverse import matrix show us the sum of imported products that have to be sold in order to increase the total production of each industry by one unit. It could be interpreted as a reduction of external dependency of a sector, as the increasing of production, decreases the use of imported inputs. Accordingly, the values obtained from the sum of reversed imported matrix row totals of sectors, and to emphasize the related importance of values numbers of importance as well as the order obtained by sorting in descending order, are shown in Table 2.

During the period in the economy, in 29 sectors out of 50 sectors it has been observed that there is growth in the uses of imported inputs in terms of the backward link effects. In the rest of the sectors during the period, the uses of imported intermediate inputs decreased. In agriculture, with a total of 7 sub-sectors, in sub-sectors of 01. agriculture, hunting and related services, and sector 03. fishery, the uses of imported intermediate inputs increased. Among these sectors, in the sub-sector of fisheries, the relative importance order also decreased. In 17 sub-sectors out of 25 manufacturing industry sub-sectors there was an increase in the use of imported intermediate inputs. In 11 out of 18 sub-sectors of service, the use of imported intermediate inputs also increased. In sub-sectors of the manufacturing industry, with an increased use of imported intermediate inputs, such as

13. Timber and the production of wood joinery
14. Production of paper and cardboard and paper products
16. Furnace coke and refined petroleum products
17. Chemical industry
22. Production of machinery and equipment

in parallel with an increase in the use of imported intermediate inputs, the relative importance of these sectors have also been increased. These sectors go forward in the ranking of importance. But in the sub-sectors such as 09. tobacco products; 21. production of ready for final metal products, despite the increase in the use of imported intermediate inputs, they have a relative position in the industry which has changed very little and has made only 1 step forward. In the textile production, despite increasing in the use of imported intermediate inputs, the relative position of the sector made 2 steps back. In sectors with the declined usage of imported intermediate inputs, the relative position of sectors also has decreased (Table 2). But in the sub-sectors of 15. issue and publishing; 24. manufacture of electrical machinery and apparatus; 07. other mining sub-sectors, despite the growth in the use of imported intermediate inputs, the relative importance of each has not changed, or has only changed by a few positions.

The first ten sectors with the highest imports according to the forward link effects are:

17. Chemical industry
22. Production of machinery and equipment
50. Other (public administration education social services)
20. Metallurgical industry
14. Production of paper and cardboard and paper products
13. Timber and the production of wood joinery
18. Production of chemical and plastic raw materials
10. Textile industry
05. Production of crude oil and natural gas extraction

According to the effects of both forward and backward links, the sectors situated in the first tens are:

17. Chemical industry
13. Timber and the production of wood joinery
18. Production of chemical and plastic raw materials
10. Textile products

Conclusion

It is well known that the economics of most countries are going through a rapid process of opening up during the process of globalization. With the increase of extensive internally and externally competing countries that are entering into the process of opening up, inevitably, with the help of increasing exports and decreasing imports, they are trying to ensure their external balance. But opening up is not always accompanied by economic growth and development. In the present condition it is impossible to completely eliminate the external dependence of the economies. However, this dependency should be withdrawn to the lowest possible level. Therefore it is important to identify industries with high back and forward link effects, and to ensure the development of these sectors. In this research the economy of Kazakhstan was investigated, which achieved its independence in the 1990s, and became an economically rich, regional leader among the Central Asian countries.

Over the period of investigation in the research, based on input and output analysis through inter sectoral uses of imported intermediate inputs, it was revealed that in the economy the dependence on imports has increased. These sectors have both forward and back link effects:

17. Chemical industry

13. Timber and the production of wood joinery

18. Production of chemical and plastic raw materials

10. Textile products

In Kazakhstan the most imported good groups are automotive and spare parts, metallurgical industry, chemical industry, mining, animal products, and forest products. An important part of Kazakhstan's' imports consist of intermediate and investment goods from these sectors. Similar results to the findings presented there were obtained. They could be stated in the terms of concentration of imports on intermediate and investment goods, which might produce the positive results with both multiplied and accelerated mechanisms in Kazakhstan and its regional economies. However, the most of the imports come from the Western countries and Russia. It is a factor that reduces the potential impact on economies of the region. For this reason, we are sure that, as regards Kazakhstan, it is necessary to implement in the sectors policies that reduce dependency on imports, and according to the regional economies (within the framework of the Customs Union created by Russia, Belarus transfer of technology, modernization of production, etc.) it is necessary to have measures for improving foreign trade with Kazakhstan.

References

Aydoğuş O., Girdi-Çıktı Modellerine Giriş, Gazi Kitabevi Ankara, 1999.

Bocutoğlu, E., Girdi – Çıktı Analizine Giriş, Karadeniz Üniversitesi İktisadi ve İdari Bilimler Fakültesi Ders Notları, Yayın No:23, Trabzon, 1990.

Chenery H.B, Clark P.E, Endüstrilerarası İktisat, (Çev. Cemil Çınar), ODTÜ, Ankara, 1965

Ersungur Ş., M., Ekinci D.,Takım A., "Türkiye Ekonomisinde İthalata Bağımlılıktaki Değişme: Girdi-Çıktı Yaklaşımıyla Bir Uygulama", *10.Ulusal Ekonometri ve İstatistik Kongresi,* Atatürk Üniversitesi İ.İ.B.F, 27-29 Mayıs 2009, Erzurum

Fleissner, P. U. A., Input-Output Analyse-Eine Einführung in Theorie und Anwendungen, Wien, 1993.

Kepenek Y. Türkiye İmalat Sanayiinin Üretim Yapısı (1963-1973), Ankara ODTÜ, 1977.

Kepenek Y., Türk İmalat Sanayiinin Üretim Yapısı, Friedrich Ebert Vakfı Araştırma Sonuçları, İstanbul, 1991.

Korum U., Input Output Analizi. Sevinç Matbaası, Ankara, 1963.

Korum U., Türk İmalat Sanayi ve İthal İkamesi: Bir Değerlendirme, Ankara Üniversitesi Siyasal Bilgiler Fakültesi Yayınları No:408, Ankara,1977.

Miernyk W.H., The Elements of Input Output Analysis, Random House, West Virginia University, 2 Printing, 1966.

Özdil T., Turdaliyeva A., Ganiyev C., "Girdi-Çıktı Analizi Yaklaşımıyla Kyrgyzstan Ekonomisinin İncelenmesi", *Atatürk Üniversitesi İktisadi ve İdari Bilimler Dergisi,* 10. Ekonometri ve İstatistik Sempozyumu Özel Sayısı, Cilt:25, Sayı:Özel, Yıl:2011, ss:353-373.

Özdil T., Yılmaz C., "Elektrik Elektronik Sektörünün Türkiye Ekonomisi İçindeki Öneminin Girdi Çıktı Analiziyle İncelenmesi", *Kyrgyzstan Türkiye Manas Üniversitesi Sosyal Bilimler Dergisi,* Sayı 21, Bişkek, 2009, ss, 117-127.

ªenesen, G., G., Türkiye'nin Üretim Yapýsý: Girdi-Çýktý Modeli ile Temel Bulgular, TÜSÝAD Büyüme Stratejileri Dizisi, No:3, Ýstanbul, 2005.

Thirlwall, A.P., Growth and Development, Fourth Edition, McMillan Education Ltd., London, 1990.

Todaro M.P., Kalkınma Planlaması (Modeller ve Yöntemler), (Çev. Orhan Sezgin), İstanbul, 1987.

Agency of the Republic of Kazakhstan on Statistics. Tables of input-output of the Republic of Kazakhstan for 2006, 2008, 2009 www.stat.gov.kz

Agency of the Republic of Kazakhstan on Statistics Kazakhstan in figures 2010. http://www.stat.gov.kz/digital/vnesh_torg/Pages/default.aspx

Agency of the Republic of Kazakhstan on Statistics. Statistical Yearbook of Kazakhstan, "Kazakhstan in 2009."Astana2010.

http://www.stat.gov.kz/Pages/default.aspx

National Bank of Kazakhstan. Balance of Payments and External Debt of the Republic of Kazakhstan for 2009. http://www.nationalbank.kz

Table 1: Effects of Back Links in the imported intermediate inputs uses of Kazakhstan's Economy (Column totals - .000 tenge)

Economic sectors	2006		2008		2009		Rate of Change 2006-09
	R_j	Rank	R_j	Rank	R_j	Rank	
Agriculture, hunting and related services	0.048	49	0.045	49	0,061	49	0,266
Forestry and related services	0.086	38	0.054	44	0,062	48	-0,279
Fishery	0.067	43	0.103	28	0,120	32	0,782
Mining of coal lignite and peat	0.128	26	0.143	12	0,122	30	-0,050
Crude oil and natural gas extraction, and prod.	0.104	37	0.099	29	0,114	33	0,105
Mining of metal ores	0.161	20	0.122	20	0,153	23	-0,045
Other mining	0.150	23	0.157	11	0,194	15	0,298
Food products and beverages	0.153	22	0.120	21	0,128	28	-0,160
Manufacture of tobacco products	0.123	28	0.167	9	0,292	6	1,374
Manufacture of textiles	0.180	13	0.139	13	0,304	5	0,689
Clothing, fur processing and dyeing	0.161	19	0.134	15	0,191	17	0,182
Leather and leather products, footwear production	0.106	35	0.086	35	0,125	29	0,172
Timber and production of wood joinery	0.105	36	0.064	41	0,284	7	1,708
Paper and cardboard and paper products	0.264	4	0.172	7	0,320	4	0,212
Printing and publishing, recorded media pl.	0.312	3	0.241	1	0,220	11	-0,297
Furnace coke and refined petroleum products.	0.173	15	0.176	5	0,147	24	-0,153
Chemical industry	0.208	7	0.168	8	0,342	2	0,647
Manufacture of chemicals and plastic raw materials	0.315	2	0.221	3	0,455	1	0,445

Other non-metallic mineral products,	0.171	16	0.123	19	0,188	18	0,098
Metallurgical industry	0.184	12	0.108	24	0,104	38	-0,431
Production of ready / final metal products	0.256	5	0.109	23	0,209	13	-0,185
Manufacture of machinery and equipment	0.165	18	0.097	32	0,192	16	0,164
Office and computing machinery manufacturing	0.399	1	0.235	2	0,071	47	-0,822
Manufacture of electrical machinery and apparatus	0.110	33	0.088	34	0,210	12	0,912
Radio, television and communication	0.143	24	0.105	26	0,221	10	0,545
Production of medical, precision, optical instruments, watches	0.195	10	0.117	22	0,168	21	-0,138
Motor vehicles, trailers and semi-trailers.	0.119	31	0.161	10	0,235	9	0,969
Production of other transport equipment	0.176	14	0.095	33	0,130	26	-0,265
Products not included in other classifications,	0.075	41	0.105	27	0,325	3	3,315
Secondary processing industry	0.160	21	0.082	36	0,080	43	-0,497
Prod. and distribution of electricity, gas, steam and hot water	0.199	9	0.132	16	0,129	27	-0,352
Water collection, purification and distribution	0.124	27	0.127	17	0,114	35	-0,085
Construction	0.203	8	0.098	31	0,171	20	-0,158
Maintenance sales and repair of motor vehicle: retail sales.	0.062	45	0.046	47	0,060	50	-0,027
Wholesale trade and commerce. mot brokerage. excluded	0.076	40	0.074	38	0,090	41	0,175
Retail trade, repair of personal and household goods	0.056	46	0.040	50	0,104	39	0,844
Hotels, motels, hostels, camping. and other lodging places	0.166	17	0.137	14	0,120	31	-0,276
Overland transport	0.131	25	0.108	25	0,147	25	0,121
Sea transport	0.213	6	0.181	4	0,114	34	-0,462
Air transport	0.122	29	0.098	30	0,177	19	0,448
Supporting and auxiliary transport activities	0.109	34	0.074	39	0,073	46	-0,335
Communication	0.078	39	0.054	45	0,108	37	0,396
Financial intermediation	0.073	42	0.075	37	0,089	42	0,223
Insurance	0.050	48	0.045	48	0,079	44	0,576

Financial intermediation and supporting operations in insurance	0.052	47	0.054	46	0,078	45	0,507
Real estate activities	0.114	32	0.072	40	0,094	40	-0,182
Rental of personal items with machine operator. and equipment	0.120	30	0.059	43	0,162	22	0,349
Activities related to calculation tools	0.194	11	0.124	18	0,112	36	-0,426
Research and development services	0.008	50	0.062	42	0,240	8	27,410
Other (Public Administration Education and Social Services	0.066	44	0.173	6	0,200	14	2,053
Total	7.213		5.667		8.225		0.140

Table 2: Effects of Forward Links in the imported intermediate inputs uses of Kazakhstan's Economy (Row totals - .000 tenge)

Economic sectors	2006		2008		2009		Rate of Change 2006-09
	R_j	Rank	R_j	Rank	R_j	Rank	
Agriculture, hunting and related services	0.007	34	0.073	20	0,237	13	33,269
Forestry and related services	0.019	31	0.000	35	0,000	43	-1,000
Fishery	0.000	37	0.025	26	0,000	42	0,433
Mining of coal lignite and peat	0.057	24	0.012	29	0,008	37	-0,854
Crude oil and natural gas extraction, and prod.	0.360	5	0.387	6	0,272	10	-0,246
Mining of metal ores	0.043	28	0.056	25	0,037	24	-0,133
Other mining	0.027	29	0.014	28	0,018	30	-0,342
Food products and beverages	0.172	13	0.360	7	0,164	16	-0,041
Manufacture of tobacco products	0.004	36	0.123	16	0,010	35	1,831
Manufacture of textiles	0.290	6	0.201	10	0,353	8	0,216
Clothing, fur processing and dyeing	0.147	14	0.012	30	0,009	36	-0,937
Leather and leather products, footwear production	0.004	35	0.061	23	0,002	40	-0,450
Timber and production of wood joinery	0.173	12	0.097	18	0,434	6	1,509
Paper and cardboard and paper products	0.238	9	0.432	4	0,535	5	1,243
Printing and publishing, recorded media pl.	0.057	23	0.065	22	0,037	25	-0,359
Furnace coke and refined petroleum products.	0.137	16	0.357	8	0,271	11	0,974
Chemical industry	0.565	3	0.686	1	1,805	1	2,193

Manufacture of chemicals and plastic raw materials	0.735	2	0.414	5	0,392	7	-0,467
Other non-metallic mineral products,	0.285	7	0.219	9	0,258	12	-0,093
Metallurgical industry	1.786	1	0.554	2	0,553	4	-0,690
Production of ready / final metal products	0.228	10	0.132	13	0,342	9	0,498
Manufacture of machinery and equipment	0.134	17	0.134	12	0,611	2	3,553
Office and computing machinery manufacturing	0.000	39	0.000	36	0,000	44	0,000
Manufacture of electrical machinery and apparatus	0.122	18	0.000	37	0,120	19	-0,016
Radio, television and communication	0.000	40	0.000	38	0,163	17	0,000
Production of medical, precision, optical instruments, watches	0.000	41	0.000	39	0,018	29	0,000
Motor vehicles, trailers and semi-trailers.	0.007	33	0.068	21	0,180	15	25,032
Production of other transport equipment	0.000	42	0.000	40	0,085	21	0,000
Products not included in other classifications,	0.056	25	0.001	32	0,008	38	-0,863
Secondary processing industry	0.000	43	0.000	41	0,000	45	0,000
Prod. and distribution of electricity, gas, steam and hot water	0.000	44	0.085	19	0,032	28	0,000
Water collection, purification and distribution	0.000	45	0.000	42	0,000	46	0,000
Construction	0.071	22	0.000	43	0,112	20	0,587
Maintenance sales and repair of motor vehicle: retail sales.	0.000	46	0.000	44	0,000	47	0,000
Wholesale trade and commerce. mot brokerage. excluded	0.000	47	0.000	45	0,001	41	0,000
Retail trade, repair of personal and household goods	0.000	38	0.000	46	0,000	48	-1,000
Hotels, motels, hostels, camping. and other lodging places	0.051	27	0.000	47	0,156	18	2,066
Overland transport	0.277	8	0.483	3	0,016	32	-0,943
Sea transport	0.075	21	0.099	17	0,003	39	-0,955
Air transport	0.147	15	0.131	14	0,011	34	-0,925
Supporting and auxiliary transport activities	0.079	20	0.001	34	0,034	26	-0,575
Communication	0.026	30	0.015	27	0,033	27	0,294
Financial intermediation	0.056	26	0.126	15	0,045	23	-0,183

Insurance	0.105	19	0.060	24	0,016	31	-0,846
Financial intermediation and supporting operations in insurance	0.000	48	0.000	48	0,000	49	0,000
Real estate activities	0.000	49	0.001	33	0,000	50	0,000
Rental of personal items with machine operator. and equipment	0.176	11	0.000	49	0,184	14	0,047
Activities related to calculation tools	0.009	32	0.012	31	0,054	22	5,244
Research and development services	0.000	50	0.000	50	0,011	33	0,000
Other (Public Administration Education and Social Services	0.487	4	0.171	11	0,593	3	0,218
Total		7.213		5.667		8.225	0.140

PART V:

GLOBALIZATION

Globalization and Central Asian Economies: Prospects for Development

Prof. Berch Berberoğlu[1]

The Eurasian region, stretching from Turkey in the West to the borders of China in the East, is one of the most important strategic regions of the world in the age of neoliberal globalization. The countries making up the core of this region, Kazakhstan, Turkmenistan, Kyrgyzstan, Uzbekistan, Tajikistan, and Azerbaijan, as well as Turkey, provide a rich mix of abundant natural resources, such as oil, natural gas, metals and minerals, industrial and agricultural infrastructure inherited from earlier periods, and a skilled work force trained under mass production in industry, agriculture, and other vital sectors of the economy.

The Soviet Legacy and the Transition to Market Economy in Eurasia

Given their historic experience under state-directed socialist development during the Soviet period, all of these countries, except Turkey, were once republics of the USSR, but have been evolving for the past two decades now as independent nation-states allied with one or another of the major powers that have strategic interests in the region. Thus, Russia, China, the United States, as well as other regional powers (such as Iran, India, and Turkey), have had and continue to have influence and impact on the development path pursued by these countries in the post-Soviet era (Kleveman 2004; Hiro 2009), one that is dominated by the forces of neoliberal globalization (the transnational corporations) and by the process that facilitates the transformation of these economies along the capitalist path (privatization of state-owned enterprises as part of the process of neoliberal globalization).

---

[1] University of Nevada, Reno, Nevada, USA

The end result of this process is the gradual integration of previously state-cantered socialist economies into the global capitalist system through a variety of means (joint-ventures with foreign capital, leasing of extractive industries, and privatization and outright sale of state-owned firms to transnational corporations). Developments along these lines over the past two decades have led to the rise and consolidation of the power of local and foreign capitalist interests, hence to the transformation of their internal social, economic, and political structure in the direction of autocratic capitalist states (Olcott 2005).

The Special Case of Turkey

In contrast, while Turkey has also followed a similar neoliberal economic path tied to the global economy, the political outcome of this process in that country has been quite different due to a variety of reasons that are specific to Turkey's historic context: (1) the legacy of statism (*devletçilik*) adopted in the early decades of the republic, and (2) the more recent rise of political Islam based on the emergence of a rival economic force (the newly rising Anatolian bourgeoisie) with broader neoliberal economic interests and linkages that go beyond a narrow religious outlook and toward greater integration into the institutions of Western economic power, i.e., the European Union (Boratav 1974; Aydin 2005). Thus, Turkey looking to the West and linking to the East has provided a combination of possibilities for social, political, and economic change that has placed the country in a unique position situated as a regional power broker that will have an important influence on countries of the Eurasian region, as this region goes through new and yet uncharted social, political, and economic transformations in the coming years.

Globalization: Its Nature, Dynamics, and Contradictions

Over the course of the past two decades of global economic transformations facilitated by the collapse of the former Soviet Union and the rise and spread of neoliberal capitalist globalization around the world, economies of the Eurasian countries have experienced the impact of this process in various ways. Before assessing the nature and depth of this impact, however, we must first examine the dynamics and contradictions of neoliberal globalization.

Main Characteristics of Globalization

A central feature of neoliberal globalization, besides its speed and intensity, is the increased privatization of various spheres of the economy and society, with a relative decline in the power and ability of the state and other political institutions to control their national economies relative to earlier periods. Under the current wave of neoliberal globalization, the state in the advanced capitalist societies (and increasingly in the less-developed ones) has lost some of its traditional power in controlling and regulating the various spheres of society, especially the economy, but also other areas such as communications, information technology, and education, where privatization has become more and more prevalent. Thus, under the current phase of neoliberal globalization, the transnational corporations have become more visible and have increasingly taken centre stage in effecting changes in the global political economy (Waters 1995; Halliday 2001; Berberoglu 2003, 2010).

Neoliberal globalization, much as during earlier stages of capitalism, is facilitated by transnational capital and is driven by the logic of *profit* for the private accumulation of capital. It is, in essence, the highest and most pervasive phase of transnational capitalism operating on a world scale. It is in this sense the most widespread and penetrating manifestation of global economic expansion that has profound social, political, cultural, and ideological impact on societies around the world (Golding and Harris 1997; Lechner and Boli 2007; Petras and Veltmeyer 2011).

Economic Basis

The export of capital by the transnational corporations to the less-developed countries around the world has historically been part of the process of economic expansion worldwide that has led to the growth of giant capitalist conglomerates, cartels, and trusts that have come to dominate the world economy over the course of the twentieth century (Magdoff 1992; Amin 1997; Petras and Veltmeyer 2001, 2007, 2011). This has facilitated the rapid accumulation of capital by the transnationals at global proportions, a process that stimulates further capital accumulation worldwide, hence further domination of the global economy by the transnationals (Siebert 2000; Munck 2002; Sklair 2002; Berberoglu 2003, 2005). It is this economic essence of neoliberal globalization, then, that has set into motion the social, political and ideological contexts in which global capitalism has come to prospers.

Social Impact

The global expansion of capital has been transforming social relations along capitalist lines, as the main class divisions in society have become wage-labour and capital. The transformation of societies around the world through this process leads to the integration of an increasing number of countries into the global economy by which they are subordinated to the transnationals, especially in terms of the exploitation of low-wage labour. As women workers increasingly constitute the bulk of the low-wage labouring population worldwide, the exploitation of the working class in this way takes on a gendered dimension (Barndt 1999; Rai 2001; Aguilar 2004; Harley 2007; Stevis and Boswell 2008).

The global domination of capital over wage-labour in this process of worldwide capitalist expansion fosters the subordination of the working class to the dictates of the transnationals who are the very source of the emerging inequalities in income, wealth, and power. These inequalities, in time, lead to contradictions and conflict in the social sphere, when class divisions become solidified to a point when class struggles between the opposing class forces begin to surface (Beams 1998; Petras and Veltmeyer 2001; Berberoglu 2009).

Political Dynamics

In the political sphere, power remains in the hands of the transnational and local capitalist classes and is exercised through the capitalist state. The control of the state and major political institutions of society by these powerful capitalist forces has led to the erosion of democratic governance and given rise to political corruption and authoritarian rule (Palast 2002; Hertz 2002; Parenti 2011). However, rather than representing the unified interests of a newly emergent global capitalist class, the imperial state of the transnationals advances only the interests of its own capitalists, as against its rivals, to secure the supremacy of its own transnationals over the global capitalist economy (Cohn et. al. 2000; Halliday 2001; Petras and Veltmeyer 2007).

Despite a temporary commercial, monetary, and even military union, however, the leading imperial state (currently the United States) continues to dominate the world political economy and dictates its terms over other states, thus giving rise to competition and rivalry between the major global capitalist powers (Hook 2001; Weber 2001; Harvey 2003). While this competition takes place at the monopoly level, between rival transnational corporations, as well as their states, it nevertheless affects the structure of social relations in general and has a direct impact on society worldwide.

As the varied dynamics of neoliberal capitalist globalization and its impact on society more and more becomes regulated by the imperial state, it is within the parameters of the state's role in legitimizing and protecting the interests of global capital that we come to understand the relationship of the imperial state to the neoliberal globalization project.

Globalization and the Imperial State

With the globalization of capital during the twentieth century, the leading capitalist state of the advanced capitalist economies (the United States) has come to assume greater responsibility in organizing and leading the global capitalist system, thus adopting the role of an imperial state charged with the control and rationalization of the global political economy to advance transnational capitalist interests (Beams 1998; Halliday 2001). It is within this context of the role of the advanced capitalist state that the imperial state confronts the contradictions of neoliberal globalization.

Crisis of the Imperial State

The globalization of capital—through the worldwide expansion of transnational corporations—has had a decisive effect on the role and functions of the imperial state, and brought to the fore new and more pervasive contradictions, leading to a crisis of management and legitimacy of capitalism on a worldwide basis. This has been the result of developments in the latest stage of global capitalist expansion, in which the monopoly fraction of the capitalist class in the advanced capitalist countries, especially the United States, has secured a thorough control of the state apparatus to advance its interests at home and abroad (Parenti 2011). And this has precipitated the crisis of the advanced capitalist/imperial state on a global scale.

The crisis of the imperial state manifests itself at different levels, ranging from international conflicts (economic rivalry, disintegration of regional political and military alliances, the inability to suppress nationalist movements and revolution, and military intervention and war) to domestic economic problems (trade and budget deficits, monetary and fiscal crisis, unemployment, recession, etc.) to national political crises (factional struggles within the capitalist class, problems of legitimacy, repression of working class and mass movements, militarization of the polity and society, and so on) (Perlo 1988; Parenti 2011).

Competition and Crises in the Global Economy

The growing prospects of economic rivalry between the major capitalist powers, backed up by their states, are effecting changes in their relations that render the global political economy an increasingly unstable character. Competition between the United States, the European Union, and China, representing the interests of their own respective elites are leading them on a collision course for world supremacy, manifested in struggles for markets, raw materials, spheres of influence in geo-political—as well as economic—terms, which may in fact lead to a new balance of forces, and consequently new alliances that would have serious political implications in global power-politics (Pieterse 2010).

As the continuing economic ascendance of the major rivals of the United States secure for themselves a prominent position in the global economy, pressures will build toward the politicization and militarization of these states from within, where the leading class forces bent on dominating the world economy will press forward with the necessary political and military corollary of their growing economic power in the global system (Hart 1992; Falk 1999; Berberoglu 2010). And this eventuality threatens the global economy with continued crises in the early decades of the twenty-first century.

The Shifting Balance of Forces in the Global Political Economy

These developments in the global political economy will bring shifts in the balance of forces among the major powers and lead to the forging of new and yet untested international alliances for world supremacy and domination in the twenty-first century. Such alliances will bring key powers such as Russia and China into play in a new and complicated relationship that holds the key for the success or failure of the newly rising imperial centres that will emerge as decisive forces changing the global economic, political, and military equation in the early decades of the twenty-first century (Pieterse, 2010).

Thus, the contradictions and conflicts imbedded in relations between the rival imperial states of the major capitalist powers will again surface as an important component of international relations in the years ahead. And it is in this context of the changes that are taking place on a world scale that the imperial state is beginning to address the current crisis of global capitalism to maintain its rule (Petras and Veltmeyer 2011; Berberoglu 2012).

The Impact of Globalization on Central Asian Economies

Becoming more and more integrated into the modalities of neoliberal globalization led by the transnational corporations, the economies of Central Asian countries have been greatly affected by the transnational oil companies that have played a central role in determining the nature and rate of economic growth and the impact on various sectors of the economy and society in each of the countries in this region.

Oil, Transnationals, and Foreign Investment

Neoliberal globalization has come to play a central role in determining the type of investment and production (mainly oil, natural gas, metals, minerals, and other natural resources extracted for export) geared to the needs of the global economy rather than the local, national economy. Thus, vast amounts of foreign capital has been invested in oil and other extractive industries by the transnational oil companies across Central Asia, with the aim of exporting these vital resources crucial for the industrial engine of advanced capitalist countries and producing high rates of profit for the transnationals (Kleveman, 2004; LeVine 2007).

Kazakhstan, the region's largest and most resource-rich country in oil, minerals, and metals attracted more than USD120 billion in foreign investment in the past two decades (Solovyov 2012). The country "is home to 3% of the world's oil, 4% of the world's coal, and 15% of its uranium. It has the world's largest reserves of zinc, lead, and chromites, and it is in the top ten for supplies of copper, iron ore, gold, and manganese" (McKeigue 2012:1). Turkmenistan is similarly rich in oil and gas, with nearly 4.5% of the world's natural gas and 500 million barrels of oil. Uzbekistan similarly has vast natural gas reserves and substantial gold, copper, lead, and uranium reserves.

The European Union and the United States are heavily involved in foreign direct investment through their respective transnational oil companies across Central Asia. The EU constructed the 1,768 kilometre Baku-Tbilisi-Ceyhan pipeline, linking the Caspian Sea and Europe through Turkey. The EU and the U.S. sponsored a second Baku-Tbilisi-Erzurum pipeline, which transports natural gas from Azerbaijan to Turkey, destined to Western Europe. These are just a few of the examples that the

EU and the U.S. are involved in when it comes to oil and gas investments linked to Central Asia.

Russia and China are likewise heavily involved in foreign investment in the oil and natural gas sector in Central Asia, and account for the biggest share of these investments in the region. Noteworthy among these are the Russian-based energy companies (e.g., Gazprom and LUKoil) and mining/metallurgical companies (e.g., MMC Norilsk Nickel Group) are heavily invested as key players in Eurasia. Like Russia, China as well is directly involved in the economies of Central Asia and greater Eurasian region. The 2,228 kilometre Kazakhstan-China pipeline, jointly owned and operated by KazMunayGaz and China National Petroleum Corporation, is one such grand project, which will transport 20 million tons of oil per year from the Aktobe, Kumkol, and Kashagan oil fields on Kazakhstan's Caspian shore to Alashankou in the Western Chinese province of Xinjiang. Another example is "the USD7.3 billion Turkmenistan-China pipeline [which] was inaugurated in December 2009, permitting the eastward transportation of Caspian gas. By 2011, 30 billion cubic meters of natural gas [was] delivered to China from Turkmenistan (along with 10 billion cubic meters from Kazakhstan)" (RSM International 2012).

Oil and natural gas investments, however, are not the only projects that have attracted China to Central Asia. Other big projects that China has undertaken across Eurasia include vast transportation networks consisting of transcontinental railway and highway projects involving road construction across several countries in the region. These include "the building of a railroad linking Kars, Turkey and Akhalkalaki, Georgia and the rehabilitation of the Akhalkalaki-Tbilisi rail line will connect Istanbul to the Caspian Sea. The Kars-Akhalkalaki-Tbilisi-Baku railway ... with onward connections from Azerbaijan to Kazakhstan [and] rail lines linking Kazakhstan and China ... will create a rail connection from Istanbul to Urumqi in China's interior"; in addition, as part of a 141,000 kilometre Asian highway project, "China is constructing 12 highways to configure Central Asia as a land bridge linking Beijing with the Black Sea. These highways will connect the Xinjiang Autonomous Region with neighbouring countries, including Russia, Kazakhstan, Kyrgyzstan and Pakistan" (RSM International 2012).

The scramble for natural resources in Central Asia that has brought a string of foreign investors to exploit the region's oil, natural gas, metals, and minerals have not translated into higher standard of living for the local population. In fact, it has opened the door for widespread corruption and criminal activity that can only be characterized as "mafia capitalism." Thus, privatization of vast natural resources of the Eurasian countries in the post-Soviet era of neoliberal capitalist globalization and transfer of this wealth to foreign capital has led to the amassing of great fortunes by some who are well connected to corrupt regimes, while the great majority of the population has experienced widening inequality and poverty in these resource-rich countries.

Corruption, Inequality, and Poverty

The penetration of Central Asian economies by foreign capital has generated immense profits for foreign corporations (U.S., European, Russian, and Chinese alike), as well as for corrupt government officials, while leaving much of the rest of the local economy unaffected and idle that has resulted in high rates of unemployment, poverty, and declining living standards for all but those directly involved with the transnationals at top levels of the state bureaucracy. The economic inequities and shortfalls created by the neoliberal policies propagated by the dominant powers and their institutions are exacerbated by Central Asian governments that are working in line with the interests of the transnationals through the corrupt policies and practices that are in their own and their collaborators' interests and not the wellbeing of their people (Olcott 2005; Hiro 2009). Thus, creating gainful employment based on skills acquired by quality education are things reserved only to a minority of the population directly linked to the political bureaucracy of the state and its immediate beneficiaries, while broad segments of the population go without access to any of the benefits accrued by the sale or transfer of vast national resources to the transnational oil monopolies. The neoliberal privatization policies in this situation come to serve both foreign and local capitalist interests that feed into the perpetual cycle of corrupt practices that local bureaucrats engage in to expand their wealth and political clout over the population, hence perpetuating inequalities that divide these societies further along class lines, thus widening the gap between the wealthy owners and the labouring poor (Sahadeho and Zanca 2007).

This is evident in no uncertain terms when one looks at the latest World Bank data on the distribution of income in all six Central Asian countries. In Azerbaijan, the lowest 10% of the population accounted for 3.4% of the total national income or consumption in 2008, while the highest 10% accounted for 27.4% and the highest 20% accounted for 42.1% of the total national income; in Kazakhstan, the lowest 10% of the population accounted for 3.8% of the total national income in 2007, while the highest 10% accounted for 25.2% and the highest 20% accounted for 40% of the total national income; in Tajikistan, the lowest 10% of the population accounted for 4.0% of the total national income in 2007, while the highest 10% accounted for 25.2% and the highest 20% accounted for 39% of the total national income; in Kyrgyzstan, the lowest 10% of the population accounted for 4.0% of the total national income in 2007, while the highest 10% accounted for 27.9% and the highest 20% accounted for 42.8% of the total national income; in Uzbekistan, the lowest 10% of the population accounted for 2.9% of the total national income in 2003, while the top 10% accounted for 29.5% and the highest 20% accounted for 47.2% of the total national income; finally, in Turkmenistan, the lowest 10% of the population accounted for 2.5% of the total national income, while the top 10% accounted for 31.8% and the top 20% accounted for 47.2% of the total national income (World Bank 2012:68-70).

While the misdistribution of income is one important indicator of the widening gap between the wealthy and the poor in these resource-rich countries, the poverty rate is certainly another measure of the concentration of wealth and income at one end and poverty and destitution at the other. Thus, as of the early 2000s, half of the population in Azerbaijan (49.6%), Kyrgyzstan (47.6%), and Tajikistan (56.6%) were below the poverty line, with Turkmenistan, Uzbekistan, and Kazakhstan not far behind at 30%, 27.5%, and 27.9% of their population below the poverty line (Dowling and Wignaraja 2006: 28). Although the situation has substantially improved in some of the countries in the region later in the decade (e.g., Azerbaijan and Kazakhstan), others (such as Kyrgyzstan and Tajikistan) have continued to remain at extremely high levels—at 43.1% for Kyrgyzstan in 2005 and 47.2% for Tajikistan in 2009 (World Bank 2012: 394-95). Moreover, nearly 30% of the population in Kyrgyzstan in 2007, 51% of the population in Tajikistan in 2004, 50% of the population in Turkmenistan in 1998, and a mind-boggling 77% of the population in Uzbekistan in 2003 earned less than USDUSD2 a day! (World Bank 2012: 394-95). In contrast, the riches accrued to the wealthy oil barons who have accumulated vast fortunes in their own private banks and commercial enterprises in these post-Soviet neoliberal capitalist states reveal the depth of the class divisions that are maintained through these authoritarian dictatorships that have managed to stay in power and squander their people's wealth for private gain.

The polarization of wealth and income that neoliberal globalization has brought to Central Asia in the wake of the privatization of state-owned enterprises in post-Soviet transformations in each of these countries making up the region have thus left their mark as a model that is contrary to the interests of the people of Central Asia and the broader Eurasian region—a situation that requires us to explore alternative paths of development that may more directly address the challenges of development in this region in the coming decades.

Paths of Development for the Eurasian Economies

Given the failure of neoliberal globalization to effect positive change in Eurasian economies over the past two decades of post-Soviet transition to a market-oriented capitalist economy across Central Asia, it would be instructive to explore alternative paths of development that would make a contribution to growth and development of these economies based on some recent examples that provide a promise for the future. Russia, China, and India on the one hand and Turkey on the other have provided paths out of alternatives to current neoliberal policies that have failed so miserably. But, ultimately, the prospects for change and development in Central Asia depend on the nature and policies of the states that are responsible for the success or failure of such efforts.

Russia, China, and India

Given both the proximity and historic relationship of these three giants of north, east, and south Asia with their growth and expansion in the midst of neoliberal forces that are always ready to derail efforts at independent development, Russia, China and India have been quite successful in escaping imperialist pressures to incorporate these states into the global economy controlled and dominated by the transnational corporations of the advanced capitalist countries, most notably the United States (Chellaney 2006; Friere and Kanet 2010). India with its heavy investment in infrastructure and industrial production and China through its state-controlled export-oriented production and trade, and Russia holding on to its vast economic base, have succeeded in escaping subordination to the neoliberal capitalist forces. Through strong state intervention and planning, these three economies and states have succeeded in managing their entry to the world economy in promoting their own interests, even if this was done through a complex web of joint-ventures, state enterprises, and private investment schemes.

While the experience of Russia, China, and India show that a strong independent state committed to advancing their national interests can provide an alternative model of development within the context of globalization and the global capitalist system, the sheer size and magnitude of their economies may not be an appropriate model for the Central Asian economies to follow, even if the latter were able to avoid problems associated with corruption and cronyism that many Central Asian states have experienced during the past two decades of transition to a capitalist economy. Given the wholesale surrender of Central Asian states of their economies to the forces of neoliberal capitalist globalization and transnational corporate control, there seem to be little or no chance for these states to emerge as independent states to re-negotiate the terms of their relationship with the transnationals and global capital, unless a major rupture takes place that changes the direction of these economies and societies in a big way.

Turkey

Turkey's links to the Central Asian states go back a long time in history, and its cultural and linguistic ties have served to open up possible economic relations that are of mutual benefit within the context of establishing and expanding a Eurasian zone of economic cooperation based on the Turkish model that may be more applicable than that of Russia, China, and India. However, as in other cases, Turkey, as well, went through a period of heavy state intervention into its economy in the 1930s that established the basis of its industrial growth and expansion in later years when the economy evolved from a state-directed, planned economy to a private neoliberal economy based on the privatization of state enterprises and public assets. The long history of state-regulated economy that provided the infrastructure and industrial base during the initial stages of its development is the basis of its more recent success in making headway even while working within the parameters of a neoliberal capitalist globalization that has come to define and set limits to its relative autonomy in economic and state policy.

The distinguishing feature of the Turkish model and its adoptability to Central Asia as an extension of the wider Eurasian region is the affinity of the two regions to the historic presence of heavy state intervention that set the stage in one case for the expanded production that followed, while failing to do so in the other, leading the latter to take a different path that led to its ultimate failure. Thus, while the statist (*devletçilik*) or state-capitalist period through state-cantered development projects produced big economic dividends in Turkey during the Atatürk era and built the basis of a strong industrial economy in Turkey that flourished in subsequent decades (Boratav 1974), the state-socialist infrastructure of Soviet era industrialization failed to translate into a strong economy in the post-Soviet transition to capitalist market economy due to heavy corruption, opportunism, and self-aggrandizement personified by the personality cults developed to serve narrow elite interests (as exemplified by the despotic regimes that have ruled this region for nearly two decades).

Perhaps the promise of the application of the Turkish model to these states would be the strengthening of ties between the countries of Central Asia and Turkey for greater cooperation, investment, and collaborative projects geared to national development that are of mutual benefit, while curbing the negative impact of the forces of neoliberal globalization that are already in the region and are destined to derail such efforts to prevent independent national economic development that may come to challenge their newly entrenched interests.

The Prospects for Economic Development in Eurasia

What are the prospects, then, for the economic development of countries spanning the Eurasian region? What would it take to set these countries on a path of development that meets the needs of their people and generate genuine development that is both sustainable and beneficial to broad segments of the population? These are not easy questions to answer, nor are the answers easy to delineate. But, given the vast natural and mineral resources of the region, and given the great potential for their development for national use, the prospects for development of these states in the near to medium term remains quite high, providing the people of these countries and the region as a whole would take charge of the commanding heights of their economy and put it all to good use for national development based on the equitable distribution of wealth and income to elevate the living standards of the people, thus eliminating poverty and destitution amidst the plenty. At the national level, further economic collaboration among countries of this region in the form of economic and political alliances that facilitate aid and investment may lead to greater links that play a critical role in promoting change. Such change, first in the economy, and later in other spheres of society, may set the Central Asian states on the road to economic recovery and democratic governance in the early to mid twenty-first century.

References

Aguilar, Delia. 2004. Women and Globalization. Humanity Books, Amherst, NY.

Amin, Samir. 1997. Capitalism in the Age of Globalization. Zed Books, London.

Aydin, Zulkuf. 2005. The Political Economy of Turkey. Pluto Press, London.
Barndt, Deborah (ed.). 1999. Women Working the NAFTA Food Chain: Women, Food & Globalization. Sumach Press, Toronto.
Beams, Nick. 1998. The Significance and Implications of Globalization. Mehring Books, Southfield, MI.
Berberoglu, Berch. 2003. Globalization of Capital and the Nation-State. Rowman and Littlefield, Lanham, MD.
—. 2005. Globalization and Change: The Transformation of Global Capitalism. Lexington Books, Lanham, MD.
—. 2009. Class and Class Conflict in the Age of Globalization. Lexington Books, Lanham, MD.
—. 2010. Globalization in the 21st Century: Labor, Capital and the State on a World Scale. Palgrave Macmillan, New York and London.
Boratav, Korkut. 1974. Türkiye'de Devletçilik (Statism in Turkey). Gerçek Yayınevi, Istanbul.
Chellaney, Brahma. 2010. Asian Juggernaut: The Rise of China, India, and Japan. Harper Collins, New York.
Cohn, Theodore, Stephen McBride, and John Wiseman (eds.). 2000. Power in the Global Era: Grounding Globalization. Palgrave Macmillan, New York.
Dowling, Malcolm and Ganeshan Wignaraja. 2006. Central Asia's Economy: Mapping Future Prospects to 2015. Central Asia-Caucasus Institute and Silk Road Studies Program—a Joint Transatlantic Research and Policy Centre publication, Washington, DC and Uppsala, Sweden.
Falk, Richard. 1999. Predatory Globalization: A Critique. Blackwell, Malden, MA.
Golding Peter and Phil Harris (eds.). 1997. Beyond Cultural Imperialism. Sage Publications, Thousand Oaks, CA.
Halliday, Fred. 2001. The World at 2000. St. Martin□s Press, New York.
Harley, Sharon. 2007. Women's Labor in the Global Economy. Rutgers University Press, New Brunswick, NJ.
Hart, Jeffrey. 1992. Rival Capitalists. Cornell University Press, Ithaca, NY.
Harvey, David. 2003. The New Imperialism. Oxford University Press, New York.
Hertz, Noreena. 2002. Silent Takeover: Global Capitalism and the Death of Democracy. Free Press, New York.
Hiro, Dilip. 2009. Inside Central Asia. The Overlook Press, New York.

Hook, Glenn D. and Harukiyo Hasegawa (eds.). 2001. Political Economy of Japanese Globalization. Routledge, New York.

Kleveman, Lutz. 2004. The New Great Game: Blood and Oil in Central Asia. Grove Press, New York.

Lechner Frank J. and John Boli, 2007. The Globalization Reader, 3rd ed. Blackwell, Malden, MA.

LeVine, Steve. 2007. The Oil and the Glory: The Pursuit of Empire and Fortune on the Caspian Sea. Random House.

Magdoff, Harry. 1992. Globalization: To What End? Monthly Review Press, New York.

McKeigue, James. 2012. "The Scramble for Natural Resources in Central Asia" Money Morning Australia (retrieved on January 19, 2012). http://www.moneymorning.com.au/20120119/the-scramble-for-natural-resources-in-central-asia.html

Munck, Ronaldo. 2002. Globalization and Labor: The New Great Transformation. Zed Books, London.

Olcott, Martha Brill. 2005, Central Asia's Second Chance. Carnegie Endowment for International Peace, Washington, DC.

Palast, Greg. 2002. The Best Democracy Money Can Buy. Pluto, London.

Parenti, Michael. 2011. Democracy For the Few, Ninth Edition. St. Martin□s Press, New York.

Perlo, Victor. 1988. Super Profits and Crises: Modern U.S. Capitalism. International Publishers, New York.

Petras, James and Henry Veltmeyer. 2001. Globalization Unmasked: Imperialism in the 21st Century. Zed Books, London.

—. 2007. Multinationals on Trial: Foreign Investment Matters. Ashgate, Farnham, U.K.

—. 2011. Beyond Neoliberalism. Ashgate, Farnham, U.K.

Pieterse, Jan Nederveen. 2010. "Dynamics of Twenty-first-Century Globalization" in Berch Berberoglu (ed.), Globalization in the 21st Century. Palgrave Macmillan, New York.

Rai, Shirin. 2001. Gender and the Political Economy of Development. Polity Press, Cambridge.

RSM International. 2012. "Eurasia in the Global Economy, June 2010" www.rsmi.com/en/global-challenges/eurasia-in-the-global-economy.aspx (retrieved on January 17, 2012).

Siebert, Horst. 2000. Globalization and Labor. Kiel Inst of World Economics, Kiel, Germany.

Sklair, Leslie. 2002. Globalization: Capitalism and Its Alternatives. Oxford University Press, New York.

Solovyov, Dimitry. 2012. "Kazakhstan Votes After Deadly Oil Town Riots" http://uk.reuters.com/article/2012/01/15/uk-kazakhstan-election -idUKTRE80E0EO20120115 (retrieved on January 17, 2012).

Stevis, Dimitris and Terry Boswell. 2008. Globalization and Labor: Democratizing Global Governance. Rowman and Littlefield, Lanham, MD.

Waters, Malcolm. 1995. Globalization: The Reader. Routledge, New York.

Weber, Steven (ed.). 2001. Globalization and the European Political Economy. Columbia University Press, New York.

World Bank. 2011. World Development Report 2012. World Bank, Washington, D.C.

—. 2012. World Development Indicators, 2011. World Bank, Washington, DC.

Role of IMF and the World Bank in Shaping Central Asian Economies

Asst. Prof. Hakan Güneş[1]

The last decade of the previous millennium gave birth to 15 new countries in the territory of the former Soviet Union. Since then, these states, including the Central Asian countries, have attempted to reform their economic, political, and social institutions. Ideological guidelines and the course of this transformation are symbolically expressed in changing the name of the official journal of the Central Committee of Communist Party of the Soviet Union (CPSU) for cadres, from Party Life (Partiinaya Zhizn') to the Business Life (Delovaya Zhizn'). Transforming party life into business life is not an easy task for the new leaderships in the offspring states. With varying levels of success, the new leaderships seek to create new institutions or reorganize the old institutions. Since new players in the business life are more open to build new relations, various governments and international organizations seek to influence this transition via commercial-economic diplomacy means, such as foreign aid, concessional loans, technical assistance, and investment promotion programs. Among other international economic and political actors, the roles of International Monetary Fund (IMF) and the World Bank (WB), the two important Breton Woods institutions, in the making of the post-Soviet Central Asia are decisive. In cooperation with other financial and developmental funds and institutions, IMF and the WB put their signature under several salient transformation moves in Central Asia.

IMF and the WB impose countries to integrate into the world economy and liberalize their markets. However, the role of these institutions is not limited to the economic sphere. IMF and the WB representatives have become increasingly explicit in articulating a certain set of political values, which go far beyond economic development goals or country assistance programs. In their relation to the Central Asian region, both institutions' goals are not only to fulfil the objective of integrating the region to the global market, but also to impose a certain set of political conditions

[1] Istanbul University, Istanbul, Turkey

aiming at re-organizing the internal political structures of these countries and at their regional and international political alignments. Looking at the recommendations in the country reports of the WB or the conditionalities in exchange of IMF loans or grants, we see a set of political impositions about governance and regional politics. Governance-related conditionalities in IMF and WB lending are focused in particular on legislative and institution-building efforts by borrowers to increase the rule of law, accountability, transparency, and participation (Kapur 2000). Conditions also push countries forward to an alternative regionalism project in accordance with the needs of the global governance and global market players. These are the invisible hands of the global market forces, mainly interfering to the region by governance conditions, loans, regionalism projects promotions, etc.

There is a wide range of issues covered by IMF and the WB programs: From energy to environment, from land administration to railways, and from urban administration to financial and administrative reforms. This powerful invisible hand approach, which is termed as proactive partnership, gives the IMF and the WB a very determining role in any underdeveloped or developing country's politics.

On the other hand, we should note that the role of international financial institutions in drawing national strategies of Central Asian countries is not an omnipotent one. Responsibility of adoption and performance of the economic receipts recommended by international financial institutions, at the last instance, belongs to national governments of the region. Turkmenbashi or Kerimov of Uzbekistan and the colour revolutionary Bakiev of Kyrgyzstan are good examples of the type of regional leaders, who at the last instance set their own rules. As Libman (2007) clearly indicated, the post-Soviet elites are willing to follow the Russian "rules of the games' (semi-authoritarian institutions), but are reluctant to support integration with Russia and, vice versa, they are willing to support EU integration, but reluctant (or unable) to live under European rules of transparency. Thus, understanding the matrices of relations between the Central Asian countries' governments and the international financial institutions requires a simultaneous analysis of both the global processes and local dynamics.

This study investigates the role and the strategies of two international financial institutions in post-Soviet Central Asia's economic and political transformation process and attempts at exploring the political nature of their structural adjustment programs, enhanced structural adjustment facilities and conditionalities of IMF and the WB in the Central Asian context. We argue that these two institutions have a twofold political agenda: The first and the general objective is to integrate the Central Asian countries to the global markets through market liberalization and privatization. The second and the more political objective is to lead these countries towards an anti-Russian integration or alliance via regionalization projects.

Economics is Political: The Bretton Woods System in Practice

In July 1944 at the Bretton Woods conference, the vision of a liberal economic order was presented: The delegates from 44 allied nations at Bretton Woods established the International Monetary Fund (IMF) and the International Bank for Reconstruction and Development (IBRD). Today, together with the four other intuitions the IBRD constitutes the affiliates of World Bank Group.

The immediate purpose of the Bretton Woods conference was to formulate a plan for post-World War II international economic cooperation. Over time, the emphasis of the IBRD has shifted from its short-term purpose of rebuilding war-ravaged economies to the promoting economic growth in developing countries. These countries were obliged to adopt a monetary policy that maintained the exchange rate by tying their currencies to the U.S. USD. The IMF was obliged to bridge temporary imbalances of payments. The currencies would be fixed in relation to each other in order to prevent a competitive devaluation which had caused the breakdown of the international order in the 1930s (Harold 2000).

The founding principles and their implementations have changed over time due to changes in global economy, political dynamics and economic ideas: Just as the founding principles based on Keynesian 1940s and 1950s have changed in the Neo-classical 1980s and the early 1990s, they have also changed in the late 1990s and 2000s (Best 2007).

In the 1950s, the WB expanded its resources and pure project lendings; and new institutions were formed: The International Finance Corporation (IFC) was founded in 1956 in order to mobilize private investment. The International Development Association (IDA) was established in 1956 to provide long-term credits to the poorest country members of the WB. The Multilateral Investment Guarantee Agency (MIGA) was formed in 1988 to stimulate foreign direct investment by providing guarantees against political risk, armed conflict, civil unrest and so forth (Woods).

The IMF and the WB underwent further changes in the 1980s. The Latin American debt crisis in the early 1980s drew them into a new role. They started to undertake more policy-based lending and expanded their focus to include rural development. When the 1979 energy crisis erupted, they initiated structural adjustment loans, which distributed aid to struggling countries while enforcing policy changes aiming at encouraging investment, production and labour-intensive manufacturing and altering the distribution of government resources. As Ngaire Woods says, these conditional structural adjustment loans required borrowers to undertake stringent measures to stabilize and ensure adjustment in their economies in order to access credit from the IMF or the WB. (Barend 1996)

Conditionalities went further to more political levels when the post-Soviet countries' transition process began. In the terminology of the IMF, *conditionality* refers to the policies the Fund expects a member to follow in order to be able to avail itself of credit from the Fund (Barend 1996). However, in practice, political and security goals are implied in many cases. Over time, the conditionalities became broader. New conceptual tools such as good governance measures, anti-corruption measures, and encouragement of the rule of law have come into prominence (Woods).

The typical set of conditionalities consists of two main elements requested from the debtor: First, liberalization of tariffs, domestic goods markets and domestic factor markets. Second, higher domestic taxes in order to improve the debtor state's fiscal position and government austerity. According to Brawley and Baerg (2007), these policy recommendations are aimed at improving the country's ability to export more goods and services while importing less by improving the competitiveness of individual domestic firms, and at improving the state's ability to service its own international debts. Similarly, Burnside and Dollar (2000) state that increasing the conditionalities of aid on policies will improve the effectiveness of aid.

However, Easterly, Levine, and Roodman (2004) find that the conclusions of Burnside and Dolar are fragile if one changes the sample period (e.g., by extending the sample up to 1997) or if one fills in the missing data for 1970–1993. The findings in Barro and Lee (2002) are even more negative; they analyse the effectiveness of IMF aid and conclude that loan participation rates reduce economic growth and investments, although they increase openness.

Moreover, according to a Eurodad survey, based on data from 24 countries including former Soviet countries, average poor countries face as many as 67 conditionalities per WB loan. Some of the countries face a far higher number of conditionalities: Uganda, for example, where 23% of the all children under 5 years old are malnourished, faced 197 conditionalities attached to its WB grant in 2005 (Kovach 2006). Another piece of research by Webb and Kapur (2000) on the number of conditionalities found that for a sample of 25 countries, with programs initiated between 1997 and 1999, the average number of conditonalities was 26. This compares to about six in the 1970s and ten in the 1980s.

Some of the conditionalities are binding and some are just advisory. The WB conditionalities are more clearly expressed in documents like grant/loan agreements and country assistance strategy papers. The main objective of the country assisted strategy papers is to set out a selective program of the WB support linked to the country's development strategy and to include a comprehensive evaluation of challenges facing the country. In its diagnosis, the country assisted strategy paper takes into account the country's creditworthiness, state of institutional development, implementation capacity, governance, and other sectoral and cross-cutting issues. From this assessment, the level and composition of the WB financial, advisory, and/or technical support to the country is determined.

Conditionalities for Central Asian countries

Central Asian countries became the neediest clients of the IMF and the WB throughout the post-Soviet period. By the end of 2011, the number of loans by the WB to Kazakhstan reached 42 (18 of them fully repaid), to Kyrgyzstan 74 (none fully repaid), to Uzbekistan 27 (none repaid), to Tajikistan 52 (none fully repaid), and to Turkmenistan 4 (almost all fully repaid).

Almost all loan projects in Central Asian countries contain the same conditionalities as elsewhere in the world. Critics of IMF and the WB conditionalities for the less-developed world and transition economies blame their general character and that they are not country specific (Vatkin 2003, Woods 2006, Caufield 1996). However an analysis of IMF and the WB agreement conditionalities reveal contrary results: For example, detailed privatization proposals for cotton farms in Tajikistan or pharmacological industry in Kyrgyzstan reveal how the two institutions work country-specific. The uncountable number of agreements and their strictly detailed entries leave no space to argue that the IMF and the WB strategies are not country-specific. However, the principle is the same for all countries: Open and liberalize the markets, integrate with the western economies, abolish the social state functions, and believe in the invisible hands of the free market.

In one of the first development credit agreements with Kyrgyzstan, it is stated that in order to strengthen the borrower's capability to carry out the program, the borrower shall implement the activities set forth in the schedule. In the mentioned schedule it is expected from the borrower to perform a study on privatization in agriculture, to draft a mining legislation to promote reform activities, to cooperate in legal reforms and to reform the health services and pharmaceutical sector. After two decades of operations in the country and after two colour revolutions in the low income Kyrgyzstan, the WB still demands to continue the privatization of public assets.

Similar recommendations can be found in almost all documents of IMF and the WB affiliates, such as IFC's Investment Climate Advisory Services Project, Central Asia Corporate Governance Project, IFC Azerbaijan-Central Asia Financial Markets Infrastructure Advisory Services Project.

However, as admitted in one of the earlier evaluation reports by the WB, privatization has never been easy to implement, even in developed market economies such as Great Britain and Canada. The total number of state owned enterprises that were privatized worldwide between 1980 and 1991, amounted to 6,832 enterprises, and the CIS countries seek to privatize over 85,000 within two years (Im 1993).

The WB clearly states that Turkmenistan, the least cooperating country in the region, will get additional support, only if the government shows strong commitment to a deeper reform agenda. According to evaluation reports, it is expected that the reform agenda should include phasing out of state order system combined with the gradual elimination of input subsidies and administrative interference with production decisions.

Regionalism Conditionalities for Central Asia

In the early years after Central Asia's independence, the international institutions paid scant attention to the region, as the focus was on a rapid recovery of Central Europe and of Russia. Among the post-Soviet countries, Russian Federation and Baltic states were the countries that most of the international aid and support were allocated to (Charles 2002). This changed after the September 11 attacks in 2001. At the beginning of the new millennium, Russia started to recover and under the Vladimir Putin administration became a rival for those who were trying to have an influential role in Central Asia, in a region called the backyard of Russia. Moscow's aim is to reintegrate Central Asia into an economic, political, and ultimately military union with Russia (Blank 2007).

China's and India's growing energy need and Putin's move back to Central Asia made European countries be more alert on Central Asian affairs. Putin's vision of energy as a weapon in international and regional politics underlined the fact that Central Asian and Caucasian energy resources are one of the most important alternatives for the European countries. The EU's aims became stability in the region, the propagation of European values, and access to Central Asian energy resources.

Moreover, awareness about these issues made European countries put more effort into encouraging the Central Asian countries in regionalism projects, which means an institutional framework set by the governments and widely accepted in international economics and international political economy. The driving force of regionalization is the internationalization of the activity of non-governmental actors and international financial institutions; and regionalism is a consequence of inter-governmental bargaining (Libman 2007). Thus, international donors accompanied Western efforts and focused on assisting Central Asia with a broader agenda of transition reforms, the building of market institutions, and provision of social and physical infrastructure (UNDP 2005).

However, Central Asia is a tough region for Western governments and institutions. There are rival regionalization projects: The USA and the EU support a regionalization project in which Central Asian countries become independent from strong neighbours, Russia and then China (Pomfret 2003).

Most of the post-Soviet integration projects are formed by Russian centric structures: The Commonwealth of Independent States (CIS), The Common Economic Space and the Eurasian Economic Community (EAEC). The political and security arm of this system is the Organization of the Collective Security Treaty (OCST), which is strongly affiliated with EAEC. The Organization of the Central Asian Cooperation (OCAC) was also established as a sub-regional integration area; however, after Russia's accession to the OCAC in 2004 it merged with the EAEC in 2005 (Libman 2007). The number of multilateral treaties currently exceeds 2,500.

The ongoing regionalization processes based on the Soviet networks is politically aimed at diversifying to two different targets. The first one is a regionalization project aiming at regions altogether integrating to the Russian Federation. The second is a projection of a regional integration model excluding Russia and other neighbouring partners like China.

Conclusion

At the beginning of the transition period in Central Asia, the main goal of IMF and the WB was to carry out liberalization reforms as quickly and as decisively as possible. This path is named shock-therapy. In almost all country reports of the WB in the first years of the reforms, the objective of the shock therapy was defined as to carry out the reforms to an irreversible point. The fear from the rise of the anti-capitalist movements and parties in the early nineties was an important factor in this motive. Obviously this was a rather more ideological-political strategy than an economic one. But in the mid 1990s and especially with the economic crisis in Russia in 1998, the side effects of the shock therapy became clear. Critics argued that the free market reform policies of IMF and the WB in practice are often harmful to economic development if implemented badly, quickly (shock therapy), or in the wrong sequence or in very weak, uncompetitive economies.

These criticisms led to a strategy change: Poverty reduction strategy and structural adjustment programs gained priority for Central Asia, as elsewhere in the world. Today IMF and the WB focus on Millennium Development Goals. This new strategy is welcomed by Central Asian governments who need loans and infrastructure support programs.

References

Barro, R., and Lee, J. W. (2002) "IMF Programs: Who Is Chosen and What Are the Effects?" NBER Working Paper No. 8951.

Best, Jacqueline, Why the Economy is Often the Exception to Politics as Usual, Theory Culture Society 2007; 24.

Blank, Stephen J., U.S. Interests in Central Asia and the Challenges to Them, Carlisle, PA: 2007.

Brawley, Mark R. and Nicole Baerg, Structural Adjustment, Development, and Democracy, International Studies Review (2007) 9, 601–615, p.603.

Burnside C., and Dollar, D., "Aid, Policies, and Growth." American Economic Review, 2000; 90 (4): 847–88.

Caufield, Catherine, Masters of Illusion: The World Bank and the Poverty of Nations. New York: Henry Holt, 1996.

CCA Highlights, http://www.imf.org/external/pubs/ft/reo/2011/mcd/eng/pdf/cca1011_hi.pdf,

Council of the European Union, "The EU and Central Asia: Strategy for a New Partnership", Document 10113/07, Brussels, 31 May 2007.

Country Assistance Strategy, http://web.worldbank.org/WBSITE/EXTERNAL/PROJECTS/

de Vries, Barend A., "The World Bank's Focus on Poverty", in Griesgraber, Jo Marie; Gunter, Bernhard G., The World Bank: Lending on a Global Scale. Pluto Press. 1996.

Development Credit Agreement(Rehabilitation Credit)between Republic of Kyrgyzstan and International Development Association, Dated May 20, 1993.

Easterly W.; Levine R.; and Roodman, D., "New Data, New Doubts: A Comment on Burnside and Dollar's "Aid, Policies, and Growth'." American Economic Review, 2004: 94 (3): 774–80.

Harold, James, "The Fall and Rise of the European Economy in the Twentieth Century" in T.C.W. Blanning (ed) The Oxford History of Modern Europe, New York: Oxford University Press, 2000.

Howard Michael C. & John E. King, "Imperialism", in Encyclopedia of Social Theory, George Ritzer (ed), Volume II, California: Sage Publications, 2005.

Im, S. J., R Jalali, J. Saghir, Privatization in the Republics of the Former Soviet Union: Framework and Initial Results, The World bank, June 1993.

Japanese Grant Agreement between Republic of Tajikistan and International Bank For Reconstruction and Development, Dated October 1, 1996.

Kapur, Devesh & Richard Webb, Governance-Related Conditionalities Of The International Financial Institutions, Harvard University, Cambridge, Massachusetts, G-24 Discussion Paper No. 6, August 2000.

Kovach, Hetty & Yasmina Lansman World Bank and IMF conditionality: a development injustice Eurodad report June 2006.

Libman, Alexander Regionalisation And Regionalism in The Post-Soviet Space: Current Status And Implications For Institutional Development, Europe-Asia Studies, Vol. 59, No. 3, May 2007, p. 412

McMichael, Philip.. Development and Social Change: A Global Perspective. Thousand Oaks, CA: Pine Forge, 2000

Ngaire Woods, The Globalizers: The IMF, The World Bank, And Their Borrowers, London: Cornell University Press, 2006.

Polak, Jacques J. The Changing Nature of IMF Conditionality, OECD Development Centre, Working Paper No:41, August 1991.

Pomfret, Richard, "Central Asia Since 1991: The Experience Of The New Independent States," OECD Development Centre, Working Paper No. 212, July 2003.

Program Information Document (PID), IDU, April 8, 2011 Report No.: AB6520

Ries, Charles (2002), .The Baltic Sea Region from a US Perspective., Speech to the Baltic Development Forum Summit, Copenhagen (15 October 2002) < http://www.cbss.st/baltinfo/2002/baltinfo_52.pdf >, accessed 9 June 2008.

Sklair, Leslie, The Transnational Capitalist Class. Malden, MA: Blackwell. 2001.

Turkmenistan, Country Assistance Strategy Document, 2000/12/22, Report Number: 21530. December 22, 2000

UNDP, Central Asia HDR 2005.

Vatkin, Sam, After the Rain, How the West Lost the East, 2nd ed. Skopje: Narcissus Publication, 2003.

Woods, Ngaire, The Globalizers: The IMF, The World Bank, And Their Borrowers, London: Cornell University Press, 2006.

Woods, Ngaire, The International Monetary Fund and World Bank.

World Bank Databases: Country Lending Summaries, http://web.worldbank.org

World Bank http://www.referenceforbusiness.com/encyclopedia/Val-Z/World-Bank.html#ixzz1fzYhR6Fn

World Economic and Financial Surveys, Regional Economic Outlook, Middle East And Central Asia, IMF, September 2006.

TURKEY AND GLOBALIZATION IN EURASIA

PROF. RECEP KÖK[1]

Introduction

In studying the geopolitical developments that have arisen due to the process of globalization in the Near East, Middle East, Central Asia, Caucasia, the Balkans, and, in short, the Islamic-Turkic world, we have to take into account the political aims and practices of all the major powers, the USA, the European Union, Russia and China, concerning this region. Is globalization a tool for these powers to administer and channel world resources to their own advantage; a tool which uses the "carrot" approach, that is, seems to offer advantages to other countries for these superpowers to attain their own aims and motives?

In the literature on globalization, several political, cultural and economic explanations have been given by different authors for its emergence. Some authors have sought the reason for its emergence in economic relations (Bauman 1999, Giddens; 1998 Hopkins-Wallerstein 1999; Wallerstein 1974, 1979, 2004; Robertson 1992, 1999; Rodric 1997; Walters 2001; Steger 2003). Some authors question whether globalization is a tool of superpowers to acquire and maintain their world hegemony. In short, they ask, whether globalization is a new form of "imperialism" (Bukharin 1994; Rupert 2000; Mittelman 2005; Steger 2003, 2009, Ritzer 2004; Robinson, 2004, 2007; Sklaire 2005; Mooney and Evans, 2007).

In this article, we will first investigate the literature on globalization, its historical frame and its reflections. Subsequently, we will open discussions for the need to introduce a new nationalistic strategy for Turkey and kin countries.

[1] Dokuz Eylül University, Izmir, Turkey

Globalization, Universalization, Internationalism and Imperialism

According to Steger (2003, 2009), globalization and universalization give rise to very important outcomes. Globalization is built on five consistent and coherent assertions (Yalçınkaya, 2010, p.90) as below:

- Globalization liberalizes and integrates the markets.
- It is inevitable and irreversible.
- Globalization is not directed by people but by markets and technology.
- Globalization benefits everyone (that is, it is a win-win situation, not a zero-sum-game).
- Globalization accelerates the spread of democracy in the world.

We need to investigate and discuss the accuracy of these assumptions, based on actual historical developments that have taken place as a result of globalization. This should enable us to avoid accepting any unverified "dogma" concerning globalization.

In our opinion, "universal" can be explained only with human nature and natural laws of motion; whereas "global" is the sum of practices that materialize the universal, that is, global is acquired. On the other hand, the form that both of the motives take when they are turned into a moving power of synergy is ideology, and it appears as imperialism in terms of the global system.

The common aspect of the characteristics of being human can be analysed philosophically with the concept "humane". Any individual, whether he or she works in an organization or not, can be "humane" if he or she strives to raise the standards of humanity. Bauman (1999), in this vein, perceives man's struggle to improve and develop civilization and to broaden unity as "humane", and he wants these efforts by individuals to continue. But, historical events show that the objective and determination to benefit humanity, that is, for individuals to be "humane", is not always the top priority.

The emergence of interdependencies and the rise in the number of ties between organizations and governments create a process of integration. The elements that gain a "global character" in this process are mutated or manipulated by human beings. Therefore, everything universal can also be global, but not the other way round.

Internationalization is a process stemming from economic, political or cultural interdependence between the individual and the society, between the society and the state, and amongst the states. Robinson (2005) underlines the importance of geographies marked by mutual interdependence and argues that transcending geographical national boundaries paves the way for the improvement of economic activities both quantitatively and qualitatively. These processes, known in economic literature either as bilateral or multilateral, form the basis of internationalization.

As long as economies are subject to an open system, relations live on differences, and even though the need of decision-making units are at the level of single relationship, the nation-society and nation-state ceilings created by mutual interactions are shaped under international economy. The process that stems from trans-nationalization weakens the nation-state structure. As transnational experiences increase, nation-states hand over some of their functions to supranational institutionalization. According to Robinson (2005), the quantitative extension that is unique to internationalization creates qualitative extension based on functional integration with a different dimension. Therefore, trans-nationalization becomes a web of global control, rather than internationalization, based on the integrated meaning of globality.

In this respect, Sklair (1999) mentions three types of approaches aimed at explaining globalization: internationalization, globalism, and trans-nationalization. Internationalization is a state-centrist approach. It is reminiscent of the centre-periphery and semi-periphery approach among powerful and powerless states. Globalism, on the other hand, is a counter-thesis to the state-centrist approach. This thesis is market globalism, which has the discourse of a borderless world that is not defined with states but - although it is hard to explain - with the concept of market forces.

Trans-nationalization, on the other hand, is a process which is defined by economic, cultural and political transnational practices and can be explained with a global system formed through a synthesis of internationalization and market globalism. This phenomenon is, in historical framework, defined as “capitalist globalization” (Yalçınkaya, 2010 p.22). Then, is it possible to speak of “socialist globalization” or “Islamic globalization”? A social element that has become global can live as an ideology only if it gains validity as a socio-economic system and carries a claim. According to Sklair (1999), the capitalist globalization that operates under the constraints of “class polarization” and “ecological unsustainability” can turn into “socialist globalization” depending on a transition stage following the process of democracy based on cooperation and participation. This view basically echoes with the Marxist doctrine. Kazgan (2000) argues that the theory of imperialism is the theory of Marxism that follows the capitalist evolution and that especially the market globalism that emerged in the post-WWII period created the notion of “neo-imperialism”. This argument is in parallel with the view of pre-

Lenin theorists of imperialism (such as, John A. Hobson, Rosa Luxemburg, Rudolf Hilferding) and of Lenin that "it is the final development of capitalism in which the domination of monopolies and the financial capital has already been established, capital exports has gained significant importance, the sharing of the world amongst trusts has already begun and the sharing of all soils of the world amongst capitalist states has been finalized" (Yalçınkaya, 2010, pp.25-28). Today, as Bukharin (1918) points, the "capitalist evolution that emerges in its commercial, industrial and financial forms" still evokes the presence of a system that overlaps with internationalization and serves for the process of finalizing globalization.

Globalization, Neo-Imperialism and Turkey

To know the cyclical causes that pave the way for crises, it is necessary to assess the process of growth of the Turkish economy, and to address the causes of overlaps and deviations between real economy and monetary economy within the framework of the negative conditions into which we have been driven. Did the rupture between forces of production and financial markets stem from lack of a political model? Why did the events go beyond financial markets, or what fed the crises so that the real (negative) impacts on employment and living standards have become continuous and often (1960, 1980, 2003) political parties that formed the coalition have fallen outside the parliament? In what conditions did the "viruses" that threaten the global economy emerge and turn into deadlock "syndromes", especially for developing countries? Should the "conventional support" for this process be searched for in the notion of globalization? Taking into consideration the consequences and intensities of the crises in Turkey in April 1994, November 2000, and February 2001, and the global crises in 1929, 1945-1947 and 2008; in what conception of reactions should we consider the newly-emerged "new world order", the position of impoverished masses and its possible consequences? What are our chances of finding a guiding light among the threat and opportunity strategies debated for Turkey and of illuminating our path with our own light? If such a chance exists, what are its driving forces?

The concept of globalization, which had not been of much importance academically until the 1980s, began to be used widely in the 1990s. The main reason this concept evokes an ideological insecurity stems from the atmosphere created by the "powerful world" that justifies the spread of the Western culture and the capitalist society and carries the claim of changing the world. When looked upon with suspicion, is globalization a process of social catastrophe in which the geographical barriers over social and cultural regulations are removed and the degree of differentiation between people's economic gains and losses are heightened, that is, the relative imbalance begins to be felt more acutely?

As for traditional imperialism, it is the sum of efforts of a state to control, or at least, supervise the resources of the world and to be influential economically and culturally over another state or a region. As long as superstates saw establishing continuous control over all lands, human production and capital powers in the world as indispensable for their hegemony and independence, they have always competed with each other in order to extend their privileges. They developed "contemporary" approaches oriented towards exploiting underdeveloped and developing countries and their regional sensitivities with the aim of assuming control over new markets and natural resources, and thus extended their global sovereignty. This development gained speed with the process of "monopolization" and the age of systematic imperialism began after 1870. Analysing the world wars and almost all local operations in the last fifty years from this perspective will contribute to the formation of healthier social theories.

The theory of imperialism, which began to gain prominence in the early twentieth century, began to have different dimensions following WWII, when colonies started to become nation-states. In fact, although it has not been perfected yet as a theory, the neo-imperialism approach, which was proposed in the 1960s, brought into question an issue that had not hitherto been included in classical theories of imperialism: methods to subordinate countries like Turkey were developed by burdening these countries with debt under the guidance of multinational corporations and various international organizations. However, in today's world in which the understanding of "interdependence" is valid even for the most developed countries, it is very difficult to estimate the dimensions of neo-imperialism; because autonomies and functions of the states are being eroded by the influences of supranational trends. Even though sensitivities about the global transformation are propounded, the economic and political integrations among the states as key units are becoming increasingly prominent. Multi-dimensional variables are the key in economic imperialism and the international allocation of resources. With the maturation of the "supra-national system", many foreign firms have developed alternatives to control and even to totally lay hands on global natural resources by employing the mediation of their protective hegemonic powers. The message conveyed to the global public through the statement made by US president Bush "Iraqi petroleum reserves are the God's bestowment on the US society" is exemplary.

Since the Industrial Revolution (1976-1840, according to Toynbee) that started in Britain, especially developed countries had undergone W. W. Rostow's "process of sustained growth" and formed the "wealthy Western club" in the 1960s, but no other country has been allowed to join it. According to Wallerstein, (1974) who analysed the world system for the period of 1945-1960 and provided his expectations for the period between 1990 and 2025, there exist only two formal possibilities: one is that the world system will keep functioning as it has been doing for the last five centuries as the capitalist world economy through certain continuous adjustments. This means that the Kontradieff cycle will turn upwards again and its longer hegemonic cycle will re-enter the process of reorganization. The other is that an ambiguous period of systemic chaos will begin as a foregone conclusion of a hegemonic downfall that began to be observed in the 1970s. As a result of this systemic crisis, a bifurcation will emerge. The hegemonic downfall will require those countries located in the centre to strive to be competitive primarily in advanced products (high technology goods). Formulae are sought towards rewarding labour in these hegemonic products. It requires a long struggle for hegemonic superiority, and if remaining at the top collides at this stage, the process may lead to a world war (Hopkins, 1998 pp.284-286).

While the cleavage between the First and Third Worlds were thought to be permanent, Asian Tigers (Hong Kong, Singapore, Taiwan and South Korea) emerged as the first flow, followed by the second flow that created the surprising rise of highly-populated economies of the South-Eastern Asia and China, and this second flow added a new dimension to the "new world order". As the 20th century drew to a close, the "firedamp" (my own term) accumulated, or a regulatory power embittered this accumulation in such a way that consecutive explosions followed a single "spark" causing radical government change-overs (the background of the changeovers experienced in the USA, England and other countries after the 2008 global crisis can be recalled).

From the point of view of Turkey's economic development; Turkey managed to survive the developments in the world through policies of self-sufficiency (with the accumulated stock of knowledge and capital) until the 1980s, although it suffered from the difficult conditions of the early 20th Century and it later "pendulated" between "right and left" under the novel conditions brought about by WWII.

In these years, financial markets, especially in developed Western countries were re-regulated; new market enterprises were initiated;

attempts were made to minimize the role of the state in the functioning of markets with the aim of improving the contracted market conditions, accelerating the slowed-down growth processes. This led to bringing into force again the monetarist policies that had lost their dynamism; and the international ties between financial markets were reinforced further. On the other hand, when foreign credits provided by international financial institutions (IMF, World Bank, etc.) to developing countries in the 1970s were faced with the risk of not returning with principal and interest beginning in the early 1980s (e.g. debt payment crises in South American countries) the issue was opened up for discussion of finding a new and lower-risk real resource to the rapidly increasing international fund surplus and what should be its instruments. Within the context of these debates, the proposal of the OECD council to put into effect the deregulation policies of 1979 in order to enhance and regulate competition paved the way for global privatization policies in the international platform. This view was also embraced by the IMF and World Bank. As a result, economic packages were prepared for the less developed countries aimed at the implementation of IMF programs that limited the implementation of statist policies, that is, public investments, interventionism and protectionism. These packages made it easier for international financial organizations and developed countries to allocate financial support to less developed member countries.

As the threat of a "radical revolution" largely shrivelled with the collapse of communism in the subsequent years (1990), investments made by the Western world to the less developed world rapidly rose under the new secure conditions provided by the Western world. In this period, therefore, interest rates in developed countries fell down and many investors began to transfer funds abroad to less developed countries in order to obtain higher yields. This situation was labelled as new financial opportunity areas and thus "emerging markets" were born. The volume of private capital flow to developing countries was as much as 42 billion USD in 1990. Investments financed by institutions like IMF and World Bank in the Third World as part of the above-mentioned developments exceeded in volume the sum of all private investments, and as of 1997, the flow of private funds reached 256 billion USD.

Therefore, although the negative effects of the "tequila crisis" were alleviated within a couple of years with the involvement of IMF and World Bank for the grand rescue, the debate on this simple question did not end: Are the costs, which are already present and may get heavier in the future, burdened with the essential aim of legitimizing Turkey's special emphasis on US interests? The crises which began in 1997, due to the competition between the USD and the yen or, as also indicated above, due to the lack of regulation and control over financial sectors, have influenced Turkey in 2000 to provide a brief evaluation related to China. The emergence of China as an Asian competitive power caused the contraction of Thailand, Malaysia, Indonesia, Hong Kong, South Korea, etc. The wave of this contraction created a panic for these latter countries which, in the end, also influenced Turkey.

Liberal Hayek sees capitalism as a system of balance and explains crises as results of periodic interventions of governments and private banks in this “fragile system” and excessive expansion in credit volume. Schumpeter’s model, on the other hand, is based on the investigation of the impacts of technological effectiveness on the general economic balance. According to him, “development” is a process of non-stop “change” stirred by innovation and it emerges as a result of the creation of new combinations. Change, on the other hand, emerges as a result of “creative destruction”. We should explain the creative destruction in the near history of the world through the conditions of birth of the Turkish Republic. Today, when we fully see the true colour of the USA’s claim of directing history, our rush to be a party to the cost to be paid and the shame of not fulfilling our role in the historical evolution will sooner or later bear heavily on Turkish intellectuals.

In economic systems, creative destruction always occurs in the form of replacement of the old system with a new one. In this economic model, it is advocated that growth without technical innovation, technical innovation without entrepreneurship, and entrepreneurship without credit are not possible. According to Schumpeter, innovations not only create the new economic process but also increase the “temperature of the economy”. A sudden slowdown will happen while innovations follow one another, the economy heads towards a new stable equilibrium. In this respect, in order not to experience unsustainable “supply shocks”, developing countries constantly export (via the mediation of international institutions) demand shocks to developing countries and these countries become a part of this “global” mechanism at the cost of saving the day trapped by the currency-interest-inflation spiral. For instance, as of February 2003, Turkey’s outstanding external debt reached 120 billion USD, and internal debt, 180 billion Turkish Liras (in terms of today’s currency remuneration), and the country fell down to 51st rank in the world league on productive efficiency. Recently, we also witnessed an historically remarkable development. In the face of the possibility of the Turkish government sending a war resolution to the Turkish Parliament, the USD depreciated and the stock index rose. However, when the possibility of the delay or cancellation of the resolution became a current issue during the negotiations, the USD appreciated and the stock index went down. This paradox is a clear indicator that could explain the chaos mentioned above that we have been driven into.

According to Schumpeter, what will bring an end to the capitalist system is not economic crises, but the rise of unequal wealth the system creates. As in the USA case, when the wave of dissatisfaction among workers whose living standards have been improved and among intellectuals who grew up in a liberal environment come together with an unequal and unfair distribution, the attained welfare is replaced by moral dissatisfaction and quest for prestige. Therefore, the September 11 Osama Bin Laden movement, linked with the organizational support (Al-Qaeda) is turned into an instrument of legitimizing the "global" system, and is principally presented as the process of transformation of the "new world order" with the support of media powers.

Turks' Mission Concerning Western Ideology and Eurasia

The Western ideology does not have the luxury to turn its back on the increasing importance of Turkey, which possesses geopolitical and strategic importance in Eurasia. Therefore, it developed two main ideological approaches in order to be able to control the "Turkish Eurasia".

The first corresponds to our description of "tough ideological approaches" and consists of practices that change the direction of history; the main proponent of which is the USA. This ideology, known as the "Carter Doctrine" proposed by Z. Brzezinski for a monopolar world, is presented to the world as the driving force of globalization. It is, in fact, a strategy aimed at stopping the rising Chinese and Indian nationalism by American capitalism. This "pre-emptive strike strategy" began with the Iraqi invasion and is shown by the "armistice press" of many countries as an inevitable reflection of success in the genetic sector and intelligent weapons. It is also based on Huntington's clash of civilizations.

The second ideological approach, that we want to include under the category of "soft ideological approaches", can be defined as the strategy of "anchoring" Turkey to Europe. The main aim of this strategy is to put into practice the "softened" institutional decisions of the EU by taking advantage and using the weakness of pro-EU Turks. In fact, Europe, which is based on "rational foundation", sees Turkey as an historical rival, because Turkey keeps hold of the epicentre of what Europe considers contemporary civilization. The high European civilization was born in the Aegean and Mediterranean and developed as Istanbul-cantered in the East-

Roman Empire. For this reason, the fact that Turkey keeps hold of this geography is kept in mind by the West as an unbearable memory and seen as a historical problem.

At the core of these ideologies, that can be explained through historical consciousness and whose actors have changed over time, lies the claim of the West to fully control the strategic resources ranging from China and India to Asia Minor and Europe, and the Silk Road that connects these resources. In this region, among the states which have controlled this road and which represented a high culture, are the Turkish states. The Turkish nation controlled the course of history for about a millennium. Since the Eleventh Century, the Great Seljuk Empire cantered in Rey/Isfahan, the Timur Empire cantered in Samarkand, the Ottoman Empire cantered in Istanbul, and today's Ankara-cantered Turkish Republic and other Central Asian economies are seen as representatives of the period that need to be called to account. Today, although this Eurasian geography, known for its underground riches, is shared by many independent states, it whets the appetite of wild Western tigers. In this context, the empowered existence of the new Turkish Republic that takes its reference point M. Kemal Atatürk, who is known with his expression "Independence is my character", is perceived as a syndrome of insecurity by the EU. Therefore, it necessitated the West to search for new approaches towards Turkey.

Those in Europe who seek dominance have found a new rational way to anchor the Turkish Eurasia to the New Europe: Turkey's EU membership. Though EU membership had been proposed with great attractions for Turkey, she was to be kept in the waiting-rooms indefinitely. This new way was at first perceived by Turks as long, narrow, dark and rugged. The regulations that assure European nations about the future keep-out of Turkey and the decisions that are used to convince Turks are based simultaneously in the EU Constitution.

These two ideological approaches that trap Turkey also force Turkey into a choice of "a rock and a hard place". The competition over the distribution of global resources is becoming clearer by means of (mostly EU- and US) multi-national corporations, roadmaps to be imposed on the world are determined in Bilderberg summits; the monopolar administrative mechanism, which is formed with the contribution of the co-opts coming from developing countries, is secured as a global power.

The ideologies that aim to change the course of history impose the following two scenarios on Turkey. According to the first of these, Turkey has the potential to control the Near East. Turkey should either be committed to the US like a mandate or be anchored to Europe without being made a full member of the EU. If the first scenario is not accepted by Turkey, a process in which agreement is rendered more difficult should be triggered: This process covers a five to ten year period marked by a policy of gaining time in order to persuade Turkey. Here, Turkey should either be forced to an ethnic civil war after preparing the political and legal foundations of it; or political plans should be put into practice, including the admittance of the so-called Armenian Genocide, that will render Turkey's fragmentation viable; or the constitutional resistance that ensures independence should be broken through processes like open-ended "democratic opening" and a society that is at odds with its state due to increased poverty should be created so that a divided Turkey emerges out of the trap of a federative government. What the above-specified tough ideological approaches have been doing in Iraq within the framework of the "Greater Middle East project" is clear.

The soft ideology is covered in the demands of the EU for Turkey's full membership negotiations. These, negotiations are open-ended (EP Decision Art. 50, EU Summit Art. 23). Thus, Greece, The Greek Cypriot Administration of Southern Cyprus and some other countries can come together and suspend the negotiations. It is difficult to estimate what compromises will be asked from Turkey and what threat strategies will be proposed in the negotiations to be held under these conditions.

Calls concerning the local population living in South-eastern Turkey, administrative reforms, recognizing Kurds' cultural rights and guaranteeing of equal treatment, and taking more effective steps towards reaching an agreement with "Kurdish forces" are striking. Expressions that tend to force Turkey to recognize Kurds as a political power should be taken into consideration along with the efforts to present the terrorist organization, that has been backed by the West and supported for years, as a legitimate political actor, although implicitly. This approach that serves the imperialist aims of the EU is hidden from the public conscience and the Turkish-Kurdish issue is kept as a bleeding wound. Therefore, the movement of secessionism is endowed with legitimacy, and the active demands of the secessionist powers in Turkey for a federative government are given support as a supranational institution.

However, it should be known that the Turkish Republic has the power and determination to protect its own citizens and to perform what a constitutional state requires. The Republic has demonstrated its power to fight against treason and negligence many times in the history and identified its Turkish ideology with human rights by saying "the people who established this republic are Turkish". The EU's approach on this issue, on the other hand, is nothing but a tool for global imperialism that reflects hypocrisy and hostility.

The directive that "Turkey should recognize the genocide on the Armenian population and encourage the process of reconciliation with the Armenian public" is important. By also considering the laws passed by French and Swiss Parliaments that prohibit the denial of the Armenian Genocide, it is not difficult to estimate how far the daring will go.

Similarly, if the extreme demands such as that of Greece of increasing its territorial waters up to twelve miles, recognition of the Greek Cypriot administration as "Cyprus Republic", and withdrawing the Turkish military presence from Cyprus are accepted, either Turkey will face the obligation to draw back to Central Asia or a satellite country will be born that is integrated with Europe as the state of Ankara.

When the impositions of EP decisions regarding Eurasia are examined, the primary question is about petroleum and water reserves. The rationales of bringing EU policies to the administration of the regional infrastructure regarding petroleum and water resources are dictated to Turkey. The off-border problems, transfer of energy resources to Europe and protection of customers are propounded to have positive and lasting impacts on European citizens. Moreover, by pointing to the fact that the water outflow from Turkey has declined after the building of Atatürk Dam, the EU is kind of using an iron hand in a velvet glove. The EU even implied the establishment of an "Ombudsman Office" monitored by the EU that will be responsible for the fair and equal distribution of rivers.

In sum, when these ideological approaches and the developments of the recent history are considered together with the practices of the US and decisions of the EU; our findings should necessitate an original way and method for Turkey. Turkish nationalists derive their current power from the will that established the Republic of Turkey; Turkish nationalism is the name of the will that shoulders the burden of history and carries it to the future by putting the essence of Islam into it. This will, which sanctifies human rights and honour, is the Turks' historical mission. Turks have managed to convey the cause of being independent; they have dignified other oppressed nations and have always accurately read the changing global conditions. In all periods of history, the Turkish nation set an example to oppressed nations and groups by fighting for its honour and independence. However, it is necessary to point to the mismatch today between the historical mission and pragmatic vision.

If we read the existing conditions correctly with respect to Eurasia and recent relations with the EU, our main duty is to develop an alternative policy/strategy against the strategy that involves ethnic conflicts and a religious paradigm, into which the USA and the EU want to drive us. The USA assumed control by ensuring the appointment of German-origin Pope

Benedict XVI in order to block the impact of Germany to make independent strategies on Eurasia and to enroot the Crusader Alliance again, despite the opposition by Italy and France. Unsurprisingly, the new Pope made his first speech giving a message to the global public: The main theme underlined in this speech is that "Jews share a common heritage with Christians".

Conclusion: A Proposal Based on Turkish-Islamic Civilization

Every social cause and imperial aim involves "human nature and economy". In order to raise the Turkish pendulum of history and to re-establish justice, we should develop the main principles and the universal determinants of a model, which we presume as "general welfare" in terms of consumption and "national regulation" in terms of production, and we should find original ways to express ourselves.

It is necessary to take into consideration the ideas based on our national existence and to embrace an enlightened scientific thinking system that is equipped with strategies to protect our independence, fed by Turkish wisdom. It is a moral and humane responsibility to convey our belief in Turks' historical mission and call the Turks of the world to revise this sacred mission.

There exists an urgent necessity for a strategic and effective regional organization in order to prevent the controlling power of the imperialist strategies and the monopolar exploitation of energy resources over the peoples of Eurasia and to fulfil our historical responsibility in front of history. This strategy should be turned into a common policy that should be embraced by all the Central Asian countries living in this geography. The more the kin states focus on this new formation, the more likely the establishment of the commonwealth of independent kin states will become.

The Turkish-Islamic civilization/modernization project that we define as the Turkish Renaissance is a project to be shouldered by every human being living in Eurasia to reconstruct himself or herself with science, wisdom and belief. We believe that anyone who opposes the enslavement of people is a civilized person. The project that turns the essence of human rights into social norms can be called Turkish-Islamic civilization. On the other hand, Western civilization sees people as material entities, through a lifestyle reduced to technology. We have to recall the three passions and three troubles that explain the social orders widely accepted but also criticized throughout the world, the necessity of the search for a new formation and the management and direction of these passions towards a new project of civilization will then become more meaningful.

These passions fed by the philosophy of the middle ages are defined as "three sins" by Saint Augustinus: money and desire to acquire property; assuming authority; and uncontrolled sexual desire. These passions create the following three troubles in practice: regulatory wars that redirect the allocation of world's resources; mass hunger, poverty, unequal income distribution and dissatisfaction that is felt more heavily through mass communication instruments; and finally diseases that carry the risk of spread that are hard to control and are rising in vehemence. Therefore, it is necessary to raise the awareness about the effective management and direction of good elements in human nature that will eliminate or at least minimize the dominance of evil elements. Searches for projects of civilization that will create a take-off of international consciousness will become more important when an assessment is made, as will be proposed below.

While imagining a world ruled by civilized states and nations; the primary condition of establishing a social order in which we could live in prosperity and peace is the desire to be civilized individuals and civilized nations/communities. In this respect, the viability of the Eurasian Union Strategy as a manageable construct depends on the capacity to orient the following three passions/principles: science, wisdom, and belief.

What is meant by science is the cultivation of the "type of human" identical to the claim of having a share in the universal values. The more a person girds himself for being a man of future, the more he becomes a person who dedicates time to explore himself and control his passions. Therefore, the individual who questions the possibilities in the nature through an effective learning/education can manage the transition from nature to humanity.

The second passion that should be managed is "wisdom", which refers to culture, civilization and sagacity. It is, on the one hand, communing with the Islamic understanding that is an inseparable part of our lifestyle and, on the other hand, achieving a synthesis with material and cultural elements. With respect to Turks, being cognizant of the Islamic essence is the internalization of being a good person. In other words, the evil elements widened in human nature should be repressed and the domain of good elements increased through education. It is adopting the combination of traditions which survived history and the culture of sharing turned into a lifestyle as the main source of Turkish culture. In short, in order to build bridges between the rationalism of reviving Turks' essential values and world rationalism, it is necessary not only to establish a method and creative force to realize technological advancement and technical development, but also to define targets in parallel with the aim of existentialism. Furthermore, conveying the "myth/red apple" to the future with a free and democratic will should be viewed as a venerable duty.

The third main principle, belief, is the interaction vector of the first two. Thus, it is the upgrade of an individual's self-confidence to the understanding of "general will" and his success in reconstructing himself. Historical experiences show that belief is the driving force of our inner world and it, therefore, should be reactivated. For Turkey, the best example of reactivation is the achievement of total independence. This spirit, which is the ideal of Atatürk and his cadres, is the best message to be given to the type of intellectual human who reads the future correctly. This message, at the same time, should be perceived as the vision of materializing Mustafa Kemal's ideal of "raising generations with free minds, free conscience and free knowledge".

When we take the expression of Confucius "the superior man is modest in his speech, but exceeds in his actions", we can understand this vision better. We should also correctly read Great Atatürk, who pointed to the Turkish nation to catch and surpass contemporary civilization. For this reason, it is necessary to bring into force a system of thought that will render sovereign the virtue in politics oriented towards establishing peace/order in society, creativity and fair distribution in the economy. In short, we, as generations living in Central Asian economies, should burden the responsibility and duty of improving the prosperity of the Turkish nation by keeping alive Ismail Gaspıralı's saying "cooperation in language, thought and practice" by giving each other a helping hand in each kin state's struggle for independence, and by striving together to catch up with the values of the time.

References

Hirshman, Albert O. (2008), Passions and Interests, Turkish Translation: Barış Cezar, Metis, Istanbul.

Bauman, Zygmunt, (1999), Globalization: Social Consequences, Turkish Translation: Abdullah YILMAZ, Ayrıntı, Istanbul.

Bukharin, Nikolay, (1918) Imperialism and World Economy, Turkish Translation: Ugur Selcuk AKALIN, Baglam, Istanbul.

Giddens, Anthony; (1998), The Consequences of Modernity, Turkish Translation: Ersin KUŞDİL, Ayrıntı, İstanbul.

Hopkins, Terence K, Wallerstein, Immanuel (1999), The Transition Age, Turkish Translation: ERSOY Nuri, et al., Avesta, 1975, İstanbul.

Kazgan, Gülten (2000), Economic Thought and the Evolution of Political Economy, Remzi Kitabevi, İstanbul.

Kök, Recep (1999), Economic Thought, Concepts' Analytical Evolution, Anadolu, İzmir.

Mittelman, James (2005), Ideologies and the Globalization Agenda, Rethinking Globalizm, Editor: Manfred STEGER, Rowman & Littlefield, Maryland, ABD.

Mooney, Anabelle and Evans, Betsy (2007), Globalization: The Key Concept, Routledge, UK.

Topçu, Nurettin, (1995), Ethics of Insurgence, Turkish Translation: Mustafa Kök-Musa Doğan, Dergah, İstanbul

Ritzer, George and Lair Craig,(2007), Outsourcing: Globalization and Beyond: The Blackwell Companion To Globalization (Editor: George Ritzer), Blackwell Publishing, ABD.

Robertson, Roland, (1995), Globalization: Time, Space and Homogene-Heterogeneity, Global Modernities (Editors: Mike Featherstone, Scott Lash ve Roland Robertson), Sage publication, London.

Robinson, William I (2005) "Gramsci and Globalization: From Nation-State to Transnational Hegemony", Critical Review of International Social and Political Philosophy Vol.8 No:4

Rodrik, Dani, One Economics, Many Recipes: Globalization, Institutions and Economic Growth, Princeton University Press, New-Jersey.

Sklair, Leslie, (1999), "Competing Conceptions of Globalization", Journal of World-Systems Research, Volume 2, Summer.

Steger, Manfred B (2004), Globalism, The New Market Ideology, Rowman & Littlefield, Maryland, AB.

Wallerstein, Immanuel, (1974) The Modern World-System: Capitalist Agriculture and Origins of The European World-Economy in The Sixteenth Century, Academic Press, New York

Waters, Malcolm,(1995), Globalization, Routledge, New-York

Yalçinkaya, Timuçin, (2010), "Analysis of the Impacts of Globalization on Economic Policies: The Turkish Case", DEU, SBE, 2010

PART VI:

ENERGY

Energy Sector in Eurasia

Asst. Prof. Yeşim Reel[1]

The integration of the Eurasian super-continent will potentially have major implications for the Eurasian region, and also for the world economy (Linn and Tiomkin, 2007). Remarkable opportunities have opened on the Eurasian continent. Not only will Greater Central Asia benefit from this, but India, Pakistan, Iran, China, Azerbaijan, and Russia have similar gains to make by engaging the region, including energy.

Opening Greater Central Asia to continental trade in energy and goods will give countries in the region greater access to foreign technology and foreign exchange revenue and increase market access (Norling and Swanström, 2007).

Moreover, potential gains in energy transit are also massive. Whether India's and Pakistan's energy needs are met by building the Turkmenistan-Afghanistan-Pakistan-India pipeline across Afghanistan or the Iran-India-Pakistan pipeline, transit states will benefit substantially. For example, it is estimated that Pakistan would gain a total of 14 billion USD in 30 years from building the Indo-Iran pipeline (Pandian, 2005).

The increasing demand for Eurasian energy is creating a very interesting dependency game involving three groups of countries. The existing dependencies are based on a number of variables (Svedberg, 2007). Therefore it is important to analyse the energy sector in Eurasia.

Current Situation

The breakup of the Soviet Union created a number of different, new stakeholders in pieces of the energy supply system, and a number of formally independent producing states. In particular, almost all Central Asian and Caucasian natural gas (and oil) initially had to pass through the Russian pipeline network to reach foreign customers. Thus Russia, through Gazprom, remained the monopoly supplier of Eurasian gas to Europe.

[1] Marmara University, Istanbul, Turkey

This situation remained essentially unchanged until the Russian financial collapse of 1998, and the subsequent economic recovery driven by a dramatic rise in oil and other energy prices. That crisis brought a change in the government of Russia, and ushered in a new era of rising energy demand and prices.

The Russian state tightened its control over oil and natural gas supplies to the rest of the world, reinforcing its monopoly over oil (Transneft') and gas (Gazprom) export pipelines. It was perceived by dependent countries as using its energy supply to gain political and other leverage. In the light of these developments, the European Union has initiated efforts to form a common energy policy and seek ways to diversify energy supplies, in particular natural gas supplies. And Russia began looking to develop alternate export routes to lucrative European markets. Thus, a complex and changing structure of interdependence has arisen (Ericson, 2009).

Based on this knowledge and also considering International Energy Annual, it can be argued that four Eurasian countries, Russia, Azerbaijan, Kazakhstan and Ukraine, have a special role in the region:

Russia holds the world's largest natural gas reserves, the second largest coal reserves, and the eighth largest oil reserves. Russia is also the world's largest exporter of natural gas, the second largest oil exporter and the third largest energy consumer. Although Russia has huge natural gas reserves, the industry will face significant investment challenges in bringing new, more challenging fields online. In the meantime, production from Gazprom's four largest fields is in decline. Russia is a major world oil producer, sometimes producing even more than Saudi Arabia. Russia's output rebounded during the early 2000s from the fall that followed the end of the old regime, but the effects of high government taxation and a mature field base threaten an overall decline in production (IEA, 2010).

Azerbaijan is emerging as an important exporter of oil and natural gas and as a transport corridor between Europe and Central Asia. Its strategic geographical location bordering the Caspian Sea has attracted significant international interest in developing its oil and natural gas reserves. Oil production in Azerbaijan more than quadrupled between 1997 and 2008 to 875,000 bbl/d and is expected to increase further. With the startup of the Shah Deniz natural gas and condensate field in 2007, Azerbaijan went from being a net natural gas importer to a net exporter, shipping increasing amounts of natural gas to Europe via Turkey. Indeed, Azerbaijan is emerging as a key player in the European attempt to diversify supply with alternatives to the supply routes originating from Russia. The Nabucco pipeline through Turkey, due to open in 2017, will start in Baku and ultimately, perhaps, in Turkmenistan as well as Iraq.

Kazakhstan has the second largest proven oil reserves among the CIS countries as well as the second largest oil production. The country also has large reserves of natural gas and is steadily increasing production, while its oil production is expected to rise substantially in the near to mid-term. With large amounts of associated natural gas at its oil fields, Kazakhstan has the potential to become a net exporter in coming years (IEA, 2011). China, in particular, has made major investments in Kazakhstan's energy sector, preparing for a time in the future when Central Asian gas and oil will be piped into western China, with a pipeline from eastern Kazakh fields already being developed (Ferguson, 2006).

Ukraine is important to world energy markets because it is a critical transit centre for exports of Russian oil and natural gas to Europe, as well as a significant energy consumer. Ukraine's gas sector has been dominated by Naftogaz. Ukraine has the seventh-largest amount of coal resources in the world, but underinvestment and a lack of progress on deregulation have made the country a net coal importer. Ukraine has sufficient generating capacity to supply more than twice its electricity needs, but the country's ageing infrastructure is in need of investment and maintenance (Heifetz, 2009; IMF, 2007). The country has one of the highest energy intensities in the world and has made some progress in reducing its energy usage from oil and coal but not for natural gas. In order to provide reliable supplies domestically and in Europe, increased investment in the Ukrainian transport network, better international cooperation, and a more transparent energy sector are all needed (IEA, 2010).

The energy data in Tables 1 to 5 gives more detailed information about Azerbaijan, Ukraine, Kazakhstan and Russia in this area (IEA, 2010; IEA, 2011).

Table 1. Petroleum Data for 2008

Petroleum (Thousand barrels per day)	Azerbaijan	Russia	Kazakhstan	Eurasia	World
Total Oil Production	874.98	9,792.33	1,429.95	12,527	85,429
Crude Oil Production	869.56	9,356.78	1,345.42	11,927	73,652
Consumption	121.00	2,916.00	244.00	4,350	85,752
Net Export/Imports	753.98	6,876.33	1,185.95	8,177	--
Total Oil Export to US	74	465	12	605	12,915
Refinery Capacity	399	5,428	345	8,205	85,460
Proved Reserves(billion barrels)	7.00	60.00	30.00	99	1,332

Table 2. Natural Gas Data for 2009

Natural Gas (Billion Cubic Feet)	Azerbaijan	Russia	Kazakhstan	Eurasia	World
Production	577	20,610	388	25,814	106,506
Consumption	367	15,524	304	21,125	107,245
Net Export/Imports(-)	209	5,085	133	4,734	--
Proved Reserves (Trillion Cubic Feet)	30	1,680	85	1,994	6,289

Table 3. Electricity Data for 2007

Electricity Billion kWh	Azerbaijan	Ukraine	Russia	Kazakhstan	Eurasia	World
Net Generation	22.88	185.06	962.07	72.41	1,412	18,795
Net Consumption	19.21	152.94	844.42	64.69	1,228	17,139
Installed Capacity (GWh)	5.73	53.95	224.68	18.73	352	4,468

Table 4. Total Primary Data for 2007

Total Primary Energy (Quadrillion Btu)	Azerbaijan	Ukraine	Russia	Kazakhstan	Eurasia	World
Production	2.231	3.266	53.679	5.275	71	473
Consumption	0.591	6.339	29.969	2.320	45	482
Energy Intensity Btu per USD	9,176	21,119	15,117	14,603	15,797	7,528

Table 5. Total Primary Data for 2009

Coal (Million Short Tons)	Azerbaijan	Ukraine	Russia	Kazakhstan	Eurasia	World
Production	0.000	60.645	304.228	111.173	498	7,546
Consumption	0.000	68.774	204.083	79.124	374	7,318
Net Exports-Imports	0.000	-2.081	92.526	32.075	121	--

The oil and gas and energy sectors have been a primary focus of attention through the years. In **2009**, for example, further to the traditionally complex Russian-Ukrainian differences cantered on the terms of purchase and transit of gas, new problems were reported in this sector. An accident on the main pipeline in Turkmenistan in April 2009 led to a break of supply of Turkmen gas to Gazprom. Friction emerged between Turkmenistan and Azerbaijan over the division of oil and gas resources in the Caspian. At the end of the year, Moscow and Minsk also had heated debates over the transit of Russian gas via Belarus and exports of oil to that country. In December, the opening ceremony of the Turkmenistan-China pipeline was held with the participation of the Presidents of Turkmenistan, Kazakhstan, and Uzbekistan, a pipeline that undermines Gazprom's monopoly in Central Asia. Indeed, all oil and gas producing countries have been making attempts to revise the format of their relations with Gazprom, a long-standing Russian monopoly. 2009 also saw a series of crises in the electrical power sector, specifically, the withdrawal of Uzbekistan from the Unified Electric Power System of Central Asia (Maqsimchook, 2010).

In **2010**, both Russia and Ukraine approved new programs that include specific medium-term targets for energy saving (Government of Russia, 2010; Government of Ukraine, 2010). There are also signs in Uzbekistan and Kazakhstan that energy efficiency is becoming a higher policy priority. Kazakhstan, for example, is assessing what would be required to meet a national target to reduced energy intensity by 25% by 2020. Each of these countries has strong reasons to realize their energy-saving potential. Greater efficiency represents a cheap source of incremental energy supply, freeing up resources either for export or notably in the case of Ukraine, as a means to reduce dependence on imports. To a greater or lesser extent, this potential has been recognized and integrated into national policy objectives. In Russia, for example, the technical potential for energy savings has been estimated at a more than 40% of total primary energy supply, or around 300 Mton, based on 2007 energy use (Government of Russia, 2010). This provides the basis for the official target to improve the energy intensity of the national economy by 40% between 2007 and 2020 (IEA, 2011).

Energy trends in Eurasia

- Slow expansion of European and Japanese demand
- Rapid expansion of import demand in China, India; recovery from depressed levels in CIS countries

- Gas demand growing more rapidly than oil demand.
- Rapid growth in electricity demand
- Rapid expansion of CIS energy exports in recent years, but now slowing down
- Russia is the main factor on the supply side (Linn and Tiomkin, 2008)

EurAsEC countries desperately need investments to realize the potential of their vast resources. Russian investments especially have been made in the energy sector and infrastructure of EurAsEC countries. Some oil and gas production projects are closely associated with the joint reconstruction of existing pipelines or construction of new ones for exporting fuel and raw materials. One of the most active Russian players in EurAsEC is LUKoil, a private company formed by the merger of three state companies in 1991. LUKoil has participated in eleven oil projects in Kazakhstan since 1995, when a contract for the development of the northern part of Kumkol was awarded. Since then LUKoil has invested over 4.5 billion USD in Kazakhstan's economy (Heifetz, 2009).

On the other hand, the investment cooperation of Russia and other EurAsEC countries faces various challenges; the most important are (Heifetz, 2009):

- Political opposition to investment expansion
- Lack of flexibility in Russian company policy
- Increasing competition
- No progress in multilateral cooperation

Governmental support for the investment expansion of Russian companies and investment cooperation in EurAsEC is inadequate. The formulation of a common policy for EurAsEC countries towards the use of energy resources and transport services and cooperation in this area are priority economic goals for EurAsEC (Heifetz, 2009).

The Dependency Game

The increasing demand for Eurasian energy is creating a very interesting dependency game involving three groups of countries: The European Union (EU) is dependent on oil and gas from countries in the Commonwealth of Independent States (CIS) for consumption, whereas the CIS countries, in general, and Russia in particular, are dependent on the EU countries for exports. Both the CIS and the EU countries are dependent on the Baltic States, Belarus, Ukraine, and Poland, for transiting energy from the former to the latter. The transit countries, for their part, are dependent on CIS energy both for domestic consumption and as a source of revenue, as the transit traffic constitutes significant shares of their GDPs. These transit countries play a crucial role in the dependency game (Svedberg, 2007).

The energy trade in Eurasia is not a zero-sum game but rather an interesting example of regional interdependence. Europe imports about 43% of its total oil and gas consumption, of which some 63% comes from the CIS. Some countries are more dependent than others. With respect to gas, for example, Finland, Slovakia, Bulgaria, Croatia, and Greece basically have no production, and import almost everything from the CIS, whereas Spain, Belgium, Sweden, and Ireland import almost no gas from the CIS, although they are completely dependent on imports for their gas consumption. Between these extremes, the UK imports about 45% of its gas, but very little of it originates from the CIS. Germany has no production of its own and imports about 40% of its gas from the CIS, a situation that is similar in Italy and France, while Poland imports 70% of its consumption, of which almost 90% comes from the CIS. The Netherlands, on the other hand, is one of the world's major gas exporters. In absolute terms, the UK, Germany and Italy are by some way the largest gas consumers in the EU, and Germany and Italy are the biggest importers of the CIS gas. Most of the Central and Eastern European countries are fully dependent on CIS imports for their oil consumption (Svedberg, 2007; Marzo, 2008; Rogers, 2011).

The transit countries in between Western Europe and Russia, most notably the Baltic States, Poland, Ukraine, and Belarus, play a crucial role in the dependency game. They are today among the most dependent countries on Russian energy imports for consumption and revenues and are, at the same time, the energy bridge between Europe and Russia. As much as 80% of Russian gas exports are transited through Ukraine and 25% of its crude oil exports.

The existing dependencies can be based on a number of variables that are very difficult to fully assess. Most analysts seem to agree that demand will remain high and growing, especially as the demand in the large emerging markets, most notably in China, is increasing rapidly. The underlying issues are related to the future supply, infrastructure, and price of oil and gas (Svedberg, 2007).

Under these conditions, while the introduction and diffusion of energy-saving policies may help, they are unlikely to relieve the upward pressure on prices. Consequently, all actors should be concerned about policies that would support and guarantee the flow of supply. While this entails, in the short term, a growing general concern for investments in existing and new oilfields as well as transport infrastructure for energy (oil and gas primarily), there are also pressures for diversifying energy dependence over the longer term. The advantage of high energy prices, on the other hand, give leverage to energy producers that they may wish to use against consumers in other areas when there is a conflict of interest (Malle, 2007).

Russia needs Europe for exports and investments. It is, therefore, more important than ever that Russia and the EU get their act together and agree on a joint energy policy based on mutual dependency. One of the most interesting outcomes of this dependency game is what role the transit countries will play, both in shaping the policy and as future energy bridges (Svedberg, 2007).

Morelli suggests that Russia, with its vast resources, especially in gas, will likely continue to be Europe's primary supplier of gas for the indefinite future. For Europe, trying to construct an overall common energy policy with a common external energy strategy, directed especially at Russia, could be critical. Since Europe understands that Russia is dependent on Europe as a stable customer for Russia's energy resources and is an eager investor in Russia's economy, the EU has several options regarding its energy relations with Russia (Morelli, 2006).

It is unclear whether the EU can adopt an effective common policy on the Russian energy question. Central and Eastern European countries within the EU want the EU to take a stronger stance against the dependence on Russia for energy. On the other hand, energy companies and other influential voices in countries such as Germany, France and Italy have forged close links with Moscow in order to secure access to Russian energy supplies and opportunities to invest in Russian energy projects (Woehrel, 2010).

At the same time, the importance of Eurasia for Europe has increased dramatically. Because membership of each new Central and Eastern European country into the EU means additional demand for energy, this in turn necessitates new supply sources. There are several prerequisites for membership into the EU, including adjustments of states' economies. It is expected that new member states adapt to economic structural adjustment programs to improve their economic performance, and economic development will also lead to a higher energy demand (Maleki, 2007).

The gas transit game represents an interesting economic phenomenon related to market structures, externalities and other emerging games. These issues often arise because producers and consumers are separated by large distances, which also tend to grow as a result of the depletion of nearby gas fields. The connection of supply with demand involves several types of problems related to politics, logistics and investments among others (Yegorov, 2009).

Diverging energy interests and challenges among the key players

- Russia:
    - Interests: Exclusive control over supply (and distribution) chain; no transit; multiple market outlets
    - Challenges: Increase production and control consumption
- Central Asia:
    - Interests: Control over national resource and transport assets; multiple transit routes and markets
    - Challenges: Increase production for local and export consumption, cooperate with neighbours
- China:
    - Interests: Dedicated supplies from diversified sources with direct control over supply chain; serve a transit corridor
- W. Europe, India, Japan, Korea:
    - Interests: Diversified, secure supplies with limited transit (Linn and Tiomkin, 2008)

Potential Gains

Opening Greater Central Asia to continental trade in energy and goods would give countries in the region greater access to foreign technology and foreign exchange revenue, increase market access, and reduce harmful effects of being landlocked. Forecasts about the positive effects of construction and restoration of road corridors suggest that there could be enormous gains (Norling and Swanström, 2007).

Potential gains in energy transit are massive. Whether India's and Pakistan's energy needs are met by building the Turkmenistan-Afghanistan-Pakistan-India pipeline across Afghanistan or the Iran-India-Pakistan pipeline, transit states will benefit substantially. For example, it is estimated that Pakistan would gain a total of USD14 billion in 30 years from building the Indo-Iran pipeline (Pandian, 2005).

Supporting energy projects in the region and regional energy integration promise to have huge potential long-term payoffs; the Baku-Tbilisi-Ceyhan (BTC) pipeline is a case in point. This pipeline not only relieved Azerbaijan from dependence on Russia, but its construction also signified a long-term commitment from the West to Azerbaijan's future. This attitude spills over into neighbouring countries, whose trust in American and/or European long-term intentions is reinforced. Similar support should be given to projects of equal weight, such as the proposed

Turkmenistan-Afghanistan-Pakistan-India pipeline, which could act as a symbol and milestone in Greater Central Asia relations, similar to the BTC's provision of a "window to the West" (Norling and Swanström, 2007).

Energy demand projections assume that the next decades will be characterized by successful reform and restructuring in Eurasia as a whole, leading to sustained investments in the energy sector, and economic development that will be reflected in the long-term improvement of energy intensities. Furthermore, that the total primary energy demand in Eurasia grows by a factor of two to three between 1990 and 2050 in these scenarios.

Eurasian electricity demand between 1990 and 2050 is expected to increase by a factor of five in the Asian part and nearly by a factor of three in the European. The challenge therefore is to match the rich energy resources of Eurasia to growing demand. Resources and demand need to be matched geographically through trade, transportation networks and energy grids. They have to be matched financially through investment flows and reforms designed to attract those investment flows. And they must be matched in terms of flexibility, convenience and cleanliness. Substantial technological and financial expertise will be needed to match the rapidly expanding energy needs of Eurasia with the required supply from its substantial resources (Klaasen, et. al, 1999).

Klaasen, et, al. (1999) suggest the following conclusions:

- Eurasia is becoming the world's largest energy consumer.
- Siberian and Caspian regions are endowed with enormous gas resources and resource availability is not expected to be a real constraint in meeting demand, but the concentration of resources in a limited number of areas is.
- Up-front investment in gas transit pipelines may constitute a significant portion of the expected investment in the energy sector in Asia with the level of investments depending on the exact network design.
- Financial risks are significant and will depend on intricate factors such as demand and supply development, technological progress, geographical and political environments, and prevailing regulatory regimes.
- Timely investments in the necessary infrastructure could imply that CIS gas exports could be ten times higher in 2050 than would be the case in business-as-usual type scenarios.

- Building of required infrastructure could have significant positive impacts on the global, regional and local environment, and also imply significant positive economic impact.

In order to make full use of the potentials in the Eurasian continent, it will continue to be necessary to strengthen cooperative mechanisms and make sizable efforts in restoring and developing infrastructure, as well as reducing border inefficiency. The scope of activity cannot be limited to Central Asia alone, especially if the region is conceived of as if still comprising part of the Soviet Union. Indeed, Greater Central Asia has as great complementarity with the economies of South Asia and East Asia as it does with Russia and Europe for that matter (Norling and Swanström, 2007).

Conclusions

Regional energy trade is seen not only as a reason for transnational linkage, but also as a major force for integration in Eurasia. Opening Greater Central Asia to continental trade in energy and goods would give countries in the region greater access to foreign technology and foreign exchange revenue, increase market access, and generally stimulate economic and other activity.

The region possesses vast resources, and the EurAsEC countries desperately need investments. Especially Russian investments have been made in the energy sector and infrastructure in the EurAsEC countries. Some oil and gas production projects are closely associated with joint reconstruction of existing pipelines or construction of new ones for exporting fuel and raw materials. Formulation of a common policy for the EurAsEC countries towards the use of energy resources and transport services and cooperation in this area are priority economic goals for the EurAsEC.

Moreover, the increasing demand for Eurasian energy is creating a very interesting dependency game. The existing dependencies between different country groups could be based on a number of variables that are very difficult to fully assess. Most analysts seem to agree that demand will remain high and growing, especially in light of the demand in the large emerging markets. Therefore, Eurasia could have an advantage, using linkages and the dependency game.

The potential gains in energy transit are massive. But there are also major challenges. Energy demand projections assume that leading to sustained investments in the energy sector and economic development will be reflected in the long-term improvement of energy intensities in Eurasia.

In order to make full use of the potentials in the Eurasian continent, however, it will be necessary to strengthen cooperative mechanisms and make sizable efforts in the areas of infrastructure restoration and development, as well as border inefficiency reduction. For all these, strong and efficient relations should be maintained, and comprehensive and efficient projects are necessary.

References

Ericson, 2009. "Eurasian Natural Gas Pipelines: The Political Economy of Network Interdependence", Eurasian Geography and Economics, 50, p.32, 33.

Ferguson, 2006. "Lecture 1: Eurasia: Super-region or Zone of Conflict?", Bond University, p.5. At http://www.international_relations .com/wbeurasia/WBEA-2006-Lec1.doc. (22/02/2011).

Heifetz, 2009. "Russian Direct Investments in EurAsEC and Their Role in Energy and Transport Infrastructure Development in Eurasia", EDB Eurasian Integration Yearbook 2009, P.130, 137-140. http://www.eabr.org/eng/publications/IntegrationYearbook/index.wbp?article-id=F591B688-BF0D-45FC-9EFD-B31E0E1E4DD7(03.08.2010).

IEA, 2010, International Energy Annual. http://www.eia.doe.gov/country_energy_data.cfm?fibs=AJ (05.08.2010).

—. 2011. Country Analysis Briefs - Azerbaijan, Russia, Kazakhstan. http://www.eia.doe.gov (27/12/2011)

—. 2011. World Energy Outlook 2011, Are we entering A Golden Age of Gas?, Special Report, France, p.55, 114.

International Monetary Fund (IMF), 2007. Ukraine: Selected Issues, IMF Country Report No. 07/47,Washington, p.20.

Klaassen, et. al, 1999. Towards New Energy Infrastructures in Eurasia: a background paper, Interim Report IR-99-17, December, p.6, 8, 27.

Linn, and Tiomkin, 2007. Economic Integration of Eurasia- Opportunities and Challenges of Global Significance, in Anders Aslund and Marek Dabrowski (ed.) Europe After Enlargement, Cambridge University Press, Cambridge, p.162.

Linn, Johannes and Tiomkin, 2008. "Economic Integration of Eurasia: Opportunities and Challenges of Global Significance", Asia Europe Journal, 4 , p.16, 19.

Maleki, 2007. "Energy Supply and Demand in Eurasia: Cooperation between EU and Iran", China and Eurasia Forum Quarterly, 4 , p.112.

Malle, 2007. "Energy and Central Asia: an Overview of Current Issues", Transition Studies Review, 14, p.149, 150.

Maqsimchook, 2010. "Chronicle of Eurasian Regional Integration 2009", in Evgeny Vinokurov (ed.) EDB Integration Yearbook 2010, Almaty: Eurasian Development Bank, p.29.

Marzo, 2008. Security of natural gas supply in Spain, at VII. ASPO CONFERENCE, October 20-21 Barcelona. http://www.aspo-spain.org/aspo7/presentations/Marzo-GasSuply-ASPO7.pdf. p.3, 5, 6.

Morelli, 2006. "The European Union's Energy Security Challenges", in Congressional Research Service Report for Congress September 11, 2006, Washington, p.12.

Norling and Swanström, 2007. "The Virtues and Potential Gains of Continental Trade in Eurasia", Asian Survey, 47, p. 369-372.

Pandian, 2005. "Energy Trade as a Confidence Building Measure between India and Pakistan: A Study of the Indo-Iran Pipeline Project," Contemporary South Asia, 14 , p.314.

Rogers, 2011. "The Impact of Import Dependency and Wind Generation on UK Gas Demand and Security of Supply to 2025", The Oxford Institute for Energy Studies, NG 54, Oxford, p.5.

Svedberg, 2007. "Energy in Eurasia: the Dependency Game", Transition Studies Review, 14 , p.195-197, 201.

Woehrel, 2010. Russian Energy Policy Toward Neighboring Countries , March 22, 2010, CRS Report for Congress, Congressional Research Service, p.4.

Yegorov and Wirl, 2009. "Ukrainian Gas Transit Game", Zeitschrift für Energiewirtschaft, 33, pp.147-155. http://www.springerlink.com/content/93x851nt4u71m431/fulltext.pdf

CHINA'S INTERESTS IN ENERGY SOURCES OF CENTRAL ASIA

ASST. PROF. DR. HASAN DURAN[1] AND KADIR KÜRŞAT YILMAZ[2]

Until the 2000s the leading countries of oil and natural gas consumption were the USA and the EU, while in the 2000s a third country, China, was added to this list. Together with her growing economy China's demand and consumption of energy have rapidly increased, which elevated her to the position of an important actor in the energy market. In 2010, China consumed more energy than the USA and become the leading energy consumer of the world, with an increase in use of all types of energy, and the worldwide energy consumption share of China went above 20% (British Petroleum 2011).

By 2004, China increased her energy consumption by 245% while her energy production during the same period increased only by 194%. The ongoing industrialization and urbanization processes increase the demand for energy while they also mark the gradual inadequacy of national resources (Bayraç 2010). That is to say, China is becoming more and more dependent on foreign resources in terms of energy needs, especially for oil and natural gas (Alkın and Atman 2006). Due to her increasing energy consumption, increasing with respect to the rapidly growing economy, China, in the five year development plan for 2011-2015, intends to limit her annual energy consumption increase rate by 4.24% (Yeşil Ekonomi 2011).

China is dependent on the petroleum from Iran and the Middle East with whom large natural gas-petroleum purchase agreements were signed. During recent years China has invested in energy in many different parts of the world, especially in the African countries Sudan and Angola. However, as the petroleum import from the Middle East is controlled by the USA, and petroleum and natural gas import from Iran is blocked, China needs to look for alternatives. While China (with India) became the

---

[1] Dumlupınar University, Kütahya, Turkey

[2] Economics and Entrepreneurship University, Celalabad, Kyrgyzstan

new petro-politically determining countries due to their increasing dependence on foreign resources, energy supply security becomes a vital issue (Stratejik Araştırmalar Enstitüsü 2011). At this point, the first alternatives appear to be Central Asia and the Central Asian economies in the region (Yavuz 2011). The attention is focused especially on Kazakhstan with her rich petroleum resources and Turkmenistan with rich natural gas resources.

China's Diplomatic Relationships with Central Asian Countries

With the great tension between China and the USSR during the 1950s, no deliberate Central Asian policies were developed by China except for securing her borders. However, during the early 1980s when the China-Soviet relationship was normalized, economic relationships among Soviet Central Asia and China gained impetus (Bekar 1995). With the collapse of the USSR, China saw Central Asia as the threshold of opening to the West and recognized all Central Asian economies at the beginning of 1992; China established diplomatic relationships, especially concerning border issues, preventing ethnic and religious conflicts in the region, and developing inter-country cooperation. China's steps might be interpreted as avoiding disturbing Russia and prioritizing the moves that would contribute to her economic growth.

No significant developments were observed in bilateral relations until 1994. However, in 1994, Chinese senior officials realized important visits to all the countries in the region. The first formal and intensive relationships were initiated by the Chinese Prime Minister Li Peng in 1994 who visited the countries in the region. During these visits Peng has asserted that with the recovery of the New Silk Road it would be possible for China to reach Europe while the same would enable the countries in the region to open to the Pacific (Bekar 1995). The main issues debated until 1996 included mutual support in the trial and extradition of criminals, cooperation in radical and separatist problems, and alleviation of border ambiguities.

With the beginning of 1996, relations between China and the Central Asian economies gained a new momentum. Russian President Boris Yeltsin was accompanied by presidents of Kyrgyzstan, Kazakhstan, and Tajikistan during his visit to China on 24-26 April 1996. During this visit various cooperation agreements were signed between the Russian and Chinese parties. This was followed by the meeting of the presidents of five countries signing an agreement on military security in the borderline in

Shanghai. Thus the assembly, called the Shanghai Five, was formed (Ekrem 2003). The issues fore-grounded by the Shanghai Organization were providing equivalent common interests and avoiding interference in the internal affairs, importance of cooperation against any type of harmful activities and the desire for a multi-polar world. During the fifth meeting in Dushanbe in 2000, a decision for enlargement was made incorporating other countries troubled with regional and global problems.

The Shanghai Five, incorporating Uzbekistan on 15 June 2001, was transformed into the Shanghai Cooperation Organization (İşyar 2010). The organization aims at establishing a common ground for cooperation among China, Russia, Kazakhstan, Kyrgyzstan, Tajikistan and Uzbekistan on political, economic, military, and energy issues (Bayraç 2010). China, through the Shanghai Cooperation Organization (SCO), has gained easier control over Kazakhstan and Kyrgyzstan, which both have Uyghur population, along with the China-Russian cooperation in Uyghur and Chechen issues and lessening USA activities in the region. Thus, China has established good relations with her neighbours concerning some troublesome issues and solved border problems, while she also increased her dominance in the region. The problems among the parties were solved, though partially, and the worries and anxieties were removed.

During recent years China's interest in Central Asia shifted from border security to energy procurement due to her increasing energy needs and consumption which would be obtained from the region. To this end, important energy investments were made in Central Asia and loans were given to countries in the region for energy investments. In 1997, shortly after the first meeting of the Shanghai Five, an agreement on drilling for oil and transportation was signed with Kazakhstan (Ekrem 2003). During Chinese President Jiang Zemin's visit to Turkmenistan on 6 July 2000, an agreement on discount loan and cooperation in petroleum-natural gas areas was signed between the two countries (Ekrem 2003). China desires to also become the economic giant in the region.

China's Central Asia Strategy

Central Asia and the Caspian Sea Region have a special place in China's new era national interest (Adıbelli 2008). The important parameters of China's concern for the region are security, commerce, and energy (Dikkaya 2010). Central Asia's geopolitical and geostrategic importance and its energy resources are of essential value for China. In this context, China first initiated petroleum trade with Kazakhstan and natural gas trade with Turkmenistan. China's concern for the Caspian resources increased the regional countries' room for negotiation (Yavuz 2009). Thanks to her insistent and decisive policies on turning the region's energy resources towards the east, China became a really influential country (Özertem 2008). However, the problem of balance between China's human resources surplus and Central Asia's excessive natural resources will possibly cause important problems in future (Davutoğlu 2004). The situation is the same for the Russian Far East. Beside the unqualified Russian population, which account for less than 10 million, there are more than 120 million (İşyar 2010).

Since petroleum production areas and transportation routes of the Middle Eastern resources are under the control of the USA, China has been developing various projects with Russia and the Central Asian countries (like Kazakhstan and Turkmenistan) for the sake of purchases from Central Asia. China is helping Armenia in some aspects not only for entering Central Asia, but also for entering the Caucasus Southern region via Armenia and being active in this region (Laçiner 2005). China aims at preventing Turkey and the western countries from reaching the east through Azerbaijan by supporting Armenia, which constitutes a natural block between Turkey and Azerbaijan (İşyar 2010).

The Central Asian economies have been striving to make the best use of the energy resources that they have. The Russian opposition, the deadlock in the Caspian Sea's status, causes difficulties in selling natural gas to the west. Therefore, new projects are blocked, and when the Iran route is considered, the USA opposes strictly. The pipelines of the Soviet Union period reach Russia and other Central Asian countries. Therefore, being able to reach Europe only via Russia brings along many problems. In order to bring up, operate and market these natural resources, investment by foreign enterprises is needed. In this context, importance of China increases and using the economic advantages supplied by her and selling natural gas to China becomes more convenient and beneficial.

Central Asian countries believe that the pipelines that reinforce the economic cooperation with China will serve the interests and wellbeing of their citizens. The line also will contribute to the stability and development in the region, and as a result enhancement of international energy cooperation and partnerships will gain great importance. Kazakhstan, Uzbekistan, and Turkmenistan would like to balance the Russian factor in petroleum and natural gas, and in this respect they consider China as the most important actor to balance Russia in economic and political terms (Bilgin 2010). The fact that China is not interested in the regimes of the Caspian Basin countries and also that not many countries are needed to cooperate for borders, make China always an attractive option.

Meanwhile, China has become more and more interested in Central Asia in order to strengthen her hand in the region and come into prominence in global competition (Tüysüzoğlu 2010). Another reason for China to enhance her relationship with the Central Asian countries is that she seeks to help the Eastern Turkistan to develop as much as the other regions.

As China aspires to turn her economic growth into a global power, she needs more and more energy. Therefore, in her foreign policies China has been taking energy geopolitics as a kind of axis. A cooperation basis was created with SCO. Whereas SCO was initially established in order to solve the border problems and reinforce regional security, later it removed the existing and foreseen safety hazards caused by China's Uyghur Region, and thus was able to keep Kazakhstan and Kyrgyzstan, where some Uyghurs are located, under control (Dikkaya 2009). Moreover SCO increased the cooperation opportunities by facilitating control of radical movements and terrorism in Central Asia. Together with the solution of the problems, the energy projects were initiated. It is possible to state that, with reference to energy, they also have a common approach about the security in Central Asia. China has been supporting the Central Asian states in terms of the fight against terrorism and fundamentalist movements. Thus, the foundation for establishment and operation of Turkmenistan-Kazakhstan-Uzbekistan-China natural gas pipeline and Kazakhstan-China petroleum pipeline, which connect the Eastern Turkistan Region and the countries in the region, was created.

Atasu-Alashankou petroleum pipeline and China-Central Asia natural gas pipeline establish the strategic connection between the Central Asian countries and Chinese economy. While the whole world was fighting with the 2008 global crisis, the Turkmenistan-China natural gas pipeline, which transfers Turkmen natural gas to China via Uzbekistan, Kazakhstan and Kyrgyzstan, was initiated. The China-Central Asia Natural Gas Pipeline ranging from Turkmenistan to China was opened on 14 December 2009 in Turkmenistan with the attendance of the presidents of Turkmenistan, Uzbekistan, Kazakhstan and China (Türkmenistan-İran doğalgaz boru hattı açıldı, 2010). Moreover, during this opening, a 4 billion USD loan agreement concerning operation of the natural gas deposits in the South Yolotan field of Turkmenistan was signed (Haber 7, 2011).

Thanks to this pipeline, Turkmenistan's dependence on Russia, to which it sells 70% of its natural gas, was decreased and demand guarantee was reinforced for Turkmenistan. China benefited with the supply guarantee due to the possibility of developing the natural gas trade already initiated with Central Asia later with Uzbekistan and Kazakhstan, reinforcing the border security of the Eastern Turkistan Region. Right after the pipeline begins operating in full capacity, Chinese firms are expected to gain great efficiency in operation of Turkmen natural gas reserve (Dikkaya 2010).

The Turkmenistan-China pipeline is important for Turkey as well because of the fact that China is going to purchase Kazakh petroleum, and firstly Turkmen, secondly Kazakh and Uzbek natural gas decreases Central Asia's need for reaching Turkey and Europe via Caucasia, at least in terms of energy. For these countries, reaching Europe via Caucasia is no more an essential need, but just one of the routes that can be considered if the conditions are convenient (Bilgin 2010).

200,000 Uyghurs live in Kazakhstan, which has rich oil fields (Çolakoğlu, 2010). About one million Kazakh population are located in China's Uyghur Autonomous Region (Dikkaya and Bora 2006). This increases Kazakhstan's importance for China. In 2009 Kazakhstan took a 13 billion USD loan from China for use in petroleum and natural gas sectors (Zaman 2010). Importance of Kazakhstan for China is increasing gradually. Thus, together with important purchase agreements in the energy sector and the loans given with the purpose of being used for energy investments and the energy sector, China has obtained a very efficient position in Kazakhstan.

Kazakhstan-China Petroleum Pipeline is a 3 stage project and 625 km (388 miles) long (Pamir 2008). It is going to be operated on a 50:50 partnership basis between the Chinese oil company CNPC and Kazakhstan's KazMunayGaz. The line from the Caspian Sea shore to China's Alashankou city goes through Kazakhstan. Construction of the Atasu-Alashankou part of the pipeline, the capacity of which counts 20 million tons, began in 2004 and the first crude oil reached China at the end of July 2006 (Haberler 2009). Actually this part is the second stage of a pipeline that will travel through Kazakhstan from one end to the other, from the Caspian Sea to Alashankou. The third stage that will integrate the Atırau-Kenkiyak line and Atasu-Alashankou line is planned to be completed in 2011. Once completed, the project is expected to meet 5% of China's energy demand. In the future, China will become a country of great economic and political influence in Central Asia, with many countries from which she supplies energy, and will have gained strategic access to the Caspian Sea (Açık İstihbarat 2009). Kazakhstan, on the other hand, will increase the number of its customers and benefit economically. Moreover, Russia is also expected to use this pipeline to sell oil to China.

Kazakhstan's National Petroleum and Gas Company KazMunayGaz and China's National Petroleum and Gas Company CNPC agreed on construction of a natural gas pipeline between China's Beyneu city and Kazakhstan's Chimkent city. For construction of the pipeline a joint venture will be established and the project will be put into effect immediately. The natural gas brought up in West Kazakhstan will be transferred to China and the project will cost about 3.6 billion USD (TRT 2010).

Investments by the Western companies in the region constitute an important guarantee for the independence and stability of Kazakhstan. Kazakhstan keeps trying to balance the Western companies and Russia with China. The trading volume between China and Kazakhstan has increased year by year. The bilateral trade volume increased by 44.55% from 2009 to 2010, and reached 20.4 billion USD (China Embassy 2011).

Kazakhstan's president Nursultan Nazarbaev, who was disturbed by the civil insurrection in Kyrgyzstan and the resulting government change in 2005, stated his idea of the Central Asian Cooperation strongly in order to strengthen his hand against the USA and the EU, who were the supporters of the velvet revolution, and attract the attention of Russia.

In addition to the Kazakh oil and Turkmen natural gas, Uzbekistan's political and strategic importance motivates China to be active in this region. After the Andican incident, China became a balancing alternative for Uzbekistan against the USA, with whom Uzbekistan's relations experienced a crisis due to these events, and Uzbekistan shut down the American headquarters. Kerimov defined China as a "reliable partner" just after the Andican incident (Laçiner 2006a). During Kerimov's visit to China in 2005 an oil-cooperation agreement was signed and an engagement was contracted for developing the bilateral relations. Nevertheless, China never meant to reflect her close relationship with Uzbekistan to the USA as a kind of defiance.

The products of Chinese origin have been getting more and more common in Central Asian markets. China's increasing influence in Central Asia has the potential to challenge Russia's economic and political influence in the region in the long term. In 2009, Kazakhstan's exports to China (13.6 billion USD) surpassed its exports to Russia (8.2 billion USD), while among the import partners of Kazakhstan, China became the second (12.6 billion USD) after Russia (31.3 billion USD) (Trade Profiles Kazakhstan 2009). The fact that China became one of the most important partners of Turkmenistan both in exports and imports by 2010, brought her to the position of a country that can balance Russia in terms of regional trade (Türkiye-Türkmenistan 2011).

Realization of the petroleum and natural gas pipelines is vitally important for China. China, who inverted the regional energy resources to the east, will as a result increase her efficiency in the region once dominated by the USSR, while meeting most of her ever increasing need for oil and natural gas. In Turkmenistan, there are 37 Chinese-invested, 30 Kazakh-invested, and 13 Uzbek-invested companies, most of which operate in the field of energy.

The strategies followed by China over energy in Central Asia can be summarized as cooperation aimed at solving the security issues caused by the Eastern Turkistan region, benefiting from the petroleum and natural gas of the region to meet her demand for energy, getting closer to Caucasia, Turkey and Europe over Central Asia. To realize these strategies, China does not want any nationalistic or Islamic trends getting stronger in Central Asia, and aspires to the existing statute that facilitates putting the energy projects into force at certain stages, to continue in stability (Bilgin 2010).

China-American Rivalry

Central Asia, which has great geopolitical importance, serves as a buffer zone for Chinese threat against Russia and the West. The same is also valid for China. However considering the USA-Russia-China relationship from an energy perspective, it might be asserted that the rivalry is based simply on energy (Ekşi 2009).

The energy resources have a special importance for the USA with regard to her policies concerning the Caspian Basin. The USA has announced that the Caspian region, which was formerly defined as an area of interest, was defined as an "area of responsibility" after 1997. Pre-9/11 policies concerning the region were performed using diplomatic and commercial channels, while the post-9/11 approach was fundamentally different. The USA tried to block Chinese energy enterprises in the region via the Indian Ocean with the intervention in Afghanistan that practically surrounded western China. Thus, Central Asia is strategically important for the USA, not only due to investment opportunities and petroleum and natural gas sale, but also for the supremacy over her rivals in natural gas and petroleum issues.

With the proximity of Central Asian economies and Iran to Russia and China, an over-powerful Russia in Europe, Iran's reinforced position in the region, China's energy procurement from Russia, Central Asia and Iran are threatening for the benefits of the USA (Stratejik Boyut 2010). The USA desires that Azerbaijan and Turkmenistan get connected to Europe and to world markets through pipelines passing from Turkey, rather than Central Asian and Caucasian energy resources, except for

Azerbaijan to stay under the monopoly of Russia and orientate towards China. Thus, Russia, China and Iran would be kept away from the control and marketing of the energy resources in the region (Bilgin 2010).

The USA aims at gaining control over the strategically important energy transportation passages from Iran to the Sea of China, and thereby subjecting China to herself in matters of energy, thus keeping hold of energy control. The conflict between the USA and China concerning the sea and energy stems from the Hormuz, Bab-el-Mandeb, and Malacca straits. China faces serious threats during the transportation of the required petroleum and natural gas to the country by sea due to the critical status of the straits mentioned, and also by land as the territory where the pipelines pass is insecure. The security of the sea routes are controlled by the American Navy, which makes China more and more subservient to the USA (Bayraç 2010).

The China-Persian energy and military cooperation is another source of anxiety for the USA. China imports 12-15% of the oil from Iran. There are various energy agreements between the two countries. In January 2000, an agreement of approximately 13 billion USD concerning search and drilling procedures to be undertaken at Zavareh and Kashan was signed between Chinese Petroleum Company SINOPEC and Iranian National Petroleum Company (NIOC). At the beginning of 2004, China signed an agreement of 20 billion USD value with Iran concerning the purchase of liquefied natural gas for more than 25 years (İşyar 2010). During autumn 2004, the two countries signed an agreement in 70-100 billion USD value concerning the purchase of petroleum and natural gas. The countries also agreed on developing the Yadavaran petroleum zone in Iran. China agreed to buy 150,000 barrels of crude petroleum from Iran after the development of Yadavaran (Laçiner 2006b). China is also expected to invest approximately 100 billion USD on the Yadavaran petroleum reserves in Iran (Alkın and Atman 2006).

Although China resisted the sanctions against Iran for an extended period of time, she unwillingly agreed on the latest decisions of the United Nations Security Council due to the uranium enrichment activities of Iran, yet by the provision that the measures would be mitigated through time (Hogg 2010). Though China supports UN sanctions against Iran, it seems quite impossible that she might discard Iran, who meets 11% of her petroleum needs. China tries to secure herself against the USA policy of naval supremacy and energy dominance in the Middle East through decreasing her dependency on the Middle East. In this context the resources in Central Asia are very important for China.

Figure 1: Countries importing oil to China

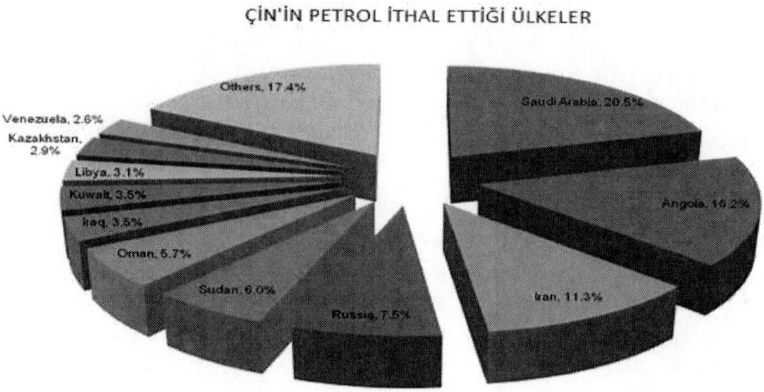

Source: Uzman Forex 2011

China-Russian Rivalry

The two countries China and Russia, which cannot agree on the Communist ideology, have enhanced cooperation during recent years in areas of mutual interest. Especially, the recent developments in their relationships through Shanghai Cooperation Organization are noteworthy (Akçadağ 2009). China desires to keep Russia by her own side and enhance cooperation in order to increase the reaction against the uni-polar world order of the USA, and increase her efficiency in Central Asia. For Russia, China is a country that would contribute to raising her political efficiency and would be cooperative in energy, arms sales, and security issues (Denker 2000). Russia has sold 69% of the arms during 2005-2009 to Asia and to Pacific countries. Russia has the highest share in Chinese arms imports (Çınar 2010).

Russia and China are in harmony, especially in defending a multi-polar world system against a uni-polar one. The Shanghai Cooperation Organization, which was initially founded to ensure border security yet later agreed on conducting military drills, has closed the gap between Russia and China. Russia and China have taken important steps in ensuring security in the region within the framework of Shanghai Cooperation Organization. At the same time both countries resisted the sanctions against Iran. The dialogue process that started off as solving border problems and opposing the uni-polar world system turned out to become a systematic cooperation model resting on the opportunities that

China's growing need for energy created in Russia (Alkın and Atman 2006). China's growing energy demand not only boosted China-Russian relationships but also created incentives for solving old and newly emerging problems.

Russia makes sufficient economic profits from the European market and thus keeps hold of the east-west energy corridor. Moreover, she desires to sell natural gas and oil to the Eastern market, which has a growing demand for energy. Russian interest in the eastern markets facilitates China-Russian cooperation. China needs the presence of a strong Russia for energy security. The treaties signed by countries in Central Asia do not suffice to bypass Russia in terms of energy security. While China wants to make further use of Central Asian natural resources, Russia serves not only as an important supplier but also as a mediator.

Russian energy sources are important in satisfying China's growing need for energy. By December 2009, 2757 km of the East Siberian-Pacific Pipeline (ESPO) was opened for use and, on completion in 2013, the 4070 km long pipeline will be the longest in the world. The Chinese section of ESPO, which will connect Russian oil reservoirs to the oil production centre of Daqing in northeast China, will boost the cooperation of the two countries (Çolakoğlu 2010). Russia accepted a USD25 billion loan from China in exchange for future oil deliveries in 2010 (Financial Times 2010).

Although cooperating with Russia in the transportation of the energy sources of the region, China wants to reduce the influence of Russia over the pipelines. Thus, China suspended the Altay Natural Gas Pipeline Project and developed the Central Asia Natural Gas Pipeline Project. The capacity of the pipeline to be supported by Uzbekistan, Turkmenistan and Kazakhstan is 40 billion m^3. The factor that caused the annulment of the former project was the disagreement between Russia and China on natural gas prices, while with the latter project China got the chance of reaching the Central Asian natural gas without turning to Russia (Okur 2009).

Medvedev's visit to China on 27 September 2010 is his second official visit to China after his taking office in May 2008. During the visit the two countries signed several cooperation treaties concerning efficient use of oil, natural gas, coal and energy resources, renewable energy resources, electric network, and the use of nuclear energy for peaceful purposes. Moreover, a cooperation protocol on fighting against terrorism, separatism, and religious fundamentalism was also signed. Russian national natural gas company Gazprom has reported that an annual amount of 30 billion m^3 natural gas will be supplied to China for 30 years (BBC 2010).

China, as a purchaser of Kazakh oil and Turkmen natural gas, would weaken Russia's strategic interests as the holder of the marketing monopoly of the resources of these countries. The rivalry that stems from Chinese moves on central Asian energy resources considerably annoys Russia (İşyar 2010). Although China supports the stability of Russia she does not want a strong Russia in the region. This might lead to great rivalry between the two in the future. To say a few words on the importance of Central Asia for Russia and China; for Russia, Central Asia is the engine of the car, while for China it is the bumper, or the backyard (İşyar 2009). In the region, an economically growing China is a candidate to replace the efficient and primary political dominance of Russia in the near future (Gürbüz 2010).

Conclusion

In recent years, entering the region with the cooperation China established with Russia, she has gained a great position there especially in terms of energy resources. China is getting more and more influential on the Central Asian economies with the investments she makes and partnerships she establishes. She has been granting loans to the countries of the region for many sectors, especially for exploration of natural resources and drilling for them. China has also been undertaking many projects in the region, especially those concerning infrastructure, thus getting more powerful day by day. Apparently, she cares about Turkmenistan and Kazakhstan more on this subject, whereas she avoids any confrontation with the USA and Russia. China is always careful about her national interests and keeps making strategic moves to protect them.

China has been developing economic cooperation with the Central Asian economies. Balancing Russia economically and politically, she has become the alternative power for the Central Asian economies against Russia. However, in the case where they face the risk of remaining beneath this power and being obliged to make a choice among the powerful countries, the Central Asian economies may find themselves in a difficult position. Moreover, China's human resources surplus and Central Asia's natural resources surplus together with the low population density are facts that will possibly cause important pressure over the Central Asian economies. With the pipelines running through the Uyghur region, China has made this region the soft belly for herself and internalized it totally.

China's inclusion in the rivalry among Russia, the USA, Turkey and Iran on the Central Asian oil and natural gas as both an investor and a customer, for them will rekindle the new great game and accelerate competition. Finally, diversion of the oil and natural gas of the Central Asian economies to the east will result in a decrease in the flow of the natural resources into the pipelines going over Turkey.

References

Açık İstihbarat, 2009. "Sincan, Pekin için ne kadar değerli" http://www.acikistihbarat.com/Haberler.asp?haber=8028. (12.08.2011)

Adıbelli, Barış, 2008. Avrasya Jeopolitiğinde Büyük Oyun, IQ Kültür Sanat Yayıncılık, İstanbul.

Ahmet Davutoğlu, 2004. Stratejik Derinlik Türkiye'nin Uluslararası Konumu, 17. Baskı, Küre Yayınları, İstanbul.

Akçadağ, Emine, 2009. "Yükselen Güç Hindistan", http://www.bilgesam.org/tr/index.php?option=com_content&view=article&id=506:yuekselen-guec-hindistan&catid=110:analizler-hindistan&Itemid=138. (01.02.2011).

Alkın, Kerem ve Atman, Sabit 2006. Küresel Petrol Stratejilerinin Jeopolitik Açıdan Dünya ve Türkiye Üzerindeki Etkileri, (Haz.), İTO Yayınları, Yayın No:2006-48, İstanbul.

Bayraç, H. Naci, 2010. "Küresel Enerji Politikaları ve Türkiye", http://www.turksam.org/tr/a1909.html. (12.03.2011).

BBC, 2010. "Çin'in İran'a Yaptırım Çelişkisi", http://www.bbc.co.uk/turkce/haberler/2010/07/100730_china_iran_sanctions.shtml. (12.08.2011)

—. 2010. "Rusya-Çin arasında yeni enerji koridorları" http://www.bbc.co.uk/turkce/haberler/2010/09/100927_china_russia.shtml. (27.09. 2010)

Bekar, Olgan, 1995, "Çin ve Batı Türkistan", Avrasya Dosyası Çin Özel, C.2., S.2., s.48.

Bilgin, Mert, 2010. "Yeni Asya'nın Enerji Paradigmasında Orta Asya ve Kafkaslar: Rusya, AB, ABD, Çin, İran ve Türkiye Arasındaki Açmazlar ve Stratejik Açılımlar", http://www.stratejikongoru.org/makaleler/103-yeni-asyann-enerji paradigmasnda-orta-asya-ve-kafkaslar.html. (08.02.2011).

British Petroleum, 2011. "Dünya Devi Çin Enerji Tüketiminde de Lider" http://www.bp.com/genericarticle.do?categoryId=9018433&contentId=7069637, (15.07. 2011),

China Embassy, 2011. "Çin-Kazakistan ortak bildirisi: İlişkiler "kapsamlı stratejik ortaklık" düzeyine çıkarıldı", http://www.chinaembassy.org.tr/tur/xwdt/t830392.htm, (10 Temmuz 2011)

Çınar, Burak, 2010. "Rus-Hint Askeri İşbirliğinin Stratejik Etkileri", http://www.21yyte.org/tr/yazi.aspx?ID=3891&kat1=1. (01.02.2011).

CNNTürk, 2010. "Türkmenistan-İran doğalgaz boru hattı açıldı". http://www.cnnturk.com/2010/ ekonomi/dunya/01/06/turkmenistan.iran.dogalgaz.boru.hatti.acildi/558 167.0/index.html. (01.08.2011)

Çolakoğlu, Selçuk, 2010. "Çin'in Orta Asya ve Kafkasya Politikası", Orta Asya ve Kafkasya Rekabetten İşbirliğine, Tayyar Arı, (Der.), MKM Yayıncılık, Bursa.

CRI Online, 2010. "Çin-Rusya Petrol Boru Hattı projesi tamamlandı". http://turkish.cri.cn/781/2010/09/27/1s128527.htm. (12.08.2011)

Denker, Mehmet Sami, 2000. 2000'li Yıllarda Asya Pasifik Güvenliği, Asam Yayınları, Uzakdoğu-Pasifik Araştırmaları Dizisi:1, Ankara.

Dikkaya, Mehmet ve Bora, Ali, 2006. "Çağdaş Kazakistan'ın Ekonomi Politiği ve Türkiye'nin Yeri", OAKA., C.I., S.2., Ankara, ss.110-127., http://www.usak.org.tr/dosyalar/dergi/2UY4CqNBcpY6XBe5SlCleeq EcVIOUp.pdf. (12.08.2011)

Dikkaya, Mehmet, 2009. Orta Asya ve Kafkasya Dönüşüm Süreci ve Uluslararası Ekonomi Politik, Beta Yayınları, İstanbul.

—. 2010. "Çin-Orta Asya İlişkilerinde Doğal Gaz Faktörü ve Muhtemel Bölgesel Sonuçları", http://www.usak.org.tr/makale.asp?id=1321. (22.03.2011)

Ekrem, Nuriye Hidayet, 2003. Çin Halk Cumhuriyeti Dış Politikası (1950-2000), Uzakdoğu-Pasifik Araştırmalar Dizisi:4, ASAM Yayınları, Ankara.

Ekşi, Muharrem, 2009. "Enerjinin Önemi ve Büyük Güçlerin Enerji Politikaları", Mostar, Yıl:5, Sayı:50, ss. 51-53.

Enerji Enstitüsü, 2011. http://enerjienstitusu.com/2011/05/22/dunya-devi-cin-enerji-tuketiminde-de-lider/, (22.05.2011) ve detaylı bilgi için bkz; British Petrolium, www.bp.com/statisticalreview" target="_blank" (12.08.2011)

Financial Times, 2010. "Russia Opens China Pipeline For Siberian Oil". http://www.ft.com/intl/cms/s/0/dd89374a-b38c-11df-81aa-00144feabdc0.html?ftcamp=rss#axzz1STKuVVZl, (18 Temmuz 2011)

Gürbüz, Vedat, 2010, "Rekabetten İşbirliğini Türk-Rus İlişkileri", Zaman, 12.01.2010.

Haber 7, 2011. "Çin'den Türkmenistan'a 4.1 Milyar USD Kredi". http://www.haber7.com/haber/20110426/Cinden-Turkmenistana-41-milyar-kredi.php, (14 .07.2011)

Haberler, 2009. "Kazakistan-Çin Petrol Boru Hattından Çin'e 12 Milyon Ton Petrol Sevk Edildi". http://www.haberler.com/kazakistan-cin-petrol-boru-hattindan-cin-e-12-haberi/. (12.08.2011)

Hürriyet, 2010. Rusya Çin'e uzanan kritik boru hattını açtı, 2010. http://www.hurriyet.com.tr/ekonet/15669318.asp. (07.06.2011).

İşyar, Ömer Göksel, 2009. Karşılaştırmalı Dış Politikalar Yöntemler Modeller Örnekler ve Karşılaştırmalı Türk Dış Politikası, Dora Yayınları, Bursa.

—. 2010. Avrasya ve Avrasyacılık, Dora Yayıncılık, Bursa.

Laçiner, Sedat, 2005. Ermeniler Bir Uluslararası İlişkiler Çalışması, USAK Yayınları, Genişletilmiş 2.Baskı, Ankara.

Laçiner, Sedat, 2006a. "Hazar Enerji Kaynakları ve Enerji-Siyaset İlişkisi", OAKA, C.1., S.1., Ankara, ss. 36-66. , http://www.usakgundem.com/makale/61/enerjide-bat%C4%B1-tekeli-kalkarken-yeni-bir-akt%C3%B6r-olarak-%C3%A7in-hindistan-ve-japonya.html. (18.07.2011).

—. 2006b. "Enerjide Batı Tekeli Kalkarken: Yeni Bir Aktör Olarak Çin, Hindistan ve Japonya", http://www.usakgundem.com/makale/61/enerjide-bat%C4%B1-tekeli-kalkarken-yeni-bir-akt%C3%B6r-olarak-%C3%A7in-hindistan-ve-japonya.html. (20.07.2011).

Okur, Eren 2009. "Enerji Kaynakları ve Orta Asya'nın Geleceği", http://www.bilgesam.org/tr/index.php?option=com_content&view=article&id=433:enerji-kaynaklar-ve-orta-asyann-gelecei&catid=83:analizler-ortaasya&Itemid=149. (12.08.2011)

Özertem, Hasan Selim, 2008. "Kazakistan: Ekonomik Kalkınma ve Boru Hatları Siyaseti", http://www.usak.org.tr/makale.asp?id=789. (09.01.2011)

Pamir, Necdet, 2008. "Küresel Enerji Görünümü Karadeniz ve Hazar Denizleri Arasında Konumlanan Türkiye'nin Rolü", http://www.tankstorageinternational.compdf08Pamir.pdf, (12.08.2011)

Radikal, 2011. "Rusya'dan Çin'e ilk petrol akmaya başladı". http://www.radikal.com.tr/Radikal.aspx?aType=RadikalDetayV3&ArticleID=1034894&Date=02.01.2011&CategoryID=81. (08.06.2011).

Stratejik Araştırmalar Enstitüsü, 2011. "Üretici Ülkelerin Petro-Politiği 2010-2025", http://www.turksae.com/sql_file/366.pdf, (15.07.2011)

Stratejik Boyut, 2010. "Çin ve İran Arasında Dev Ortaklık". http://www.stratejikboyut.com/haber/cin-ve-iran-arasinda-dev-yakinlasma--40746.html, (18.07.2011)

TRT, 2010. "Kazakistan'dan Çin'e Yeni Doğalgaz Hattı".

http://www.trt.net.tr/haber/HaberDetay.aspx?HaberKodu=6cbafcc1-35c2-4e4e-a1a6-39ddbe9d1ba0. (12.07.2011).

Türkiye-Türkmenistan 2011. "Türkmenistan'ın En Fazla İthalat Yaptığı Ülke Türkiye", http://turkiye-turkmenistan.com/News.aspx?id=202, (12 .07.2011)

Tüysüzoğlu, Göktürk 2010. "Orta Asya'da Çin Etkinliği ve Küresel Oyun", http://www.stratejikboyut.com/haber/orta-asyada-cin-etkinligi-ve-kuresel-oyun--29654.html. (11.05.2011)

Uzman Forex 2011. http://www.uzmanforex.com/emtia-analizi/%C3%A7in%E2%80%99-libya%E2%80%99daki-duruma-bak%C4%B1%C5%9F%C4%B1-ve-bunun-petrol-arz%C4%B1na-olan-etkisi, (18 July 2011)

World Trade Organization, Trade Profiles Kazakhstan, 2009, http://stat.wto.org/CountryProfile/WSDBCountryPFView.aspx?Language=E&Country=KZ, (15.07.2011)

Yavuz, Celaleddin, 2011. "Türkiye ve Asrın "Stratejik"Enerji Hatlarına Gelinen Aşama", http://www.enerji2023.org/index.php?option=com_content&view=article&id=275:tuerkye-ve-asrin-qstratejkq-enerj-hatlarina-gelnen-aama&catid=15:stratej&Itemid=126, (10.07.2011)

Yavuz, Celalettin, 2009. "Rusya-Türkiye Yakınlaşması: Jeopolitik Bir Değerlendirme", Jeopolitik, Yıl: 8, Sayı:65, İstanbul.

Yeşil Ekonomi, 2011. http://www.yesilekonomi.com/cin-enerji-kullanimina-kota-getiriyor.html, (29.12.2011)

Zaman, 2010. "Çin'den Kazakistan'a 13 Milyar USD Kredi". http://www.zaman.com.tr/haber.do?haberno=995249, (15.07.2011)

CONTRIBUTORS

Dr. Kamiljon T. Akramov
Prof. Ömer Önder Arı
Assoc. Prof. Ahmet Ay
Dr. Murat Ozan Başkol
Prof. Berch Berberoğlu
Asst. Prof. Alkan Çelik
Asst. Prof. Abdüllatif Çeviker
Assoc. Prof. Mustafa Kemal Değer
Asst. Prof. Dr. Hasan Duran
Prof. Ömer Selçuk Emsen
Asst. Prof. Mustafa Ersungur
Dr. Junus Ganiev
Assoc. Prof. Günseli Mine Gerni
Asst. Prof. Hakan Güneş
Prof. Mükerrem Hiç
Dr. Kamalbek Karymshakov
Prof. Sadık Rıdvan Karluk
Asst. Prof. İsmail Koçak
Prof. Recep Kök
Prof. Turar Koichuev
Assoc. Prof. Akın Marşap
Asst. Prof. Hanifi Murat Mutlu
Assoc. Prof. Müslüme Narin
Zamira Oskonbaeva
Asst. Prof. Volkan Öngel
Dilek Özdemir
Asst. Prof. Tuncer Özdil
Prof. Jusup Pirimbaev
Asst. Prof. Yeşim Reel
Prof. Selahattin Sarı
Dr. Ercan Sarıdoğan
Asst. Prof. Fahri Solak
Asst. Prof. İlyas Sözen
İsmail Taş
Asst. Prof. Can Tansel Tuğcu
Ainura Turdalieva
Kadir Kürşat Yılmaz